BASIC HTML TAG REFERENCE

HTML	Description
<!--text-->	Commented out text
<A HREF="sample.html text</A>	Hyperlink
<B>text</B>	Bold
<BODY>text</BODY>	Body of Web page
 	Line break
<CENTER>text</CENTER>	Center
<CODE>text<CODE>	Monospaced font
<HEAD>text</HEAD>	Document header
<H1>text</H1>	Large heading
<H2>text</H2>	Medium heading
<H3>text</H3>	Small heading
<HTML>text</HTML>	HTML page start and finish
<I>text</I>	Italics
<HR>	Hard rule, line
<IMG SRC="sample.gif ">	Image
<OL><LI>text</OL>	Numbered list
<P>text</P>	Paragraph
<PRE>text</PRE>	Pre-formatted text
<SCRIPT>code</SCRIPT>	Client-side script
<TITLE>text</TITLE>	Title of document
<UL><LI>text</UL>	Bulleted list

HTML SPECIAL CHARACTERS REFERENCE

Character	Numeric Entity	Named Entity	Decription
"	"	"	Quotation mark
#	#	None	Pound
$	$		Dollar
%	%		Percentage
&	&	&	Ampersand
<	<	<	Less than
>	>	>	Greater than
@	@		At
•	•		Bullet
–	–		En dash
—	—		Em dash
™	™		Trademark
©	©	©	Copyright
®	®	®	Registered Trademark
°	°	°	Degree
¶	¶	&#para;	Paragraph Symbol
é	é	é	Lowercase e acute

HTML BASIC STRUCTURE REFERENCE

Table

```
<TABLE CELLPADDING = "0" CELLSPACING = "0" BORDER = "0">
<TR>
<TD>..</TD>
</TR>
</TABLE>
```

HTML Page

```
<HTML>
<HEAD>
<TITLE>..</TITLE>
</HEAD>
<BODY>
..
</BODY>
</HTML>
```

SAFE WEB BROWSER COLOR VALUES FOR RGB SETTINGS

Decimal	Hexidecimal
0	00
51	33
102	66
153	99
204	CC
255	FF

Webmaster

Answers!
Certified Tech Support

About the Author . . .

Christopher Ditto is a Webmaster at Ikonic in San Francisco. Besides answering questions every day on everything from Web servers to browsers and scripting languages, Christopher designs, codes, and manages the development of Web site projects for a number of Fortune 500 clients. Additionally, Christopher writes a monthly column, "Ask the Expert," for *Web Informant Magazine* and has published a number of articles on various Web-based technologies.

Webmaster

Answers!
Certified Tech Support

Christopher Ditto

Osborne **McGraw-Hill**

Berkeley • New York • St. Louis • San Francisco
Auckland • Bogotá • Hamburg • London
Madrid • Mexico City • Milan • Montreal
New Delhi • Panama City • Paris • São Paulo
Singapore • Sydney • Tokyo • Toronto

Osborne/**McGraw-Hill**
2600 Tenth Street
Berkeley, California 94710
U.S.A.

For information on translations or book distributors outside the U.S.A., or to arrange bulk
purchase discounts for sales promotions, premiums, or fund-raisers, please contact
Osborne/**McGraw-Hill** at the above address.

Webmaster Answers!
Certified Tech Support

1234567890 AGM AGM 901987654321098

ISBN 0-07-882459-1

Publisher	**Copy Editor**
Brandon A. Nordin	Peter Weverka
Editor-in-Chief	**Proofreader**
Scott Rogers	Joe Sadusky
	Pat Mannion
Acquisitions Editor	
Joanne Cuthbertson	**Indexer**
	Valerie Robbins
Project Editor	
Claire Splan	**Computer Designer**
	Michelle Galicia
Editorial Assistant	Roberta Steele
Stepane Thomas	
	Illustrator
Technical Editor	Arlette Crosland
Alan Herrick	
	Series Design
	Michelle Galicia

This book is dedicated to the millions of people around the world who are contributing to the community, the value, and the manifest destiny of the World Wide Web.

—*Christopher Ditto*

Contents @ a Glance

Contents

Acknowledgments

My inspiration for writing a Webmastering book came from the success of my "Ask the Expert" column in *Web Informant* and *Microsoft Visual J++ Informant* magazines. My column, and permission to reprint material from it, have been made possible through the generosity of Editor in Chief Jerry Coffey and Managing Editor Lori Ash.

The opportunity to write *Webmaster Answers* would not have been possible without the keen sheparding of Joanne Cuthbertson, Acquisitions Editor. The Answers series was brought to life by Scott Rogers, Editor in Chief, and it is a pleasure to contribute a book to such a successful series. Alan Herrick, Technical Editor, and Peter Weverka, Copyeditor, both contributed a great deal to the book's final form through their insightful and sharp editing talents. Stephane Thomas, Editorial Assistant, and Claire Splan, Project Editor, made the project run more smoothly than I could have imagined through the entire publication process.

A technical book that covers as broad a range of topics as this book could not have been created without the helpful advice and direction of some very talented specialists. The following individuals generously helped in reviewing the book and offering constructive, concrete feedback: Gregg Butensky, Anita Corona, Brian Davila, Dennis Kurimai, Mark McCormick, Graham Neumann, Evangelo Prodromou, Bill Schaefer, Jon Thompson, Clayton Tucker, and Mark Ward.

Writing a book on a tight deadline while holding a full-time job was only possible through the generosity of Ikonic's CEO, Robert May. Many thanks, Robert, and may Ikonic continue to build successful businesses on the Web.

Introduction

The value of the World Wide Web as a resource is no longer questioned. Businesses, organizations, and individuals have all flocked to establish a Web presence to attract new eyes and new customers from the millions who are already online. But before a site can succeed on the Web, there are a whole range of challenges that first need to be tackled. Everything from getting a domain name to setting up your server and developing your site needs to be addressed before a Web server logs the first visitor to a new site.

But the work doesn't stop there. In order to continuously attract new sets of eyes and keep them coming back, your site needs to be competitive. Upgrading and managing content, keeping your server online, and remaining ahead of new technologies are all abilities that are crucial in the online environment. No one can go through this crazy process without first asking some difficult questions.

Webmaster Answers is a collection of the most common questions and answers faced in the world of Web site development, deployment, and maintenance. As Webmaster of one of the largest and busiest Web development firms in the World, I can honestly say that these questions have all been asked many times before.

Webmaster Answers is intended to help answer the questions of anyone involved in the Web site process. The questions included in this book have come from graphic artists, programmers, writers, and online advertisers, as well as the companies who hire them.

The answers themselves are the result of years of accumulated experience garnered from working on many of the most popular Web sites on the Internet. But experience and inside knowledge doesn't always translate into neat, elegant solutions that will work for any site running on any browser. Answers often come in the form of tricks, tips, and hacks that help make up for the fact that the Web isn't a single software application. The Web is a wide mix of protocols, languages, browsers, and servers that all work together to create an experience for the end user.

This book answers your questions with advice that will take you and your Web site one step closer to success. With source code, trivia, real Web development examples, and, most importantly, clear, well-tested explanations of the topics, the book should give you the answers you need.

Webmaster Answers is divided into 20 chapters covering 19 different topics. Each topic is subdivided into sections to further organize the questions that are answered. If you can't find the question that you need answered in Chapter 1's Top Ten Frequently Asked Questions, try looking under the chapter title that most closely matches your question. Use the table of contents to find your question's chapter topic and beginning page number.

Use the @ a Glance section at the beginning of each chapter to narrow your search down to its subtopic. But don't stop there. Take a look at some of the similar questions, and I'm sure you'll find plenty of additional information and support. Even if you don't know exactly what question to ask, browse through each chapter to find plenty of tips, notes, warnings, and sidebars, all intended to enhance your ability to set up, develop, improve, or maintain a successful site on the World Wide Web.

CONVENTIONS USED IN THIS BOOK

Webmaster Answers uses several conventions to make it easier to read and find the information you need on a particular topic or area. Among the conventions you will see are:

- **Bold Type**, which is used for text that is entered from your keyboard.

- *Italic Type*, which emphasizes certain important words or phrases that you need to know.

- SMALL CAPITAL LETTERS, which are used to differentiate the keys on your keyboard. For example, you will see the words SHIFT and ENTER when those keys need to be pressed.

Chapter 1

Top 10 Frequently Asked Questions

Answer Topics!

The Top 10 Frequently Asked Questions @ a Glance

In the process of developing and maintaining a Web site there are always certain questions that come up more frequently than all of the rest. The questions in this chapter are ten of the most frequently asked questions and a great starting point for anyone looking for answers.

The questions themselves all fall within categories which are discussed in greater detail in other chapters throughout the book. If your question isn't here, try looking it up in the chatper that is titled closest to your question's topic.

? 1. How can I tell if a domain name is taken?

Before you apply for a domain name, check to see if anyone else has claimed it already. To do so, simply type in the domain name you want as a URL beginning with http://www. If a Web page comes up, your domain has been taken and is being used by someone else. URLs are bought and sold all the time, so don't let the fact that a URL is already taken discourage you. If typing the URL does not make a page appear with the name you want, however, the URL may still be taken. You still have investigating to do.

To find out for sure if a domain name has been taken, you have to query the InterNIC database. InterNIC was formed in 1993 by the National Science Foundation to handle the overwhelming problem of how to assign and register domain names. The easiest way to query InterNIC is to either use a whois application or visit a Web site that acts as a front-end to whois and type in the domain name you want. If your name isn't taken and isn't in the process of being registered by someone else, you should be able to claim the name by filling out a form and paying InterNIC a registration fee.

Online you can query InterNIC's database as many times as you wish at the InterNIC whois page shown in Figure 1-1. The whois Web page can be found at http://rs.internic.net/cgi-bin/itts/whois.

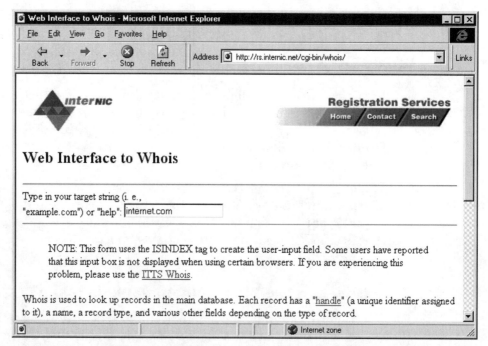

Figure 1-1   The InterNIC whois Web page allows visitors to enter domain names to determine whether they are currently registered

Simply submit something like *YourName.com* and conduct the search. To search without a Web browser, you need to install a whois application (it most likely requires a Web connection). For a locally run Windows 95 whois application, download Netcop from http://www.shareware.com. Most whois applications require an Internet connection to run.

2. How can I tell what Web server software other sites are using?

Whenever a Web server requests a page, certain information is sent back with the HTTP headers. Every server sends back different types of header information, but most return a server header that indicates what software is being used.

To view a site's HTTP headers, telnet to port 80 of the Web server you are investigating. From Windows 95 or Windows NT, go to the command prompt and enter

TELNET www.microsoft.com 80. On a PC, a default telnet client opens to the correct location. Next, type **get / http/1.0** quickly and hit return twice (if you don't it won't work).

In most cases, the Web server returns the name and version of its server software. The Web server usually cuts off the connection if the request takes more than a few seconds, however, so it is important to hurry. Following is a set of HTTP headers from www.ibm.com:

```
HTTP/1.0 200 Document follows
content type: text/html
server: IBM-Planetwide-Server/4.1
date: Wed, 31 Jul 1997 01:15:10 GMT
```

The server header may indicate which software the site uses, but not which operating system. Some Web server software is platform-specific. For example, Internet Information Server, a Microsoft Web server, only runs on Windows NT. If you are really curious, try hyperlinking to a page or two on a site, changing the capitalization of the Web document in the URL line, and hitting return. If a message appears and states that the page was not found, you are probably looking at pages served by a UNIX server or Macintosh server. Both UNIX and Macintosh file systems are case-sensitive, so requesting document.html is not the same as requesting Document.html, for example. Microsoft Windows operating systems are less picky and have no trouble serving up documents with different capitalization schemes.

3. What should a document be named for the specific filename to be unnecessary in the URL line?

When a Web page comes up that hasn't been specifically named in the URL line (the home page of www.apple.com, for example), a default document for the directory referenced in the URL has been set. The actual filename for the default document of a directory, or *directory index file* as it is also known, is set in the Web server itself. The most common filenames for default documents on Web servers are index.html, default.htm, and welcome.html.

For large Web sites, the problem with default document names is that as many as fifty files named index.html may have to be present for every directory to have a default document. To solve this problem, many sites create aliases that map index.html (or the appropriate default document name that is specified in the server) to a document that shares the directory's name but has *.html* on the end. A default document in a directory named employees, for example, would be named employees.html and have an alias sitting at the same directory level named index.html that points to it.

Follow the instructions for your server to see which file is currently set as your default document or to change your default document to a different filename.

Netscape Enterprise Server

For Netscape servers, the default document at the time of installation is index.html. Follow these steps to change this filename:

1. Go to the Enterprise Server main administration screen.
2. Select the Web site you want to edit (there may only be one).
3. Select Content Management from the menu.
4. Select Document Preferences from the menu on the left.
5. Enter the name of the default document you want to apply in the Index Filenames text box. For multiple default document names, separate the names with commas and prioritize them from left to right.
6. Click OK.
7. Select Save and Apply from the Save and Apply Changes page.

Microsoft Internet Information Server

On Microsoft's Internet Information Server, the default document at the time of installation is default.htm. Follow these steps to change the default document:

1. Open the Internet Service Manager and double-click WWW Service.
2. Select the Directories tab.
3. Enter the default document name in the Default Document text box. Make sure that the Enable Default Document check box is checked off.

4. Select OK and then Apply.

With version 3.0, Microsoft added the ability to specify a number of different default documents in order of priority. To set multiple documents in Internet Information Server, simply separate the names with commas (index.html, default.htm, index.htm, and default.html, for example) and insert them into the default document field.

Apache and NCSA

Edit the server resource management file, srm.conf, by using the following syntax for multiple default documents:

```
DirectoryIndex index.html default.htm
```

 Note: *Referring to a default document by filename also works perfectly well. For example, http://www.apache.org/index.html brings up the same Web page as http://www.apache.org.*

? 4. What are the most common causes of Web server failure?

The following problems may cause a Web server to stop responding or to stop altogether:

- **Full hard drive** is often a result of Web server log files that have not been removed from the server. Some operating systems have difficulty starting without enough hard drive space. Some Web servers also require hard drive space in order to operate.

- **Programming error** caused by a custom application such as a CGI. Even though a crashing CGI shouldn't directly effect the Web server, it may crash the operating system or overutilize the system resources.

- **Too many requests** cause many Web servers to crash. You can fix this problem by optimizing your site for performance. See Chapter 5 for details.

- **Memory leaks** can be caused by any server application including the operating system itself. Memory leaks can be cured temporarily by rebooting the server. To permanently cure memory leaks, eliminate or update the offending program.

● **Free server software expires** and so cannot be used. It may sound obvious, but it isn't uncommon for companies to rely on free, time-limited trial versions of software. Mark your calendar a week in advance of the date that free software expires and do what needs to be done to remove or properly register the software.

5. What is the HTML <META> tag, and how do I use it?

The <META> tag sits at the top of the HTML document between the <HEAD> and <TITLE> tags and provides information that is invisible to the user. The <META> tag is usually used for defining page topics for search-engine robots, setting cookies on a user's browser, and setting the page to refresh itself in the number of seconds that you specify. Newer browsers interpret <META> tags as if they were HTTP response headers. More recent uses of the <META> tag include setting the RSAC content rating, specifying who created the page, and defining the document's content type.

To correctly use <META> tags on a site, you can either learn the various attributes and formats pertaining to each type of <META> tag you want to implement or you can copy and adapt a tag that has already been formatted. Because <META> tags use many formats, especially within the CONTENT attribute, simply copying pre-existing tags is quite a bit simpler.

Following are many of the uses for <META> tags along with examples and explanations.

Defining Content

<META> tags allow you to define the content of your pages with both key words and a description.

```
<META NAME="Keywords" CONTENT="Computers, Sales,
Intel, Compaq, Discount">
<META NAME="Description" CONTENT="We sell discount
computers on the Web!">
```

These lines of HTML summarize the page for a search engine by listing key words. The key words help place the page properly and competitively in site listings such as Excite, Alta Vista, Lycos, and InfoSeek.

Recreational Software Advisory Council Rating System

You can set an RSAC rating for your page by using the <META> tag as follows:

```
<META http-equiv="PICS-Label" content='(PICS-1.1
"http://www.rsac.org/ratingsv01.html" l gen true
comment "RSACi North America Server" by
"inet@microsoft.com" for "http://www.microsoft.com"
on "1997.06.30T14:21-0500" r (n 0 s 0 v 0 l 0))'>
```

The Recreational Software Advisory Council rating system provides a standard to rate the content of Web sites. Users can set Microsoft Internet Explorer 3.0+ to exclude sites that contain such topics as nudity and violence. This example HTML is from Microsoft's home page. In the code, the r (n 0 s 0 v 0 l 0) indicates that the page contains zero nudity (n), sex (s), violence (v), and obscene language (l). For more information on RSAC ratings, visit the RSAC site, shown in Figure 1-2, at http://www.rsac.org/.

Controlling the Caching of Pages

Microsoft Internet Explorer supports a <META> tag that defines the date on which the content expires:

```
<META HTTP-EQUIV="expires" CONTENT="Mon, 12 May 1998
00:36:05 GMT">
```

Microsoft Internet Explorer, if set to first look to the browser's cache, uses a cached version each time a visitor revisits a page until the expiration date set by the <META> tag is reached. For pages that you don't want cached, set the expiration date to a previous date.

Setting a Page to Change or Refresh the URL

You can use the <META> tag to change URLs in a specified number of seconds:

```
<META HTTP-EQUIV="refresh" CONTENT="5;
URL=http://host.domain.com/index.html">
```

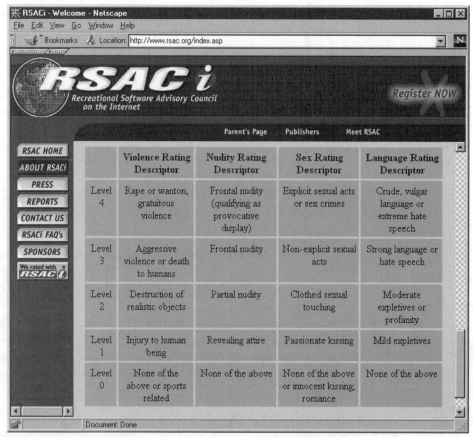

Figure 1-2 The RSAC Rating System's online reference

This example calls a new page five seconds after the current page has loaded. This can also be set to the same page that the <META> tag is on to allow the page to refresh itself.

Language

The <META> tag allows you to set the language:

```
<META HTTP-EQUIV="content-language" CONTENT="en">
```

English is en, French is fr, and esperanto is eo. For a complete listing, visit http://vancouver-webpages.com/multilingual/iso639a.txt.

Robot Information

It is possible to tell friendly robots to index a page but not follow the links:

```
<META NAME="ROBOTS" CONTENT="INDEX, NOFOLLOW">
```

Other options for the CONTENT attribute include NOINDEX and FOLLOW.

Cheating on <META> tags

To avoid the trouble of constructing your own <META> tags from scratch, visit http://www.apple.com and http://www.aol.com and view the HTML source for some great examples.

Another option is to visit the META builder page shown in Figure 1-3. On this page, you can construct <META> tags by simply filling out forms. The META builder page can be found at http://vancouver-webpages.com/VWbot/mk-metas.html.

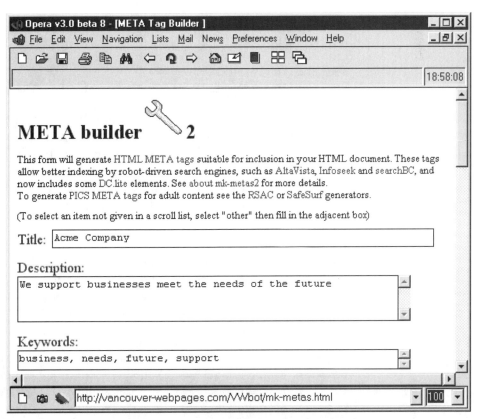

Figure 1-3   On the Meta builder page, you can build your own <META> tags online by using simple form input fields.

? 6. How do I add the current date to a page with JavaScript that includes the day of the week or month by name?

By default, JavaScript stores the date in the following format:

Day Month Date Hour:Minute:Second Time Zone Year

The default date format may be written with the following code:

```
<SCRIPT LANGUAGE="JavaScript">
<!--
var todaysdate = new Date();
document.write(todaysdate);
// -->
</SCRIPT>
```

Depending on the browser, one of the following formats will be used:

```
Fri Dec 10 19:00:12 PDT 1997
Fri Dec 10 19:00:12 Pacific Daylight Time 1997
```

To specify the full name for the month or day of the week, you need to create your own conversion lookup table. Retrieving the day of the week by number is possible, but it is important to note that the numbers begin at zero. Following is an example of a lookup table that converts the month from a number to a full month name:

```
<SCRIPT LANGUAGE="JavaScript">
<!--
var todaysdate = new Date();
var todaysmonth = todaysdate.getMonth();
var todaysday = todaysdate.getDate();
var todaysyear = todaysdate.getYear();

if (todaysmonth == 0) todaysmonth = "January";
else if (todaysmonth == 1) todaysmonth = "February";
else if (todaysmonth == 2) todaysmonth = "March";
else if (todaysmonth == 3) todaysmonth = "April";
else if (todaysmonth == 4) todaysmonth = "May";
else if (todaysmonth == 5) todaysmonth = "June";
else if (todaysmonth == 6) todaysmonth = "July";
else if (todaysmonth == 7) todaysmonth = "August";
```

```
else if (todaysmonth == 8) todaysmonth = "September";
else if (todaysmonth == 9) todaysmonth = "October";
else if (todaysmonth == 10) todaysmonth = "November";
else if (todaysmonth == 11) todaysmonth = "December";
document.write(todaysmonth + ' ' + todaysday + ', 19'
+ todaysyear);
// -->
</SCRIPT>
```

This script produces a date in a format that resembles the following:

```
January 12, 1998
```

+ ***Tip:*** *Like a number of programming languages, JavaScript stores dates internally as the number of milliseconds since the very first moment in 1970. If you want to complete date calculations for dates before this time, you either have to add years to put the date past 1970 or calculate dates without using the date functions provided by JavaScript.*

? 7. How do I specify alternative content for non-Java-enabled browsers?

Any HTML included between an <APPLET> and </APPLET> tag that does not fall within a <PARAM> tag is displayed by non-Java browsers. For example, to create an HTML message for non-Java browsers that provides a hyperlink to www.browser.com, use the following HTML:

```
<APPLET CODE="MyJavaApplet.class"
CODEBASE="/media/JavaApplets" Width="83" HEIGHT="33">
<H2>Your browser does not support Java.</H2>
Information on the latest browsers are available from
<A HREF="http://www.browser.com">Browser.com</A><BR>
</APPLET>
```

? 8. How can I design a Web page that prints well from a printer?

When you print a page from a Web browser, the page is converted from HTML (the language was never intended to be a publishing or printing language) to PostScript or your printer's proprietary language. HTML is intended to be window size-independent, whereas the language that a printer uses must provide exact sizes for printing.

Browsers assume that Web pages are printed on paper that is 8.5 inches, or about 600 pixels, wide. Converting the data from HTML to PostScript or your printer's proprietary language doesn't always go smoothly. Designing a page that prints well from different browsers and on different printers requires a little trial-and-error experimentation. Netscape Navigator 3.0 and 4.0 both include a print preview feature for viewing a page before actually printing it.

Graphics from a Web page always print poorly because they are optimized for file size and a 72 dpi monitor. Most printers support much higher resolutions (300 to 600 dpi), so printed Web graphics often look blocky.

Printing from frames also causes a few more headaches than one might expect. Printing more than one frame at a time, from either Microsoft Internet Explorer or Netscape Navigator, is simply not possible. For a specific frame within a page to be printed, the frame must be the last one clicked. You make a frame active simply by clicking the background of that frame's Web page.

9. How can I tell when a page was last modified?

If you are looking at a document from the Web server itself locally or through FTP, you can identify when it was last updated by examining the attribute that the operating system assigned to the file. From a Web browser, the task can be tricky and the results not always accurate. Server applications such as CGIs always generate content dynamically, with the result being a last file modification date that either is not specified by the file or is the same date that your request was made.

Here's a tip: use a Netscape Navigator browser and go to the page you want to check. Next, add about: before the http:// part of the URL line, as in the following example. Netscape Navigator will list a number of attributes including the last modification date if it is available. For example, entering **about:http://www.mcgraw-hill.com/** in a Netscape browser will give all sorts of information on the McGraw-Hill home page.

Here are some other tricks you can do with a Netscape browser:

about:cache	View the attributes of cached files.
about:global	See a history of your browser activity.
about:image-cache	View images and information regarding images that have been cached on your browser's hard drive.
control-alt-f	Navigate to Netscape's Amazing Fish Cam page.
control-alt-s	Cause the status bar to disappear or reappear.
ftp://username @ftp.domain.com	Log onto a secure FTP server (use this format when using your Netscape browser). Files may be uploaded by selecting Upload File from the File menu. Although it isn't documented, Microsoft Internet Explorer also allows access to secure FTP directories using the syntax ftp://*username*:*password*@ftp.*domain*.com in the URL line.

10. How do I add a page counter to my site?

Page counters have become a common feature across the Internet. Counters simply count the number of requests that have been made for a page since a specific date and list the number of requests. Page counters are either numeric text that is included on the page or they are text strings in the form of image tags that reference a different graphic for each digit (e.g., 12 is represented as <IMG SCR="1.gif"> <IMG SCR="2.gif">). Regardless of which style is used, the basic process behind both page counter display types is very similar.

To include a counter on your page, you can either use a counter service or your own script to track the number of visits to your site and publish the results. A counter service takes care of the work for you for free or at a small cost. If your site is hosted by an ISP, a counter service may already be available to you at no cost and with minimal effort from the ISP.

If you want to use your own script, it is simply a matter of executing a script, which is easily done through a server-side include tag such as <!--#include virtual="/cgi-bin/counter.cgi"-->. Keep in mind that not all servers provide built-in server-side include support. For more information on server-side includes, read the server-side include section in Chapter 11.

Most counter CGI scripts simply open a text file, read the number that it currently stores, increment the number by one, update the text file with the new number, and output the number through standard output for inclusion on the page. If you want to use graphical numbers, such as those shown in the following illustration, output each number individually with <IMG SRC= preceding the digit and .gif BORDER=0> following it. A comprehensive collection of graphical digits is available from http://www.counterart.com/.

Commercial services are available from the following sites:

- http://www.digits.com/
- http://www.asoftware.com/

Web counter scripts are available at these sites:

- Kira's Web Toolbox: http://lightsphere.com/cgi/#lk3
- Matt's Script Archive: http://www.worldwidemart.com/ scripts/counter.shtml

---

* *Note:* *If you are placing several adjacent graphics on a page and you want to eliminate the spaces between them that appear on Netscape browsers, you need to use tables. For instructions on how to do this, see Chapter 8.*

Chapter 2

Planning a Site

Answers Topics!

Planning a Site @ a Glance

Building a site requires planning. You have to complete a number of key steps. As you plan, it is important to think strategically in terms of what you want to accomplish and concretely in terms of what must be done to make it happen.

This chapter focuses on the planning and domain registration phases of building a site. By carefully stepping through the planning phase, you save significant amounts of time in the long run.

Starting Out covers why establishing an online presence is so important. It outlines the necessary steps involved in constructing a site. This section also describes the role of the Webmaster and explains what the different sections of a URL address are.

Domain Names describes what you need to know about domains, including the importance of choosing a good name, what it costs to acquire a name, and how to register a name. Securing a domain name early in the site development process is a critical step, and this section explains why.

Planning Your Site helps you determine what skills you need to develop a site and which milestones you must reach in order to develop a successful site. Also in this section are the basic rules of Web etiquette that every site should consider following or flaunting.

STARTING OUT

❓ What are the advantages of having a Web site?

Each Web site has its own agenda. Earning profits, advertising, public service, product distribution, information distribution, or just for fun are all excellent reasons for having a Web site. The Web presents a very inexpensive way of getting exposure for yourself and your company and reaching a niche in the marketplace.

Unless your company's business model centers on having a Web site, you shouldn't see a Web site strictly as a source of revenue. A Web site can also be a means of enlarging your customer base. A toll-free number doesn't always generate profits for a company, but the benefits to customers of having the number make the cost of providing the service worthwhile.

Getting on the Web early can be a big advantage. By securing a domain name and establishing a presence online, you acquire real-world experience with the Web. Even if your reasons for establishing a site are unclear, you may consider getting on the Web anyway, because establishing a strong foothold in a quickly growing marketplace is a safe bet for the future.

Consider this quote by Stu Malin, taken from http://www.webmaster.org/training/infra.html:

"There will always be ambiguity in building a Web site. The challenge is to continue moving forward in spite of ambiguity."

❓ What are the key elements of a Web site?

In order to build a site and make sure that others can find and access it from the Web, every site needs these key elements:

● **An address:** Any server hooked up to the Web should be accessible through its IP address, but domain names are how people remember a site's address. Whether you acquire a domain name or simply a directory that falls under someone else's domain name, an address is a key element of any site.

● **Hardware:** Every site needs a computer on which to sit, and that computer, in turn, must be connected to the Internet. As to hardware, you can go the simple route and use the preconfigured system at an Internet service provider (ISP), or go the complex route and set up a system of your own.

● **Software:** At an absolute minimum, every Web site needs Web server software. A Web server is necessary to accept requests for your Web pages and send the pages to the right location on the Web. ISPs provide Web server software.

● **Content:** Of course, a Web site requires *content*— graphics, text, and other collateral. Without content, a Web site is merely a bunch of empty pages.

● **HTML:** Without HTML (hypertext markup language), the Web would be just a networking protocol, like FTP, for delivering files. HTML is what displays the graphics and text on the screen and defines the links between the pages.

● **Webmaster:** Someone needs to be assigned the responsibility of maintaining the site. At the very least, this person ensures that the bills are paid and the site is still running.

？ What is the role of the Webmaster?

The *Webmaster* is the person who coordinates and manages a Web site. The name comes from "postmaster," a title adopted by systems administrators in charge of running an e-mail server for a particular domain. Evidence of the old Postmaster title is still seen in the contact address, usually in the format postmaster@domain.com, for problems or questions related to e-mail. As the Web became more popular and more complex, the need arose for a position similar to that of the postmaster. A Webmaster ensures that everything a visitor sees through his or her browser—everything from the Web server to the Web page— works the way it was intended to work.

According to the Webmaster's Guild, the task of a Webmaster is to design, implement, and maintain an effective World Wide Web site. What design, implement, and maintain means is the tough question. Usually, it means that the Webmaster must understand and communicate effectively with the content developers, such as writers and programmers, who create the site. On smaller sites, a Webmaster is often called upon to do everything from creating graphics to maintaining the Web server. At the very least, every Webmaster should understand the factors involved in each step of the process.

Note: *Some people consider "Webmaster" a masculine title. Many women prefer the title Webmistress. Other names for the Webmaster include Webgoddess, Weblord, Webwizard, Webmeister and Manager of Internet Operations.*

What are all the different parts of a URL?

Getting a URL (uniform resource locator) is similar to buying a house. When you buy a house, you acquire an address that people can visit. In the case of the Internet, the address is a URL. By typing your site's URL into a Web browser, anyone in the world connected to the Internet can visit your Web site. For example, http://www.shareware.com is a URL run by C | Net.

Protocol

The *http://* section of the URL, which stands for *hypertext transfer protocol,* is present at the beginning of every address on the World Wide Web. Fortunately, the major browsers today, such as Microsoft's Internet Explorer and Netscape Navigator, enter the http:// part of the address for you, so you don't have to type it yourself. FTP and gopher are examples of two other Internet protocols. Respectively, *ftp://* and *gopher://* appear at the beginning of their URL addresses.

The Server, or Host, Name

After the *http://* section of the URL is the server, or host, name. Not all servers are named *www*; some have no name at all. For example, http://backoffice.microsoft.com and http://www.microsoft.com are different sets of machines that host different sites maintained by the Microsoft Corporation.

On the other hand, http://news.com has no specific server name mapped to it but is directed to the same server as http://www.news.com.

Domain Names and Suffixes

Following the server name is the domain name and a suffix. A *domain name* is the section of the URL that is uniquely registered to one company, one organization, or one individual. In the United States, domains are almost always one word in length and are followed by one of six suffixes:

- .com for businesses
- .edu for educational institutions
- .net for sizeable ISPs or businesses
- .gov for government agencies
- .org for organizations
- .mil for the military

Netscape.com, for example, is the registered domain name of Netscape, a company, while whitehouse.gov is the registered domain name of the White House.

Because we are slowly but surely running out of domain names, plans are being made to create additional suffixes so that names can be recycled and used again. Suggestions for new suffixes include .store for online commerce, .nom for personal names, and .info for informational sites.

Two-Letter Country Codes

Outside of the United States, URLs get a little more complicated. The domain names of most international sites and even some U.S. sites end in a two-letter country code. Australian domains, for example, end in *.au*. French domains end in *.fr*. A Canadian site such as http://www.wave.ca includes the *.ca* country code.

What often confuses things is that, in international domain names, an extra two-letter suffix is frequently inserted between the name section of the domain name and the country code. For example, http://www.cranbrook.co.nz is a company in New Zealand, and http://www.essexx.gov.uk is a government page tied to a region in the United Kingdom.

Path Information on Web server

The server name and domain name define where a site is located on the World Wide Web. After the domain name comes the section of the URL that refers to specific pages, graphics, files, or scripts. When nothing appears after the domain name, the Web server has found a document that has been named in such a way that it matches the default document naming conventions mapped within the Web server. For more information on directory paths, see "File Path and URL Line" in Chapter 4 of this book.

DOMAIN NAMES

What should I consider when I choose a domain name?

In a survey conducted by Nielsen Media Research and CommerceNet Consortium to determine what leads people to visit Web sites, a full 8.5 percent answered "newspapers and magazines," and another 3.6 percent said "television." These days, URLs often appear in advertisements, and consumers are clearly visiting sites whose URLs they got from the print media and television. However, in order to bring in visitors with print and TV advertisements, you must choose a domain name that no one needs to write down in order to remember.

Since all World Wide Web URLs begin with *http://* and most also include the letters *www*, most Web surfers understand that they only need to remember the unique section of the name—the section they see in the advertisement. A savvy Web user only needs to remember *browser.com* in order to find http://www.browser.com on the Web, for example. For this reason, having registered a domain that is as memorable as wired.com, for example, helps to bring in more site visitors.

Another thing to consider when you choose a domain name is what happens when you move your site to a new server or even a new ISP. If you choose a name carefully, you can move your site without having to give out a new URL. The sidebar explains how.

You Don't Have to Have a Domain Name

Technically speaking, you don't actually need a domain name. Any Web site can be found by simply entering its Internet Protocol or IP address. When you enter a domain name for the first time, a domain name server looks up the domain name in its database and converts the name to an IP address so that the address can be found on the Internet. Since the conversion is done behind the scenes, many people don't realize that entering **http://205.139.115.8**, for example, takes you to the same Web site as entering **http://www.ikonic.com**.

Unfortunately, not only are IP addresses hard to remember, but they make it difficult to move a site between servers. Changing the IP address associated with a domain name is usually more feasible than changing an IP address of a server. The IP address associated with a domain can be changed by simply filling out a form and submitting it via e-mail to InterNIC.

? What if the domain name I want is taken?

Some companies buy domain names with the intention of selling them or leasing them to interested parties. If a company that brokers names owns the domain you want, it shouldn't be difficult to buy the name. Prices for domain names start at a few hundred dollars and go up to $15,000 for popular names such as divorce.com.

If the domain name you want is owned by a company that isn't looking to sell, try running a whois search on the domain name, and then contact the party whose name appears in the search results. If the domain name you want happens to be your company name or a name that your company has trademarked, you might be able to persuade the other party to give up the name, although you might have to threaten legal action to do so. A company that owns the trademark to a name stands a very good chance of winning the right to use the name as a domain name. Unfortunately, many disputes over domain names have resulted in legal action. In legal disputes over trademarked names, the party that owns the registered trademark usually wins. In disputes over names that are not trademarked, it is hard to tell where the court will side.

Domain.com

Many books, software applications, and Web sites use
"user@host.domain.com" as a sample e-mail address. Domain.com is
actually a registered domain name with an associated mail server.
What began as a trickle of e-mails a few years ago has skyrocketed to
approximately 3500 e-mails a day.

? How do I register a domain name that is not already taken?

There are two ways to register a domain name. You can
either register the name yourself through InterNIC, or you
can partner with an ISP or hosting service and register the
domain name that way. The latter is by far the easiest route
for a person or company that is registering a name for the
first time. The questions you have to answer when you
register a name are hard to answer if you are not technically
familiar with how or where the site will be initially set up.
An ISP is forced to register names as part of doing business
and should be intimately familiar with what is required to
register a domain name.

Registering a domain name is now an almost completely
automated process and can be handled via e-mail. Registering
a name can take up to three weeks, and if any mistakes were
made on the e-mail form, getting it right may take a few
attempts. Phone support is very difficult to obtain, and if you
do speak to someone by phone, he or she usually advises you to
resubmit the e-mail form with better information.

To register a domain yourself, you need to know the
following pieces of information:

● The name of the domain you want to register

● The name of an administrative contact and technical
contact, as well as the person's phone number and
e-mail address

● The IP addresses of a primary and secondary domain
name server (a *domain server* is a database—typically
part of your network or your ISP's network—that points
Internet queries directly to your Web server)

The potential downside of using an ISP to register a domain name is cost. ISPs occasionally charge from $25 to $75 above what the InterNIC charges. It is always a good idea to compare what a few different ISPs charge before you select one to register your domain name.

Download a registration form from http://rs.internic.net/cgi-bin/itts/domain/.

? How much does it cost to register a domain?

Educational, military, and government domains are paid for by the National Science Foundation, but .com, .org, and .net domains cost $100 for the first two years and $50 per year thereafter. It is important to note that changes in physical address and e-mail address can make it quite difficult for InterNIC to bill you. Keeping the contact information that you give InterNIC when you register up to date is important.

Free Domain Names

If you are concerned about the price of registering a domain, consider registering with a .us domain for free. The following illustration shows a page on the U.S. Domain Registration Services site which explains the naming structure of the .us domain name system.

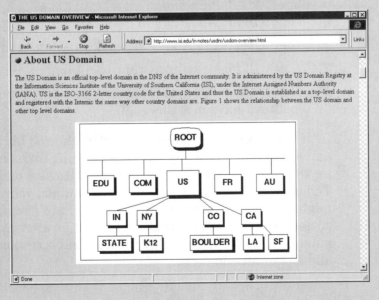

U.S. companies use .com addresses far more often than they do .us addresses, but other than aesthetics there is no difference between the two addresses. However, .us domains do need to be localized with a regional suffix. The city of Pasadena, California, for example, uses the URL http://ci.pasadena.ca.us. To register .us domains, visit the U.S. Domain Registration Services site at: http://www.isi.edu/cgi-bin/usdomreg/template.pl.

PLANNING YOUR SITE

❓ What kind of planning makes for a successful site?

Some of the most successful Web sites started as class projects or hobbies; some of the biggest flops occurred despite hundreds of thousands of investment dollars. So what determines the success of a Web site? Although there is no definitive answer, asking the right questions before you start building a site goes a long way toward building a successful site instead of a flop.

Ask yourself these questions before you start building your site:

● Who is my audience?

● What will draw visitors to my site?

● What aspects of my site will make visitors want to stay?

● What will make visitors want to return?

● What is the main goal of the site, and how can I measure whether I have met this goal?

These kinds of questions should be thoroughly considered and answered before any concrete building plans are drawn for the site. Think of the plan for your site as a business plan. The plan may be easy to define. For example, your goal might be "to promote our corporate brand to as many Web surfers as possible." Or your goal might be as complex as "to make a profit through highly targeted subscription services and electronic commerce."

? What aspects of a site can be counted on to attract a large percentage of return site visitors?

Assuming you have figured out who the target audience is, put yourself in the shoes of a visitor to your site and write down in one column of a sheet of paper what you expect from a site of this type. Next, write in another column what you would like to see at the site. In a third column, list the features that you would find both surprising and pleasing in the site.

Below are some broad ideas for a site that will keep visitors coming back for more:

- **Make it attractive:** Most visitors to a site associate the quality of the graphics with the quality of the content. In the same way that a magazine with poor photographs rarely sells many copies, an unattractive site rarely retains visitors.

- **Make it flashy:** Use the latest and greatest Web site gimmicks to attract attention to your pages, but still make sure to use technology that is compatible with the hardware and browsers that the majority of your visitors have. If you "go over your visitors' heads" and use technology that they can't access, many visitors will be alienated or confused by warning windows and missing functionality. If your site requires a plug-in that most visitors don't have, don't assume that visitors will download and install the plug-in so they can visit your site. Most of today's browsers support JavaScript and Java, so try using these technologies to enhance your site. Adding alternative features or text for browsers that do not support your flashy enhancements is also a good idea. Also keep in mind the file size and the speed under which some technologies operate.

- **Keep it current:** Visitors are less likely to come back to a site if they discover that it hasn't changed since the last time they were there. Whether your new content is as simple as a stock ticker or live Web camera, or as ambitious as providing up-to-date news, keeping a site current attracts return visitors.

- **Provide valuable content:** Content is ultimately what makes visitors remain loyal to a site. Valuable content can be anything from an HTML reference guide to entertaining stories or statistics. Look at the sites that you bookmarked in your browser and count how many have weak content.

- **Give visitors what they were looking for:** If most visitors come to your site to get your address and phone number, put it prominently at the front of the site along with a map. If your site attracts visitors who are looking for great graphics, surprise them with insightful articles. Put yourself in a visitor's shoes before you try to out-fancy the competition. Survey your audience to find out what else they would like to see. Let them join a mailing list for updates to your site. Interaction and feedback allow you to tailor your site to your clientele and build an online community based around your site.

- **Make it fast:** Large graphics, Java, and many plug-ins can make visiting a site a painfully slow experience. Choosing a maximum page size in kilobytes before you start building is also a good idea.

- **Keep it free:** Don't expect to attract any visitors if you charge to visit your site from the beginning. Very few companies have made a profit by charging for their sites in the first six months.

+ ***Tip:*** *If you are new to building Web sites and you have an idea that you've never seen done before, try to figure out why it hasn't been done before. Learn the limitations of the current browsers and technology. HTTP protocol, file size, and browser compatibility alone often limit the potential functionality of sites.*

? What skills do I need for a successful Web site project?

Having these skills helps immensely when you develop a Web site:

- **Understanding of Web servers:** For your site to be accessible, either you should know how to install and test a Web server, or you should be able to interface with the ISP that will host your site.

- **Ability to create Web graphics:** Graphic design skills and an understanding of Web graphics formats are necessary if you intend to create a site that arrives quickly on-screen and is visually compelling.

- **Ability to write for the Web:** Copy that reads well in a brochure usually doesn't come across very well online. An understanding of online editorial issues is a great asset to any Web project.

- **Site architecture and layout skills:** An effective site needs an intuitive layout for both the navigation elements and the locations of pages themselves. A site with pages buried too deep or a difficult navigation design will not retain visitors.

- **HTML talent:** HTML is the glue that binds all the qualities of a Web site together. The ability to generate error-free HTML that is compatible with target browsers is an absolute necessity.

- **Site administration skills:** Often referred to as "Webmastering skills," being able to manage a site after it is constructed (and maintaining the Web server if the site is not hosted at an ISP) is necessary. Webmastering skills rely to some degree on a basic understanding of all the skills mentioned here, as well as a knowledge of FTP and Internet diagnostic tools such as ping, trace route, nslookup, finger, and whois.

- **Programming experience:** For dynamic sites and interactive sites, it is often necessary to customize server scripts or compiled applications specifically for your Web server. With dynamic HTML and the recent expansion of the JavaScript programming language, programming experience is necessary for highly interactive pages. An experienced programmer is a great enhancement to almost any team.

? **What are some good milestones for a company or organization that is building a site for the first time?**

Create a calendar and try to match a set of goals and objectives with a timeline for building your site. View the process as an evolutionary one and allow for changes in strategy and purpose even after the first release of the site. Many new sites begin with a set of milestones such as the following:

1. **"Coming Soon" page:** Start with a single page that says "Coming Soon" to make sure that the domain is listed and your Web server and connection are reliable. If a "Coming Soon" page goes down for a little while, it isn't that big of a deal.

2. **"Phase one" site:** Keep your first site simple, but make sure that phase one provides something useful. Even an address, phone number, and driving directions can make a site worth visiting. From a "phase one" site, you may be able to figure out what is of most interest to visitors. For example, you can find out what the most popular pages are or listen to user feedback. A few product pictures, prices, and a phone number may generate enough business to encourage an online commerce component in "phase two." To point is, "phase one" is when you begin publicizing yourself.

3. **"Phase two" site:** Build a site that addresses the needs and goals of your organization. Add the features that are necessary to attract visitors and keep them coming back. Try to build anticipation for the launch and then go live with a splash.

? **What kind of Web etiquette should be factored into the design and construction of a site?**

No matter how hard you try to conform to rules, written or unwritten, critics will find something to harp on in a Web site. Most unwritten rules of the Internet—called *netiquette* in some circles—apply more to newsgroup postings and e-mail than they do to Web sites.

You may also rest assured that many popular sites on the Web have cast convention aside, increased site traffic, and set industry trends at the same time. However, these sound, practical words of wisdom should at least be considered before being broken:

- Avoid excessive use of the <BLINK> tag. Simply put, people hate it and it is a distraction.

- Include a "mailto:" tag on your welcome page as a direct link to the person who administers your site. If something breaks on your site, a visitor is the first to notice. An e-mail link to someone who administers the site is a great first line of defense.

- If you ask users to submit e-mail addresses on a form, ask them as well if they would like to be e-mailed. Everyone hates unsolicited e-mail. In fact, many users make up an e-mail address to keep from being spammed as the result of a form that they filled out on a site. If you do have an e-mail list, give recipients an easy way to remove themselves from the list.

- Avoid using the REFRESH attribute of the <META> tag with the time set to zero seconds. This effectively disables the Previous button in a number of different browsers, including Netscape Navigator 2.0.

- Don't open up a new window for every hyperlink that leads out of your site.

- Try to avoid making site visitors scroll horizontally.

- Verify links to ensure that they aren't broken. Use a tool or a service, if necessary, to ensure that both the hyperlinks and the graphics are all still intact.

- When you move and rename popular pages, provide either an alias to the new page or a "page has moved" notification with a hyperlink to the page's new location.

- Offer file sizes and creation dates for downloadable files as a courtesy.

- If people frequently confuse your Web address with another address, provide a friendly link to the the other address. (See http://www.altavista.com for an example.)

Chapter 3

Web Server

Answers Topics!

Web Servers @ a Glance

A Web server is a crucial element in the delivery of Web content. Which server you choose and the environment in which it lives determine how fast, flexible, and functional your site is. There is a big difference between a server that you maintain and a server that is hosted by an Internet service provider. Understanding the advantages and disadvantages of hosting a Web site will help you to make the best hosting decisions.

You have to make other decisions as well. For example, you have to decide what your server's connection speed to the Internet will be, which operating system to use, and which software to use. Changing Web servers after a site launch is difficult and risky, so knowing beforehand about servers will help make your site a success. Poor decisions made at the outset can affect a site over a long period of time.

This chapter covers the following important topics:

Web Server Basics explains what happens when a hyperlink is clicked or a URL is entered, as well as the pros and cons of using an Internet host provider for your Web site.

Hosting with an Internet Service Provider covers the ins and outs of using another company to host your Web site and keep your Web site running.

Hosting a Site Yourself explains the important decisions you have to make if you want to play host at a Web site. It explores selecting a connection, hardware, and software for the site.

Selecting a Web Server discusses what you should look for when you select Web server software. You also find out how to tell what Web server software other sites are using.

WEB SERVER BASICS

? What happens when a URL is entered or a hyperlink is clicked in a Web browser?

This may sound like a simple question, but it really isn't. When you type in a URL from a Web browser or click a hyperlink on a Web page, the Web browser converts a string of characters into a correctly formatted HTTP GET request. Through the Internet connection, the string of characters—they essentially ask for a page, graphic, or other kind of file—is sent. The domain name section of the URL (http://www.news.com, for example) is converted into an IP address by the nearest domain name server. A domain name server is essentially a large, frequently updated database. A domain name server matches IP addresses to domain names. After the request has been converted to an IP address, it travels across the Internet to the Web server that has been assigned a matching address.

As soon as it receives the correctly formatted request, the Web server reads the rest of the URL line and finds the corresponding document or file. A correctly formatted request always includes a return IP address. The Web server reads the return IP address and simply sends the file back to the person who requested it.

When a request is made to executable programs such as search engines, chat servers, bulletin boards, and online form submissions, a server script or compiled application is triggered. The application may search a database, send e-mail, or read a text file. However, it must send back text of some sort, or there is an error. The text that is sent from a server application may be as short as a single-line redirection to another URL or as long as HTML for an entire Web page.

Web servers not only handle Web page requests, they also help organize and set attributes to different types of content. Web servers are used to set virtual roots, to set security for secure Web sites, and to set which directories comprise executable content and which do not.

❓ Is it better to host my own site or to select a host provider such as an ISP?

Hosting your own site is a reasonable option under these conditions: you have a continuous connection to the Internet, you know how to maintain a Web server, you can afford a domain name, and you have Web server software and all the necessary hardware. Installing the necessary hardware and software is not enough, because the Web server still needs to be connected to the Internet via a constant or dial-up connection.

For companies with a strong MIS department and a long-term dedication to serving a site, hosting a site internally is not a bad option. What's more, if your site requires a large amount of custom configuration, using an ISP may not be an option, because finding an ISP to host your site at a reasonable cost may be too difficult.

Hosting a site externally, with an ISP, presents different considerations. Most ISPs have a standard configuration for their servers, and they want their customers to stay within the standard configuration. As long as you follow the rules laid down by the ISP, your site will probably receive the following services:

- 24-hour monitoring
- Up-to-date software patches for firewalls and Web servers
- Preconfigured servers
- Fast Internet connections for your site's server
- Dial-in accounts
- E-mail addresses
- Log file analyses for site statistics
- Preconfigured MIME types

Some ISPs offer special functionality such as search mechanisms, streaming audio, and bulletin boards. However, Web site owners have to pay extra for these services.

HOSTING WITH AN INTERNET SERVICE PROVIDER

? **What qualities should I look for in choosing an ISP?**

Every site has different needs, but every ISP shopper should look for these qualities in an ISP:

- **Support:** How long do you have to wait for a tech person to pick up the phone at the ISP? Are the hours reasonable? Response speed is critical when things go wrong, so on-site, 24-hour support is a great feature. If a Web server goes down at an ISP, you likely will not have access and be able to solve the problem yourself remotely. The importance of good support from an ISP cannot be overemphasized.

- **Location:** Is the ISP a local call away? If you use the ISP for dial-up connections, the long distance charges start to add up. And many people feel more comfortable using an ISP that is within driving distance. The odds of actually having to visit your ISP are probably low, but if you do need to pay a visit to the ISP, its proximity is important.

- **Similar sites:** Find out if the ISP hosts sites similar to your own, and if it does, call or e-mail the Webmasters to find out if they are happy with the service. You will hear it from a frustrated Webmaster if he or she has had problems with the ISP.

- **Speed:** Web servers at the ISP should be connected to the Internet with a fast connection such as a T1 or T3 line. It helps if the connection to the Internet is as close to the Internet backbone as possible. The more servers between your ISP and the main Internet trunk, the longer the lag time is for each request to the server.

- **Hidden costs:** Make sure that requesting small things such as adding MIME types to the Web server does not result in ridiculous charges. Many host providers allow a certain number of megabytes to be downloaded each month from your site before they charge extra. If your site is particularly popular one month, you could be charged a lot for downloads. Also make sure that your site is given an adequate amount of hard drive space. ISPs frequently charge more per month for sites that are over 20 to 25MB in size; some ISPs set the file size limit as low as 5MB. Calculating your space requirements early and managing space well can save big in the long run.

● **Security access:** What sort of access do you get to the server? You should have permission to place CGI scripts on the server. You should also have authorization to change security permissions on your own files. Most important, others should not have access to your files. If you can access the files on other sites, then they may very well have access to yours. Ask the ISP if you have the option of setting up an anonymous or password-protected FTP directory that is separate from your Web files. An FTP directory is a valuable asset to a business that wants to share files remotely.

● **Perks:** Many ISPs offer perks such as e-mail, real audio streams, search engines, registration services, lots of scripting language options, and databases. Whether an ISP offers perks is indicative of its willingness to offer cutting-edge technologies as they appear. If you want to expand or enhance your site with added functionality, look for an ISP that could potentially fulfill your wish list.

● **Tracking and reporting:** Many ISPs do not offer tracking and reporting statisitics on the number of visitors to a site. Others charge for the service. Find out whether the ISP performs log-file analyses and whether it charges for this service. At minimum, an ISP should give you access to your raw standard log files. With your raw files, you at least have the ability to perform statistical analyses on Web site traffic and performance at your site.

? What kinds of Web server and platform choices will I have if I host my site at an Internet service provider?

For sites hosted on a shared server along with other sites (the least expensive route), most ISPs do not offer a choice of

Web servers or platforms. For ease of maintenance and security, most ISPs stick to one platform and one Web server for shared machines. Most ISPs use UNIX as the operating system, and either Apache, NCSA, or Netscape Web servers. Recently, many ISPs have begun offering Microsoft Windows NT hosting, with Microsoft Internet Information Server as the Web server.

By looking carefully, you can find a variety of configurations, especially from small ISPs. National ISPs tend to be conservative in the server configurations they offer because they have to follow broad corporate policies on adopting new server configurations. Look carefully and you will find a provider with the resources that you need. Start by looking on ISP Web sites. Configuration options are almost always listed on the Web.

Dedicated server hosting is becoming a popular option for medium to large sites that require 24-hour support. Many ISPs let businesses and individuals place their own servers alongside the ISP's servers for increased bandwidth and to allow for 24-hour maintenance. ISPs are usually quite flexible about server platform and software choices in this type of arrangement, but most ISPs only support environments with which they are familiar. Dedicated server hosting is a more expensive option than sharing server space, but if your site requires a highly customized server configuration or requires special attention, a dedicated server may be the only way to go.

HOSTING A SITE YOURSELF

What is involved in hosting a site myself?

To host a site yourself, you need all of the following:

- A Web connection through a network access provider
- Web server software on a machine that is connected
- A domain name server that directs HTTP traffic to your server

❓ What kind of connection do I need?

Two types of connections are available: *dial-up,* also known as an *on-demand connection*, and *continuous,* also referred to as a *dedicated connection.* The basic difference is that, with an on-demand connection, a connection between the Web server and the host provider is established only when necessary. With a continuous connection, the connection is always on and the line is never dropped, even when the network is inactive.

Dial–up connection

For on-demand connectivity, a connection is created between your Web server and your network access provider when a page or graphic is requested from your Web server. After a set period of network inactivity, the line is dropped and your server remains physically disconnected from the Internet until another Web page or graphic is requested. The period of inactivity may range from a few minutes with regular phone lines to 15 seconds with connections such as ISDN, which are much faster at re-establishing a connection to a network access provider. Each time a connection is re-established, a delay occurs. Delays range from less than a second with some ISDN connections to as much as five seconds with some regular phone connections.

Continuous connection

For a continuous Web connection you need, at a bare minimum, a computer hooked up to a network access provider. Some network access providers offer a firewall, a primary or secondary domain name server for your Web server, and a dedicated IP address. Many large ISPs provide basic network access services. For continuous connections, the line is not dropped and connections can be made instantly. Leaving a line constantly connected can be expensive but is usually a good option for sites with significant traffic.

Table 3-1 lists the services and rates for dedicated Web connections.

Name of Line	Line Capacity	Description	Approximate Price of Dedicated Connection
T3 or DS1	45 million bits/sec 5625 KB/sec	Equivalent to 673 regular phone lines, is used only by the largest Web sites and ISPs. An extremely expensive option, but the fastest option currently available. In many regions, connections faster than T1 are not available.	$2100–$4000/month
T2 or DS2	6.3 million bits/sec 788 KB/sec	Composed of four T1 lines, is the equivalent of 96 regular phone lines. Usually the price difference between T2 and T3 is small enough to warrant using a T3.	$1800–$3800/month
T1 or DS1	1.5 million bits/sec 187 KB/sec	Uses what is, in essence, 24 normal telephone lines bundled together. A good option for larger businesses. Many ISPs use one T1 to connect all their Web sites to the Internet. T1 connections do not suffer from the speed hit of using a modem; as a result, they are faster than simply operating many phone lines in parallel with modems.	$800–$2000/month

Table 3-1 Services and Rates for Dedicated Web Connections

Name of Line	Line Capacity	Description	Approximate Price of Dedicated Connection
ISDN	Max 128,000 bits/sec (depending on the configuration)	Most regions in the U.S. now offer Internet Services Digital Network connectivity to the office or home. Costs vary drastically by region. Areas in which ISDN is most common tend to be the least expensive. Probably the fastest and most cost-effective Internet connection available to the home.	$100–$500/month
Normal Phone Line	33,000 bits/sec 4 KB/sec two-way 55,000 bits/sec 7 KB/sec optimized for one direction	Regular phone line, also known as twisted pair.	$15–$25/month

Table 3-1   Services and Rates for Dedicated Web Connections (*continued*)

 Note: *When choosing a connection, note the difference between T and DS connections. T, as in T1, refers specifically to bundled telephone wires. DS, or Digital Service, refers to the speed and capacity of the connection and is a unit of measurement that is the equivalent to the throughput of its matching T number. A connection may be defined as DS3, but if it uses fiberoptics or bundled ISDN, it is not a T3 connection.*

? What does Web Server Software do?

At its simplest level, a Web server is merely a piece of software that responds to requests for documents, images, and other files via HTTP. Web servers can be run on almost any operating system. With small numbers of requests, a Web server can run even on slow desktop computers. Currently, most Web servers are UNIX-based, but Windows NT is rapidly becoming a popular Internet server platform alternative. A number of Web server applications are also available for the Macintosh and most other popular operating systems.

Web server software receives requests for Web pages, graphics, and other files and either executes CGIs or simply finds the files on the hard drive and delivers them with correctly formatted HTTP headers.

? What other equipment may be required for hosting my own site?

To host your own Web site, you may also need this equipment:

● **Routers:** The role of a *router* is to route information between two networks. Routers are usually in the form of a box with cords going in and out. Internally, routers perform very complex tasks. The easiest way to think of a router is as a bridge. Routers not only direct information, they may also convert analog signals into digital data.

● **DNS (domain name server):** A domain name server is basically just a database of domain names and their associated IP addresses. Often organizations point their domain name to a DNS server, and the server then points to the actual machine on which the site is hosted. When a Web site changes IP addresses, the domain name associated with the site stays the same. Simply updating your DNS server to point to the new IP address of the Web server is all that is necessary. DNS servers also allow you to split one domain into multiple hosts. Search.yahoo.com, for example, is a different host server than www.yahoo.com.

● **Modem:** A server on a dial-up connection requires a modem. When a server gets a request after a certain period of inactivity, the ISP's computers literally call the server to establish a connection.

SELECTING A WEB SERVER

? **What types of Web servers are available?**

Web servers come in different shapes, sizes, and prices. Popular Web servers are designed to meet the common needs of Webmasters, but other servers are highly specialized and are meant for specific activities. Following is a list of common Web server features:

● **Speed/load:** The ability to serve pages to high numbers of simultaneous Web site visitors as quickly as possible.

● **Database connectivity:** Linking content from databases to Web pages.

● **Commerce:** Securing financial transactions for online commerce, such as the kind of transactions done on the Wells Fargo Web site shown in Figure 3-1.

● **Custom scripting:** Built-in server-scripting languages or APIs for server scripting. With custom scripting, server-side applications can be built more quickly and can run more efficiently than standard CGI.

A number of Web servers try to include as many features as possible, such as the kind shown in Figure 3-2, but often the best Web server is the one that was designed for a specific type of functionality. For specialized tasks, you can modify existing Web servers. For example, ad servers, ISP servers that host multiple domains, and search engine servers are often mainstream Web servers that were heavily configured to do specific tasks.

? **What should I look for when I choose a Web server platform?**

As you choose and evaluate Web servers, determining which features you need or may need in the future is important.

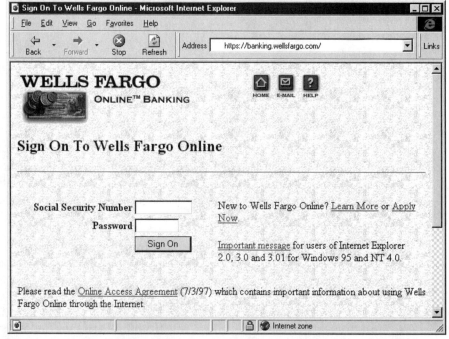

Figure 3-1   The www.wellsfargo.com site specializes in secure Web transactions. Thanks to secure sockets and Netscape Commerce Server, private bank account information can be sent securely over the Internet.

Changing Web servers is usually more difficult than a standard software installation. Because a large percentage of Web servers are either optimized for one operating system or only run on one operating system, choosing an operating system first is a good idea.

First, inventory your hardware and determine whether it is powerful enough to handle the number of simultaneous requests that you expect your site to receive. If you anticipate no more than 10 to 20 visitors at the same time and your site is made up mostly of HTML pages and static graphics, any reasonable desktop computer will suffice. Web servers are available for every major operating system, but sticking with the platform with which you are most familiar is a good idea. Problems with Web servers are often caused

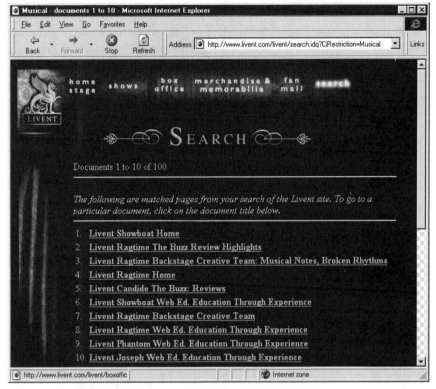

Figure 3-2   The www.livent.com site uses Internet Information Server's
Active Server scripting to provide server-side e-mail, an
online quiz, and up-to-date stock price listings.

by operating system configurations such as network settings
and security settings. Familiarity with the operating system
is often a prerequisite for debugging problems.

If your existing computer has an Intel or Intel-compatible
chip set, you should probably choose Microsoft Windows NT
or IBM's OS2 Warp. Most people in the business world are
familiar with the Windows 95/NT interface, so Windows NT
is the operating system of choice. Another option for Intel
PCs is to use Linux, a freely available version of UNIX.
However, beware of the large number of publicly released
security holes in Linux that could effect your Web server.

For Motorola PowerPC computers, Macintosh OS and
OS2 Warp are both good choices. Consider what type of
support you are able to get—both in-house support and
vendor support—for both platforms. Pick the one you feel
most comfortable with in a crisis.

When you choose a UNIX operating system for a Web Server, consider the security issues and the optimization issues. If the source code for the operating system is available, problems can often be exploited more easily, but also fixed more quickly. Operating systems such as Sun's Solaris and Silicon Graphic's Irix are both heavily optimized for each company's respective computers. As a result, these operating systems are less likely to encounter stability problems and will likely run faster than other operating systems.

? What should I look for when I choose a Web server application?

If you are fortunate enough to have a popular operating system, the number of Web server applications you can choose from is quite large. A quick visit to http://serverwatch. internet.com/ will reveal exactly how many choices are available. Here are some things to consider as you look for a Web server application:

- **Support:** If things go wrong, can you rely on tech support? How about eager teams of newsgroup and mailing list junkies who would love a chance to help you? If your site is mission-critical, try to get 24-hour support or at least a tech support staff in the same time zone that you are in. Don't be afraid to call tech support before you purchase a product to find out how long it takes to get support.

- **Security:** For Internet Web servers, an important consideration is how much time passes on average between the time that security holes are found in the Web server and the time that update patches become available online. Security holes often become public knowledge before patches are available, and the time that it takes for patches to become available can be a dangerous time for your server. Also, determine if the source code of the Web server is available. If so, ask yourself if you are comfortable with this; a large percentage of Webmasters are not. Selecting a well-documented Web server is a good idea in terms of setup and use, as well as in terms of patches and fixes. In general, the more popular a Web server, the easier it is to learn about problems in advance and fix those problems.

● **Installation:** Many UNIX Web servers need to be compiled in order to run. Some Windows servers require a DOS-based installation. Is the installation process easy enough to ensure that security and configuration problems will not appear? If you are worried about installation, stick with a platform that you know. Few will argue that Macintosh-based Web servers, although not as common as other servers on the Web, are among the easiest to install.

● **Administration:** Administration interfaces for Web servers range from command-line and Telnet, to HTML, to full Windows-based applications. A bad interface causes problems, wastes time, and can potentially lead to misconfiguration and security holes. A knowledgeable Web site administrator can configure a server for security and efficiency, as well as identify problems as they arise. Being informed will help you identify problems and suggest solutions to ISP technicians even on a site that is hosted on a shared server at an ISP.

● **Features:** If your site requires server-side e-mail, a search engine, or database connectivity, you need a server that supports those features. If the server does allow for the functionality, find out how easy the features are to add to the site. Adding a "search our site" feature can take anywhere from a few hours to a few days, depending on the method and software you use. Your Web server may narrow the list of software options to only a few. If possible, narrow your site's features before you select a Web server or ISP. If you don't know what features you need, make sure that your Web server is flexible.

● **Performance:** A great number of Web server benchmarks have been published. Compare the load and performance specifications for the servers that are available for your platform. Will the server deliver enough simultaneous connections for the type of work it will be doing? How much will a search-engine search or database request slow it down? For example, a site that anticipates a great deal of traffic and a large number of pages dynamically generated from a server application should stay away from Web servers that only support the basic CGI interface for server applications.

Security and performance are discussed in more detail in later chapters.

✱   ***Note:***   *Security and performance concerns make dedicating at least one machine as the Web server a good idea. If price is an issue, save money on the monitor and keyboard, and don't worry about a sound card or expensive graphics board. A dedicated Web server that runs well should not require much hands-on attention.*

Popular Web Servers for the Major Operating Systems

Web server software is available for every major operating system. There are well over a hundred Web servers available, but only a handful of industry leaders dominate the market for each platform. If you are considering adding a Web server to your server, you should consider the market leaders for your server's operating system. The following is a list of operating systems and associated Web server software:

Operating System	Web Server
BSD UNIX/Red Hat	Apache
	Netscape
	NCSA
Solaris	Apache
	Netscape
SGI	Apache
	Netscape
	Web Force
Windows NT	Microsoft Internet Information Server
	Netscape
	Web Commander
	Web Site
Macintosh	WebStar

❓ How can I tell if my Web server can be seen from the Internet?

If your Web server is installed but is not responding to HTTP requests, you can run a number of different tests to locate the problem. First, try pinging the computer by using its IP address. If your requests go through a firewall, your ping requests may be blocked. If the server is responding, you at least know that there is an established network connection with the server. Depending on your network setup, a successful ping from outside your network may give you a more accurate reading of whether the server can indeed be seen from the Internet and not just your network.

Essentially, a *ping* is simply a string of data sent to a server. The server responds to the ping after it has received all of the data. Ping applications usually tell you either how long each ping took or whether your request timed out. A timed-out request does not necessarily mean that a server is down. A successful request, however, means that the server is at least connected to the network. The time it takes to return a standard ping request can also be a useful diagnostic tool. Anything over 300 milliseconds is considered way too long for a Web server on the Internet. If your server is nearby, response times should be under 200 milliseconds.

To ping a server from Windows 95, Windows NT, and most UNIX platforms, simply enter the word **ping** followed by the server's IP address from a command prompt, as shown in Figure 3-3.

To determine if the Web server is running, request a page from the Web server using a Web browser on the Web server itself. First, try using the machine's name or IP address (http://www or http:// 198.137.240.92, for example). If your server's browser gets no response from its Web service, the Web server software is either not running, or it has been misconfigured. If the test does work, try requesting a page from the Web server using a browser on a separate machine using the server's IP address instead of its full domain name. For example, entering http://198.81.129.99/ in the URL line returns the same page as entering http://www.odci.gov. If entering an IP address from a Web browser on a separate machine works, try accessing it over the Internet. If there is no response then the problem is most likely a networking problem.

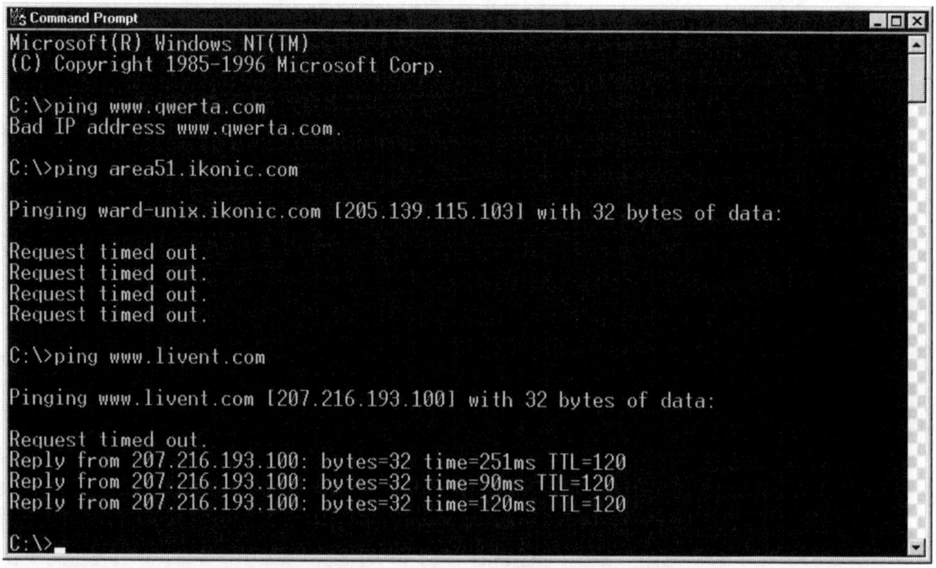

```
Command Prompt                                                        _ □ ✕
Microsoft(R) Windows NT(TM)
(C) Copyright 1985-1996 Microsoft Corp.

C:\>ping www.qwerta.com
Bad IP address www.qwerta.com.

C:\>ping area51.ikonic.com

Pinging ward-unix.ikonic.com [205.139.115.103] with 32 bytes of data:

Request timed out.
Request timed out.
Request timed out.
Request timed out.

C:\>ping www.livent.com

Pinging www.livent.com [207.216.193.100] with 32 bytes of data:

Request timed out.
Reply from 207.216.193.100: bytes=32 time=251ms TTL=120
Reply from 207.216.193.100: bytes=32 time=90ms TTL=120
Reply from 207.216.193.100: bytes=32 time=120ms TTL=120

C:\>
```

Figure 3-3 Pinging a server is one of the quickest and easiest ways to check if a server is connected to the network or Internet.

A Web server that responds locally to a Web page request made to its IP address but not from the Internet has a networking or firewall problem. You will get a warning from your browser that says the server is not responding. If you don't trust your browser, you can telnet to the correct port on your Web server by using the technique described in "How can I tell what Web server software other sites are using?" in Chapter 1.

If the Web server does respond to a request made over the Internet to its IP address, try using the domain name. If using the domain name fails to return a Web page, the problem can be narrowed down to your local domain name server or InterNIC's information regarding your domain. Check to make sure that you are up to date with any fees to InterNIC. You can check out the information that InterNIC keeps on your domain using a whois search. For more information on using whois, see "How can I tell if a domain name is taken?" in Chapter 1.

The most common reason for your Web server failing to respond is the fact that it needs to be started. Many computers reboot after losing power, but do not restart their

Web services. Try following your Web server's instructions for restarting the server. For a list of common Web server problems, see the list of problems described in "What are the most common causes of Web server failure?" in Chapter 1.

If problems persist, you may need a network engineer to debug your connectivity problems.

Connecting a Web Server to the Internet Using a Modem

Using a dial-up or dedicated connection between a Web server and a network access provider over a regular phone line requires a Serial Line Internet Protocol (SLIP) or Point to Point Protocol (PPP) connection. Your Web server may require special software that creates data packets so that the data packets can be sent via modem and conventional phone lines. PPP software is preinstalled on the latest Apple Macintosh and Microsoft Windows operating systems. You have to install the software on other operating systems.

Chapter 4

Managing a Web Server

Managing a Web Server @ a Glance

Managing a Web server involves more than just allowing pages to be served. For many Webmasters, managing a Web server— or a cluster of servers—is a full-time job. As a site grows and new technology is added, a number of server tasks need to be performed. Whether it is adding MIME types and virtual roots, or analyzing a site's log files, the role of managing a server is crucial.

Many people make the mistake of thinking that the Webmaster is involved with configuring the Web server from the beginning. That may have been the case a few years ago, but today most Webmasters inherit a server that has already been built and configured. As a result, it is important to not only be able to set up a site, but also to be able to deconstruct and understand a site that has been around for a while.

This chapter covers the following important topics:

File Path and the URL Line takes some of the mystery out of how URL lines are configured and how they relate to the actual location of files on a Web server. Setting up virtual roots and tracking down your files on the server, as well as other common problems, are also covered in this section.

Configuring Server-Generated Pages explains how to configure automatic directory listings for directories in your Web site. You also learn how to customize and understand the error messages that are generated by the Web server.

Site Tracking and Reporting covers the nitty-gritty details of log file formats, what information they store, and what type of information you can garner from them. This section also includes useful tips for finding and using tools that analyze and generate reports on Web site statistics.

FILE PATH AND THE URL LINE

?
How does the URL line relate to the location of a document on the Web server in a basic server configuration?

Figuring out a URL path to a file sitting on a Web server, such as the one shown in Figure 4-1, can be surprisingly difficult, depending on how the Web server is configured. Understanding how the URL line is constructed is a big step toward figuring out the correct URL path to a file. A Web URL is usually constructed in the following format:

http://host.domain.com/directory/filename

Domain

All path information through the end of the domain name, *.com* in the case of the example URL listed above, is a reference to the server. Note that some sites include a port number after the domain name, usually to reference a specific Web server on a machine, to help you to find the

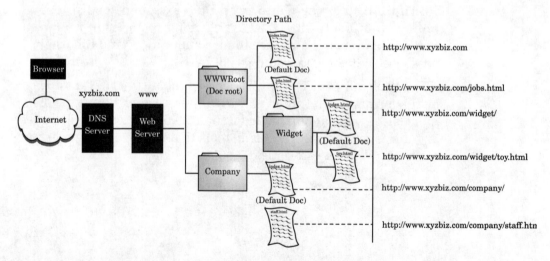

Figure 4-1 The relationship between the URL line and the actual directory path to a document on the Web server can be deceiving.

correct configuration files, and so on. Port names appear in this format:

http://host.domain.com:port/

For *multi-homed* Web servers (Web servers that host sites with different IP addresses and domain names), you need to find the configuration files for the domain name or IP address associated with your domain on the Web server.

Document root

Next, determine the file path for the *document root,* also referred to as the *home directory,* of the Web server. You need to check your Web server's configuration files or administration interface to find the document root.

If your file sits within your Web server's document root directory, the URL path is

http://host.domain.com/file.html

Suppose the file is in a directory named "products" within your document root. In that case, the path is

http://host.domain.com/products/file.html

? What are virtual roots, and how are they referenced in the URL line?

If a Web file does not sit somewhere in the document root of the Web server, it is probably located in a directory that has been set to be a virtual root of the server. *Virtual roots* are directories that are aliased by the Web server and may sit anywhere on the Web server's hard-drive. On the URL line, virtual roots are treated as if they sat within the document root of the server.

A directory can be set as a virtual root with a different name. For example, a directory named "CompanyEmployees" may be set as a virtual root named "people." The URL path to a file that sits in the directory CompanyEmployees would be

http://host.domain.com/people/file.html

Virtual roots are set on servers for a number of reasons, but usually they are used for directories that have different security access permissions or for directories that have executable permissions. To create a hyperlink from any HTML document on the server to the file listed, as in the example above in the people virtual root, use the following syntax:

<A HREF="/people/file">Link</A>

Note: *Giving virtual roots different names from the directories to which they are mapped is usually a poor idea. Giving them different names can make it extremely difficult to find files and determine the correct syntax for hyperlinks within a site. It is also a poor idea to give a virtual root a name with forward slashes—people / business /, for example—because many Web servers are incapable of handling them. Different names and forward slashes needlessly make it more difficult to determine the correct URL paths for documents and directories.*

How do I set a virtual root for my Web server?

To set a virtual directory, you first need to know the file path to the actual folder you want to alias and the alias name you want to associate with your virtual root. Read on to find out how to set these attributes in a Web server.

Netscape Enterprise Server

Follow these steps to set a virtual root with Netscape Enterprise Server:

1. Go to the Enterprise Server main administration screen.
2. Select the Web site you want to edit (there may only be one).
3. Select Content Management from the menu.
4. Select Additional Document Directories from the menu on the left.
5. Under URL prefix, enter the name of the virtual root you want to add.
6. Enter the file path to the directory under Map To Directory.

7. Select OK.

8. Select Save and apply from the Save and Apply Changes page.

Apache and NCSA

To set a virtual root in Apache and NCSA, edit the server resource management file, srm.conf. The following syntax aliases a directory path outside of the document root of the Web server to create a virtual root named "people":

Alias /user/local/html/people/people

Microsoft's Internet Information Server

To set a virtual root with the Internet Information Server:

1. Open the Internet Service Manager and double-click WWW Service.

2. Select the Directories tab.

3. Click the Add button and enter the file path to the folder you want to link to your virtual root. You may select Browse to find the directory.

4. Enter the name of your new virtual root in the Virtual Directory text box.

5. Select whether the directory will be executable, read-only, or both read and execute by clicking the check boxes at the bottom of the window.

6. Select OK and then select Apply.

How can I tell where on the Web server hard drive a file is sitting based on its URL line?

The simplest way to find a file on a UNIX machine is to do a UNIX search from a shell account on the Web server. To find a file named class.html, for example, use the following syntax:

```
find / -name class.html -print
```

If you don't have shell access to your server and you rely on FTP to search directories, you are stuck and have to find the file yourself.

Starting with the filename, keep in mind that the name could be an alias on the server to a different file name at a different location. This possibility is particularly true with UNIX servers. If you are looking for an HTML file, remember that when no filename exists on the URL line, the actual file name matches the name of the default document setting on the Web server. The file is usually named index.html, default.htm, or welcome.html, although the server may have been configured differently.

If you can't find a directory name, the file sits at the document root directory for the Web server. Obtaining the absolute file path to this directory from your Web server's administration interface should be easy. If there is directory information, the path is most likely a reflection of either an actual path that starts in the document root directory or a virtual path that has been specified in the Web server's administration interface or configuration file. Common names for document root directories include wwwroot, htdocs, docs, web, and www.

Start by looking for a virtual root in the Web server that is named after the directory in the URL line, and, if it exists, use the file path specified in the server. If no virtual root is specified, search for a directory that matches the URL line in the document root of the Web server.

Pay attention to directory names that begin with / ~*directory*. A tilde (~)—pronounced til-DA—at the beginning of a directory name is often used in Apache to map users' home directories. For these directories, you should consult the Apache documentation. Also, be aware that, with UNIX, directories can be aliased on the file system as well as on the Web server. After you have found the correct directory referenced by the Web server, you may need to see if it actually points at a file system level to another directory on the hard drive of the Web server.

? What should a document be named for the specific file name to be unnecessary in the URL line?

When a Web page comes up that hasn't been specifically named in the URL line (the home page of www.apple.com, for example), a default document for the directory referenced in the URL has been set. The actual filename for the default document of a directory, or *directory index file* as it is also known, is set in the Web server itself. The most common filenames for default documents on Web servers are index.html, default.htm, and welcome.html.

For large Web sites, the problem with default document names is that it may be necessary for as many as fifty files named index.html to be present for every directory to have a default document. To solve this problem, many sites create aliases that map index.html (or the appropriate default document name that is specified in the server) to a document that shares the directory's name but has *.html* on the end. A default document in a directory named employees, for example, would be named employees.html and have an alias sitting at the same directory level named index.html that points to it.

Netscape Enterprise Server

For Netscape servers, the default document at the time of installation is index.html. Follow these steps to change this filename:

1. Go to the Enterprise Server main administration screen.
2. Select the Web site you want to edit (there may only be one).
3. Select Content Management from the menu.
4. Select Document Preferences from the menu on the left.
5. Enter the name of the default document you want to apply in the Index Filenames text box. For multiple default document names, separate the names with commas and prioritize them from left to right.
6. Click OK.
7. Select Save and apply from the Save and Apply Changes page.

Microsoft Internet Information Server

On Microsoft's Internet Information Server, the default document at the time of installation is default.htm. Follow these steps to change the default document:

1. Open the Internet Service Manager and double-click WWW Service.
2. Select the Directories tab.

3. Enter the default document name in the Default Document text box. Make sure that the Enable Default Document check box is checked off.

4. Select OK and then Apply.

With version 3.0, Microsoft added the ability to specify a number of different default documents in order of priority. To set multiple documents in Internet Information Server, simply separate the names with commas (index.html, default.htm, index.htm, default.html, for example) and insert them into the default document field.

Apache and NCSA

Edit the server resource management file, srm.conf, by using the following syntax for multiple default documents:

```
DirectoryIndex index.html default.htm
```

Note: *Referring to a default document by filename also works perfectly well. For example, http://www. apache.org/index.html brings up the same Web page as http://www.apache.org.*

CONFIGURING SERVER-GENERATED PAGES

How can I make my server automatically list all the documents in a directory?

When no document is specified as part of a URL request, the Web server looks for a default document. And if no default document is available, most Web servers either create a directory index with hyperlinks to the individual documents or send a 404 page not found error response. A setting in the Web server determines whether or not a directory is listed when a default document does not exist.

Netscape Enterprise Server

Follow these steps to add directory indexing to your Netscape Enterprise Server:

1. Go to the Enterprise Server main administration screen.
2. Select the Web site you want to edit (there may only be one).
3. Select Content Management from the menu.
4. Select Fancy or Simple under Directory Indexing.
5. Click OK.
6. Select Save and apply from the Save and Apply Changes page.

Microsoft Internet Information Server

Follow these steps to add directory indexing to your Microsoft Internet Information Server:

1. Open the Internet Service Manager and double-click WWW Service.
2. Select the Directories tab.
3. Select the Directory Browsing Allowed check box.
4. Select OK and then select Apply.

Apache and NCSA

To add directory indexing to your Apache or NCSA Web server you will need to modify the IndexOptions setting in the server resource management file, srm.conf. For example, IndexOptions FancyIndexing generates an index with the contents of a directory.

? When I request some pages, I get messages such as HTTP://1.0 404 Bad Request. What do the different error codes mean?

When a Web page that does not exist is requested, an HTTP status code is generated that reports the error. Some Web servers send site visitors to a friendly page that states that the page they are looking for does not exist. All too often, however, an HTTP status code simply appears in the Web browser with little or no explanation as to what it means.

HTTP status codes are generated every time a Web page, graphic, and so on is requested from a Web server. Contrary to what Web surfers may think, not all status codes are bad.

In fact, the vast majority of status codes users receive are 200 codes, which indicate that everything is fine. To view status codes that have been generated by your server, you need to look at your log files. In almost every Web server log file format, log status codes are logged. For performance reasons, some Web servers offer a setting by which the logging of successfully served documents is turned off. When this is the case, only true errors and unusual events are recorded.

Table 4-1 lists the HTTP status codes and their definitions.

Category	Error Code	Error Meaning
1XX Informational	100	Continue. The server has received the first part of its request and the request is being processed.
2XX Successful	200	OK. The request was successful.
	201	Created. This code follows a POST from a Web page. It indicates that a document was created.
	202	Accepted. The request has been accepted, but it is not known if any action was taken.
	203	Partial Information. Not all the information was returned following a GET request.
	204	No Response. The server received the request, but no information was returned.
3XX Redirection	301	Moved Permanently. This code is for pages that have permanently moved to a new location.
	302	Found. The requested item was found, but it resides in a different location. Often used for pages that have temporarily moved.
	303	Method. The document has not been modified since the date in the If-Modified-Since field in the request.
	304	Not Modified. The requested document exists, but it has not been modified since the date specified in the request.

Table 4-1 HTTP Status Codes

Category	Error Code	Error Meaning
4XX Client Error	400	Bad Request. Most likely bad syntax or unacceptable characters in the URL.
	401	Unauthorized. Security permissions prevent the page from being sent out.
	402	Payment Required. Requires an acceptable "Charge To" header.
	403	Forbidden. The request has been forbidden for reasons other than insufficient authorization.
	404	Not Found. The item requested was not found on the server.
5XX Server Error	500	Internal Error. The server could not fulfill the request because of an internal error.
	501	Not Implemented. The server does not support the request method that was made.
	502	Service Temporarily Overloaded
	503	Gateway Timeout.

Table 4-1　HTTP Status Codes (*continued*)

How can I customize the page that my server displays for different error codes?

Browsing the Web, you no doubt requested many pages that did not exist, and you may have noticed the variety of ways that such pages are displayed. At worst, you see Web server default error pages or pages that are hard-coded into the Web server software. The prettiest and most helpful pages, however, have been customized, such as the Yahoo! page shown in Figure 4-2.

To customize a server's error messages, you may need to edit your Web server's preferences or add functionality to the Web server by means of software modifications. For examples of custom error pages, try entering a URL for a page that doesn't exist on a popular site (for example, http://www.yahoo.com/hoohoo.html). Keep in mind that an error page is still exactly that—an error page. Visitors with slow connection speeds would rather see a lightweight page than wait for large error graphics to download.

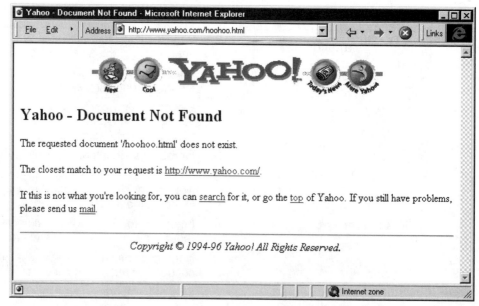

Figure 4-2   A customized error page that Yahoo! kindly provides helps visitors to the site get back on the right track.

Netscape Enterprise Server

The following steps will allow you to customize your Netscape Enterprise Server error responses:

1. Go to the Enterprise Server main administration screen.

2. Select the Web site you want to edit (there may only be one).

3. Select Server Preferences from the menu.

4. Select Error Responses from the menu on the left side of the screen.

5. For each error message, enter the file path to the document or CGI to which you want to point the user. For CGIs, you need to check the CGI check box.

6. Select Save and Apply from the Save and Apply Changes page.

Apache

Apache can be similarly adapted to return custom messages and local HTML pages, or to redirect the user to a different page outside of the domain. Instructions for customizing error messages with Apache can be found at http://www. apache.org/docs/custom-error.html.

NCSA HTTPd 1.4

NCSA HTTPd 1.4 allows a CGI to redirect users who have requested bad pages. A public domain Perl script that allows hyperlinking back to the referring URL is available at http://hoohoo.ncsa.uiuc.edu/cgi/ErrorCGI.html.

Microsoft's Internet Information Server 2.0 and 3.0, O'Reilly WebSite

Microsoft's Internet Information Server 2.0 and 3.0, WebSite 1.1, and WebSite Professional do not have built-in functionality to redirect broken links or offer customized error pages. To add this functionality to your WebSite or IIS server, you must write (or download and install) a custom ISAPI or WSAPI filter. These filters sit on the Web server and wait for requests to meet certain criteria, such as file suffixes, or environment variables, such as error codes. When requests meet the criteria, these filters are able to customize data as it leaves the server.

Documentation and uncompiled source code for creating a custom ISAPI filter to redirect broken links is available at http://www.avatarmag.com/columns/serverside/default.htm.

For a compiled WSAPI filter that should also work with IIS, visit http://wgg.com/hal.html.

SITE TRACKING AND REPORTING

? What are my server's log files, and what do they track?

Whenever someone visits a Web site, a number of variables are invisibly passed as part of the request header from the browser to the Web server. The server responds to the request by generating response headers, which are sent back to the browser along with the requested file. This process takes place for every graphic, HTML page, Java applet, sound, and so on referenced in the Web pages.

Some HTTP request headers are essential if a file is to be returned successfully to a Web browser. Other headers, such as cookies or the URL that hyperlinked someone to your site, are not required, or, in some cases, are not even officially part of the HTTP specification, but are often sent along with the request anyway. Each request and each response can be seen as one transaction. As long as logging is active, the Web server records a number of these response variables.

Some Web servers allow log data to be written directly to a database, but most simply append a text file with a new line for each transaction. The most common text log file formats are NCSA httpd, Combined Log Format, Common Log Format, and Microsoft's Standard Format. These formats all append text (.LOG) files with variables separated by commas.

Lots of software is available for generating customized server log files and reports. Many servers even allow Webmasters to choose among different formats and scheduling options. Log files that are set to generate a new file for each day of the week are usually given a name that includes the date, such as in120197.log. Table 4-2 lists the variables that are frequently included in log files.

Typically, most of the variables are found in log files. The variables in Table 4-2 were taken from Microsoft Internet Information Server 3.0 using Standard Format logging, with extended variable tracking using newlog.dll, as shown in Figure 4-3.

***

✱ ***Note:*** *The variable names in Table 4-2 are not Standard Environment Variable names. A number of the variables are HTTP variables, but the list also includes system variables and Web server variables. HTTP variables are usually written as HTTP_USER_AGENT, SERVER_NAME, QUERY_STRING, etc. System variables do not have standard naming conventions.*

What kind of information are log files capable of revealing?

Deriving meaningful information from log files is all too often overlooked. Log files can tell you all sorts of

Variable	Description	Sample Data
Bytes Received	Size of URL line including variables	459
Bytes Sent	Size of file sent	1698
Client Host	IP address of client (browser)	205.139.115.17
HTTP Referer	Referring URL, if available to the server (not all browsers report this variable)	http://www.yahoo.com/Science
Log Date	Date user visited the site (different date formats for different servers)	03/01/97
Log Time	Time request was made (sometimes combined with Log Date)	10:45:16
Machine	Name of server computer	WebServer6
Operation	Type of request	GET
Parameters	Variables sent using the GET method, if any (after the *?* in the URL)	name=jon&id=4
Processing Time	Number of milliseconds to process and send the requested file	2068
Server IP	Server's IP address	205.139.114.3
Service	HTTP, FTP, gopher, etc.	W3SVC
Service Status	HTTP status codes (the numbers correspond with messages such as OK or Page Not Found)	200
Target	File requested	/wwwroot/index.html
User Agent	Client browser (Mozilla is Netscape Navigator)	Mozilla/2.0 (compatible; MSIE 3.0; Windows NT)
User Name	User name entered in password-protected sites (usually anonymous)	Administrator
Win32 Status	File IO status from operating system	0

Table 4-2   Variables Frequently Recorded by Log Files

```
🗎 in971101.log - Notepad                                                        _ □ ×
File  Edit  Search  Help
193.92.228.9, -, 11/2/97, 23:57:52, W3SVC, PAN, 205.139.114.3, 12125, 416, 12085, 200, 0, GET,
/img/web5.gif, Mozilla/2.0 (compatible; MSIE 3.01; Windows 95) via Harvest Cache version 1.4p13,
http://www.ikonic.com/ikonia/webpersonal.htx, -,
193.92.228.9, -, 11/2/97, 23:57:59, W3SVC, PAN, 205.139.114.3, 15, 422, 3608, 200, 0, GET,
/ikonia/ikonia.htx, Mozilla/2.0 (compatible; MSIE 3.01; Windows 95) via Harvest Cache version 1.4p13,
http://www.ikonic.com/ikonia/webpersonal.htx, name=unknown,
193.92.228.9, -, 11/2/97, 23:58:08, W3SVC, PAN, 205.139.114.3, 3234, 416, 6939, 200, 0, GET,
/img/homindex1.gif, Mozilla/2.0 (compatible; MSIE 3.01; Windows 95) via Harvest Cache version 1.4p13,
http://www.ikonic.com/ikonia.htx, -,
193.92.228.9, -, 11/2/97, 23:58:16, W3SVC, PAN, 205.139.114.3, 0, 418, 8053, 200, 0, GET,
/ikonia/clients.htx, Mozilla/2.0 (compatible; MSIE 3.01; Windows 95) via Harvest Cache version 1.4p13,
http://www.ikonic.com/ikonia/ikonia.htx, name=unknown,
193.92.228.9, -, 11/2/97, 23:58:30, W3SVC, PAN, 205.139.114.3, 890, 415, 1079, 200, 0, GET,
/img/pacbell.gif, Mozilla/2.0 (compatible; MSIE 3.01; Windows 95) via Harvest Cache version 1.4p13,
http://www.ikonic.com/ikonia/clients.htx, -,
193.92.228.9, -, 11/2/97, 23:58:30, W3SVC, PAN, 205.139.114.3, 5735, 415, 2181, 200, 0, GET,
/img/clihead.gif, Mozilla/2.0 (compatible; MSIE 3.01; Windows 95) via Harvest Cache version 1.4p13,
http://www.ikonic.com/ikonia/clients.htx, -,
193.92.228.9, -, 11/2/97, 23:58:30, W3SVC, PAN, 205.139.114.3, 953, 414, 855, 200, 0, GET,
/img/sprint.gif, Mozilla/2.0 (compatible; MSIE 3.01; Windows 95) via Harvest Cache version 1.4p13,
http://www.ikonic.com/ikonia/clients.htx, -,
130.236.232.115, -, 11/2/97, 23:58:32, W3SVC, PAN, 205.139.114.3, 0, 253, 111, 404, 2, GET,
/img/bbridge.gif, Mozilla/3.01Gold (X11; I; Linux 2.0.20 i586),
http://www.lysator.liu.se/~samir/kamera.html, -,
193.92.228.9, -, 11/2/97, 23:58:33, W3SVC, PAN, 205.139.114.3, 734, 414, 872, 200, 0, GET,
/img/virgin.gif, Mozilla/2.0 (compatible; MSIE 3.01; Windows 95) via Harvest Cache version 1.4p13,
http://www.ikonic.com/ikonia/clients.htx, -,
193.92.228.9, -, 11/2/97, 23:58:34, W3SVC, PAN, 205.139.114.3, 3922, 413, 913, 200, 0, GET,
/img/cover.gif, Mozilla/2.0 (compatible; MSIE 3.01; Windows 95) via Harvest Cache version 1.4p13,
http://www.ikonic.com/ikonia/clients.htx, -,
193.92.228.9, -, 11/2/97, 23:58:34, W3SVC, PAN, 205.139.114.3, 2609, 209, 3066, 200, 0, GET,
/img/GammaButton.class, Java1.0.2 via Harvest Cache version 1.4p13, -, -,
193.92.228.9, -, 11/2/97, 23:58:34, W3SVC, PAN, 205.139.114.3, 5375, 410, 598, 200, 0, GET, /img/ms.gif,
Mozilla/2.0 (compatible; MSIE 3.01; Windows 95) via Harvest Cache version 1.4p13,
http://www.ikonic.com/ikonia/clients.htx, -,
193.92.228.9, -, 11/2/97, 23:58:37, W3SVC, PAN, 205.139.114.3, 703, 205, 383, 200, 0, GET,
/img/nwlpeople.gif, Java1.0.2 via Harvest Cache version 1.4p13, -, -,
193.92.228.9, -, 11/2/97, 23:58:40, W3SVC, PAN, 205.139.114.3, 625, 203, 359, 200, 0, GET,
```

Figure 4-3   A log file for Microsoft Internet Information Server that was
customized in order to record additional data such as Web
browser types.

information about a site. Some information, such as the type
of browser that visitors to the site used, is not tracked by
default with many Web servers, but tracking as many
variables as possible is important if you want to know who
visits your site. Unless variables are logged by your Web
server, you can't get information about visitors. Log files are
the only means of doing it. Fortunately, most Web servers can
be modified quite easily to include variables that are not
logged by default.

Following is a short list of interesting questions that
analyzing a log file can answer:

● How many different IP addresses visited my site last
week or month?

● How many pages were served from my site?

● How many impressions of the ad banner on my home
page were delivered?

- What are the ten most popular and least popular pages on my site?
- What percentage of site visitors used Netscape 3.0?
- What percentage of visitors used a Macintosh?
- What are the most requested graphics and pages on the server that don't actually exist?
- What are the top ten pages that linked to my site?
- What domains link to my site most frequently?
- How long did the average visitor spend on each page in my site?
- Which users accessed the password-protected pages of the server?
- What is the most common path through my site?
- What is the most popular exit point?

Because the answers to these questions are based on data that may be incomplete, the answers are often good estimates, not answers per se. Learning to read the statistics in log files correctly is a very important skill. Reporting inaccurate statistics is an easy mistake if you don't have a clear understanding of the variables being measured. For example, 400,000 hits in a month sounds impressive until you realize that the number breaks down to 80,000 actual Web pages served in over 9,000 different user-sessions to a mere 4,500 different people.

What Is So Special About Virginia?

To determine how many visitors came from each state and country, many log file analysis tools use a technique known as *reverse DNS* to look up the IP addresses of site visitors. Because AOL uses Reston, Virginia as its gateway to the Internet, Virginia is frequently listed as the top state from which visitors come. Reston is frequently listed even when no Visitors actually live in Virginia.

? What is the easiest way to generate a report on site statistics and visitor information?

Web servers are essentially just flat-file databases, so gathering data from Web servers is essentially the same as running queries to gather data from a database. Flat-file databases are uncommon nowadays. Very few tools are available for running SQL or similar queries on flat-file databases.

Even if you could import log file data into a database, running reports and generating useful graphs to represent the data would be quite difficult. As for converting the reports and graphs into HTML and Web graphics (like that shown in Figure 4-4) and uploading the HTML and Web graphics onto a secure server, that is quite a task indeed.

Fortunately, generating reports and graphs about site statistics has been designed into dozens of log file analysis tools. The tools are available on a variety of platforms. A few

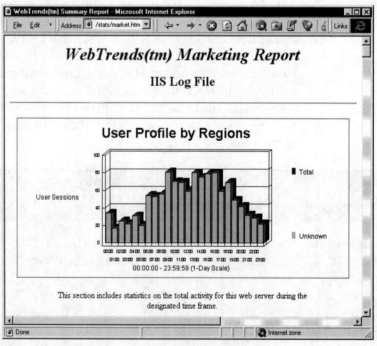

Figure 4-4 An HTML report generated by Web Trends

log file analysis tools even convert analysis results into Microsoft Word format. They also offer high-resolution color charts that print well in Word documents.

Is it possible to determine which domain or which geographic location a particular site visitor is from?

Every person who successfully requests a page from a Web site must provide an IP (Internet Protocol) address before the information can be returned. Every IP address is unique to one particular computer at one particular time on the Web. The Web server's log files track IP addresses. By using techniques such as reverse DNS lookup and whois to analyze IP addresses, you can gather basic information about the domains from which users access the Internet.

Many think that reverse DNS (Domain Name Server) lookups present a small invasion of privacy. But for a Webmaster, DNS lookups can be extremely useful. After you learn the IP address of the site visitor whom you wish to further identify, follow these steps to determine his or her domain location:

1. Download an NSLOOKUP (Name Server Lookup) application from a shareware site, or visit a Web front end to NSLOOKUP such as these:

   http://www.hood.edu/cgi-bin/nslookup.sh.cgi
   http://www.dinet.de/cgi-bin/nslookup

2. Enter the IP address into the NSLOOKUP application. Do this in order to determine the domain name or IP address of the server that was used by a visitor as his or her gateway to the Internet. Below are two different NSLOOKUP results:

NSLOOKUP	205.139.114.8
Server:	Localhost
Name:	himalia.ikonic.com
NSLOOKUP	194.22.188.199
Server:	Localhost
Name:	t12o1p11.telia.com

3. Run a whois application or use the Web front end to whois at this address:

   http://rs.internic.net/cgi-bin/whois

4. Enter the domain name that was given under the NSLOOKUP results under *name*. In the previous two examples, ikonic.com and telia.com are the domains to use with whois.

   A whois query on the domain name, such as the one shown in Figure 4-5, offers some indication of the physical location of the server that your Web visitor used as his or her gateway to the Internet. The query should list the company or organization's address, the name of the technical contact, and, occasionally, a range of IP addresses associated with the company.

```
Command Prompt                                                    _ □ ×
C:\>whois livent.com
Livent Inc. (LIVENT-DOM)
   165 Avenue Road  Suite 600
   Toronto, ON M5R 3S4
   CA

   Domain Name: LIVENT.COM

   Administrative Contact:
      Yazdi, Fardad  (FY9)   admin@LIVENT.COM
      416-324-5462
   Technical Contact, Zone Contact:
      Cheong, Raymond  (RC768)  tech@LIVENT.COM
      416-324-5436
   Billing Contact:
      Yazdi, Fardad  (FY9)   admin@LIVENT.COM
      416-324-5462

   Record last updated on 19-May-97.
   Record created on 03-Nov-95.
   Database last updated on 7-Oct-97 05:29:57 EDT.

   Domain servers in listed order:

   NS1.OTTAWA.ISTAR.NET            198.53.64.7
   NS2.OTTAWA.ISTAR.NET            198.53.64.14


The InterNIC Registration Services Host contains ONLY Internet Information
(Networks, ASN's, Domains, and POC's).
Please use the whois server at nic.ddn.mil for MILNET Information.

C:\>_
```

Figure 4-5   A whois query run from the DOS command prompt with a whois application

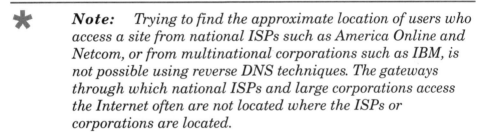

Here are the results of a sample whois query on informant.com:

```
WHOIS informant.com
Informant Communications Group, Inc. (INFORMANT-DOM)
10519 East Stockton Blvd Suite 100
Elk Grove, CA 95624-9703
Domain Name: INFORMANT.COM
Administrative Contact, Technical Contact, Zone Contact:
Bleecher, Micah (MB265) micah@DB.COM
609.227.202 (FAX) 609.374.1704
NSLOOKUP tools can be downloaded from:
PC: http://www.globsol.com/nslookup.html
Macintosh:
ftp://ftp.euro.net/Mac/infomac/comm/inet/dns-lookup-092.hqx
```

✱ ***Note:*** *Trying to find the approximate location of users who access a site from national ISPs such as America Online and Netcom, or from multinational corporations such as IBM, is not possible using reverse DNS techniques. The gateways through which national ISPs and large corporations access the Internet often are not located where the ISPs or corporations are located.*

❓ Certain, less common, file types are not working when served from my Web server. How can I fix this problem?

When files are sent from a Web server, a series of HTTP response headers are sent along with each file. Included in these headers is a content-type header that helps the Web browser determine what type of content each file contains and, correspondingly, how to display or play each file.

The content-type header defines the MIME type of the document. MIME (multipurpose Internet mail extensions) is to the Internet what file extensions are to the PC and the resource fork is to the Macintosh. MIME headers help the Web browser or operating system choose what application or plug-in to use when displaying or playing the document's content on the Web server. Because Web servers are set up to deliver HTML pages and standard Web graphic file formats, no special configuration is required for sending HTML content. HTML is automatically sent with the following HTTP response header:

content-type: text/html

Likewise, most Web servers don't require any special configuration to automatically serve .JPG and .GIF files, which are usually sent, respectively, with these two headers:

content-type: image/jpeg
content-type: image/gif

Nonstandard content, such as Shockwave and Real Audio files, usually requires a special MIME-type configuration on a Web server. Web servers handle MIME-type configurations through the mapping of file extensions to MIME types. QuickTime movies, for example, need the file extensions .MOV and .QT to be mapped on the Web server to the MIME type video/quicktime. By convention, MIME types that have not yet been registered are usually appended with the letter x. Director files, for example, are MIME-encoded with application/x-director.

Read on to find out how to add MIME types for your server.

Netscape, Apache, and NCSA

The following steps will allow you to add additional MIME types to your Netscape, Apache, or NCSA Web server:

1. Find the file named mime.types (shown in Figure 4-6) that is associated with your server and open it.

2. Copy the formatting of other existing MIME types to associate new file extensions with MIME types.

Microsoft's Internet Information Server 2.0 and 3.0

Editing or changing MIME types for IIS involves editing your server's registry, as shown in Figure 4-7. The format of registry entries for IIS MIME types has changed with Service Pack system updates that may or may not correspond with your IIS version number. Please refer to your IIS documentation for up-to-date instructions. Mistakes made in editing an NT Server's registry may damage system settings and require you to reinstall the operating system.

To find the MIME type appropriate for your content, contact the vendor or creator of the content type. For information about the addition of Macromedia Director Shockwave MIME types, visit http://www.macromedia.com/support/director/how/shock/config.html.

mime.types - Notepad

File Edit Search Help

```
#--Netscape Communications Corporation MIME Information
# Do not delete the above line. It is used to identify the file type.

type=application/octet-stream  exts=bin
type=application/astound       exts=asd,asn
type=application/fastman       exts=lcc
type=application/java-archive  exts=jar
type=application/java-serialized-object   exts=ser
type=application/java-vm       exts=class
type=application/mac-binhex40  exts=hqx
type=application/x-stuffit     exts=sit
type=application/mbedlet       exts=mbd
type=application/msword        exts=doc
type=application/oda           exts=oda
type=application/pdf           exts=pdf
type=application/postscript    exts=ai,eps,ps
type=application/rtf           exts=rtf
type=application/studiom       exts=smp
type=application/timbuktu      exts=tbt
type=application/vnd.ms-excel  exts=xls,xlw,xla,xlc,xlm,xlt
type=application/vnd.ms-powerpoint  exts=ppt,pps,pot
type=application/vnd.ms-project exts=mpp
type=application/winhlp        exts=hlp
type=application/x-javascript  exts=js
type=application/x-asap        exts=asp
type=application/x-csh         exts=csh
type=application/x-dot         exts=dot
type=application/x-dvi         exts=dvi
type=application/x-earthtime   exts=etc
type=application/x-envoy       exts=evy
type=application/x-excel       exts=xls,xlc,xll,xlm,xlw
```

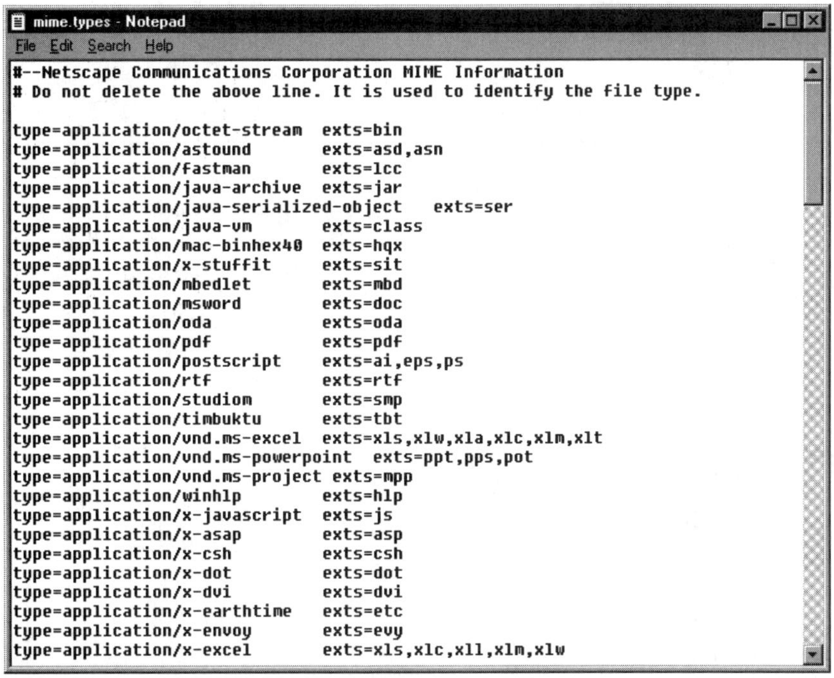

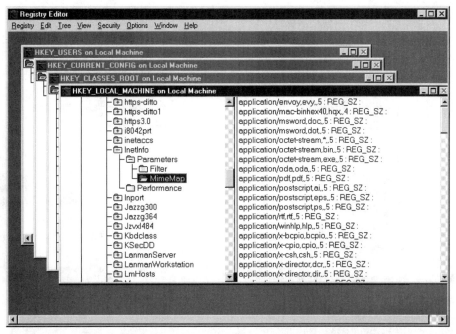

Figure 4-6 A mime.types file for editing the MIME types for many Web servers

Figure 4-7 The Windows NT Registry screen for adding MIME types for IIS 2.0 and 3.0.

Chapter 5

Optimizing Server Performance

Answer Topics!

Optimizing Site Performance @ a Glance

● A site's performance can be measured in a number of ways, but ultimately it boils down to the user's perception of how fast a site appears onscreen. People who surf the Web are, in general, impatient. If your site appears to be slow, you will lose visitors. Narrowing down the factors that effect the speed of a site can be intimidating. The number of steps between clicking a hyperlink and viewing a complete Web page makes debugging performance problems an art.

● The ability to both anticipate and diagnose performance problems in advance is critical for a successful site. Site performance is one of the most common complaints regarding the Web. In general, there are two categories of performance problems: problematic content and slow servers. Problems related to slow connection speed fall in the slow server process category in this chapter.

● Believing that all performance problems are simply related to the connection speed and processor speed of the server is a common misconception. Actually, dozens of variables influence the speed of a Web site, and any one variable is capable of seriously hindering site performance.

● This chapter covers these important topics:

● **Overview of Performance Problems** explains the basic problem areas that can cause a slow site. This section explains how to tell if your site has a performance problem and how you can use benchmark software to find out what that problem is.

● **Slow Content** describes the types of problems that arise when content is too large. You also learn which types of content may display slowly in many browsers.

CPU Speed and Memory Utilization offers tips on how you can determine if your Web server needs to be upgraded with a faster CPU or more RAM.

Disk Access Speed explains how disk access problems can result in a slow Web site. This section offers a number of ways to cut back on disk access and optimize your hard-disk configuration.

Server Configuration and Custom Application Implementation discusses different Web server options that reduce the required processing time for delivering Web content. Also listed in this chapter are a number of techniques for speeding up CGI scripts.

Network Card, TCP/IP Stack, and Internet Connection Speed explains how you can determine whether your Internet connection is fast enough for your site and how your TCP/IP stack and network card may influence the performance of your Web server.

Too Many Hits addresses a problem that most Web sites would love to have—too many hits. This section offers techniques for dealing with server performance problems that result from too many site visitors. A comprehensive checklist for optimizing your site's performance is included at the end of this section.

OVERVIEW OF PERFORMANCE PROBLEMS

How can I tell if my Web site is performing poorly?

The simplest way to tell if your Web site is performing poorly is to delete all of the cached pages and graphics in your browser and visit your site at its peak request time (probably sometime around mid-day). Use a connection method and hardware configuration similar to that of your minimum supported user. If people regularly dial in to your site from home with old computers, a minimum supported user might be defined as one who runs Windows 3.1 and dials in with a

14.4-baud modem. If you are hosting your own site, connecting to the site through your own network may result in unrealistically speedy performance. Connect to your site the way a user would by dialing into an outside ISP or through a different network.

Time how long it takes for a response from the server and how long it takes for all of the graphics to appear on each page as you click through a typical path through your site. Five seconds is a reasonable response time from a server; 20 to 30 seconds is the maximum time that should be allowed for a complete page to load on a low-end target computer. Keep in mind that Java applets and Shockwave movies, on some systems, take a number of seconds to initialize. Some developers swear by a less scientific test that involves holding your breath while your page loads. If you can comfortably hold your breath for the time it takes the page to load, you are probably doing OK.

If you are still uncomfortable with your site's performance, try analyzing your site with performance benchmark software (keep reading).

? What is a performance benchmark?

Benchmarking software simulates a heavy load on your Web server over a specific period of time and measures server performance. It is impossible to test a Web server under heavy usage conditions by hand. A Web server performance tool provides better test conditions and allows you to compare servers. Some Web server packages come bundled with benchmarking software, but for those that don't, a wide variety is available for free on the Web.

The best way to imagine how benchmarking software works is to imagine a room full of people who repeatedly request pages that you specify from your site. If no errors or extended server response times are recorded, more people are added to the room until a maximum sustainable number are present. Benchmarking software simulates this scenario and maintains the maximum sustainable level to measure performance over time.

The key variables on which to concentrate in benchmark results are server response time and server throughput. *Response time,* generally measured in milliseconds, is the amount of time it takes a server to process a single request. *Throughput* is generally measured by the number of HTTP requests made to a server in a given period of time. In general, as the number of requests per second increases, throughput and server response time increase as well. By determining what the maximum acceptable response time and the corresponding throughput are, you arrive at the maximum number of connections per second your server can handle.

? In general, what causes a Web site to run slowly?

In general, five things can cause a Web site to run slowly from the user's point of view:

- Slow content
- CPU speed and utilization
- Memory size and utilization
- Disk access speed
- Server configuration and custom application implementation
- Network card, TCP/IP stack, and Internet connection speed

The following sections address each of these areas in detail.

WWW-SPEED

WWW-SPEED is a mailing list dedicated to the notion that the Web is "just too darned slow." The mailing list takes a lighthearted approach to a difficult subject. WWW-SPEED lists among its subscribers and supporters an impressive list of Internet names. To find out more about the group, visit the WWW-SPEED home page at http://sunsite.unc.edu/mdma-release/.

SLOW CONTENT

? Why is my site slow even though a benchmark performance test on my server indicated that it is running great?

To put it simply, one of the most common site performance problems is too many kilobytes per page. Take a page that loads slowly and add the file size of the HTML document to the file size of any graphics, applets, or movies that the page contains. A good rule of thumb is to keep the total kilobyte count below 30 to 40KB per page.

Site Technologies' Site Sweeper and Microsoft's Site Analyst, shown in Figure 5-1, are two site analysis tools that

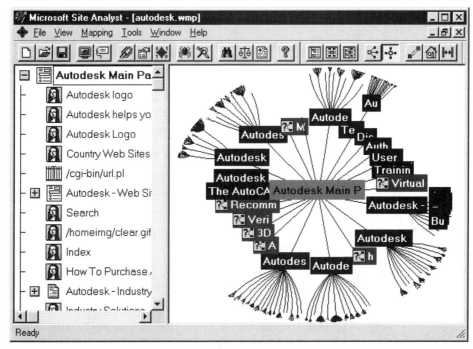

Figure 5-1   Microsoft's Site Analyst maps an entire Web site remotely and provides a detailed report on page content and total page size in kilobytes.

add up the total number of kilobytes for each page in a site. These utilities also check for broken links and gather useful site statistics.

? How long does it typically take users with different connection speeds to download content from a site?

Different browsers use different methods to request content for a Web page. As a result, accurately determining how long a Web site takes to download without timing it is difficult. Most Web browsers request an HTML document, scan it for images and other Web content that is needed to render the page, and request only a few pieces of content at a time so as not to overload the server with requests.

Though transfer rates can vary significantly, the transfer rates of different connection types typically fall into the following ranges:

Connection Type	Transfer Rate (KB/Sec)
14.4	0.8 - 1.2
28.8	2.0 - 2.5
56K	4.4 - 5.2
ISDN	5.2 - 10.4
T1	40 - 144

+ ***Tip:*** *A useful tool for measuring the time it takes to load a Web page is the Opera Web browser by Opera Software. The Opera browser automatically displays a timer each time a page is requested.*

? Why does my forms-based page load so much more slowly than other pages on my site?

In some browsers on some platforms, pages with many form elements can take considerably longer to load than pages without form elements. The best way to test the load time of a forms-based page is to save the Web page to a local hard drive and open the page locally in your browser. If the page is slow, the problem lies with the version of browser you are using. The only fix is to reduce the number of form elements on the Web page, perhaps by splitting them over multiple pages.

Macintoshes have a particularly tough time rendering form elements to the screen quickly for the first time. Pages with large numbers of check boxes, text-entry fields, drop-down menus, radio buttons, and so on have been known to take over 20 seconds to simply appear onscreen. This problem has been eliminated in recent browser versions.

? Why do my site's Java applets run so slowly?

Slow-running Java applets are caused by a slow computer and/or a slow Java virtual machine. Java applets run locally from the hard drive once they have been downloaded, so a Java applet that responds slowly to user events, such as clicks or mouse-overs, is probably not indicative of a slow connection speed or slow Web server. Other than optimizing your applet to perform faster, the only solution to a slow-running applet is to increase the processing power of your computer or upgrade the browser you are using.

Whether or not to use applets based on your target audience is a very important item to take into consideration. When targeting low-end Macintosh or Windows 3.1 users with old machines and browser versions, avoiding the use of Java applets in your Web pages is a good idea.

? Most of my pages appear quickly, but those written by CGI scripts are extremely slow. Why is that?

One of the most common problems with site performance is caused by slow CGI scripts. CGI scripts run slowly for a number of different reasons, most of which are better addressed in Chapter 11. However, the basic culprit is often the CGI protocol itself. The CGI protocol requires a new server process to be spawned each time a server script is called on the Web server. By spawning a new process each time, poorly written code only kills the process, not the Web server when it crashes. Unfortunately, each time a new process is spawned, a certain time hit and processor hit occurs. This hit can result in Web server response times that are fifty times as long as those of conventional HTML pages.

Reducing your script's reliance on large libraries, external text files, and databases increases performance. For a more drastic increase in performance, consider multi-threaded programming interfaces such as Java

Servlets for most of the major Web servers, FastCGI for Apache and NCSA Web servers, NSAPI for Netscape servers, or ISAPI for Microsoft's Internet Information Server. Many other Web servers offer their own scripting language or protocol that eliminates the need to spawn a new process each time a Web site executable is requested.

Another option is to use client-side JavaScript where possible to acquire functionality that would normally require the use of CGIs. Browser detection, initial levels of form verification, online quizzes, writing cookies, and time-stamps are all types of functionality that are easy to handle by means of JavaScript. By using client-side JavaScript, the processing load is shifted from the Web server to the computer on which the browser is running, the client. Since JavaScript is integrated into the browsers that support it, using JavaScript rarely results in performance delays that are any longer than a static HTML page. Remember that browsers must support JavaScript for JavaScript features to work.

The following techniques help increase CGI performance:

- **Choose an optimized programming interface:** If possible, use a language or programming interface that has been optimized for your server. Multi-threaded processes that do not require a new process with each request are almost always faster than straight CGIs. Multi-threaded processes are capable of running in a loop and waiting for the next request. Single-threaded applications, on the other hand, quit when they are finished and must start again with each new request.

- **Avoid disk access and database calls wherever possible:** If one CGI stores information in several text files, try to reduce it to one. If database access is required every time a script is run and the database is updated infrequently, consider writing another script that writes the needed content to a much faster static text file every ten minutes or every hour. This new script could be scheduled as a batch operation from the operating system and thereby decrease the speed hit involved in querying a database.

- **Avoid cross-dependencies:** Cross-dependencies between scripts or applications may result in multiple processes per request. Cross-dependencies can easily increase a script's processor time several fold.

● **Do not use large programming libraries:** If your script only requires one function from a large programming module, copy the function and place it in your script, if possible. Large libraries slow scripts down, especially in CGI applications.

CPU SPEED AND MEMORY UTILIZATION

? How can I tell if my Web server's CPU is too slow?

One problem that occurs occasionally with Web servers is the overuse of processing time. When a computer is faced with a number-crunching task or simply too many tasks, the processor speed may restrict the Web server's performance. To tell whether your Web server's CPU is too slow, use a utility such as Norton System Doctor (shown in Figure 5-2) that charts CPU utilization and also runs a benchmark performance test on your server. Your CPU is inadequate if CPU usage is over 80 percent at peak times. If your Web server is only serving static Web pages and it runs on a reasonably fast machine, processing time is probably not a bottleneck for speed.

In general, the faster the processor, the faster the Web server runs and the more connections the server can handle. Operating systems that are able to optimize applications for multiple processors allow Web servers on multi-processor machines to run faster than single processor machines. Since the cost difference between a single and dual processor machine is slight, choosing a multi-processor option is often a wise performance decision.

? What signs indicate that my server is in need of more RAM?

Adding RAM to a Web server is a very inexpensive option for improving or fixing speed and other performance problems. Most of the popular Web servers cache as much content as possible in RAM in order to reduce hard drive access. Use a system tool to find out how much RAM your Web server software is using.

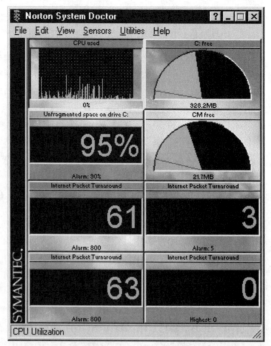

Figure 5-2 Norton System Doctor is a useful utility that tracks CPU usage over time, available disk space, and a number of other useful diagnostic measurements for Microsoft Windows NT machines.

If your server is forced to use virtual memory or is using close to the maximum amount of RAM in the machine, it is time to add more RAM. Running numerous software packages at the same time on a server reduces the amount of memory available for other functions. VRML servers, streaming audio servers, and chat servers all increase a server's RAM requirements. There is no such thing as too much RAM for a server, so don't worry about adding too much.

Some operating systems, such as the Macintosh operating system, hard-code the amount of RAM allocated to applications. If your server's operating system allows it, allocate more memory to your Web server.

Note: *Both the Windows NT and UNIX operating systems dynamically allocate RAM to applications. Memory configuration is done automatically.*

DISK ACCESS SPEED

? How does increasing disk access speed help Web site performance?

Ideally, a well-designed Web server running with lots of RAM only needs to access the hard drive once to access pages, graphics, and scripts. After the content has been accessed once from the hard drive, the content is cached in RAM, where it can be accessed significantly faster. Unfortunately, not all Web servers are designed to work this well, and other variables prevent disk access from being removed as a factor in optimizing Web site performance.

Log file records are generated every time a piece of Web site content is served. If your server is set to generate log files (almost always a good idea for tracking, reporting, and problem solving), your server frequently needs to write data to a hard drive. Nearly all Web servers batch-write their log files, so the server's log files are not updated every time a request is made to the Web server. Instead, every minute or every few minutes the Web server updates the log file all at once with the latest information. This update requires accessing the hard disk, which momentarily slows down the processor and takes up hard drive time. The more visits to a site, the more information needs to be appended to the log files. Minimizing the number of variables that are tracked in a log file or turning off logging completely helps to increase performance, but it also reduces the amount of tracking and reporting of Web site statistics that can be done later.

? What solutions are available for increasing disk access speed?

Fast SCSI-2 hard drives are more expensive than the more common IDE hard drives, but they greatly improve data transfer rates and reduce the amount of time that the drive is tied up with each process. When you select a hard drive or hard drives, pay attention to *seek times,* the average time it takes for the hard drive to get to the first data bit, and transfer rates, which are usually measured in megabits per second. Look for a fast seek time—under 11 milliseconds— and a high transfer rate—at least 10 megabytes a second.

These numbers are usually provided by the drive manufacturer and are often measured under ideal conditions, but the numbers do provide a strong measure for comparing drives.

Some Webmasters swear by multiple drives as a means of splitting requests between hard drives. The multiple drive method works similarly to load balancing between Web servers. However, it only works to help reduce overlapping requests for drive access.

Dedicating a hard drive to log files helps eliminate the delays that result when pages or scripts are requested that require use of the same drive. Separating large files onto different drives can also help reduce perceivable delays in receiving lighter content such as HTML pages.

Dedicating a drive for one task also helps for database storage. If you are stuck using the Web server as a database server as well, try using a different hard drive for the database and the Web content.

SERVER CONFIGURATION AND CUSTOM APPLICATION IMPLEMENTATION

? **Does using one server for multiple Internet-related services affect Web site performance?**

It is surprisingly common for Web sites to be served from machines that also serve mail and database content. The more processes that are running on a machine, the longer the response time for Web pages. Think of it as a desktop computer: If you initiate a search and try to open a large word processing document or graphic file, you notice your computer's response time slows down. Removing news servers, mail servers, and database servers from computers that host Web sites is a good idea if speed is a concern.

Even services directly related to the Web server affect performance. Search engines usually operate as services or daemons and constantly catalog new Web site content. Whenever they are running, chat servers, ad servers, real-time log file analyzers, and push servers all take up processor cycles and slow down Web site performance. However, these services can be run from different hard drives for increased performance.

? How does server directory and virtual root configuration influence Web site performance?

To satisfy a request for a Web page, a server processes the request in different ways, depending on how the server is configured. If the request is made for a file sitting in an executable directory, the server executes the file. Even if the file is very small and simple, the act of executing the file involves a performance hit.

Some Web servers contain settings or are configurable with additional software so that they can execute CGIs from any directory. Internet Information Server, for example, offers a read-and-execute option for Web directories. CGI-anywhere for Netscape server allows CGIs to be executed from any directory. Microsoft's Internet Information Server allows directories to be set for read and execute. Both of these options reduce overall server performance when static documents are requested from read-and-write directories and increase the likelihood of security holes in the Web server.

Another configuration option is to set a directory or group of directories to be parsed for server-side includes (SSI). Server-side includes are a somewhat standard set of tags that are parsed from a file on its way out of a Web server. The tags that are parsed out are replaced with data either from the operating system (time-stamps, the time the file was last updated, file size, and so on) or from the execution of a specified CGI. The act of a server parsing files for SSI tags decreases performance even if no tags are present in the HTML. (Make sure that directories specified for SSI only include files that need to be parsed.) Also, any server-side processing that can be done on the client end through JavaScript or a client-side VBScript reduces the processing requirements of the Web server.

 Tip: *Avoid using directories for Web site content that include more than a hundred or so files. Depending on how your Web server's operating system stores directory information internally, extremely large directories can increase the time it takes to open a file. Reducing the number of files to less than 100 is often a simple way of increasing file seek times.*

AltaVista Optimizations

With Digital's AltaVista search engine, visitors can search 60GB of indexed data in a matter of seconds. To accomplish this, Digital outfitted its Web servers with an extremely impressive list of equipment along with a very fast Internet connection. Below is a list of the equipment that AltaVista's Web servers use:

- 16 AlphaServer 8400 5/300 computers
- 10 processors per computer
- 6GB of RAM per computer
- RAID hard drives
- 100MB per second access to the Internet
- Customized software applications written in C that take advantage of multi-threading

? How can I tell whether replacing my Web server software will increase performance?

If you suspect that your Web server is not performing optimally, try reproducing the published benchmarks for your server software on a similar hardware platform on the same operating system. If your scores are roughly equivalent to the benchmarks, the chances are good that other servers perform on your platform at the speeds that their benchmarks indicate. If your scores do not match up, your speed problem may not be caused by your Web server software. Try stepping through the checklist at the end of this chapter to find your server's performance bottleneck.

Another factor you may wish to consider is the HTTP version that your server software supports. The most recent wave of Web servers all support HTTP 1.1 and offer significant speed advantages over HTTP 1.0 servers. By using a different connection method, HTTP Keep-alive, HTTP 1.1 servers can support a much larger number of consecutive users. HTTP Keep-alive allows persistent connections between a browser and the Web server. These connections time-out after a specific amount of time to reduce the total number of consecutive connections. The bottom line is that by using HTTP Keep-alive, you can reduce download times by 50 percent, especially for pages with lots of external content such as graphics.

For a site that compares different Web server applications with a common set of benchmark tests, visit open.specbench.org/osg/web96/results/.

? How can trimming HTTP response headers increase the performance of my Web server?

HTTP response headers are lines of text that precede content information as it is sent over the Internet. HTTP protocol only requires the content-type header for the transmission of files. By default, most Web servers include at least four or five response headers. By eliminating all but the content-type header, you can decrease the size of every file by something in the neighborhood of 50 to 200 bytes. Fifty to 200 bytes may not seem like much, but multiply that amount by every file request in a day and the savings potentially can be measured in megabytes. Figure 5-3 shows an example of a file with minimal HTTP headers.

! **Warning:** *Incorrectly editing your HTTP response headers may result in incorrectly formatted data that cannot be correctly interpreted by Web browsers.*

NETWORK CARD, TCP/IP STACK, AND INTERNET CONNECTION SPEED

? What is my TCP/IP stack, and how does it affect Web server performance?

Your system's *TCP/IP stack* is a software module that is specific to your operating system and can be replaced and/or optimized on most systems. The TCP/IP stack coordinates the transmission of TCP/IP packets between applications and the server's line out to the Internet or network. For

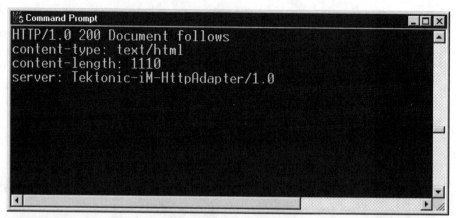

Figure 5-3 The Whitbread Round the World Race at www.whitbread.org uses Tandem's Tektonic server to deliver content with low HTTP header overhead.

optimal server performance, it is essential for HTTP packets and FTP packets to transfer between your operating system and your Web server application as quickly as possible. All Web requests and content are chopped up into small TCP/IP packets for delivery over the Internet. Once they reach their destination, the packets are reassembled. For optimal server performance, it is essential that HTTP packets are assembled and transferred from the operating system level to your Web server application as smoothly and quickly as possible.

? When is it appropriate to increase the bandwidth of a server's Internet connection?

There is a physical limit to the amount of data that can be sent across an Internet connection over a given period of time. Many log file analysis tools provide a total kilobyte count of all files sent from a Web server on a given day. Figure out how many kilobytes were served from your site on average each minute, and then multiply your site's per-minute average by 10 to 15 to calculate the demand on your Internet connection during peak hours. If the number you come up with is close to or matches the maximum capacity of your server's Internet connection, it is probably time to increase the speed of your server's Internet connection.

Check with your network access provider about options for better connectivity to the Internet. Switching to a better connection may be inexpensive or even free.

!

Warning: *Beware of fractional T1 connections. It is impossible to evenly split a T1 connection that is being shared by many organizations. Heavy use by another company can result in slower transfer rates for you. ISPs and Telcos are notorious for overselling bandwidth on fractional T1 lines. Be wary of offers that promise specific transfer speeds over shared lines. If you can, make the provider declare transfer speeds in writing, and test your transfer rates occasionally to make sure that your Internet provider is honest. Divided properly between businesses, fractional T1 lines can be an inexpensive way to connect to the Internet at very fast speeds.*

? What problems are indicative of a slow network card?

Unless your Web server is connected to the Internet through a modem, your server has a network connection. Very few computers have integrated network capabilities built into their motherboards, which means that most Web servers have network cards. Assuming that your Web server uses a network card, all communications between your server and the Internet must travel through this card. Speed deficiencies in your server's network card can cause a speed bottleneck. If you try different options in an attempt to speed up your server, changing your network card should not be your first option. Detecting whether your server has a slow network card can be very difficult. Any diagnostics beyond installing new cards and benchmarking the server requires the skills of someone who is knowledgeable in networking issues.

TOO MANY HITS

? **Everything seems to check out just fine with my server, but it is simply receiving too many hits. What should I do?**

Receiving too many hits is a problem that most sites would love to have. It is also, however, a problem that needs to be solved, and to solve it you can choose between two general methods: increasing the speed of the server hardware and using multiple Web servers.

The first possibility is to scale the server hardware to a level that supports all of the requests. This solution may require purchasing an expensive, top-of-the-line multiple processor server with a large bank of RAM. The benefit of this solution is that one server is, in general, easier to maintain than several. Also, personalization systems that track user sessions may only perform on single servers, depending on how the personalization system was implemented. Unfortunately, single-server systems only scale to a point. Ultimately, the number of requests and processing any one server can accomplish is limited.

A more scaleable solution, the second possibility, uses multiple Web servers and distributes the load among them. When distributing requests among servers, it is impossible to balance requests and processing requirements evenly. Following are a number of different solutions to the problem of server load distribution.

Dividing Content

The easiest solution is to simply divide content between servers with different names. The challenge is to estimate how the files can be divided in such a way that the server load is split as evenly as possible. Dividing content poses a problem if any one file becomes extremely popular. If that happens, one server takes a larger percentage of requests.

Load-Balancing Software

With the load-balancing software solution, a small piece of software is installed on every Web server to monitor server performance over time. Every Web server contains the entire contents of a Web site. Whenever a request is made, an application sends the request to the server that has the lowest demand at the moment. Accurate load balancing based on server demand can be extremely difficult because Web demands often cause processor spikes rather than steadily increasing and decreasing processor usage. The inherent difficulty in balancing loads accurately makes load balancing solutions very difficult to optimize and configure.

Round-Robin DNS

Round-robin DNS involves allocating the IP address of a different server each time a request is made to the site's domain name. The round-robin system rotates through each server before going back to the first server. Adding a new server to a round-robin system is as easy as adding a new IP address to a domain name server, if it supports round-robin. You may also use BIND (Berkeley Internet Name Daemon) to add round-robin functionality to your domain name server.

? My Web server's performance is suffering from a large number of hits from robots. How can I keep robots out of my site?

Web robots, or *crawlers* as they are often called, request pages from sites and chop up the text for entry in search engine databases. Robots determine what pages to visit based on hyperlinks in the pages that they request. If your page isn't listed on any search engines and isn't linked from any other site on the Web, robots are unlikely to visit your site.

When robots do visit your site, however, they can be as unintrusive as regular visitors, or they can wreak havoc by continually requesting pages. Depending on how the robot was written, it may or may not follow certain protocols.

Adding a robots.txt page to the default directory of your domain (it lists the pages that you don't want indexed) should keep friendly robots out of your site. Unfriendly robots simply ignore the file and continue to hit your pages. However, two effective methods can help keep robots out of your site: browser detection and JavaScript.

Browser detection

The browser detection method requires a script or executable of some sort on the Web server. Check the HTTP_UserAgent variable for every page request from your site and compare it with a list of known browser types. If the variable matches, then serve the page, but if it doesn't match, send an apology page that contains no other links to your site. However, this method is ineffective against robots that have been designed to fake common browser UserAgent headers such as Netscape's Mozilla 3.03 (Win95), for example. The browser detection method is also unfriendly to users with unconventional browsers.

JavaScript

Another method of hiding links from robots is to write links from within JavaScript. For this method to be effective, all hyperlinks should be split, then concatenated together, as in this example code:

```
<SCRIPT><!--
A = 'MyPage';
B = '.html';
document.write('<A HREF=' +A + B + '>This is a link
hidden from robots</A>');
--></SCRIPT>
```

For more information on excluding friendly robots from your site, visit http://info.webcrawler.com/mak/projects/robots/norobots.html.

Robot-Trapping IP Addresses

One way to keep robots from a site is to include an invisible graphic that links to a page on your site that is specifically designed to attract robots but not visitors. Visitors to your Web site do not see the link and therefore do not follow it. Robots, on the other hand, see the link and follow it as they do any other link. The page that is designed to trap robots should be a script that records the robot's IP address and either blocks it from accessing other pages on your site or appends a text file that you can manually add to your Web server's list of blocked IP addresses. Another possible feature is to add e-mail functionality to the script that notifies you when a robot has visited the site. Keep in mind that any CGIs that run on your server can be a performance hit in themselves. If you link robots to a CGI page and simply log the information, server performance does not speed up until you actually reduce the number of robots that visit your site.

? A number of people are downloading files from my Web site. Without optimizing my server, what can I do to increase download speeds?

First, compress your downloadable files to make them smaller. ZIP is the standard compressed file format for the PC and Stuff-it is the de facto standard for the Macintosh.

To accelerate the file transfer rate of files downloaded from your Web page, place your downloadable files on an FTP server. Files downloaded from an FTP server are significantly faster than files downloaded from a Web server due to the way the data packets are designed. FTP divides content into faster UDP packets, while HTTP splits content into the slower TCP packets. To use this method, simply include tags in your HTML such as the following:

```
<A HREF="ftp://ftp.domain.com/filepath/file.zip">My File</A>
```

Make sure that your file is stored in the correct location on the FTP site and in a directory that allows anonymous read access for files. Both Microsoft Internet Explorer and Netscape Navigator allow files to be downloaded from anonymous FTP sites from a hyperlink in an HTML document using the format listed above.

Checklist for Optimizing Your Web Site's Performance

Following is a checklist for optimizing your Web site's performance. The steps are roughly arranged by order of difficulty to implement and effectiveness.

1. **Check content:** Check the file sizes of the content that is being served. Keep file sizes low.

2. **Optimize executables:** Check any executables to see if they hold back server performance. Eliminate unnecessary cross-dependencies, database connections, and external file access in scripts. Use the fastest protocol available for your Web server.

3. **Configure executable directories:** Make sure that your server isn't looking at every file to check whether it is executable or contains server-side include information (SSI). Put executable content in execute-only directories, SSI content in SSI directories, and read-only information and graphics in read-only directories.

4. **Remove non-Web server-related services and daemons:** Web servers run faster if no other processes, such as mail and news servers, are running on the same machine. Note that most search engines and chat servers run as constant processes and slow down a Web server.

5. **Add RAM:** Adding RAM is inexpensive, requires no special server configurations, and speeds up servers by reducing disk access.

6. **Allocate more memory to your Web server:** Some operating systems automatically restrict the amount of RAM allocated to Web servers. Increase this to the maximum reasonable amount.

7. **Check the connection speed:** Physical limitations delay the amount of content that can be transferred over a period of time at certain connection speeds. Increase your connection so that it supports the transfer capacity needed during peak hours.

8. **Evaluate your Web server software:** Your server software may require special configuration to support many consecutively connected users. Your software may also simply be too slow or in need of an upgrade or patch. Installing service patches or updates may not result in obvious changes to your server software, but the patches may very well update key files that are used behind the scenes by your software applications or operating system.

9. **Trim your HTTP headers:** If your server allows you to customize HTTP headers and you know what you are doing, try eliminating some of the headers. They decrease the available space in every HTTP packet.

10. **Evaluate your hardware:** A fast multiple processor machine running on an operating system that takes advantage of multiple processors is optimal. Fast SCSI-2 hard drives and RAIDs allow faster disk access than standard SCSI or IDE drives. Also, make sure your server has a fast network card.

11. **Use load balancing:** At a certain point, a server simply cannot handle the load regardless of optimization. Distributing the load among multiple servers offers a scaleable solution for large amounts of site traffic.

12. **Distribute servers geographically:** For massive sites, locating servers closer to site visitors increases response times. Mirror sites and co-location are two common solutions for geographic distribution.

Chapter 6

Server Security

Answer Topics!

Server Security @ a Glance

"You give me a select group of ten hackers and within 90 days I'll bring this country to its knees. The chaos that could be created is enormous."

> —Jim Settle,
> retired director of the FBI's computer crime squad

Whenever someone can access a computer, whether physically or remotely, there is a security risk. Web sites on the Internet are, by nature, accessible remotely from around the world and are, therefore, a security risk for any organization. By taking a number of precautions, however, you can give your site a reasonable level of security.

For better or for worse, an entire subculture lives by the adage "all information just wants to be free." By balancing the number of potential Web site security holes with the necessary functionality for your site, you can construct a security barrier. How strong the barrier is depends on your operating system, firewall, installed server software, computer's scripts, and computer's physical security.

Every aspect of the design, development, and deployment of a Web server and its scripts should take into account the security of the overall site. Attacks against Web server software may come in the guise of forged HTTP requests, illegal form submission data, FTP access to a CGI-bin, and even malicious hands-on access to the server itself. Root-level access, which is most commonly gained through inadequate protection, will leave an entire collection of data vulnerable.

Security violations such as the copying of data from a Web server or the posting of unauthorized pages on a site may be the least of your worries. Depending on how your Web server is set up, intruders may be able to wreak havoc across your whole network anonymously from halfway around the world.

This chapter covers the following important topics:

Physical Security discusses the importance of physically securing your computer at its location. It offers methods of storing and hiding user names and passwords from potentially malicious users.

101

- **Configuring your Web Server Software Securely** covers the different configuration options that are available on most major Web servers and the security threats that they pose.

- **Security Between Client and Server** covers the situations in which secure connections are important. The section focuses on Secure Sockets Layer and how it works.

- **Firewalls** explains what firewalls are and whether your server needs a firewall on your network. Included are descriptions of network topologies that are commonly used to connect LANs with a firewall and a Web server to the Internet.

- **CGI Security** lists the different methods of access that can be gained to a Web server through CGIs and how to avoid them.

PHYSICAL SECURITY

How is physical security a threat to my Web server?

Intruders with hands-on access to a Web server can bypass a number of restrictions that keep intruders from accessing a site remotely. The ability to place disks into a server's floppy drive, change system settings, remove and add hardware, and even the ability to reboot a server, are all potential threats to a server's security.

If you host your own Web site, keep your Web server in a locked, climate-controlled room. Keep physical access to the computer to a minimum as well. A janitor vacuuming near the electrical outlet or a careless user can cause a Web site to go off-line.

When you select an ISP, ask about the location of the servers. Ask if employees have undergone background checks and which employees actually have physical access to the server. Also ask about backup power supply. An uninterruptable power supply makes a server less vulnerable to weaknesses during brownouts and blackouts.

Is locking my server with the built-in lock in the case a reasonable form of protection?

The vast majority of locks that are built into computer cases are extremely easy to bypass. Inside the computer's case, two small wires connect the back of the computer's built-in lock to the motherboard. If either of the two wires is disconnected from the motherboard, which is usually a matter of simply unplugging them, the lock ceases to perform its function.

? How can I safely store my Web site and Web server passwords?

Securing passwords in the vicinity of a computer is usually not a good idea. Secure your passwords in a locked room or closet. If you feel comfortable storing hard copies of user names and passwords, avoid describing what the list contains on the document itself. A document that begins, "Memo: the following is a list of valid user names and passwords for the Titan administration Web server at port 8004" could potentially be used by anyone who finds it. Simply listing the server name, user name, port, and password without putting a heading at the top of the page is a much better idea.

If you must store user names and passwords electronically, avoid storing them in a format that can be searched. UNIX allows system-wide searches for ASCII and binary strings. Windows NT and Windows 95 allow system-wide searches for strings stored in text files and in Word 97 and Word 95 format. Even simple encoding, such as ROT 13, which shifts ASCII characters 13 places over, can help hide data on a hard drive. Also, avoid file names with any strings that may indicate the document's contents. Encrypting documents that contain passwords is your best

Steganography

Steganography is the hiding of data within other file formats. A list of passwords and URLs, for example, can be hidden invisibly in a JPEG photograph with imperceptible changes in the quality of the JPEG image. Using steganography, data can be effectively hidden within sound files, video clips, and other media. The main advantage of this type of encryption is that no one knows that encrypted information is embedded in the file. Many countries restrict or prohibit the possession of encrypted data. Steganography isn't cryptography, per se, but functions very similarly. For more on Steganography visit http://members.iquest.net/~mrmil/stego.html.

bet, but with this method you are left at the mercy of having to remember one password or private key.

Typically, users gain unauthorized access to a password list by stumbling upon it in a section of the hard drive that is not as secure as the parts of the hard drive to which the passwords give access.

? Is my operating system's security effective against people who have physical access to my Web server?

Using your operating system's built-in security features is a good first level of protection. Ultimately, however, almost any OS-level security feature can be bypassed within a matter of hours. Even the strongest operating system security feature can often be bypassed simply by booting the machine with a different OS that is designed to read the file system and ignore the security features.

Commonly Used Passwords

Following is a list of the most commonly used passwords and types of passwords according to Deloitte & Touche LLP, a leading professional services firm:

- Your first, last, or child's name
- The word *secret*
- Stress-related words (*deadline, work*)
- Sports teams and terms (*Bulls, golfer*)
- The word *payday*
- The word *bonkers*
- The current season (*winter, spring*, and so on)
- Your ethnic group
- Repeating characters (AAAAA, BBBBB)
- Obscenities and sexual terms

Other common passwords include *god, love, romance*, strings of adjacent characters on the keyboard such as *qwerty*, birth dates, and words that have to do with a topic such as a server name, product name, or company name.

The technique of using a BIOS-level password to circumvent the operating system can also be foiled rather quickly. In most motherboard designs, you can move or remove a hardware jumper in the computer and thereby bypass any BIOS-level security.

? What other services are a threat to my Web server?

Any service that is accessible from the Internet is a potential threat to your Web server. Whenever multiple services are running on one machine, a weakness in any service can bring the whole machine down. The following services invite Web server security violations:

- SMTP services for receiving e-mail
- Network services, such as Samba and NFS
- finger, shell, and whois

For example, a mail server that crashes or seriously hampers the server's performance when the hard drive is full is a potential problem for your Web server. Even reliable services such as ping an be a potential threat when malicious users send ping packets that are over 64 kilobytes in size (ping packets of that size are known as "death pings").

Ports on Your Server

Ports on your server are like doors for different services. Most operating systems contain a very large number of doors that are not used. The most common services, such as FTP, HTTP, and ping, all have port numbers that are considered standard ports.

Malicious users can exploit weaknesses in ports that have been overlooked. If someone merely telnets to the correct Windows NT port and enters ten or more characters, your Web services can hang. Many operating system services provide information about a server's system and configuration that is useful to hackers.

To secure your server, blocking certain unused ports or turning off services that are not being used is a good idea. Ports can be blocked easily with a firewall if firewall software lies between your server and the Internet. Here is a list of standard ports and their services:

Port Number	Service	Description
7	Echo	
9	Discard	Dev/null
11	Systat	Information on users
13	Daytime	Time and date at computer's location
15	Netstat	Information on networks
19	Chargen	Stream of ASCII characters (press ^C to stop)
21	FTP	Transfers files
23	Telnet	Where you log in
21	SMTP	Mail
37	Time	Time
39	Rlp	Resource location
43	Whois	Information on hosts and networks
53	DNS	Domain Name Server
70	Gopher	Out-of-date information browser
79	Finger	Information on users
80	HTTP	Web server
110	Pop	Incoming e-mail
119	NNTP	News server
512	Biff	Mail notification
513	Rlogin	Remote login
	Who	Remote who and uptime
514	Shell	Remote access without password
	Syslog	Remote system logging
520	Route	Routing information protocol

CONFIGURING YOUR WEB SERVER SOFTWARE SECURELY

? What does it mean to configure a Web server for security?

In terms of security, the easiest way to view a Web site is to think of it as a bank. The public can anonymously walk through the front door of a bank and look around. Bank officers with the proper identification have access to secured data such as account information and content based on the privileges that have been assigned to them.

In a well-designed Web server, like a well-designed bank, only authorized individuals can enter protected areas, and a reliable set of procedures has been established for verifying authorization. Suppose that the authorization procedure at a bank is to ask for the customer's name, enter the name into a computer, and have the teller look at the password and ask the customer what his or her password is. There is a weakness in this authorization procedure. If the customer can see the teller's computer screen, he or she can also see the password. Computer security is very similar to this model. You must be able to break down every transaction into small steps and scrutinize each step for access points. If a bank were to leave a door that leads to a vault open and that door was right next to the public bathroom, it would be a security weakness. Similarly, providing a publicly available FTP directory on a Web server that is accessible through an HTTP server is a potential security weakness.

On a well-configured server, important data is placed behind security safeguards, and all other possible methods of entry are closed off. The main areas of concern for a Web server are

- Anonymous FTP directories that are accessible through a Web server
- Executable permission set to all, or large numbers of, directories
- Automatic executable permissions based on file extension rather than operating system file permissions
- File system privileges that are too generous for default (anonymous) users who access the computer via the Web server and FTP
- Directory tree misconfigurations
- Storing command interpreters in a Web-accessible executable directory
- Allowing more optional Web server features than are necessary

? What options does my Web server software allow that are potential security risks?

Four options that Webmasters should be wary of are available on many Web servers:

- Automatic directory listings
- Symbolic links
- Directories that are both readable and executable and server-side include directories
- Logging to an area within the document root of your Web server

Automatic Directory Listings

When no default document is provided, a server configured with automatic directory listings lists the contents of Web directories. The names of documents and directories that are not linked from the Web site are accessible remotely. Any sensitive data that is hidden from users who simply don't know the address is available through directory listings. Directory information is a useful entry point for hackers who want to break into a server.

Symbolic Links

Many Web servers are configured to allow directories and files, aliased by the operating system, to be recognized and followed when used in the URL line. The weakness in this configuration is the potential threat posed by someone who accidentally provides a shortcut to an area of the server that is not intended to be accessed through a Web browser. Similarly, symbolic links through FTP have the potential to be dangerous. Firewalls work to reduce the security risk associated with symbolic links.

Read and Executable Directories and Server-Side Include Directories

Server-side includes, read and write permissions for the same directory, and software that allows CGIs to be executed from any directory, all present the same threat. Many assume that if someone only has access to a standard readable directory that is within the document root of the server, the worst that hackers can do is post undesirable pages or delete the contents of those directories. However, if the readable directories allow the <#include exec> style tags, a malicious user can delete the server hard drive or gain access to restricted areas. Software that allows CGIs to be run from any Web directory, and Web servers that allow directories to be configured so that they are both readable and executable, offer similar security dangers. By overlapping content areas that simply deliver static Web content with executable files, anyone who gains access to the directory can run scripts or potentially execute shell commands.

The CGI-bin directory should be write-protected. If a script needs to write files locally on the server, access to the directory that contains those files should be strictly limited. The less your Web server knows about the network it is connected to, the better. Cross mounts and other operating system-level links between the Web server and other systems are strongly discouraged. If your Web server is linked directly with other servers, an intruder can access other computers on the network.

Logging to an Area Within the Document Root of Your Web Server

Log files record all Web pages that were requested from a Web server. In many log file formats, when a secure area of the server is requested, the user name that is used to request the page is also logged. Log files within the document root of your Web server are accessible to anyone via a Web browser, so potential intruders have access to protected page names and user names. In this scenario, all a hacker needs is a password to view protected pages.

? Should I restrict access to my Web server's administration server based on IP address, or should I use user name and password verification?

For optimal security, you should use both IP restriction and user name and password to restrict access to a Web server—if your server allows these options. Tricking a Web server into thinking that you have someone else's IP address, known as *IP spoofing,* is a common method by which hackers gain access to a computer. In general, the more levels of security you place on important areas, the more secure they will be.

? How can I apply simple security to one section of my site?

Secure connections between a browser and server, such as Secure Sockets Layer, are often unnecessary when the site requires only a simple form of user name and password protection against certain content. When someone enters an insecure area of a Web site, a default user name and password are given out at the operating system level. The file permissions given to this anonymous user are usually minimal and allow only read permissions on most directories and execute permissions on executable directories.

When an anonymous user is not allowed access to a directory being requested, most browsers ask for a user name and password. If the user name and password are accepted, the browser remembers these and resends them with every request that is made for content in this secure area. Unfortunately, this user name and password combination is only lightly encoded and, as a result, is easy to decrypt if the information is intercepted on the Internet. For most situations, this is a possible but unlikely scenario.

To add basic directory security to your site, one of two methods are generally used: operating system level security and Web server software security.

OS Level Security

Operating system level security, also known as *system-wide security,* uses the server's operating system's built-in security to secure content and scripts over the Web that sit in Web-accessible directories. To apply this form of security, simply remove access to the files for the user that has been defined within the Web server software as the anonymous Web user. Add user rights to the files for the user name and password combination of your intended recipient.

This form of security, as shown in Figure 6-1, is the only form of security for many Windows NT servers, including Microsoft Internet Information Server.

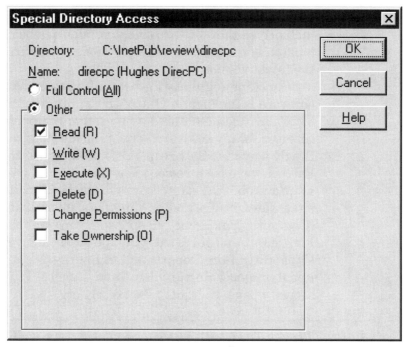

Figure 6-1   Windows NT security offers a window where read, write, execute, and delete privileges can be set.

Web Server Software Security

Many Web servers, including Netscape servers and Apache, allow documents and directories to be secured by user names and passwords that have been set within the Web server itself. For Apache and NCSA servers, this security can be set within the .htaccess file. For Netscape servers, a new database of valid user names and passwords can be created and applied to directories through the administration server's Web-browser-based front end.

? What are update patches, and how important are they for my server?

Weaknesses in Web server software are often found after the software is released. A weakness may affect more than one Web server, especially if the weakness is in the operating system. To fix weaknesses quickly, commercial software vendors and organizations that distribute free Web servers and operating systems distribute patches. A *patch* is a software fix that remedies vulnerabilities and other problems. Usually, the changes introduced in a patch are included in the software's next version release. Occasionally a patch is released for older versions of servers but not for the latest version.

Checking regularly for new software updates for server software is important. One of the advantages of registering software is being notified when software updates are released. Many software vendors pride themselves in the timely way that they respond to problems in their software. Patches have been released on the Internet a matter of hours after a problem became known. Besides checking vendor sites, newsgroups, and mailing lists, investigate the CERT (Computer Emergency Response Team) Web site, shown in Figure 6-2, and the CIAC (Computer Incident Advisory Capability of the Department of Energy) Web site for updates concerning problems and patches. To visit CERTs security page, visit: http://www.cert.org.

+ *Tip:* *The CERT Web site regularly posts methods and weaknesses by which hackers have exploited Internet-based systems. The descriptions CERT provides are quite detailed and very useful in pinpointing where a security problem may lay on your server. Unfortunately, by offering detailed descriptions of security holes to the public as soon as they are detected, CERT also offers the information to hackers. This makes it doubly important for Webmasters to be well-informed of security problems soon after they are discovered.*

? **How can overlapping FTP directories and Web server document roots or CGI directories put my server at risk?**

The easiest and most common method used to break into Web servers is to exploit a misconfiguration in a server's directory tree. Allowing a CGI directory or an SSI (server-parsed HTML) directory to be writable from an anonymously accessible FTP directory opens up one of the most common security holes on the Internet. A script may be placed in an executable directory via FTP and executed, via the Web server, by simply requesting the CGI through the URL line of any Web browser.

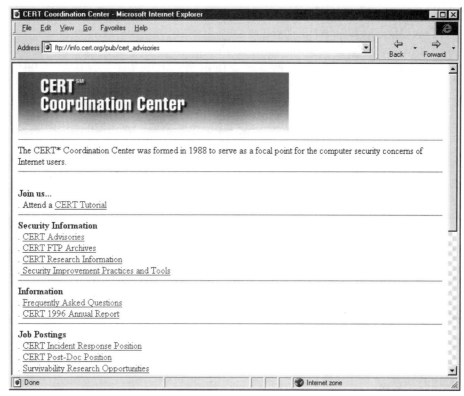

Figure 6-2 The CERT Web site offers up-to-date security advisory warnings.

Security Analysis Software

Security analysis software is one of the easiest and quickest ways to test a server against a range of attack methods. Just as virus-checking is a good but not guaranteed way of checking a server for viruses, security analysis can provide a reasonable level of assurance. The following software is designed to test a Web server against a range of hacker attacks:

● **Crack:** Crack simply tests a server's passwords against the massive number of words and word combinations in its dictionary. Leave the software running overnight and Crack will try literally thousands of word combinations and log any server passwords it manages to decipher. Make sure that Crack's output file of discovered passwords is stored in a very secure area or removed completely from the Web server.

● **SATAN:** SATAN (System Administrator Tool for Analyzing Networks) is a set of scripts that try a wide range of methods to gain access to a server. Results of the tests are logged. SATAN is controversial in that it can be used by both system administrators and malicious attackers. To defend against a SATAN attack, use an application on your server such as Courtney that looks for malicious TCP/IP behavior.

● **Courtney:** To detect malicious attacks, a Perl script known as Courtney was developed by programmers at the University of California's Lawerence Livermore National Laboratories. Courtney works by looking for suspicious requests to a server as well as high numbers of requests over a short period of time. Courtney requires Perl 5.0 or higher and runs on UNIX servers.

In addition to free software, a range of commercial software and services are available for thoroughly testing a server's security.

SECURITY BETWEEN CLIENT AND SERVER

? **Why would my Web site need a secure connection between browser and server?**

When data is sent over the Internet via HTTP, it is sent as plain text. If the packets that are being sent between a Web browser and Web server are intercepted, they are readable without any special translation tools. If you used the standard directory security provided by your Web Server or operating system to add password protection to an area of your site, the password is lightly encoded (and easily decoded), but the information being sent is not. If data being sent is sensitive, it needs to be encrypted. Particularly sensitive data includes the following:

● Online transactions
● Online orders
● Personal information
● Financial information
● User names and passwords

? How is security between the client and server provided?

A number of different types of encryption have been developed. Each type uses a different technique for securing a connection between the user and server. In its simplest form, all data sent from a Web server is encrypted. The site visitor's operating system or Web browser then decrypts the information so it can be read. Information sent from the browser to a secure server, including form-submitted information, is similarly encrypted by the client and decrypted at the server. Packets that are intercepted between the client and server are indecipherable to those who do not have the key to unlock them.

? What is Secure Sockets Layer?

SSL (Secure Sockets Layer) protocol is used for encrypting information between Web browsers and Internet servers. Credit card orders or any other highly confidential information should be passed using SSL. The protocol allows client/server applications to communicate in a way that is designed to prevent eavesdropping, tampering, and message forgery. SSL was developed by Netscape Communications and is based on public-private key cryptography developed by RSA Data Security. It is currently being evaluated by the Internet Engineering Task Force as an inter-operable, open security standard.

? What services does Secure Sockets Layer provide, and how does it work?

SSL provides three fundamental security services:

- **Mutual authentication:** SSL 3.0 allows the identities of both the server and client (although the client phase has yet to be widely implemented) to be authenticated through the exchange and verification of their digital IDs.
- **Message privacy:** All traffic between an SSL server and SSL client is encrypted using a unique session key. The server's key-pair is used to encrypt the session key itself when it is passed to the client.

● **Message integrity:** SSL protects the contents of
messages exchanged between client and server from
being altered en route.

The protocol is composed of two layers. At the lowest
level, on top of a reliable transport protocol (e.g., TCP/IP),
is the SSL Record Protocol. The SSL Record Protocol is
used for encapsulating various higher-level protocols,
as shown in Figure 6-3. One such encapsulated
protocol, the SSL Handshake Protocol, allows the
server and client to authenticate each other and to negotiate
an encryption algorithm and cryptographic keys before the
application protocol transmits or receives its first byte of
data. One advantage of SSL is that it is application
protocol-independent. A higher-level protocol can reside
on top of the SSL Protocol transparently.

The SSL Handshake Protocol consists of two phases,
server authentication and client authentication, with the
second phase being optional. In the first phase, the server
sends its certificate and its cipher preferences in response to
a client's request. The client then generates a master key,
which it encrypts with the server's public key, and transmits
the encrypted master key to the server. The server recovers
the master key and authenticates itself to the client by
returning a message encrypted with the master key.
Subsequent data is encrypted with keys derived from this
master key. In the optional second phase, the server sends a
challenge to the client. The client authenticates itself to the

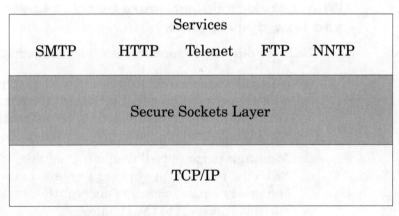

Figure 6-3 The position of the SSL layer on a server

server by returning the client's digital signature on the challenge, as well as its public-key certificate.

? What methods of encryption and verification does SSL offer during the "handshaking" process?

SSL supports a variety of cryptographic algorithms. During the "handshaking" process, the RSA public-key cryptosystem is used. After the exchange of keys, a number of ciphers are used, including RC2, RC4, IDEA, DES, and triple-DES. The MD5 message-digest algorithm is also used. The public-key certificates follow the X.509 syntax.

Server SSL Certificates allow Web sites to identify themselves, as well as enable secure communications with customers. In fact, a server Digital ID is necessary to establish SSL connections. Software publishers can also benefit from SSL Certificates by ensuring customers that the software they download is authentic and unmodified.

A Digital ID provides an electronic means of verifying that the individual or organization with whom you are communicating is the person that he or she claims to be. The identity of the Digital ID owner is bound to a pair of electronic keys that can be used to encrypt and sign digital information, thereby assuring that the keys actually belong to the person or organization specified. A Certification Authority (CA) such as VeriSign attests to the right of an individual or organization to use the keys by digitally signing the Digital ID after verifying the identity information it contains. The assurance provided by the Digital ID depends on the trustworthiness of the CA that issued the Digital ID and the integrity and security of the CA's practices and procedures.

When a connection is established between a client and a secure server, the client software automatically verifies the server by checking the validity of the server's Digital ID. The key pair associated with the server's Digital ID is then used to encrypt and verify a session key that is passed between the client and server. This session key is then used to encrypt the session. A different session key is used for each client-server connection, and the session key automatically expires in 24 hours. Even if a session key is intercepted and

decrypted, which is very unlikely, it cannot be used to
eavesdrop on subsequent sessions.

? What are the advantages of using SSL over other security protocols?

SSL isn't the only way to secure communications between a
Web browser and a server. However, it offers significant
advantages over its competition:

● SSL is widely supported by both server and
browser vendors.

● SSL can be used for protocols other than just HTTP.

● SSL is relatively easy to implement server-side as well
as client-side.

● SSL is based upon accepted, proven cryptological
technology.

● SSL prevents eavesdropping, tampering, and forgery.

Many solutions do one or two of these things, but not all
of them. A solution may prevent hackers from gaining the
passwords necessary to see protected information, but it
doesn't, for example, protect the ensuing communications
between client and server from capture or alteration. Some,
like PGP, may encrypt transmissions, but are unsuitable for
Web-based applications.

Similar solutions, such as S-HTTP, do exist, but SSL
has almost complete market dominance among both server
and browser vendors. Encryption of the transport layer
makes SSL application-independent, whereas S-HTTP is
limited to the specific software by which it is implemented.
The protocols adopt different philosophies toward
encryption as well, with SSL encrypting the entire
communications channel and S-HTTP encrypting each
message independently. S-HTTP allows a user to produce
digital signatures on any messages (not just specific
messages during an authentication protocol), a feature SSL
lacks. However, SSL retains the key advantage of market
support, rendering it a clear first choice for secure
communications between browser and server.

FIREWALLS

? What are firewalls, and what do they do?

A *firewall* is basically a wall between one network and another that regulates traffic with an eye to security. Firewalls are systems that screen data coming into and/or leaving a network. Typically, an Internet firewall is a piece of software that sits on a server and decides which types of network traffic to allow through. A firewall can allow a network of computers to see the Internet without others on the Internet being able to see them. Similarly, a firewall can protect a company from internal threats by restricting the type of traffic that is sent out. Data is better secured in a company that doesn't allow FTP connections to the Internet and doesn't allow floppy disks to be removed from the building.

When all traffic between a network and the Internet goes through one firewall server, malicious users can be blocked at a single point, ports can be closed, and certain types of traffic can be regulated. A firewall can also be seen as a window on all traffic that goes through it. If strange activities are occurring between your organization and the Internet, the firewall may very well be the place to find out about them.

It is possible to configure some firewalls to allow the transfer of information with secure network keys. A firewall that doesn't allow throughput of FTP information, for example, may be configured to allow FTP with a secure network key. Firewalls frequently disallow certain data types because of potential security threats. SNKs help reduce the risk associated with any data type.

? Does my server need a firewall?

Because Internet Web servers typically wait for requests and then respond to them, they are usually left outside of existing firewall structures. To place an Internet Web server inside a firewall, the typical setup is to "bore a hole" in the firewall so that the server can receive and respond to outside requests. This "hole" may open up other computers on the network to a security threat through the Web server.

Intranet Web servers, on the other hand, need to be behind a firewall in order to remain hidden from the Internet environment, where data can be potentially accessed by anyone with an Internet connection.

Server Configurations

The network designs shown in the following illustration are typical of organizations that host their own Web sites:

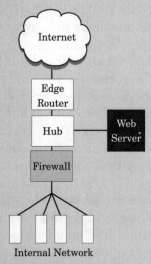

Open services architecture with little security risk to the internal network but less protection for the Web server.

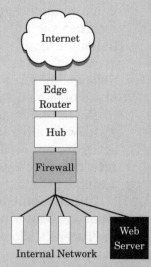

Closed services architecture with less security risk for the Web server but greater risk for the internal network.

● When a Web server is placed behind the same firewall as the network, greater access is available through the firewall. The Web server is better protected against attacks while it is behind a firewall, but the rest of the network is less secure.

● Keeping a Web server outside of the firewall is a safer scenario for the network, but leaves the Web server with only its own operating system and services to protect it.

CGI SECURITY

? What are the major security concerns when creating and running server scripts?

All custom applications on a Web server can potentially do a great deal of harm. On the lesser end, a script that receives unexpected parameters may simply use too much processing power and slow down or stop a Web server. On the more complex end, a script may allow user-specified commands to be executed on the server with root permissions.

Because server scripts are usually used for very simple tasks, the temptation is strong for programmers to write very short and very simple solutions from scratch. This practice, known as "rolling your own," is a great way to learn programming but often creates dangerous access points to a server. Keeping the core of a CGI program simple and commenting programming code liberally are two very good practices. Certain small tasks, however, such as verifying whether a URL is in the correct format or whether a link to another CGI should be trusted, should not be treated as simple problems. All data that is not hard-coded into the CGI itself should be considered suspect. Using well-tested, publicly available libraries often helps to keep your codes "core simple."

Just to execute, every script needs stronger file permissions than the security permissions given to an anonymous Web user. Exploiting this weakness, which is inherent in all scripts, can potentially lead to server access with as many privileges as the CGI has been given.

The general categories of CGI weakness are as follows:

● Executing shell commands from within a CGI based on user-entered information

● Overloading databases or text files on the server

● Trust based on IP address

● Potential to trigger processor-intensive operations

? ## What general methods can be used to prevent CGIs from being used maliciously?

A number of different techniques can be used to minimize the risks to your server from an attack that is initiated through your server's CGIs. Following is a list of these techniques:

- Cap the time that your CGI has to execute.
- Use libraries that have been successfully used by others.
- Place programming libraries and run-time engines in directories where they cannot be modified.
- Test your code with several requests at once.
- If one CGI calls another, make sure that there is a strong basis for trust.
- Scrub all form input data.
- Avoid cross-dependency.

Cap the Time That Your CGI Has to Execute

A CGI that takes too long to execute can slow down your whole server. Extended processing time may be caused by a full hard drive or an infinite loop. By starting a timed event that kills your CGI after a specific number of milliseconds, you reduce the risk of runaway or blocked programs.

Use Libraries That Have Been Successfully Used by Others

Tried-and-true programming libraries are far less likely to give you problems than libraries written from scratch that are being used for the first time. Popular, well-tested libraries are available for a variety of different CGI functions in a number of different programming languages.

Place Programming Libraries and Run-Time Engines in Directories Where They Cannot Be Modified

Be sure that any script interpreters, virtual machines, and associated libraries are installed in directories where they cannot be modified by anyone other than the server administrator. Requiring that scripts on your server use a specific, well-tested library for certain functions only works if that library is left unedited. Modifying a library may lead to security holes in another script or cause it to stop working altogether. Also, a malicious user who has access to your programming libraries but not your scripts may still be able to affect the behavior of any program that calls your scripts.

Test Your Code with Several Requests at Once

Multi-threading and the concurrent execution of a CGI program present special challenges to the programmer. Plan for multiple copies of your program to run concurrently. Be sure to lock files as they are being modified. Provide a means of recovering locked files if your script crashes. Avoid creating "deadlock" situations where two processes require a lock on a set of resources but both can only obtain a subset of the resources.

If One CGI Calls Another, Make Sure That There Is a Strong Basis for Trust

If one CGI requires the output of another, build in a reliable form of trust. Use encryption or a hash algorithm to verify that another CGI is what it claims to be. All too often trust is based on a server name or IP address alone.

Scrub All Form Input Data

A program written without data-checking fail-safes is inherently dangerous. The format of user-entered data should never be trusted. Programs that trust incoming information are often called "brittle" because they often crash when unexpected data is submitted, data in the wrong format or wrong order is submitted, or changes in the run-time environment are made. A secure, robust program is made so because data is checked at all stages of processing. For example, the input parameters of the user (or the parameters sent by the browser) are checked, as are the data that is sent to OS calls, the return values from OS calls, the data returned to the user, and internal state variables.

Don't assume, for example, that just because your HTML form only allows eight characters to be entered, a maximum of eight characters will be submitted. A malicious user can easily create a similar HTML form with no character limitations and overload your script by sending potentially thousands of characters. Use JavaScript form verification strictly as an aid for the user. JavaScript form verification is easy to bypass.

Checking individual characters in form data is particularly important when form data is used in shell-executed lines. Any characters that are not expected in form-submitted data should be removed, including perhaps the following characters: | # < - ;. If your form only expects numbers, letters, and periods, either deny illegal data or convert it to legal characters before executing it.

Add logging functionality that flags suspicious data that has been received. Check the error logs for the techniques that were used to try to get past your security.

Note: *Implementing a system that involves the review of code and formal quality assurance testing is highly recommended. Programmers in general are notoriously poor at thoroughly testing their own code for bugs and security holes. To provide a level of security against "back doors" and "time bombs" that are maliciously left in live code, as well as accidental bugs and security holes, every piece of code should be reviewed by at least one person who was not its primary developer.*

Also, for medium to large projects, a clear and complete design document is essential. This document should describe your program, its inputs and outputs, what files or services it can access or use, potential error conditions, and error handling. The design should be written in clear English and should also contain any algorithms, but without code. A change in the behavior of the program should ideally be prefaced by writing that changes in the design document.

Cross-Dependency

Creating a number of CGIs that all rely on each other in order to properly execute is a bad idea. Using common libraries is an acceptable coding practice, but calling other executables from your script can create an extremely complicated and vulnerable process. Understanding a CGI process that involves many scripts can be very difficult and confusing. It is best to keep CGI functions self-contained where possible. This practice will also make moving your site's scripts between Web servers a much simpler process.

How can crashing a server application bring down a Web server?

The CGI format was intended to protect Web servers from crashing when a poorly written CGI script crashes. Many of the new server programming interfaces have been optimized for speed to the point that the separation between the server and custom application is obscured. When applications are written for specifications such as the Netscape Server API (NSAPI) or the Internet Server API (ISAPI), crashes are far more likely to bring down the whole server. For CGIs, the danger often lies not so much in a crash, but rather in a loop or process that simply monopolizes CPU time. This CPU utilization danger can even cause static pages and graphics to be delivered very slowly or not at all.

★ ***Note:*** *If your system is receiving persistent attacks from the same IP address (this should be evident from log files or security software), block the IP address from your Web server and try to identify the individual from his or her IP address. In Chapter 4, the section "Site Tracking and Reporting" offers techniques for identifying a visitor's IP address. From the IP address you should be able to identify the domain, allowing you to contact a technical person and notify them of your problem.*

Chapter 7

Promoting Your Site

Answer Topics!

Promoting Your Site @ a Glance

- Web site publicity is all about driving traffic to your site. Only two factors determine whether traffic on your site is increased. The first factor is new visitors. Get more people to the site and traffic will go up. The second factor is getting those people to come back more often. Providing good content may be the best way to get return visitors, but publicity is the best way to attract first-time visitors to your site.

- Whether it is a listing in a popular search engine or a URL at the bottom of print ads, how to publicize a Web address is a step that every successful site has been forced to tackle. There isn't a five-step process for successfully promoting a Web site. The best advice is to simply hit as many areas as possible with publicity and hope for the best.

- This chapter addresses the following important topics:

- **Linking to the Site** discusses how Web surfers generally link to new sites for the first time. You also learn how to find out who is linking to your site.

- **Search Engines** solves the mystery of how to get listed on search sites on the Web. Search engines drive the vast majority of first-time traffic to most sites, so getting listed and getting listed well are very important topics.

- **Awards** explains the types of awards that are given on the Web, how awards can help drive traffic to a site, and what you need to do to get your site considered for an award.

- **Promoting Sites Online** describes different methods of promoting your site on the Internet. Newsgroups, mailing lists, and exchanging links with other sites are discussed.

- **Cross-Promoting Sites** contains valuable information on approaching other sites directly and using banner exchange services for cross-promotional advertising exchanges.

- **Promoting Sites Offline** explains the basic methods of offline promotion and what you can do to drive people to your site with traditional media.

LINKING TO THE SITE

? Where does most site traffic originate?

In order to publicize a site, it is useful to find out how visitors found it in the first place. Once you've discovered how visitors found your site, the next question is, how do those who haven't yet found your site find new sites on the Web? By comparing the two answers, you can get a rough idea of what areas you need to target to publicize your site.

To find out how visitors came to your site in the first place, a trip to the server log files is worthwhile. Even better, take a look at the log file analysis report that was run on your Web server's log files. If your server is logging enough variables, a detailed analysis should reveal which sites are linking to yours. This data also helps to reveal where your site visitors are *not* coming from. If no links were made to your site from the Yahoo! search engine, for example, check to see if you are listed there and, if you are listed, make sure that you are listed under the appropriate category.

Figuring out how visitors got to your site helps establish a basic user demographic. If your visitors frequently link from golf sites, for example, your demographic may be as simple as people who like golf. Once you know where visits come from, you can add content that caters to their interests.

? Where do most Web surfers find out about new URLs?

CommerceNet Consortium and Nielson Media Research conducted a survey in which respondents were asked what led them to most of the Web sites they visit. The results of the survey were reported in the July, 1997 edition of *Webmaster* magazine. As shown here, the results indicate that the overwhelming majority of surfers use search engines to find sites on the Web (some respondents chose more than one method; as a result, totals add up to more than 100 percent):

Method by which Respondents Found New Web Sites	Percent of Respondents
Search engines	71%
Friends and relatives	9.8%
Newspapers and magazines	8.5%
Links from other Web sites	8.4%
Browsing or surfing around	8.1%
Television	3.6%
Printed Internet directories	3.3%

The simple fact is that most new site traffic comes from search engines. Although they were not specifically mentioned in the survey, ad banners are another very popular source of first-time site visits. On some sites, banners are responsible for large percentages of site traffic. Banners are particularly useful in publicizing sites that have live content, since print ads and search engine results are not good at conveying when an event on a site is a live event. Auctions, Webcasts, and similar events are prime targets for banner ads.

? How can I determine which Web sites offer hyperlinks to my site?

Even though determining which sites link to your site falls under the category of "ego-surfing" (searching the Web for references to yourself), figuring out who is linking to your site can be extremely useful. Seeing which sites link to yours is also an easy way to find out if any links to pages that no longer exist on your site are found on other sites. You can find these dead links without having to dig through your server's log files.

Most people don't realize that many search engines allow you to search for hyperlinks. Currently, Digital's AltaVista search engine is the best search engine for finding links to your site. From http://altavista.digital.com, fill in the search window with the following:

+link:yoursite.com –host:yoursite.com

All Web pages in the AltaVista database that contain links to your site will be listed, excluding pages in your site, as shown in Figure 7-1.

The Inktomi search engine at http://www.hotbot.com has more of a MadLib-style interface. With the Inktomi search engine, you manipulate the drop-down menus to create the following phrase:

links to this URL

Search: the Web http://www.yoursite.com

Hotbot, shown in Figure 7-2, doesn't offer wildcard matching, so it is necessary to enter an exact URL. Using Hotbot usually results in fewer hits, but the results come back with a relevancy ranking.

There is, however, a chance that many pages that link to your site haven't been assimilated into the major search

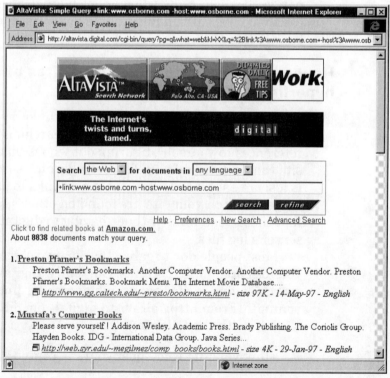

Figure 7-1   AltaVista allows you to search for pages that link to your site and exclude pages in your site from the results.

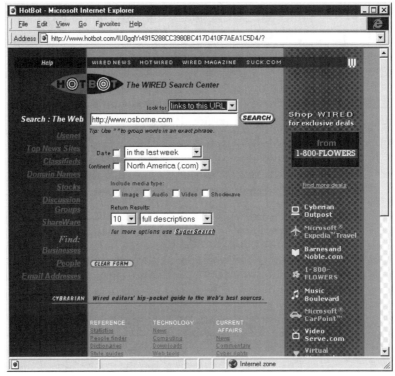

Figure 7-2   Hotbot allows searching for links to specific pages in your site.

engines. The only way to find these sites is to search the HTTP_REFERER variable in your Web server's log files. Unfortunately, not all Web servers record this variable, and not all Web browsers report it to your server, so there is no guaranteed way of determining from your log files where all of the links to your site are located.

SEARCH ENGINES

How can I list my site with all of the top search engines?

Search engines have robots, or *crawlers* as they are often called, that request pages from the Web, process the pages for keywords, parse the hyperlinks, and place the information in a searchable database. To request and parse new pages, the robots look to the hyperlinks that have already been parsed. The robots are usually automated scripts that, essentially, crawl around the Web and determine where to go next by analyzing the hyperlinks that they find along the way.

If enough hyperlinks to your site are found, it's a safe bet that your pages will eventually be assimilated into the top search engines. To ensure that your pages are listed in the proper categories and are associated with the correct search words, register your pages directly with every search engine with which you want to be listed.

Services are available to help list sites with a number of search engines at one time. Http://www.submit-it.com (shown in Figure 7-3) and http://www.register-it.com are both popular services for automatic search engine registration.

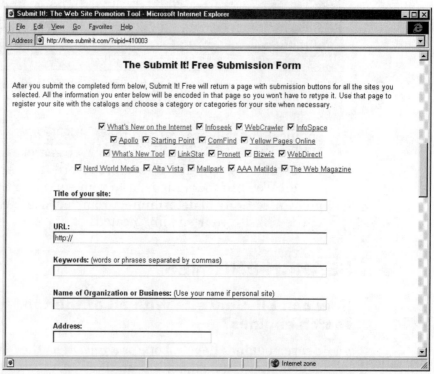

Figure 7-3 Submit It provides a free registration service by which you can fill out one form and register your site with a large number of major search engines.

Note: *Don't expect your site to be included in a search engine right away. The turnaround time is often extremely slow and can take one to two months for some of the major listing services. Be sure to keep track of where you have registered your site so that you can follow up later and make sure your site is listed.*

Now that my site is listed with a number of search engines, how can I be listed closer to the top of the pages that search engines return?

The major search engines have two types of listings: directory and keyword. *Directory listings* allow site visitors to click down through progressively more specific categories until they reach the site listing they want. *Keyword directories* are listings of pages that match user-entered parameters.

Directory Listings

To get to a listing of search engines, for example, a Web surfer may need to select Business and Economy, Companies, then Internet Services, and then Search and Navigation to obtain a listing of sites that are of interest.

Owners of sites that are listed high on the page in directory listings often pay for their positions or receive their positions as a bonus for placing ad banners on the search site. Other enhanced directory listing features include a "new" graphic or bold print that makes a site stand on a list.

Keyword Directories

Keyword directories display "search results" based on user-entered keywords or search parameters. Searching for "Internet and Shockwave and Java," for example, may return sites in an order of preference, a percentage of likelihood, or a relevancy ranking that relates to the search criteria. Search engines usually take into consideration the following factors in ranking a site:

● <META> tag keywords
● Total number of times a word has appeared in the page

- Words that appear between the <TITLE> and </TITLE> tags of the page

- The number of hyperlinks to the site from other sites

When you create a page, including a keyword <META> tag at the top of your HTML like the following is always a good idea:

```
<META Name="Keywords" Content="book, internet,
magazine, advice, tips, webmaster, search engine" >
```

See AltaVista's help page for assistance in constructing <META> tags at http://www.altavista.digital.com/cgi-bin/query?pg=h&what=web#meta.

Ever Wondered What Other People Search for Online?

A number of major search engines allow you to watch what others are currently searching for on their sites. Although it probably doesn't help make your site any more searchable, it is certainly interesting to watch how others search for information online. The following is a list of sites that offer this voyeuristic feature:

- http://voyeur.mckinley.com/cgi-bin/voyeur.cgi
- http://webcrawler.com/Games/SearchTicker.html
- http://search3.metacrawler.com/perl/metaspy

? **Does repeating the same word a number of times in a page help to prioritize page listings in search engine results pages?**

Blending the same word or words into your content helps move your page up in search engine results on many search sites. However, you can use a number of sneaky techniques to enhance a page's relevancy ranking without necessarily displaying more content.

When Web-based search engines were new, the practice of repeating keywords in <META> tags was one way of getting pages to the top of search engine listings, as is done in the Microsoft Expedia page shown in Figure 7-4. Here is an example of repeating keywords in a <META> tag:

```
<META Name="Keywords" Content="book, book, book,
book, internet, internet, internet, internet">
```

However, the major search engines have caught on to this practice, which is also known as keyword spamming. Now the major search engines either cancel the search of your page or count the practice heavily against you, since it is often the mark of an unprofessional site.

Another practice for hiding more words on the page for search engines to find involves repeating keywords within a Web page's HTML without the words being visible to site visitors. By selecting a font color that matches the background color of the page, keywords can be listed many times but be invisible as well. However, a few search engines have also caught on to this practice. If you use it, be sure and employ slightly different colors that display the same (such as < BODY BACKGROUND=#FFFFFF> for the page

Figure 7-4   Microsoft's popular Expedia travel site contains comprehensive <META> tag information on its front page so that the site is listed prominently by search engines.

background and <FONT COLOR=#FFFFFE> for the hidden text). You can also use a tiled, solid-color GIF as a background texture.

Note: *Another common practice for prioritizing page listings is to include your competitors' names in your site's content <META> tag. By doing so, you increase the chance of your site appearing when someone does a search on a competitor's name. Avoiding this practice is strongly recommended because its legal status is currently being contested in U.S. courts. For the best results from search engines, stick to clear, concise, descriptive, useful <META> tag information.*

AWARDS

How does winning an award help a site?

A number of popular Web sites and Internet magazines offer awards to sites that they have judged attractive, useful, or fun. There are two main types of awards: industry awards, which seek to recognize the designers and owners of Web sites, and "cool site" awards, which serve more to recommend great sites to Web surfers than to recognize industry excellence. Both types of awards bestow attention, hyperlinks, and most important, publicity on a site.

Industry Awards

Organizations such as the Internet Professional Publisher's Association offer awards to sites for excellence in design and function. These types of awards rarely attract large numbers of visitors to a site directly through hyperlinks. However, they generate attention both online and in the print media. Many organizations that sponsor industry awards allow winning sites to display a trophy graphic to indicate that the award has been won. Awards can serve to increase a site's legitimacy and standing. Another important aspect of industry awards is the encouragement they offer to Web site designers and programmers.

"Cool Site" Awards

"Site of the day" awards are usually given for the benefit of the Web surfer who is looking for a new site to visit. These awards are given frequently, and the fact that they were given is soon forgotten. A "cool site" award can, however, cause a surge of site traffic. In fact, the awards have been known to cause unanticipated increases from new traffic on the server load. Awards such as Netscape's "What's Cool" listing (shown in Figure 7-5), Yahoo's "Cool Links" listings, and the "Cool Site Award" can give a big boost to a site that needs publicity.

New Zealand Tourism Board

The New Zealand Tourism Board site at http://www.nztb.govt.nz has won a number of awards, but only a handful increased traffic noticeably. Fortunately, however, a well-placed award can substantially increase traffic. When the New Zealand Tourism Board received Yahoo's "Pick of the Week" award, the site experienced a 500-percent increase in traffic for the duration of the award and an overall increase in traffic in the months that followed.

❓ How can I get my site reviewed for an award?

First, put together a list of sites that offer awards. Sites that offer these lists can be found at the following addresses:

- http://www.yahoo.com/Computers_and_Internet/Internet/World_Wide_Web/Best_of_the_Web/Awards/
- http://www.infoseek.com/Internet/Searching_and_exploring/Best_of_the_Web/Web_awards
- http://www.freelinks.com/awards.html

Next, simply fill out the necessary forms. Avoid writing advertising prose when you describe your site on online contest submission forms. Instead, list the site's best features

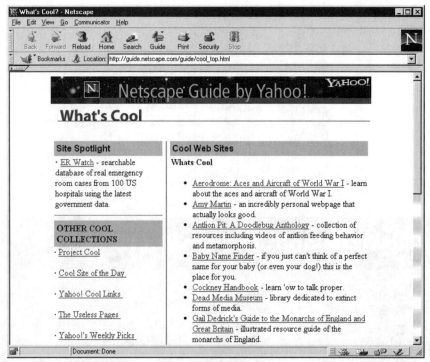

Figure 7-5 Web sites such as Netscape's "What's Cool" page help bring traffic to featured sites.

and technologies. Check back occasionally if you don't win an award. Resubmit a submission form when you change the look and feel of your site or when you add new attractions.

PROMOTING SITES ONLINE

Besides getting listed with the major search engines, how can I publicize my site online?

Besides search engines, sites can promote themselves in a number of different areas online. As a warning, whenever you enter a new area of the Web, such as a new mailing list or newsgroup, be sure to read the frequently asked questions or rules that apply to the forum. In some areas of the Web, the line between promotion and spamming is considered very fine indeed. Following are areas where you can promote your site online:

- Newsgroups
- "What's new" Web pages
- Mailing lists (LISTSERVs)
- E-mail signatures
- Online magazines and newsletters
- Web rings

Newsgroups

Literally thousands of newsgroups can be found on the Internet. They cover every topic you can think of. Newsgroups function as discussion areas and are usually an acceptable area to post new Web sites as long as they may be of interest to the newsgroup's subscribers. Find newsgroups whose topics are similar to that of your site. You may also want to post a message on the newsgroup comp.infosystems .announce, a newsgroup that has served as a popular announcement locale for Websites for a number of years.

"What's New" Web Pages

Some sites offer a page for new links. Try to get your site posted on these sites by e-mailing the site's Webmaster or by filling out a submission form if one is provided. Utilizing new technology such as dynamic HTML and Java often increases a site's chances of getting listed. Obviously, a link from a site that attracts the same type of visitor as your site is more likely to be a good referrer of visitors. Popular "what's new" pages include Netscape's Cool Site of the Day at http://home.netscape.com/home/whats-cool/ and Project Cool's listing at http://www.projectcool.com/sightings.

Mailing Lists (LISTSERVs)

Mailing lists are a very effective method of reaching a large number of eyes. First, find e-mail lists whose subscribers may want to visit your site, and then subscribe to those lists. A comprehensive list of mailing lists and methods for subscribing are available at http://www.liszt.com/.

Simply evangelizing your new site with a mailing group posting may anger subscribers, so try a more subtle approach. Take a little time to actually participate in a mailing list, and then drop your URL wherever you can into the messages that you post. Don't be afraid to drop a direct plug for your site at the bottom of a legitimate message. People are less offended by seeing a URL in a legitimate e-mail message than they are an online advertisement.

E-mail Signatures

Add your URL prominently to your e-mail signature. To bring traffic to their sites, some companies require employees to add their Web address to their e-mail signature. Most of the newer e-mail clients automatically turn URLs into hyperlinks. When these automatic hyperlinks are double-clicked, the default browser is opened automatically to the correct page.

Online Magazines and Newsletters

Send a press release that boasts about your new site to electronic publications. As long as you write a clean press release that doesn't sound too much like an advertisement, you may be able to convince publications to post it online with little or no editing. Check out a comprehensive list of electronic magazines at http://webreference.com/magazines.html.

Many magazines review sites as well as award prizes to sites. Try to convince publications to review your site. Most critics prefer to write positive reviews, so bad reviews rarely get published.

Web Rings

Web rings are groups of sites that have banded together (like the one shown in Figure 7-6), the idea being that anyone who accesses one of the sites in the ring can also take a tour of the other sites by following the hyperlinks. Recently, Web rings have become quite popular with site visitors. For more information on web rings and a listing of Web rings that have already formed, visit http://www.webring.org/.

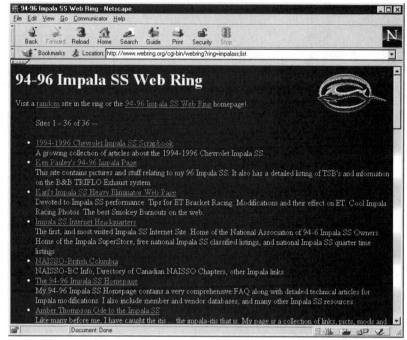

Figure 7-6   Web rings are a new way of grouping similar sites. The 94-96 Impala SS Web ring brings together 36 Chevy Impala SS Web sites.

? What are some techniques for increasing the number of links to my site?

Sites link to one another for a number of reasons. Typically, links are formed when one site offers the other one or more of the following elements:

- Reference material/advice
- Humor
- Complementary products or related subject matter
- Cross-promotional material

- Up-to-date information/dynamic content
- Monetary enticements for links that result in sales
- Obligation from a link exchange
- Services that other sites cannot offer themselves

So whether it is content, monetary promises, or an exchange, the more sites that link to yours, the higher the amount of traffic you will likely get.

Revenue Sharing for Hyperlinks

Amazon.com has implemented an interesting approach to increase traffic to its site. Amazon offers up to 15 percent of revenue from books sales to sites that send paying customers their way. If you have an Amazon partnership site that contains a link to a specific book that is sold at Amazon.com, and the person who clicks the link buys the book, you could receive up to 15 percent of the revenue from the sale of the book.

Amazon's approach is encouraging other sites to not just link to them, but to send paying customers their way. If you visit major publishers' Web sites, you will likely find links to Amazon.com.

? What are some good ideas for starting a site with a splash?

Launching a site with a splash is a sure way of drawing visitors to your site from day one. The difficulty with a site launch is in getting large numbers of people to the site at the same time. Launch events that are time-dependent, such as the following, are a popular way to attract a large number of site visitors to a site on the same day.

Live Web Broadcasts

Use streaming audio on your site to broadcast live events. Hotwired has a streaming audio music channel that broadcasts live over the Internet and provides phone numbers so that listeners can call in and participate. Live pictures of events that are taking place can be another great attraction. Live images have appeared on the Web to publicize events ranging from trade shows to the docking of the space shuttle with the space station Mir.

Contests and Sweepstakes

Contests can be an effective way of collecting demographic data from site visitors. Site visitors are more willing to fill out online questionnaires when there is a chance of a reward. Keep in mind that you must abide by a number of sweepstakes rules and regulations to promote a contest in the United States and Canada. Some of the rules are quite odd. For example, you have to provide an alternative means, such as by snail mail, of entering the contest. Be prepared to receive a large volume of both site hits and letters from people who want to enter your contest.

Live Chat Room Chats with Famous People

If your server includes a chat area, consider drawing people to your site for a live chat session with someone who is well-known. Chat promotions on America Online have drawn thousands of visitors to the same online area of the service. Chat room sessions can be a great source of community-building and dynamic content. Try scheduling regular guests for the chat areas on your site. Enticing guests is often easier than you may think. After all, guests do not need to leave home to participate.

The Deja News Tornado

During a fierce Texas tornado, parts of Austin and Cedar Park lost power. As a result, the Deja News Web site went offline for a number of hours, and several hundred thousand requests went unfullfilled. The following day, Deja News posted a small tornado graphic that linked to a picture of the storm, an explanation of why the site went offline, and an apology.

A full 10 percent of site visitors visited the Deja News tornado page the day after the storm. The high level of interest in the page and the story that it told inspired C|Net to write a story that congratulated Deja News for not trying to hide what had happened. The tornado page and the apology turned what would normally be considered a Web-site public relations nightmare into a publicity success story.

CROSS-PROMOTING SITES

? **Is it acceptable to approach another site directly with an offer of cross-promotion?**

One of the cheapest and simplest ways to promote a site is to exchange banners or traditional links with other sites. Under this scenario, you host a banner that links to another site and, in exchange, the other site displays a banner that promotes and links back to your site. Trading banners is a good and free way for two sites to mutually promote one another. The best way to set up this sort of an exchange is to find a site that you think would be a good match for a cross-promotion and e-mail the Webmaster. Once the banner is set up on the other site, check your log files from time to time to get an estimate of how much traffic is coming from the other site. Make sure your Web server is logging the HTTP_REFERER variable so you can determine from which sites your visitors came.

Trading Content for Links

To increase traffic to its site, White Palm offers other sites free daily cartoons in exchange for links back to its site. To promote the cartoon offer, White Palm used Link Exchange, at no cost, to reach sites all around the Internet. By trading dynamic content to other sites in exchange for links back to its own site, White Palm increased its site traffic by a factor of three.

? **How can I determine how many site visitors exit my site through a particular ad banner?**

A good technique for determining how many visitors left your site through a particular ad banner is to use a redirection application or script. Instead of linking an ad banner directly to another site, send the visitor to a redirection program on your site along with a variable that tells the redirection program where to redirect the visitor. A site visitor who clicks the ad can't tell the difference between linking directly to a site and redirecting through a program. The advantage of this technique is that the link is logged in your Web server's log files and therefore can be tracked. Visitors who click through an ad banner can be counted without your having to rely on the destination site to track the number of visitors.

? Are there services that allow me to exchange banners on my site with other sites on the Web?

A number of companies now offer banner exchange services. Most of them follow a similar business model. The service takes a banner of yours and posts it on a number of different sites with a link that you specify. You are then given a line of HTML to insert into your page that allows ads to be served to your site. Banner exchange services make money by interspersing the ads that they sell with the ads that are exchanged. Different services have different formulas for determining how many ads on your site are shown as compared to how many ads for other sites are shown. Most services display around two ads on your site for every ad of yours that is displayed elsewhere.

Sites that offer exchange services include the following:

- Link Exchange: http://www.linkexchange.com/
- SmartClicks: http://www.smartclicks.com/
- Banner Swap: http://www.bannerswap.com/

? What dangers should I be aware of when considering banner exchange services?

Before jumping headfirst into a banner exchange program, doing a little research is worthwhile. Here are a number of pitfalls to consider before participating in a banner exchange:

- Avoid exchange services that don't limit the kilobyte size of the ads being served. Large file sizes seriously affect the performance of a site, especially when the site attracts a lot of modem users.

- Check which sites are involved in the exchange. Make sure that your banners will not be displayed in areas of the Web where you don't want them to be displayed. This advice also applies to banners that your site will host. A suggestive banner to an adult-oriented site, for example, is quite embarrassing on a site that targets a family-oriented crowd.

- Check the quality of banners that other sites post. A poorly constructed banner can distract from any site.

Co-branding

Another way to bring visitors to a site is *co-branding*. Co-branding is a strategy to increase the value of one company's brand to consumers by associating it with another. This strategy is intended to be perceived by consumers as offering something of value from both companies, but in a non-competitive manner. American Express Travel has a number of partners on the Web whose sites feature American Express Travel "book-it" buttons. The American Express Travel site is co-branded with the logo of the site from which it was linked each time someone presses a book-it button. A site visitor that links to American Express Travel from AT&T's site, for example, sees AT&T's logo at the top of the page.

PROMOTING SITES OFFLINE

? **Where is it appropriate to list my URL in print material?**

Wherever you list your address and phone number, you should add your URL. Place your URL on business cards, stationary, brochures, billboards, print advertisements, and so on. Treating your online address as important as your street address is not inappropriate. The more places your URL is seen, the more likely your Web site will be visited.

? Do URL references in magazines and newspapers generate hits?

As long as the context in which a URL is mentioned is of interest and the URL is memorable, a mention in the media is likely to attract new visitors. To increase the likelihood of people remembering your URL, using a simple and memorable domain name is particularly important. If a specific page in your site is going to be mentioned in the press, try moving or copying the page to a location in your site that will create the simplest URL for a reader to remember.

Just one mention in a nationally distributed publication can potentially drive significant numbers of visitors to your site. Press releases about your site and any events that it hosts often provide great material for magazines and newspapers. Craft your press releases in such a way that they can be republished with minimal editing.

Chapter 8

Web Graphics

Answer Topics!

Web Graphics @ a Glance

Creating Web graphics can be a difficult task. The basic problem lies in the fact that graphics may be viewed in a number of different Web browsers, on different operating systems, with different monitor settings, over a range of connection speeds. You need patience and a variety of skills to create effective graphics for the widest possible audience.

The print publishing world only needs to accurately match colors for one printer, since all copies of all graphics are viewed as printouts from that printer. Web publishing is fundamentally different in that there is no way to guarantee that every pixel will be displayed exactly as you want it. Each Web site visitor is likely to have different hardware, monitor settings, display drivers, browser software, etc. The challenge in Web publishing is to minimize the graphical variations visitors see by creating graphic files that are as compatible as possible with different setups. A second challenge is to keep file sizes small at the same time to accommodate those with slower connection speeds to the Internet. Although there is no substitute for experimenting and testing for quality assurance, methods have been devised for creating compelling Web-compatible images that nevertheless keep to reasonable file sizes.

This chapter covers the following areas of Web graphics:

File Formats helps you choose a file format for your images and offers a little background for each option. This section covers the GIF, JPEG, and PNG file formats.

Affecting How Images Appear addresses the factors that control how a graphic looks on a page.

- **Reducing Download Time** covers techniques for minimizing the file size of static Web images. The section offers techniques to help browsers display images before they are fully downloaded.

- **Hyperlinking from Graphics** covers how to create client-side and server-side image maps and how to combine the two. Also covered is the matter of how to display graphics that touch horizontally or vertically without a gap.

- **Graphic Techniques** helps solve common problems that often get in the way of creating effective Web graphics.

- **Protecting Images** explains how to protect your images from being used elsewhere without your permission. This section also explains what images are permissible to use on your site.

- **Dynamically Generated Images** discusses the difference between dynamically creating a graphic that is sent directly to a browser and using a graphic that is cached first and then referenced through HTML.

- **Web Animations** discusses the different methods of creating Web-based animations. In this section are tips for reducing the file size of animated GIFs.

FILE FORMATS

? ### What graphic file format should I use on my Web pages?

Although PNG (portable network graphics) is a likely candidate for Web publishing in the future, for now GIF and JPEG are the only two options available to Web developers who want to support the majority of Web browsers. Many mistakenly believe that choosing a file format for Web graphics is a simple choice between GIF and JPEG, but deciding which format to choose is far from simple. Consider these attributes when you make your choice:

Attribute	GIF	JPEG
Colors	256 color palette maximum	16.8 million
Image quality	Lossless (no data lost)	Lossy (some original data lost)

Attribute	GIF	JPEG
Animation support	Yes	No
Transparency support	Yes (1bit)	No
Streamable (whether a graphic can display before it is fully downloaded)	Yes (interlaced GIFs)	Yes (progressive JPEG)

A good rule of thumb is to use JPEG for:

- Graphics with gradients, watercolor effects, and blur effects
- Graphics with fuzzy edges, drop shadows, and so on
- Photographs

Typically, GIFs are better for:

- Images with blocks of color
- Animations
- Graphics that contain sharp edges
- Graphics with text
- Black-and-white images
- Graphics that require transparency
- Images in which exact color representation is important for those with 256-color monitor settings

Ultimately, you should simply try both formats and select the one that offers the best file size-to-quality comparison.

? Is the GIF file format patented? Do I have to worry about royalties?

The GIF file format, as originally defined in 1987, includes a patented form of file compression called LZW. As the Web took off, manufacturers built their browsers to support only GIF and JPEG graphics. Consequently, GIF quickly became a very popular file format. Following a controversy over the

GIF file format patent and how to enforce it, Unisys and CompuServe announced, at the beginning of 1995, that they would ask for royalties for programs that create GIFs.

Does this mean that people who use GIFs have to pay royalties? The answer is no. If you create software that allows users to save images in GIF format, however, you should first get permission from CompuServe or Unisys. Also, if you have a server application that generates dynamic GIF images, such as time-stamped photos, you need to obtain, and possibly pay for, permission to use the server application.

? What is the PNG format for graphics?

Many predict that the PNG (portable network graphics) format will replace GIFs and JPEGs as the predominant file format on the Web for non-animated graphics. PNG, a well-thought-out format, offers the following advantages:

- **Lossless:** Unlike JPEG files, PNG files don't lose any color information when they are saved.

- **Better compression:** PNG offers better compression than GIF.

- **Bit transparency:** PNG offers alpha-channel blending of graphics allowing 256 levels of transparency. This means that one graphic may have many different levels of transparency, allowing graphical elements such as drop shadows, fades, and anti-aliased text to blend smoothly with the background.

- **Gamma correction:** PNG is the first graphics format to correct monitor gamma settings so that colors look the same on all platforms.

- **Free:** Unlike the GIF format, which has patented elements, PNG is patent-free.

- **True color:** The format supports both limited color palettes and true color display.

Unfortunately, Netscape Navigator has not supported the PNG format natively as of version 4.0. However, Netscape has indicated that it will support PNG in the future, and a number of plug-ins are available for Netscape Navigator going all the way back to version 2.0. Microsoft Internet Explorer 4.0 contains built-in support for the PNG format. Microsoft Internet Explorer 3.0 supports PNG with a plug-in as well as an ActiveX control that was developed to support PNG.

AFFECTING HOW IMAGES APPEAR

? What color palette should I use for GIF images?

Choosing the right color palette is extremely important for graphics that will display on 8-bit (256-color) monitors. A monitor that can only display a maximum of 256 different colors must reserve a certain number of colors for icons and desktop patterns, as well as the brower's buttons and window artifacts. All of these elements may be visible at the same time, which means that many different colors are kept in reserve.

If you see strange color flashes on your browser window or on the wondows behind your browser when your monitor is in 8-bit color mode, you know what happens when a browser tries to cope with too many colors at once.When the Microsoft Windows 95 monitor settings are in 8-bit color mode and you try to view GIFs that display many colors, you may see a severe color drop out across the desktop. Usually a color drop out results in incorrect colors being used by the computer to display desktop colors, icons, and other windows that are not in the foreground. In extreme cases, you need to restart your computer to fix the problem.

Because different operating systems reserve different colors for icons and desktop patterns, creating a color palette that works on the largest number of platforms and still presents the colors you want in your graphics can be tricky. Fortunately, Microsoft Internet Explorer and Netscape Navigator reserve the same set of 216 colors for Web site developers, so the 216 preset colors are safe to use in GIF files.

If you take the color values 0, 51, 102, 153, 204, and 255 and combine them in every possible way for red, green, and blue values, you come up with the 216 preset colors. The 216 colors represent what is often called the "Netscape color cube." Equilibrium's Debabelizer does a particularly good job of defining custom, Web-compatible palettes for multiple images.

The remaining 40 undefined colors are for use by the operating system. Graphic artists who define color palettes may also use the 40 undefined colors to create custom colors. If you decide to make use of the undefined colors, don't use many on any single page. Depending on the platform, the color of items on the screen such as buttons and icons may change drastically if you use the undefined colors.

Unfortunately, as long as people use different platforms and different browsers, 8-bit color displays are bound to display inconsistently.

? How do I make my GIFs and JPEGs transition from fuzzy or blocky to sharp?

With an interlaced GIF, the image displays in low resolution as it is downloading, and then a final, sharp image appears. Progressive JPEG images are capable of the same functionality, but they appear fuzzy or blurry as the file is downloading, as shown in Figure 8-1a, before they display as sharp images such as Figure 8-1b. The positive aspect of a low resolution-to-high resolution image display is that users see something before the image is finished loading. The downside is that the file size is always slightly larger.

Interlaced GIFs simply store the information that describes each row of pixels in a different order. After the first row is sent, every eighth row is sent to the browser. This provides enough information for the browser to stretch the pixels it has and display a very blocky graphic, as shown in Figure 8-2a. Next, every eighth row starting with the fourth row is sent, the result being that 25 percent of the graphic is sent, as shown in Figure 8-2b, and the graphic looks clearer. Two more passes and 50 percent, then 100 percent of the graphic is displayed, resulting in a complete image such as that shown in Figure 8-2c.

Progressive JPEG images have a very complex internal structure, but they function very similarly to interlaced GIFs and offer the same advantages. Like using a low source for graphics (a subject discussed later in this chapter), interlaced GIFs and progressive JPEGs benefit users with low bandwidth Internet connections.

A

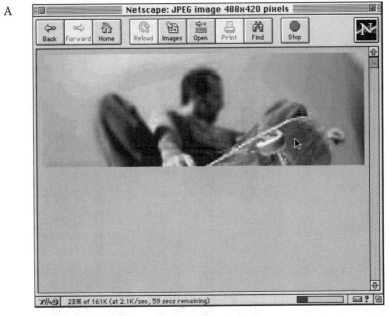

B

Figure 8-1 Progressive JPEG images transition from fuzzy to sharp the first time they are downloaded.

A

B

C

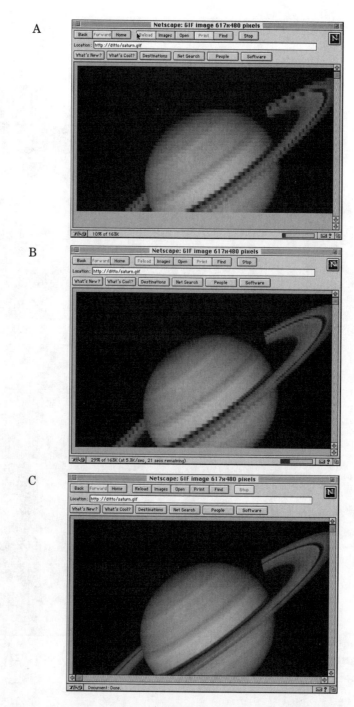

Figure 8-2 As an interlaced GIF downloads, the image appears fuzzy or blocky and then comes into sharp focus.

To save an image as a progressive JPEG or interlaced GIF, you need an image editor that supports these file formats. With most editors, all you have to do is check a box when you save the graphic to save it in the JPEG or GIF format. There is no variable that can be set to control the speed or number of transitions for either image format.

Use the ALT Attribute Within the IMAGE Tag

Using the ALT attribute along with HEIGHT and WIDTH attributes is highly recommended for all image tags. Using the ALT attribute offers four advantages:

- Visually impaired visitors who use browsers that can read page text and graphic descriptions aloud will understand your Web pages better.

- In Microsoft Internet Explorer, a yellow box with alternative text appears when the pointer rests on a graphic. The yellow box explains images and navigation elements to Microsoft Internet Explorer users.

- Browsers whose graphics display setting has been turned off and browsers that do not support graphics need an alternative to graphics on-screen. Browsing the Web with the graphics display setting turned off makes browsing go faster, but browsing a site is difficult when users can only navigate by means of graphics and the graphics do not offer alternative text.

- Browsers with slow Web connections display the alternative text until graphics are fully downloaded. If you do not provide interlaced GIFs or progressive JPEGs for site visitors with limited bandwidth, alternative text helps keep visitors' attention.

Following is an example of an image tag with an ALT attribute:

```
<IMG SRC="return.gif" HEIGHT=50 WIDTH=450 ALT="Return to Main Page">
```

? How do I create graphics that are partially or completely transparent?

Unfortunately, the JPEG image format does not allow for transparency. GIF, however, has allowed transparency since the GIF 89a format was approved in 1989. The GIF 89a format allows a 1 bit alpha channel so that one color may be chosen from a GIF's palette to be the transparent color. Unfortunately, transparent pixels must either be completely transparent or completely opaque in the GIF 89a file format.

Transparent GIFs are the best way to display non-rectangular images over a textured background when you wish the textured background to be visible. Figure 8-3 shows the disadvantage of using an opaque GIF over a textured background when the desired effect is to see the texture within the rectangular boundaries of the image. A GIF that contains some transparency is shown in Figure 8-4.

Most of today's browsers support transparent GIFs. Finding a graphics application that allows GIFs to be saved with transparency is difficult. PhotoShop 4.0 supports transparency with GIFs, but version 3.0 requires a plug-in (the plug-in is available from Adobe's Web site). On the Macintosh, Graphic Converter is one of the more popular graphics utilities and is available from most popular archives on the Web. To help create transparent GIFs on the PC, Lview Pro is available for download from many anonymous FTP sites.

Figure 8-3 On this Web page, a large opaque GIF is displayed over a textured background.

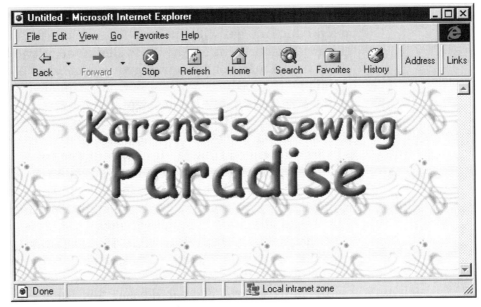

Figure 8-4 With Transparent GIFs, background textures appear behind nonrectangular images.

REDUCING DOWNLOAD TIME

❓ Why is reducing the file size of Web graphics so important?

Minimizing the file size of even a handful of Web graphics on a site can eliminate hours of cumulative waiting on the part of visitors. Suppose you were to reduce the size of each graphic on your Web site by 10 percent. Multiply the number of kilobytes saved by the number of times each graphic is requested, and the reduction in transferred kilobytes and the savings in time are surprisingly high. Reducing the file size of graphics can also help to reduce the load on a Web server, because the number of bits that the server has to send out with every page request is reduced.

❓ How do I minimize the file size of my GIFS?

Optimizing GIFs, especially animated GIFs, is considered by many to be a black art. Competitions between individuals and software manufacturers to see who or what application can produce images with the smallest possible file size are not uncommon. Spending hours to shave one or two kilobytes off an image may not seem worthwhile, but when a palette or technique that reduces the size of GIFs is applied to an entire site, the savings can be significant.

For all GIFs, the first challenge is to reduce the total number of colors to as few as possible. GIFs use a form of compression called LZW. With LZW, a row of pixels of the same color compresses far more easily than a row with several different colors. By replacing blocks of dithered colors with a solid color, total file size can be reduced. Also, if an image uses less than 128 colors, the palette that is being used for the image should contain less than 128 as well. Eliminating at least 128 colors from a palette results in a smaller image file size.

If you have already created a common palette (also known as a super-palette) for your graphics, you may be able to trim a small amount of file size by eliminating unused colors from the palette of each graphic. To do this in Photoshop, take the graphic that has already been assigned a super-palette and return it to RGB (palette-free) mode. Then select Indexed color from the Mode menu and map the graphic to the exact colors it uses without dithering. The graphic should look the same onscreen, because the colors have not actually changed. The palette, however, is reduced from the entire super-palette to a subset of the super-palette; the subset contains only the colors that are actually being used by the graphic. Equilibrium's Debabelizer does a great job of creating Web-compatible super-palettes and minimizing palettes as it saves graphics.

Avoid dithering GIFs if you can. *Dithering* is the speckling of colors to approximate another color or set of colors. Since speckled colors result in several different colors on the same line, compressing an image that has been speckled, or dithered, is not as effective. Unfortunately, most graphics look better when they are dithered. If a graphic contains areas that need to be dithered as well as large blocks of the same color, dither the graphic and then remove the dithering from the large blocks of color with image-editing tools.

? How do I minimize the file size of my JPEGs?

Not much can be done to reduce the file size of a JPEG other than adjusting the quality settings when you save it. Try saving different versions of a graphic at different quality settings to find a balance between quality and image size. To retain image quality, it is important not to open a JPEG and save it a second time. Since JPEG is a lossy file format, opening and saving a JPEG file degrades the image and lowers its quality. Saving a TIFF image in JPEG format typically reduces the total file size by 10:1 to 20:1. The higher the compression setting, the greater the loss in original graphic data. A TIFF image, such as the image shown in Figure 8-5a, may result in a reduction in file size as effective as 40:1, as shown in Figure 8-5b, when saved as a highly compressed JPEG.

? How do I make a graphic with a small file size display until the browser downloads the larger, final graphic?

Making a small graphic display until its larger version is downloaded is only possible with Netscape Navigator. People accessing a site through a low bandwidth connection such as a modem really appreciate being able to see the small graphic, however. Because large JPEG images and animated GIFs are frequently necessary for site navigation or key information, providing an identically sized graphic with a much smaller file size as a low source is often a good idea. Low-source graphics, such as the graphic shown in Figure 8-6a, are often only two colors for two reasons. First, it is easier for a site visitor to tell that a two-color image is not the final graphic. Second, two-color GIFs are usually extremely small, so they load more quickly. Figure 8-6b shows a page after the low resolution graphic has been replaced with a high resolution graphic.

A

B

Figure 8-5 This 877KB TIFF image (above) was reduced to just 20KB when it was saved in JPEG format with high compression (below).

A

B

Figure 8-6   Here, low-source images supplement the larger animated GIF image to accommodate those who visit the site by way of a modem.

To add a low source to your Web page's graphics, use HTML in the following format:

```
<IMG SRC="BigAnimation.gif" LOWSRC="BlackAndWhite.gif">
```

Always Specify Height and Width for Web Graphics

A Web browser needs an HTML file to figure out which graphics to request from a Web server. Since HTML files are always requested first and tend to be small in size, HTML files almost always finish downloading before the associated Web page graphics. As long as you specify the height and width attributes in an image tag in HTML, most browsers will display the HTML before the graphics are finished downloading and leave a correctly sized space for the graphics. As a result, users see a correctly laid out page that they can read and link from before the graphics have finished downloading.

Different browsers give different results if height and width tags are not specified within a Web page's HTML. When Netscape Navigator 2.0 reaches an image tag without height and width attributes, it stops displaying HTML and waits for a graphic to at least partially download. Microsoft Internet Explorer 3.0 assumes that graphics are a certain size and shape (square) and displays the page anyway. As graphics download, the layout of the page changes to make room for the new graphic size.

The simplest way to determine the size of a graphic is to open it or drag it onto an open Netscape Navigator 2.0 or 3.0 window. The height and width appear in the bar across the top of the browser window. If a graphic is already being displayed on a Web page, right-click the graphic (Option-click it on the Macintosh) and select the View Image command. This technique also reveals the file type.

HYPERLINKING FROM GRAPHICS

? How do I put a single image with more than one clickable area on my Web page?

The best solution for putting more than one clickable area on a Web page graphic is to use both server-side and client-side image maps. An *image map* is a set of coordinates by which clickable shapes and corresponding hyperlinks for Web page graphics are defined. Users cannot see the clickable shapes.

Server-side image maps use text files on the Web server to determine which part of the image was clicked. Client-side image maps, on the other hand, look up the coordinates in the HTML of the current page and then navigate directly to the intended destination.

Server-Side Image Maps

Older browsers such as Netscape 1.1 only support server-side image maps, but newer browsers support both client- and server-side maps. Select View | Source on an HTML page that uses server-side image maps to see a series of tags similar to these:

```
<A HREF="/cgi-bin/ImageMap.map">
<IMG SRC="Image.gif" ISMAP></A>
```

The ISMAP attribute in the <IMG> tag tells the browser to collect the vertical and horizontal coordinates of the mouse as it travels over the picture, then send the coordinates to the server as soon as the button is pressed. Figure 8-7 shows an example of a server-side image map with coordinates visible in the browser's status bar.

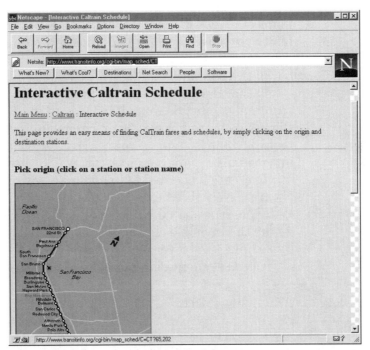

Figure 8-7 This commuter train Web site uses a server-side image map so that travelers can click on the train route and plan a schedule.

The map file is simply a text file formatted to be either NCSA- or CERN-compliant. In the text file are coordinates associated with destination URLs. Check your Web server's documentation to determine which formats the server supports (NCSA is usually a safe bet). Also, make sure that your image map is set to be executable on your Web server. The server-side image map is essentially a script whose sole function is to determine an appropriate destination URL. Keep in mind that a handful of little-used Web servers do not support server-side image maps.

Tools such as LiveImage by Media Tech allow image maps to be created graphically and easily. To use these tools, you don't need a strong knowledge of NCSA or CERN file formats.

For information on server-side file formats, visit http://www.ihip.com.

Client-Side Image Maps

Client-side image maps are a more recent development. Both Microsoft Internet Explorer 2.0 and later and Netscape Navigator 2.0 and later support client-side image maps. The maps offer two distinct advantages. First, they offer a much faster response time. Second, most browsers list the destination of each section of the graphic along the status bar of the window.

Rather than using a server process, where mouse-click coordinates must be sent all the way to the Web server, client-side maps handle the processing in the browser, requiring one less step. Browsers that support client-side image maps experience much faster response times.

To create a client-side image map, insert <MAP NAME="NameOfMap"> and </MAP> tags in your HTML. <AREA> tags should be inserted between the MAP tags to define the invisible clickable shapes and associated hyperlinks that cover your graphic.

A typical client-side image map looks like this:

```
<MAP NAME="MyMap">
<AREA SHAPE="CIRCLE" COORDS="33,31,28" HREF="http://www.yahoo.com">
<AREA SHAPE="RECT" COORDS="72,15,188,65" HREF="http://www.lycos.com">
<AREA SHAPE="POLY" COORDS="82,129,119,94,159,124,148,170,95,171,80,129"
HREF="http://altavista.digital.com">
<AREA SHAPE="DEFAULT" HREF="http://www.infoseek.com">
</MAP>
<IMG SRC="/img/welcome.gif" WIDTH="480" HEIGHT="262" USEMAP="#MyMap">
```

Combining Client- and Server-Side Image Maps

Combining a client-side and server-side image map is quite simple:

1. Create a server-side image map and verify that it works correctly.

2. Add USEMAP="#MyMap" as an attribute to the <IMG> tag next to the server-side ISMAP attribute. Newer browsers overlook the ISMAP attribute if USEMAP is present.

3. Add <MAP NAME="MyMap"> and </MAP> tags to your HTML.

4. Add <AREA> tags to define the appropriate shapes and destinations. The easiest way to create <AREA> tags is to use an image map tool.

A combined client- and server-side image map looks like this:

```
<MAP NAME="MyMap">
<AREA SHAPE="CIRCLE" COORDS="33,31,28" HREF="http://www.yahoo.com">
<AREA SHAPE="RECT" COORDS="72,15,188,65" HREF="http://www.lycos.com">
<AREA SHAPE="DEFAULT" HREF="http://www.infoseek.com">
</MAP>
<A HREF="/cgi-bin/ImageMap.map"><IMG SRC="/img/welcome.gif"
WIDTH="480" HEIGHT="262" ISMAP USEMAP="#MyMap"></A>
```

Mapedit, Web Map, and LiveImage are free image-map utilities available for the PC.

Many people don't realize that image maps can be mapped to e-mail addresses. To add this functionality, simply replace a standard http://www.domain.com style destination with mailto:user@domain.com. For example:

```
<AREA SHAPE="RECT" COORDS="72,15,188,65"
HREF="mailto:president@whitehouse.gov">
```

? I would like several graphics to sit side-by-side without gaps. How can I do this?

Microsoft Internet Explorer allows you to place graphics side-by-side, vertically or horizontally, without spaces by using the <IMG> and <BR> tags. Netscape, however, makes this simple request surprisingly difficult. In short, everything must go into a carefully authored table.

First, create a table for your graphics with the following attributes in the <TABLE> tag:

```
<TABLE CELLPADDING=0 CELLSPACING=0 BORDER=0>
```

(Adding a COLS attribute is also acceptable.) Next, place each graphic in a different cell and add WIDTH and HEIGHT attributes to every <IMG> tag or every <TD> tag. Make sure that, within the HTML document, every <IMG> tag is adjacent its associated </TD> tag. Line breaks or spaces between the two tags create a gap between the graphics. If you are still having problems, try eliminating all spaces and line returns between all the tags in your table.

+   ***Tip:*** *A frequent problem with hyperlinked graphics in Netscape Navigator is the small red line that appears in the bottom-right or top-left corner of graphics. This problem occurs when hyperlinked graphics have a space or hard return between the <A HREF> tag and the <IMG> tag or the <IMG> tag and the </A> tag. To eliminate the red line, simply eliminate the spaces or the hard return.*

GRAPHIC TECHNIQUES

? **Is it possible to position graphics to exact coordinates in a way that is compatible with both Microsoft Internet Explorer 4.0 and Netscape Navigator 4.0?**

Both Netscape Navigator 4.0 and Microsoft Internet Explorer 4.0 have introduced the ability to position graphics at exact coordinates on a page. The trick is done with cascading style sheets, also known as CSS. The following HTML allows you to position images at specific screen coordinates for both Microsoft Internet Explorer and Netscape Navigator:

```
<HTML>
<HEAD><TITLE>Absolute Positioning Page</TITLE></HEAD>
<STYLE>
.spin{
```

```
position:      absolute;
top:           150px;
left:          150px;
visibility:    visible;
}
</STYLE>
<BODY>
<DIV CLASS="spin">
<IMG SRC="/img/ufospin.gif" WIDTH=144 HEIGHT=52 BORDER=0>
</DIV>
</BODY></HTML>
```

For more information about style sheets and browser-compatible positioning and animation, read Chapter 15 about dynamic HTML.

? Why do my transparent GIFs sometimes have a halo of color around them?

The halo problem typically occurs when a high-resolution image is converted to a 72dpi image with a 256-color or less palette. Resizing an image or remapping the colors to a limited palette often cause colors to blend. This blending, or *anti-aliasing* as it is called, is especially noticeable along sharply contrasting borders.

To apply transparency in GIFs, only one color can be selected; that color becomes the transparent area. Though this works fine with graphics that have not been anti-aliased, as shown in Figure 8-8a, problems occur with graphics that use anti-aliasing such as the graphic shown in Figure 8-8b. Because anti-aliasing blends colors along sharp edges, pixels are often mapped to a color in the palette that falls between the transparent color and the opaque color of the edge.

Anti-aliasing and transparency can be made to work together if the Web page background that is visible through the transparency matches the color that is set to be transparent in the GIF. A background that shows a strong texture pattern or different color, unfortunately, still causes a visible halo to appear around the edges of a graphic, such as the graphic shown in Figure 8-9a.

If the background of the original graphic is not a similar color to the final background or texture, fixing the halo is probably a simple matter of recreating the GIF from its

A   B

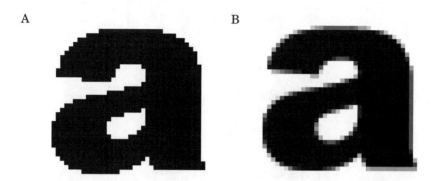

Figure 8-8   The graphic on the right has been resized with anti-aliasing, but the graphic on the left has not.

high-resolution original and changing the graphic's background color to match the Web page before resizing the graphic and remapping the palette. Doing so is still likely to cause a halo, although this time the halo should match the background of the page better, thereby allowing the edge of the graphic to blend nicely.

If the graphic still has a visible halo or if you want to place the graphic over a background tile with a large number of colors, you have two options:

- Assuming you still have the original, high-resolution piece of art, you can go back to the original and redo any image resizing with anti-aliasing off. Doing so should eliminate blurring around the edges of the graphic and will result in a graphic with transparency such as the gray section of the graphic in Figure 8-9b. To turn anti-aliasing off when you resize a graphic, change your PhotoShop preferences for resizing from bi-cubic or bi-linear to nearest neighbor. If this makes the graphic look too blocky, try the second option (read on) or else try de-selecting the dithering feature when you remap the palette.

- Take the GIF into a photo-editing program such as PhotoShop or PaintShop Pro and remap the palette to no palette. To do that in PhotoShop, reset the image from indexed color to RGB mode. If you do not have a copy of the palette, you may save the palette first so you can reapply it later. Next, using a selection tool such as PhotoShop's magic wand, adjust the tolerance so that it selects enough of the blurry edge to minimize the halo. Fill the selection with the color you wish to be transparent and remap the graphic to the same Web-safe palette that was previously applied to the graphic. This should result in a transparency effect such as that shown in Figure 8-10. If the magic wand tool doesn't get all of the halo pixels, try restepping through this process, but this time set the tolerance of the magic wand tool to a higher level.

With the GIF 89a Export function in Photoshop 4.0 and the similar plug-in in Photoshop 3.0, you can select the colors you want to make transparent in a GIF file with the eyedropper tool. There is no limit to the number of colors you can select. By using this method to select the colors that create the halo, the halo effect can be completely eliminated quickly and easily, and you don't need a high level of know-how, either.

? How can I overlap graphics on a Web page?

Different techniques can be used to make graphics overlap on a Web page. Which techniques you use depends on which browsers you want to support.

A 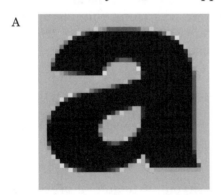 B

Figure 8-9 After the white pixels have been made transparent and a new graphic has been inserted behind, the anti-aliased graphic develops a halo (left). The aliased graphic does not develop a halo (right).

Figure 8-10 The halo effect was removed from this graphic by increasing the tolerance on Adobe PhotoShop's magic wand utility.

Netscape Navigator 2.0 to 3.0 and Microsoft Internet Explorer 2.0 to 3.0

Until the release of Netscape Navigator 4.0 and Microsoft Internet Explorer 4.0, the only way to overlap Web graphics with HTML was to use a tiled background image on the Web page and place an <IMG> tag between the <BODY> and </BODY> tags. Netscape Navigator 2.0 and later, and Internet Explorer 2.0 and later, all support the BACKGROUND attribute of the <BODY> tag, which tiles graphics across a Web page background. Keep in mind that the image is tiled over the entire background, no matter how large the background is; it is not possible to tile part of a background. The following HTML places the TopLayer.gif graphic over the Background.gif graphic:

```
<HTML>
<HEAD><TITLE>Test Page</TITLE></HEAD>
<BODY BACKGROUND="Background.gif">
<IMG SRC="TopLayer.gif" WIDTH="100" HEIGHT="100">
</BODY>
</HTML>
```

Unfortunately, if you try to align a graphic with a tiled image, you usually run into more problems than you bargained for. A number of factors make aligning graphics accurately and background tiling difficult. The following factors should be considered:

- Netscape Navigator and Microsoft Internet Explorer apply different pixel spacing between graphics.

- The size of default text on different operating systems is not consistent. This inconsistency affects all image tags that are placed after text on pages.

- Users can configure the window size of their browsers (unless a client-side language is used to open a new, nonresizeable window).

Due to the different display factors, accurately aligning background tiles with graphics in <IMG> tags is not possible with older browsers if you wish to support more than a few browser versions.

Netscape Navigator 4.0+ and Microsoft Internet Explorer 4.0+

With the 4.0 browsers, there are a number of ways to display overlapping images., Unfortunately, there is no graceful degradation for displaying images in earlier browsers. Earlier versions simply display both graphics without overlapping them. The easiest way to overlap two graphics in a way that is compatible with both browsers is to use absolute positioning and layering with both graphics. Use the code example explained earlier in this chapter under "Is it possible to position graphics to exact coordinates in a way that is compatible with both Microsoft Internet Explorer 4.0 and Netscape Navigator 4.0?"

? How can I accurately space my graphics apart from each other or accurately space my text from my graphics without using tables?

A trick that works well for accurately spacing graphics and text on a Web page involves using a completely transparent GIF. By placing a small and completely transparent GIF on a page and adjusting the height and width specified for its <IMG> tag, you can accurately space graphics and text.

To make a transparent GIF, simply create a graphic with one solid color and, when you save it as a GIF, select its only color as the alpha channel. By keeping the graphic as small as a few pixels, you can reduce the image size to less than 1

KB. Note that older versions of PhotoShop have been known to have trouble creating completely transparent graphics.

If support for Microsoft Internet Explorer 4.0 or Netscape Navigator 4.0 browsers is all that is needed, try exact positioning, which is available through dynamic HTML or cascading style sheets. For more about exact positioning read the first question in this section.

? How can I get an image onto a Web page without a scanner?

Before you can add any image to a Web page, it needs to be in a digital format so it can be converted to a Web-ready format such as JPEG or GIF. Scanning is the most popular method of digitizing images; many photocopy shops offer digitizing services as well. If you do not have access to a scanner, you can digitize an image by using a digital still or digital video camera.

Digital Still Cameras

Digital cameras record images in a digital format. Resizing these images and converting them to standard Web-compatible file types is easy. Most digital camera software includes conversion utilities by which digital camera images can be converted to the JPEG or GIF format.

Digital Video Cameras

Many digital video cameras offer reasonable resolution and quality for single-frame takes. If you have a digital camera, simply shoot the scene from which you wish to create a still image and download the frames to your computer. Video editing and graphics packages such as Adobe Premiere allow you to save single frames, which are easy to convert to a Web graphics format.

Royalty-Free Images

Royalty-free images, which are available on CD-ROM and from online graphic libraries, are a great starting point for obtaining graphics for a Web site. Also check out the royalty-free clip art libraries that are included with many image-editing software packages. If a commercial graphics application is installed on your computer, royalty-free artwork may already be on your hard drive without your realizing it.

Why Are Page Background Colors Often Described in Both Characters and Numbers?

Unfortunately, hexidecimal RGB (red, green, and blue) is the description format used to define background colors and text colors for Web pages. Recently, browsers acquired the ability to use 216 colors, including such esoteric colors as fuchsia and lime. To ensure that your Web page backgrounds are compatible with the widest range of browsers, you need to find a way to convert your RGB values to hexadecimal.

Note: Hexadecimal is a numerical system that uses 16 numbers (base 16) instead of the traditional 10. Where the decimal system counts from 0 to 9 before reusing digits, hexadecimal uses 0 through 9 and the letters a through f. Following is a sample conversion chart:

Decimal	Hexadecimal
0	0
8	8
10	A
15	F
21	F6
255	FF

The easiest way to convert numbers back and forth between decimal and hexadecimal is to use a conversion tool. A number of Web sites offer hexadecimal conversion tools, and you can also find shareware utilities that convert numbers offline. An online color conversion tool is available at http://www.inquisitor.com/hex.html. RGB Color Mixer, a useful shareware utility, is available from http://www.shareware.com.

PROTECTING IMAGES

What images can be legally used on my pages?

Making sure that the images you place on the Internet do not violate existing copyrights is very important. Clip art CDs and Web sites frequently contain copyright-free and royalty-free images. Taking a photograph yourself, scanning it, and placing it on a page is about as safe as you can get with regard to copyrights. Because of the ease with which graphics can be copied from the Web, copyright infringements are commonplace. For more information on copyrights read Chapter 20, which covers legal issues.

+ ***Tip:*** *Follow these steps to copy an image from a Web page with Netscape Navigator: On a PC, right-click the image and select Save Image As; on a Macintosh, hold down the mouse button until a menu appears and select Copy Image. Follow these steps to copy an image from a Web page with Microsoft Internet Explorer: On a PC, right-click the image and select Save Picture As; on a Macintosh, click and hold down the mouse button over the image, and then select Download Image to Disk from the pop-up menu.*

? How can I prevent my images from being used by other sites?

A savvy user can always copy your Web site's graphics and use them. Fortunately, you can take a few precautionary measures to find and identify copies of your graphics on the Web.

Unique Filenames

Giving graphics unique filenames that are unlikely to be used elsewhere on the Internet is one preventative measure. Many search engines allow you to search their databases for graphics with a specific filename and exclude your own site from the search. The search engine looks for sites where files under the name are located—it doesn't look for files that are being served from your site. Although it is easy enough to simply rename a graphic to keep from getting caught, it is surprising how often others steal graphics without renaming them.

Watermarking

Watermarking is a new technique for protecting copyrights. It involves hiding information that identifies the image's origin in the graphic's file format. One particular type of watermarking, developed by Digimarc and built into Adobe PhotoShop 4.0 and CorelDraw 7.0, retains information that describes the creator of the graphic even when the graphic is edited, cropped, and transformed in other ways.

 Tip: *To find copies of a uniquely named graphic on Web sites other than your own, go to http://altavista.digital.com and use the following syntax in the search field:*

```
+graphic:mygraphic.gif -site:mydomain.com
```

Enforcing Watermarks

The first major independent effort to track down and expose copyright infringements by means of digital watermarks was undertaken in Europe by the TALISMAN project (Tracing Authors' Rights by Labeling Image Services and Monitoring Access Network). One of the aims of TALISMAN is to recommend a method for marking online documents to let others know who owns their copyrights. For more information on the Talisman project, visit http://www.tele.ucl.ac.be/TALISMAN

DYNAMICALLY GENERATED GRAPHICS

What are dynamically generated graphics?

Dynamically generating graphics for the Web can be defined as any Web server process that involves automatic image manipulation. Up-to-the-minute time-stamps on pictures, adding a logo to an image from a live Web camera, and automatically adding a form-entered word or phrase to a Web page graphic are all examples of dynamically generated graphics.

To add dynamically generated images to a site, two methods may be used. The first method sends a graphic directly to a browser, and the other saves a graphic to the hard drive and references it from an HTML page.

? What is involved in sending a dynamically created image directly to the browser?

With this technique, every time the browser requests a dynamic image, a script or application is triggered on the Web server. A custom graphic is created on the server but never saved to the hard drive. Instead, the graphic is sent directly to the browser along with the corresponding graphic format's HTTP header information. The whole process is very similar to that of a standard CGI application, except graphical data rather than standard HTML-formatted ASCII is the resulting output.

! Warning: *GIFs created dynamically from a Web server application are subject to the same copyright agreements as custom desktop software that allows images to be saved in the GIF format. Getting permission from Unisys or CompuServe is recommended before creating your own dynamic GIF application.*

Creating dynamic JPEGs, on the other hand, requires no special licensing or special permissions.

? How are dynamically cached images included on Web pages?

Including dynamically cached images on Web pages is similar to sending a dynamically created image directly to a browser, except the process is instigated by an event other than a graphic request itself. A timed server event (a batch file operation, for example) or a Web page form submission can be used to trigger an application that creates a custom graphic and saves it to the Web server's hard drive. The image is then referenced, like any other graphic, from an HTML document.

The Gd 1.2 programming library allows dynamically generated GIFs to be created from Perl or C applications. AspImage 1.0 is a dynamic image extension for Active Server Pages.

WEB ANIMATIONS

? ## What are animated GIFs?

Animated GIFs are GIFs that store more than one image frame along with timing and repetition information. The timing and repetition information determines how long each frame is displayed and how many times the animation is looped. The effect is an animation that may play once, twice, or endlessly on a Web page. Animated GIFs can be as simple as blinking dots or as complex as software tutorials.

To create an animated GIF, use an animated GIF application such as GifBuilder or GIF Construction set. These tools allow static graphics to be imported into an animation and positioned accurately. After the animated GIF has been built, including it on a Web page is no different than referencing any other GIF; simply include an <IMG> tag that references the animation in the HTML of your Web page.

★ *Note:* *Not all browsers that display GIFs can display animated GIFs. Browsers that can't display animated GIFs simply display the last frame of the animation. For the benefit of Web site visitors who are using older browsers, many GIF animations include either a full picture or all of the relevant text information in the animation in the last frame.*

? ## How can I optimize my animated GIFs?

Creating an animated GIF that works is the easy part. Reducing the GIF to a reasonable file size can be one of the most difficult tasks in creating a Web site. Many of the popular GIF animation tools offer a range of methods for reducing even large animations to a reasonable file size.

To optimize an animated GIF, try using these techniques:

● **Minimize the dimensions of the entire GIF animation:** If your animation shows a face with a winking eye, for example, create an animated eye and use tables or dynamic HTML to place the static graphics that compose the face.

● **Don't interlace the frames:** Interlacing can increase total file size and distract from the animation the first time it plays.

● **Take advantage of transparency wherever possible:** If every frame has a textured background, using transparency significantly reduces the total file size. Transparency also allows graphical elements from previous frames to continue being displayed in later frames of the animation.

● **Crop every frame as much as possible:** Before you import graphics into your GIF animation tool, make sure that each graphic is cropped as much as possible. If the third frame of a 50-by-50 pixel GIF animation only involves changes to a 4-by-4 pixel area, for example, only import a 4-by-4 pixel graphic.

● **Use the same optimized color palette for all frames:** Use color optimization methods to create the smallest Web-compatible palette with adequate colors for all frames, and then apply this palette to each graphic before you import it into your GIF animation tool. Double-checking the palette that is used in the animation is worthwhile, because many animation tools default to the Netscape 216 color palette if a palette isn't specified.

● **Minimize the total number of frames in the animation:** An animation that displays thirty frames over a period of one second is probably just as effective visually with as few as six to ten frames. Cutting out frames can drastically reduce overall file size.

● **Experiment with different tools:** Although different GIF animation tools may produce animations that look the same, the animations may be drastically different in file size.

? Is it possible to create Web page animations with JavaScript?

You may use JavaScript to create animations, but JavaScript offers limited browser support. By triggering a timed event with the onLoad parameter of the <BODY> tag, you can activate a series of animation frames that display at specific times. Unfortunately, only Netscape Navigator 3.0 and later and Microsoft Internet Explorer 4.0 and later support this feature.

The advantage of JavaScript animations is that they can be triggered by other JavaScript events, such as mouse-overs, mouse-downs, and form selections. Due to the limited support for this animation technique, JavaScript animations are rarely used.

? Are animations possible using Java?

With the arrival of the new Java animation tools, using Java animation applets has become a viable option for nonprogrammers. Netscape Navigator 2.0 and later and Microsoft Internet Explorer 3.0 and later both natively support Java applets. Java offers the advantage of increased user interactivity with the animation. Animations can change as a result of mouse-clicks and mouse-overs.

Tools designed for creating Java animations include Astound Web Motion, Aimtech's Jamba, and Macromedia's Flash.

Chapter 9
Audio and Video

Answer Topics!

Audio and Video @ a Glance

Audio and video are used far less frequently on the Web than in CD-ROM-style multimedia applications. They are the forgotten elements of the Web, but they have the potential to breathe life into static pages. Audio and video put the "multi" in multimedia, yet the vast majority of Web pages today don't offer sounds or video images. Critics argue that audio and video files are simply too large for the benefits that they add to a Web page. Though file sizes are often large, they don't have to be, and everything that is needed to experience audio and video is already built right into the Web browsers that most people use.

Both Microsoft Internet Explorer and Netscape Navigator now support a number of different audio formats without additional ActiveX controls or plug-ins. In addition, adding additional video support such as QuickTime or Video for Windows to platforms that don't provide built-in support has become exceptionally easy. As multimedia-equipped computers and higher bandwidth connections become more commonplace, expect to see a higher percentage of pages that feature audio and video content.

This chapter covers these important topics:

Sound Basics describes the major sound file formats and how they differ. A chart is provided to show which sound formats are supported by default in Netscape Navigator and Microsoft Internet Explorer.

Sound Solutions discusses solutions to the most common problems related to getting sound onto a Web page.

Streaming Basics addresses the most common types of streaming and the advantages associated with each. Also covered are multicasting and unicasting, as well as the Multicast Backbone (MBone).

Streaming Sound covers the ins and outs of adding streaming sound to your site and discusses the steps involved in live audio transmissions on the Web.

Adding Video to a Page describes the most common video formats, what you need to view video in these formats through a Web page, and what the issues are in providing video on your site.

Synchronizing and Streaming Video covers the latest streaming technology for video on the Web, as well as synchronizing soundless video with a separate audio track.

SOUND BASICS

? Why is audio on the Web so uncommon?

Audio is not as prevalent on the Web as it is in other multimedia platforms such as CD-ROMs for a number of reasons. Following are the drawbacks that limit sites from adding audio content to their pages:

- **Not all computers on the Web have sound cards:** Browsers that don't have sound cards may have to wait for sounds to download even though they cannot play the sounds. Some methods serve errors to computers that do not have sound cards.

- **Sound files are large:** Built-in sound formats do not compress sound very effectively. Until browsers provide built-in support for a heavily compressed audio format, including long sound clips on Web pages will not be a reasonable option.

- **Sound can distract from page content:** Many Web surfers prefer not to hear background sounds because they are distracting. Poorly made sound can be very disturbing and can ruin a Web page experience. Many liken looped MIDI sounds to the background Muzak heard in supermarkets.

- **Sounds with reasonable file sizes are harsh sounding:** To reduce a sound file to a reasonable file size for the Web, quality has to be sacrificed, often resulting in hisses, crackles, and popping noises. Some feel that no sound is better than low-quality sound.

- **Many don't realize that sound is an option:** Since most sites do not include sound, many Web site builders simply don't realize how many browsers offer built-in support for sound.

? What are the most common sound formats, and how do they differ?

Here is a list of the most common sound formats:

AIFF   Apple developed this sound format for a variety of settings. However, it does not allow for compression.

AIFF-C Also known as AIFC, this format is the same as AIFF, only it supports a very effective but lossy form of file compression.

AU   This is one of the most cross-platform, Web-compatible sound formats. Different types of compression are available for AU files, but μ Law (pronounced mu-law) compression is the most common.

MIDI   Technically speaking, this isn't a sound format as much as an interface for musical instrument communication. MIDI is better described as a method of storing sheet music and the instruments that play it. Modules are a form of MIDI that include snippets of recorded sounds along with digital signal processing information. In MIDI, it is as if the sound an instrument makes is stored along with its sheet music. MIDI and modules both have extremely small file sizes.

WAV   This format, first seen in Windows 3.1, is predominantly a PC file format. The WAV format is similar to AIFF in terms of its flexibility in settings. The WAV format offers similar file sizes to the AIFF format.

? What audio file formats do Netscape Navigator and Microsoft Internet Explorer support without plug-ins or additional ActiveX controls?

If you want your Web audio files to be compatible with both Microsoft Internet Explorer 3.0 and Netscape Navigator 3.0 as well as later versions for both, without users needing browser add-ons, you are limited to just three audio file formats: AIFF, AU, and WAV. These formats are all supported by both browsers. Navigator 3.0 also offers built-in support for MIDI sound; Internet Explorer also supports the SND format. Table 9-1 indicates which formats are automatically supported on Netscape and Microsoft browsers.

! **Warning:**   *Microsoft Internet Explorer has been known to have problems when playing AIFF files, so sticking to WAV or AU is probably the safest bet.*

	AIFF	AU	MIDI	SND	WAV	AIFF-C
Internet Explorer 3.0+	√	√	À	√	√	√
Netscape 3.0+	√	À	√		√	

*Internet Explorer 3.0 supports MIDI files in the <BGSOUND> tag but not in an <EMBED> tag.

Table 9-1 Audio File Formats That Netscape and Internet Explorer Support

? What does psychoacoustic mean when referring to sound compression?

When certain sounds are played next to or at the same time as other sounds, they cannot be heard. Sounds that are only slightly different from each other are not necessarily distinguishable. *Psychoacoustic compression* takes human psychological factors and hearing limitations into consideration when reducing a sound to a smaller file size. Just as JPEG compression eliminates colors that the eye cannot distinguish between, psychoacoustic compression techniques strip out imperceptible data from sound files. As I explain later in this chapter, the MPEG, RealAudio, and Shockwave Audio formats all use psychoacoustic methods to compress audio files.

SOUND SOLUTIONS

? How can I get sounds into my computer in the first place?

The easiest way to digitize sound is to record it directly to your computer. To record sound on a computer you need the following:

- A microphone
- A sound card (if you have a PC)
- Software that allows you to save sound files

As long as your sound card and microphone are working, recording sounds directly into your computer should be quite simple. If you already have sounds on an audio CD, it is possible on most systems to open the files in an audio application directly from your CD-ROM drive, edit the sounds, and save them in a Web-ready format.

★ ***Note:*** *Unless you paid for the rights to use a sound or music or you created the sample completely on your own, you may not have the rights necessary to use an audio file on your site. The same copyright laws that apply to using audio on the Web also apply to sampling for use in original pieces. Royalty-free CDs and sound libraries are two popular ways of getting sound files for Web sites. For a large variety of sound files, visit the WWW Sound Library at http://www.comlab.ox. ac.uk/archive/audio.html.*

? What settings should I choose for my sound file before saving it and putting it on my Web site?

Making the tradeoff between file size and audio quality is tough. When it comes to sound quality, you must consider three sets of options: the number of channels, the number of samplings per second, and the sampling size.

The first decision to make is to select the number of channels. This decision usually is restricted to mono (one channel) or stereo (two channels). Mono is like listening to sound that comes through only one speaker. Audiophiles scoff at the thought of combining a stereo signal into a single mono channel, but because stereo usually doubles the size of files, nearly all Web files are recorded in mono or converted to mono for size considerations. Mono offers no advantage in sound quality.

The second sound quality option setting has to do with *Kilohertz* (kHz), or samplings taken per second. This setting is similar to the dots-per-inch setting by which graphics are described. The more dots per inch, the higher the quality of the image. For sound on the Web, the choice is typically 22kHz, 11kHz, or 8kHz. An 8kHz sound simply stores less information than a 22kHz sound. No sound quality advantage comes from using 8kHz settings, only a reduction in file sizes. CD audio, by comparison, is very high quality and uses 44.1kHz sound.

Bit rate or sampling size is the third sound setting. The *sampling size,* also known as the *sample resolution,* is simply the number of possible increments between the base and the peak of a sound wave. This setting is similar to the color depth setting in graphics. When the resolution of a sound is lowered, fewer variations are available to define it. Eight-bit sounds offer far fewer variations than 16-bit sounds, but result in much smaller file sizes.

To be blunt, 8kHz, 8-bit mono audio is very poor quality. Converting sounds down for file size often results in scratchy- or choppy-sounding audio files with an added noise referred to as "the 8-bit whine." Unfortunately, the difference in file size between the different settings is large enough that most sounds on the Web usually go with the 8kHz, 8-bit mono options.

Like graphic file settings, trial-and-error experimentation is the best way to go when trying to determine the best way to save a sound file. Save the same sound in a number of different settings and in different formats to compare sound quality and file size. Listening to the sounds on different target systems and in different browsers is also a good practice. Make sure you use the highest quality original sound file possible each time you convert a sound file to different settings, or sound quality will deteriorate with each conversion.

How can I edit out silence in sound files?

When you record a sound, silence is inevitably recorded at the beginning and end of the clip. However, if you look closely at the clip within a sound-editing program, you see that "silence" is actually a series of very quiet sounds. Since very quiet sounds often increase file size as much as regular sounds, trimming them out is a good idea. Most sound-editing applications allow you to highlight a section of sound that you wish to remove (as shown in Figure 9-1) and either cut it out or simply delete it.

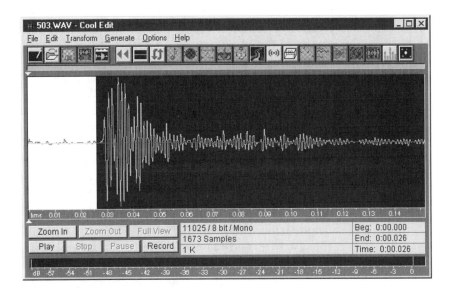

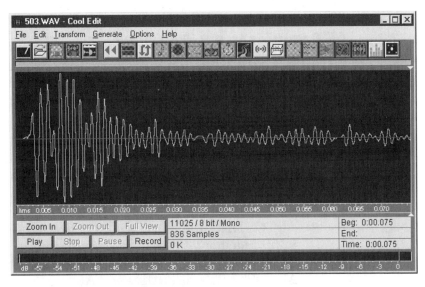

Figure 9-1 A sound file with the section of silence highlighted in white (top); the same sound file with the silence at the beginning and end removed (bottom). The total savings in file size is 11KB.

? Why do my sound files sometimes have popping sounds or loud static sounds when I convert them between formats?

Popping sounds and static at the end of a sound file are typical symptoms of a bad sound file conversion. When sounds are converted poorly, artifacts often enter the file and corrupt the sounds. There are two options for eliminating artifacts. If the popping or static sound comes during a segment of silence, simply cut out the offensive sound segment and replace it with silence. The second method is to simply reconvert the original sound file by using a different application or convert it to a different, preferably lossless, format first and then convert it to its final form. The best way to diagnose a sound file is to open it in a sound editor that allows you to view sound files in wave form.

? What is the best way to play WAV, AU, MIDI, and AIFF sounds in my Web page?

To include WAV, AU, or AIFF sounds on a Web page in a way that is compatible with Microsoft Internet Explorer 3.0+ and Netscape Navigator 3.0+, use the following syntax:

```
<EMBED SRC="sound.au" AUTOSTART="TRUE" LOOP="1" HIDDEN="TRUE">
```

Following are explanations of the different EMBED parameters for embedding sound files in a Web page:

- SRC is the location of the sound file.

- AUTOSTART indicates whether the sound starts when fully loaded or whether the sound is played when the user presses the Play button. The options for AUTOSTART are TRUE and FALSE.

- LOOP specifies the number of times the sound file plays. TRUE loops the sound forever, while any integer specifies the number of times the sound file will play.

- WIDTH specifies the width in pixels of the sound controller.

- HEIGHT specifies the height in pixels of the sound controller.

Figure 9-2 The <EMBED> tag may be used to add sound to Netscape Navigator 3.0 and higher browsers and Microsoft's Internet Explorer 3.0 and higher browsers. The control panel on the left is used by Netscape; the one on the right by Microsoft.

- HIDDEN may be set to TRUE to play a sound with no visible controller, or left out altogether to allow the user to pause, play, and stop the sound.

- CONTROLS may be set to a number of different options in Netscape Navigator, including CONSOLE and SMALL CONSOLE. Microsoft Internet Explorer uses one standard controller if the controls are visible. Figure 9-2 shows the standard Netscape and Microsoft controllers.

For more information about Netscape's EMBED tag options for sound, visit http://search.netscape.com/comprod/products/navigator/version_3.0/multimedia/audio/how.html.

✱ ***Note:*** *The above method also works on Netscape Navigator with MIDI files. Unfortunately, Microsoft Internet Explorer 3.0 only supports MIDI files through the <BGSOUND> tag.*

Why do my static sounds fail to work after they have been put up on a Web server?

Sound files, like most Web content, need MIME types mapped on the Web server. Doing this usually means associating a sound file extension with an appropriate MIME type. For more on associating MIME types with your content, see Chapter 4, which offers more information about configuring a server to support new MIME types. Table 9-2 explains the file formats and their associated MIME types.

File Type	Extensions	MIME
AIFF	.aiff, .aif, .aifc	audio/x-aiff
AU	.au	audio/basic
MIDI	.mid, .mod	audio/x-midi
Real Audio Plug-in	.rpm	application/x-pn-realaudio-plugin
Real Audio/Real Video	.ram, .ra, .rm	application/x-pn-realaudio
WAV	.wav	audio/x-wav

Table 9-2 Audio File Formats and Their Associated MIME Types

STREAMING BASICS

What is the difference between streaming and nonstreaming file formats?

The basic difference between streaming and nonstreaming content is that streaming content begins playing before it has finished downloading. Two different types of streaming can be applied to content: basic static streaming and synchronized streaming.

Basic Static Streaming

Many conventional sound and video files can be played as soon as the first file segments are received by the browser. Unfortunately, many files download more slowly than they play, so viewers have to wait until as much as half to three quarters of the file has downloaded before they can play the file. Sometimes they have to wait for more of the file to download before the clip is finished playing. QuickTime uses this method of streaming for both movies and sound files.

Synchronized Play and Transfer Rates

If a file transfers at the same rate at which it plays, then a streaming file can begin playing and continue to play for the entire length of the file. A five-minute audio clip, for example, may take a very long time to download and play at almost any connection speed. For a streaming file that plays and downloads at the same speed, the length of time it takes to play doesn't matter. A five-minute streaming audio clip that has synchronized play and transfer rates should take around five minutes to download, but the user will only experience a short delay as the sound starts.

However, the synchronized method of playing content often suffers from scratchiness and missing chunks of sound or missing video frames because parts of the file have to be dropped for the file to keep playing at the correct speed. A video file cannot slow down once it starts playing. To keep from slowing down, a video file skips frames to give the perception of a constant speed. At the same time, however, image quality is often significantly diminished. This method of streaming content is essential for live video and audio Web casts.

Real Network's Real Video offers both synchronized audio and video play and transfer, such as the Real Video movie shown in Figure 9-3. Macromedia offers synchronized play and transfer for audio and basic streaming for video, animations, and other interactive content.

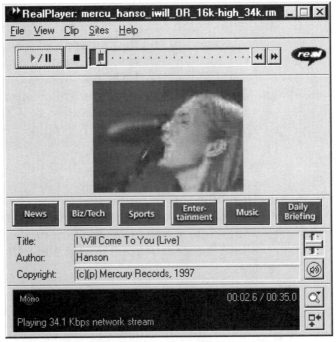

Figure 9-3   Real Network's Real Video allows video and audio content to stream over the Web continuously at the same speed at which it is being played.

✱ *Note:* Keep in mind that while content is streaming in, other content is transferring at a slower rate. Streaming content takes up a share of the bandwidth. While it is downloading, other requests—such as requests for graphics—must utilize what is left of the bandwidth. If you are going to stream sound or video, doing it after the rest of the Web page has finished loading is a good idea. Keep in mind that content that is streaming into one frame on a Web page still affects the download time of content that is being requested by other frames.

? What is the difference between multicast and unicast for streaming media audio and video broadcasts on the Web?

Multicast and unicast are different delivery methods for a server and result in different play options for the end user. For unicast content, a server sends a separate stream to every computer that requests the content. This delivery method is similar to regular content in that the content can be cached on the end user's hard drive and viewed or heard at any time. Unicast video, depending on the format, can be stopped and restarted while it is streaming from the server.

Multicast broadcasts differ from unicast in that the server sends out one constant stream to any number of computers. This delivery method is more like a live radio or television broadcast, since the single stream cannot be rewound or paused. For truly efficient multicasting, the Internet suffers from hardware limitations. Ideally, the multicasting server could send one packet of data that would only split into multiple packets when necessary as it approached the "tuned-in" destination computers. Unfortunately, many standard Internet routers do not allow this form of packet addressing.

Multicast Backbone (Mbone)

The Multicast Backbone is best described as a layer that sits on top of the Internet infrastructure. Mbone is essentially a set of nodes that are linked to each other and support IP multicasting. Although not yet a widely used system, the potential of Mbone is exciting. A computer that is linked to the Internet with a clean 28.8 modem connection could potentially deliver a live 2KB/Sec audio or video stream to thousands of computers without any bandwidth problems on the server end.

STREAMING SOUND

? How does live streaming audio work on the Web?

Live audio on the Web goes through the following steps:

1. The sound enters a microphone or is played in a device that is linked to a computer.

2. An application takes the audio feed, encodes and compresses it, and sends it to a server.

3. A server application continuously streams sound to browsers that request it.

4. Browsers receive the sound and play it through an appropriate browser plug-in or ActiveX control.

The most difficult part of setting up live audio on the Web is properly setting up the server and encoding software. The two main products that offer live streaming audio for the Web today are Real Network's Real Audio and Xing Technology's Streamworks.

? **Why does live streaming audio on the Web not work for some visitors to my site, even if they have installed the right software?**

Just because you can hear a sound or video clip with synchronized download and play features built in over the Internet doesn't mean everyone can hear it. Problems with streaming media of this sort are almost always a result of firewall configuration.

Unfortunately, HTTP is the protocol for sending packets of Web data. With HTTP, if a packet of data is sent but doesn't get to the end user, the packet is sent again. This system requires some overhead in all of the checking that takes place, but it is great for guaranteeing successful data transfers. For streaming audio or video that involves synchronized download and play rates, however, HTTP overhead and guaranteed packet delivery are not as important. If a movie frame is not received in time, not playing it at all is better than sending it too late. A movie frame that is re-sent usually shows up late and takes up valuable bandwidth that could be better allocated to upcoming frames.

In order to bypass HTTP speed deficiencies, vendors use different methods to transfer information packets. UDP (User Datagram Protocol) is the clear winner for streaming content. Unfortunately, however, UDP presents one small problem: Many corporate firewalls are not set up to accept UDP packets. As a result, many Web site visitors do not hear streaming audio. If your browser is having problems with UDP packets, you need to allow UDP packets to go through at least one port on your firewall.

? **How do I play a continuous sound between HTML pages without the sound stopping and starting again?**

There are two methods for playing a continuous sound over two or more Web pages: either play a sound in a floating window or play it in a different frame in the same browser window. By placing the sound in a one-pixel-high frame or a floating frame, a site visitor can hyperlink around a site and listen to uninterrupted sound as he or she does so.

Which method you choose to play your sound does not matter as long as your target browsers support the method. Simply place the appropriate tags within the HTML of your sound frame. If you wish to play different sounds based on a site visitor's mouse-clicks, simply target the sound frame with an HTML file that plays a different sound file. If the HTML file is already cached, the sound should play immediately.

If you use Shockwave Audio, try placing a two-by-two pixel Shockwave movie that plays a Shockwave Audio (SWA) file in a frame that is approximately five pixels high, such as the Web page shown in Figure 9-4. Keep in mind, however, that Shockwave movies must be visible on the screen to play sound. Depending on the browser, the frame in which the movie is placed may have to be five pixels high to guarantee that all Shockwave-compatible browsers display the Shockwave movie.

Figure 9-4 The Livent Web site at www.livent.com features streaming Shockwave audio that spans multiple pages and uses a separate frame for the sound.

ADDING VIDEO TO A PAGE

? Which video file options for the Web don't require plug-ins or ActiveX controls?

The two main formats for downloadable video on the Web are AVI and QuickTime. Each format offers a few advantages over the other.

AVI

The AVI format is native to Windows. Playing AVI video on a Mac requires a Video for Windows Apple Macintosh utility or QuickTime 3.0 to be installed. AVI claims that it is better for synchronizing sound with video frames, but AVI lacks the compression benefits of QuickTime movies. AVI movies that play in a Web browser window also offer fewer options for playing. Often, users can't rewind a movie part way.

QuickTime

QuickTime, an Apple technology, has become the de facto standard for small-scale desktop video production. QuickTime movies run natively on Macintoshes and play on Windows machines if QuickTime for Windows has been installed. It is common for multimedia applications to install QuickTime for Windows, so many Web surfers who use Windows have QuickTime already installed without realizing it. QuickTime offers much better compression-to-quality comparisons than AVI and has recently added streaming capabilities. Streaming allows QuickTime movies to begin playing before they have started downloading.

? Is full-motion, full-screen video possible on the Web?

The number of megabytes required for even a few seconds of full-motion, full-screen video is enormous. Even highly compressed broadcast-quality video usually requires files that are between 2 and 6MB for each second of video. Many computers cannot even support transfer rates of that speed from their own internal hard drives.

In the near future, we will likely see broadcast-quality images through television tuner cards in our computers. These images will run from computer DVD or CD-ROM players, or perhaps they will run in the form of vector graphics, such as cartoons, and in so doing bypass the need for a high-bandwidth Internet connections. Macromedia's Flash offers a different solution for vector animations such as cartoons: by storing vector information rather than full-frame information, playing full-screen vector animations over the Web with Flash, such as the animation shown in Figure 9-5, is possible today.

? What do users see if they don't have the necessary software to see a movie?

On the Windows platform, a user who links to a QuickTime movie but does not have QuickTime installed sees a floating window with a message and an offer. The message explains that it is necessary to download QuickTime for Windows, and the offer suggests linking to Apple's Web site.

Macintosh users who do not have Video for Windows or QuickTime 3.0 installed get either of two messages,

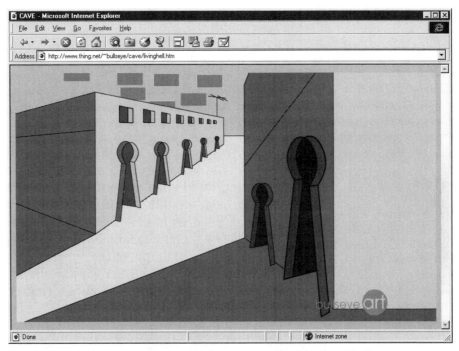

Figure 9-5   Bullseye Art has created a reasonably sized full-screen animation using vector graphics and Macromedia Flash.

depending on the software that has been installed. One states that the browser doesn't recognize the file type. The other announces that the computer will attempt to convert the AVI to QuickTime format and play it.

If a QuickTime movie has been placed within a Web page using the <EMBED> tag, an optional PLUGINSPAGE attribute is available to link browsers that are lacking the necessary components to the correct download page.

How do I include an AVI or QuickTime movie on my Web page?

There are two ways to play an AVI or QuickTime movie from a Web browser: use an <EMBED> tag or use an <A HREF> tag. The <EMBED> tag embeds a movie within the HTML of your page. The syntax of an <EMBED> tag is close to that of the <IMG> tag but adds a few extra parameters. The options for the <EMBED> tag are as follows:

```
<EMBED    SRC=[NAME and location of Movie]
          HEIGHT=[NUMBER for pixels NUMBER% for percent]
          AUTOPLAY=[TRUE, FALSE]
          CONTROLLER=[TRUE, FALSE]
          LOOP=[TRUE, FALSE, PALINDROME (forward then backward)]
          BORDER=[NUMBER of pixels for border if tag is hyperlinked]
          PLUGINSPAGE=[URL of page you wish to link to for incompatible browsers]
          HIDDEN [Simply hides the movie, usually used for QuickTime audio clips]

     >
```

If you want to specify an ActiveX control for Microsoft Internet Explorer to play your movie and let Netscape default to its associated player, you need to wrap your <EMBED> tag inside <OBJECT> and </OBJECT> tags. The parameters specified in <PARAM> tags for the ActiveX controls are specific to whichever control you choose. Following is an example of the syntax for combining <OBJECT> tags that specify a Microsoft NetShow movie and <EMBED> tags for Netscape browsers that point to a QuickTime movie:

```
<OBJECT    ID="NetShowPlayer"
       WIDTH=150
       HEIGHT=150
```

```
        CLASSID="CLSID:2179C5D3-EBFF-11CF-B6FD-00AA00B4E220"
CODEBASE="http://www.microsoft.com/netshow/download/en/nsasfinf.cab#Version=2,0,
0,912"> <!--Gets Netshow Player if not installed-->
        <PARAM NAME="FileName" VALUE="Microsoft.asx">

    <EMBED SRC="Netscape.mov"
      PLUGINSPAGE="http://www.netscape.com/ "
      WIDTH=150
      HEIGHT=150>
    </EMBED>

</OBJECT>
```

Flattening QuickTime Movies Made on Macintoshes

For QuickTime movies that have been made on Macintoshes to play on PCs, the movie must be "flattened." Flattening refers to the process of removing data from a file's resource fork (a Macintosh-specific file data storage area) and copying it into a file's data fork. Flattening is also known as making a QuickTime movie "self-contained."

Apple's Movie Player allows you to flatten movies by saving them as "Self-Contained." Movie Cleaner Pro is another popular video-editing tool. You can use it to generate cross-platform, Web-ready QuickTime movies without special configuration.

To download Internet Movie tool, another tool that flattens QuickTime movies, visit http://quicktime.apple.com/sw/sw.html.

? What is MPEG, and who can see MPEG movies?

MPEG is a compressed video file format defined by the Moving Pictures Expert Group. MPEG comes in two types, an older MPEG-1 and a newer, more highly compressed MPEG-2. MPEG is a lossy form of video compression, so some of the original data is sacrificed for higher compression ratios. Even with lossy compression, the quality is high enough that it can be used to create laserdisc-quality video and CD-quality sound. Viewing an MPEG movie requires either a software MPEG decoder or, for larger files, a hardware

MPEG decoder (usually in the form of an MPEG card for your computer). The QuickTime MPEG extension supports MPEG-1 movies.

? How can I minimize the file size of my QuickTime or AVI movie?

Minimizing the file sizes of movies is an extremely technical subject. However, following are some basic techniques for reducing the file size of video on the Web:

● **Minimize the number of frames per second:** Eliminating frames reduces file sizes significantly. Movies accompanied by audio can often get away with lower frame rates than can movies without audio. A movie set to eight to ten frames per second that runs at 160 by 120 pixels requires a transfer rate of around 2.5 to 5 KB/Sec in order to stream at the same speed it is playing.

● **Minimize the dimensions of your movie:** Reducing the pixel dimensions of a movie results in a significant reduction in the total file size.

● **Compress your movie as much as is reasonable:** For the Web, quality settings are often set as low as is possible without significantly diminishing the effect of the movie. Different software packages provide different amounts of compression. If file size is crucial, use a high-end video tool such as Cinepak or Indeo to reduce file size. Also, consider sending your movie to a service shop that can compress it for you using high-end tools.

SYNCHRONIZING AND STREAMING VIDEO

? How can I synchronize my audio file and soundless video file on a Web page?

Unless you are using a proprietary format such as Real Audio or Shockwave, you can't synchronize a sound and video file perfectly. The only method is to simply play both files and hope that they start at the same time or near the same time. For a large video file, consider delaying the start of the sound file. One way to play both files at the same time is to instruct the Web page visitor to manually start both the movie and sound file. Of course, you have to provide a play button for both files and change the AUTOSTART attribute of your audio <EMBED> tag from true to false. The best solution is to use a movie-editing tool and "marry" the sound to your video file.

? Is it possible to stream video at the same speed at which it is playing?

To stream video at the same speed it is playing, you need a product such as Real Network's Real Video or Microsoft's NetShow. Both products offer high levels of compression and streaming capabilities over connections speeds as slow as 28.8KB per second.

The drawback to both of these solutions has to do with the physical limitations of sending video over a Web connection. Modem users are limited to only a few kilobytes per second. A video that plays with sound at a transfer rate of 2 to 2.4KB per second (28.8 modem speeds) has to be either extremely small in terms of pixel dimensions or have very few frames per second and poor sound quality. Just getting the technology to function has been quite an impressive feat for both Microsoft and Real Networks. Unfortunately, unless the bandwidth limitations that hamper most Web surfers today go away, we will continue to face difficulties in transmitting smooth video and audio over the Web at the same speed at which it plays.

Chapter 10

HTML

Answer Topics!

HTML @ a Glance

HTML forms the basic building blocks of the World Wide Web. At the very heart of every Web page sits text that instructs the browser where to grab elements such as graphics and sounds, what text to display on-screen, and how the page should be formatted and displayed. The recent introduction of dynamic HTML makes HTML more important than ever on the Web.

Whether you're a Web developer, administrator, designer, or hobbyist, understanding HTML and its limitations helps immeasurably. Anyone with a basic text editor and a Web browser can create a rudimentary Web page in just a few minutes. Re-creating a complex design in HTML, however, requires quite a bit of practice. Because every major operating system can display HTML in a number of different Web browsers, thoroughly understanding the tricks of the trade requires a great deal of hands-on experience.

This chapter covers these important topics:

HTML Basics covers the basic HTML questions asked by new Web authors. This section explains what HTML is and what tags are. It offers an HTML example for a minimal Web page.

Tags outlines the most and least commonly used HTML tags and answers common questions about Web page authoring.

Frames explains how to make a simple frames-based page, eliminate frames, and open up a new browser window from a hyperlink.

Forms discusses the many issues that arise when adding forms to pages. Drop-down menus, text-entry boxes, and e-mailing the contents of a page are all discussed in this part of the chapter.

Techniques offers tricks and tips for HTML authors. Validation of HTML, converting other file formats to HTML, and pre-loading images are all covered in this section.

HTML BASICS

? What does HTML have to do with a Web page?

On a Web page, Hypertext Markup Language (HTML) describes the text, graphics, and other embedded media and their positions on the page for the Web browser. A Web page is defined by a standard ASCII text file that includes special sets of characters written in the HTML language. These special character sets define font sizes, colors, graphics, form elements, line breaks, Java applets, and so on. When browsers receive a Web page, they read the HTML. The page is then displayed in the browser window.

Because HTML is the defining language of all the pages on the Web, HTML is considered the Web's cornerstone. HTML was never designed to be a programming language or a print publishing language. HTML was designed to be what it is today, a display and linking language for digitally stored documents.

Because HTML is merely a markup language, learning HTML basics is extremely simple. HTML is also made easier by the fact that it was designed to be resistant to mistakes. If you misspell a special HTML tag, the browser doesn't crash, but merely ignores the mistake. The newest browsers by Netscape and Microsoft include error-correction mechanisms. If you leave out an important tag, these browsers can make a rough estimate of what you want to do and do their best to display it. For example, if you put text or images into a grid but forget to put in a tag that ends a row, the browser may very well ignore your mistake. Incorrectly formatted HTML has the potential to crash some browsers, however. Testing and HTML verification (discussed in the "Technologies" section of this chapter) are highly recommended.

You can view the HTML that defines a page in a Netscape Navigator or Microsoft Internet Explorer Web browser. To do so, select Source, Page Source, or Document Source (depending on the browser and version) from the View menu.

✚   ***Tip:***   *With Netscape Navigator browsers and Internet Explorer 4.0, you may enter **view-source:** in the URL line preceding a URL to automatically view a document's source, like so: **view-source:http://golf.yahoo.com/***

? What are HTML tags?

HTML for formatting text and adding elements to a page is enclosed in less than (<) and greater than (>) characters. Strings of characters enclosed in < and >—for example, <HR>— are known as *HTML tags*. There are close to a hundred tags in the HTML language. Not every browser supports every tag, and some browsers offer a number or proprietary tags to enhance the language. Text that appears between the < and > characters should not appear on Web pages. When browsers do not understand text within the characters, they simply ignore it.

Tags either stand by themselves or are used in pairs. For example, the <BR> tag stands by itself and specifies that a line break should occur. An example of a tag that is used in pairs is <B>, to begin bold formatting, and </B>, to end bold formatting. In a small number of instances, several tags are required to create a single feature, as is the case with a table (grid). If its associated tag does not appear, a tag that requires a closer causes problems.

The World Wide Web Consortium (W3C) maintains an official list of defined HTML tags. There are different versions of HTML, each building on a previous version. Browsers usually tout themselves as being compliant with a version of the HTML language defined by the W3C. HTML pages that only use correctly formatted, W3C-endorsed tags are considered W3C-compliant.

? What are HTML tag attributes?

Many HTML tags offer a number of options. To set these options, you use *attributes*. Attributes are sometimes optional, but more often they are necessary for a screen element to display or a formatting option to appear correctly.

The <HR> tag, for example, draws a horizontal rule across the Web page. As an option, you may define the horizontal rule to span only part of the page. To set this option, you need to add the WIDTH attribute to the <HR> tag and either specify the percentage of the window that the horizontal line should span (with a number less than 100 and a percentage sign following) or specify the line's exact width in pixels. Following is an <HR> tag that spans 400 pixels:

```
<HR WIDTH="400">
```

HTML attributes are often enclosed in double quotation marks ("). When attributes contain spaces, double quotation marks are necessary. Otherwise, double quotes are optional, but using double quotation marks around all HTML attribute values is considered good form. Many tools that check HTML syntax give a warning when double quotation marks are not present.

---

*   ***Note:***   *HTML tags are case-insensitive. Using <code>, for example, is the same as using <CODE>. Different people prefer different capitalization in tags. In this book, all HTML tags and attributes are in uppercase.*

When referencing external elements such as graphics and Java applets, file names and file paths should be written in the correct case. Although Windows operating systems are case-insensitive when it comes to file paths, screen elements and hyperlinks may not work if your files end up on a UNIX server, which is sensitive to case. For simplicity, many Web page authors use all lowercase letters for directories and graphic names. Following is a sample image tag that refers to an image directory and file with lowercase names:

```
<IMG SRC="images/titlebar.gif">
```

Values associated with the TARGET and NAME attribute in the <A> tag are case-sensitive. These attributes are discussed later in this chapter. TARGET="_Top", for example, is not the same as TARGET="_top".

? What is the bare minimum HTML needed to define a page?

First, create a text file in a text editor and give it a name that ends in .html or .htm. Next, add the following text to your document:

```
<HTML>
<HEAD>
<TITLE>Browser window title goes here</TITLE>
</HEAD>
<BODY>
Insert Main content here
</BODY>
</HTML>
```

Note that line returns do not matter in HTML. Line returns are considered the same as spaces in most browsers. Also, two or more blank spaces are ignored. For example, entering "*Hello* followed by several spaces and the word *there*", as in the first line shown here, is rendered without the spaces on the Web page (and without double quotes as well), as in the second line shown here:

```
"Hello          there"
Hello there
```

? What are WYSIWYG HTML editors?

WYSIWYG stands for What You See Is What You Get. WYSIWYG HTML editors are graphical HTML creation and editing tools with which you can create Web pages without having to type HTML code. By dragging images onto the page and formatting text with traditional, word processor-like controls, you can create HTML pages quickly and easily.

A large percentage of pages on the Web can be created or duplicated quickly and easily with a good WYSIWYG editor such as Macromedia's Dreamweaver, shown in Figure 10-1. Unfortunately, however, studying the actual HTML of a page when you need to add a page element that your WYSIWYG editor doesn't support is often necessary. You also have to study the HTML when you try to remove HTML tags that don't work in some browsers. Even when you use a graphical HTML creation tool, understanding the basics of HTML helps a lot. Popular WYSIWYG editors include Macromedia Dreamweaver, Adobe Pagemill, Netscape Navigator Gold, and Microsoft Front Page.

What is XML, and how does it relate to the Web?

Extensible Markup Language (XML), a new specification, is designed to extend HTML with a great deal of functionality. The W3C is currently working on defining an XML standard. Jon Bosak of Sun Microsystems describes the reasoning behind XML this way:

"To address the requirements of commercial Web publishing and enable the further expansion of Web technology into new domains of distributed document processing, the World Wide Web Consortium has

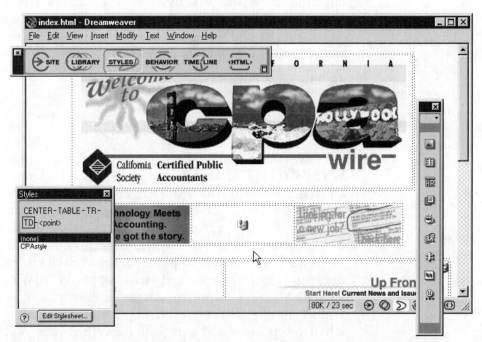

Figure 10-1 Macromedia's Dreamweaver, a WYSIWYG HTML editor, can help beginners who don't know HTML create Web pages and also help professionals edit and create pages quickly.

developed an Extensible Markup Language (XML) for applications that require functionality beyond the current Hypertext Markup Language (HTML)."

Both Microsoft and Netscape have added some XML functionality to their 4.0 Web browsers. However, full XML implementations are not likely until future versions of Netscape and Microsoft Web browsers are released.

To read Jon Bosak's paper "XML, Java and the Future of the Web," visit http://sunsite.unc.edu/pub/sun-info/standards/xml/why/xmlapps.htm.

TAGS

Common HTML Tags

There are a large number of HTML tags. The following list is intended as a reference and is not comprehensive. This list is also included in the insert in the back of this book:

Tag	Tag Name
<A HREF="">...</A>	Hyperlink
<B>...</B>	Bold
<BODY>...</BODY>	Body of Web page
 	Line break
<CENTER>...</CENTER>	Center
<H1>...</H1>	Large heading
<H2>...</H2>	Medium heading
<HEAD>...</HEAD>	Document header
<HR>	Hard rule line
<HTML>...</HTML>	HTML page start and finish
<I>...</I>	Italics
<IMG SRC="">	Image
<OL><LI>...</OL>	Numbered list
<OL><LI>...</OL>	Auto-numbered list

Tag	Tag Name
<P>...</P>	Paragraph
<PRE>...</PRE>	Preformatted text
<SCRIPT>...</SCRIPT>	Client-side script
<TABLE><TR><TD>...</TD></TR></TABLE>	Table
<TITLE>...</TITLE>	Title of document
<UL><LI>...</UL>	Bulleted list

PC users can download the extremely useful Microsoft HTML reference in Microsoft Help format (HTMLRef.zip) from http://www.microsoft.com/workshop/author/newhtml/ default.htm.

A number of online HTML references are available on the Web. One of the better lists is the Sandia National Laboratories HTML Elements List located at http://www.sandia.gov/sci_compute/elements.html.

? How do I specify fonts in HTML? And what if a browser does not have a font installed?

The <FONT> tag was first supported in Netscape Navigator 2.0 and Microsoft Internet Explorer 3.0 browsers. The <FONT> tag allows color, font, and font size to be specified with the COLOR, FACE, and SIZE attributes, respectively:

● **COLOR:** Color may be defined in either hexadecimal RGB values with a preceding # character (see Chapter 8 for more information about hexadecimal color values) or as one of a number of different color names. The default colors for regular text, hyperlinks, and visited hyperlinks can be defined in the <BODY> tag. Specifying a font color with the <FONT> tag overrides the color specified in the <BODY> tag.

● **FACE:** This attribute specifies the font face that is used. A number of different fonts may be listed as long as they are separated by commas. If the browser that is looking at a page does not have access to the first font, it goes to the next, and then the next until it comes to a font that it does have. If no font is available, the page's default font is used.

 SIZE: Unfortunately, the SIZE attribute does not refer to font size in points as people are accustomed to seeing it in word processors and other publishing tools. SIZE can either be set to an absolute value from 1 to 7, with 1 being the smallest, or size can be set relative to the current font size. Relative size is established with a + or − sign along with a number to increment up or down the 1 to 7 font-size scale. Whether absolute or relative sizing is used, all font sizes are relative to the default font size set that the user has set within the Web browser. Specifying <FONT SIZE="3">, for example, displays text at different sizes if a browser's default font size is changed.

Following are several examples of font definitions:

```
<FONT COLOR="#FF0000" FACE="Arial, Helvetica, sans-serif"
SIZE="6">Big red sans serif font.</FONT>

<FONT COLOR="magenta" FACE="Times New Roman, Times, serif"
SIZE="-1">Small magenta serif font.</FONT>
```

Microsoft Internet Explorer 4.0 and Netscape Navigator 4.0 have introduced features whereby fonts can be packaged and installed on clients' machines. With these features, Web sites can display text in any font they wish.

✱ ***Note:*** *If you define a font with the <FONT> tag outside of an HTML table, the settings defined in the <FONT> tag may not apply to the text within the table. To specify font attributes within a table a separate <FONT> tag must be included within each table cell that contains text. Following is a simple table that contains text with special font styles applied to each cell:*

```
<TABLE>
    <TR>
    <TD><FONT FACE="Arial, Helvetica, sans-serif">Hello</FONT></TD>
    <TD><FONT FACE="Arial, Helvetica, sans-serif">Cell</FONT></TD>
    </TR>
</TABLE>
```

Style sheets may also be used to globally add text style information to a document. Style sheets are discussed in detail in Chapter 15.

? How do I include special characters in a Web page?

The only part of the HTML language that does not require the < and > characters is the syntax by which special characters are defined. Anyone who has copied special characters such as the trademark (™) or copyright (©) character between platforms has probably seen special characters change.

To get around this problem, special characters are defined by {, where 123 is the ISO number for the character. For example, © represents ©, and ™ represents ™. A number of special characters may also be defined with characters that are easier to remember instead of ISO numbers. For example, © displays the © symbol. For a listing or common tags, see the section in this chaper on HTML tags. Not all characters with corresponding numeric entities need to use this special syntax. The percent (%) and at (@) characters, for example, display perfectly well as text characters.

Table 10-1 lists common special characters.

? What is the best way to indent paragraphs?

As odd as it may seem, there is no simple way to indent paragraphs such that the paragraphs display similarly in different browsers. Netscape introduced the <SPACER> tag for setting widths, but, unfortunately, it was not adopted by other browsers. If you use the <SPACER> tag to indent paragraphs, non-Netscape browsers simply ignore the tag and do not indent the paragraph.

Probably the most common solution is to add a string of nonbreaking space ISO characters to the beginning of the paragraph, like so:

```
    This is the start of an indented paragraph.
```

However, the nonbreaking space character is not consistently the same width across operating systems and

Character	Numeric Entity	Named Entity	Description
"	&#034;	&quot;	Quotation mark
#	&#035;	None	Pound
$	&#036;	None	Dollar
%	&#037;	None	Percentage
&	&#038;	&amp;	Ampersand
<	&#060;	&lt;	Less than
>	&#062;	&gt;	Greater than
@	&#064;	None	At
•	&#149;	None	Bullet
–	&#150;	None	En dash
—	&#151;	None	Em dash
™	&#153;	None	Trademark
©	&#169;	&copy;	Copyright
®	&#174;	&reg	Registered trademark
°	&#176;	&deg;	Degree
¶	&#182;	&#para;	Paragraph symbol
é	&#233;	&eacute;	Lowercase e with acute accent

Table 10-1   Common Special Characters

browsers. If you use this method, make sure to test it on all of your target platforms with different browser default text-size settings.

Using an invisible GIF as a spacer is another option. This method is compatible with all of the common browsers. For more on creating completely transparent GIFs as spacers, see Chapter 8. Here is a sample <IMG> tag for the beginning of a paragraph:

```
<IMG SRC="clear.gif" WIDTH="20" HEIGHT="1"> This is the start
of an indented paragraph.
```

To indent the left margin of an entire paragraph, you may use <UL> and </UL> tags around the paragraph or tables to create the added space. With tables, simply create a table with two table cells and no border. Following is a sample table set up to give a paragraph or entire body of text a 20-pixel left margin:

```
<TABLE BORDER=0>
<TR><TD WIDTH="20"></TD>
<TD>
```

Insert the indented paragraph here:

```
</TD></TR>
</TABLE>
```

? How do I include comments in a Web page that do not display on the screen?

There are a number of ways to enclose comments in HTML without the text appearing on the screen. The correct way is to enclose comments within <!— and —> tags. Many HTML syntax validation tools give errors or warnings when HTML tags are placed within a comment. Certain little-used browsers have trouble when they reach a > character within a tag that does not represent the closing of the tag. Newer browsers have no problem with other HTML tags being included within comment tags.

A correctly formatted comment is as follows:

```
<!--This is a correctly formatted comment-->
```

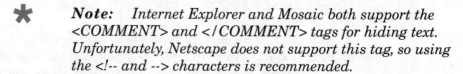

Note: *Internet Explorer and Mosaic both support the <COMMENT> and </COMMENT> tags for hiding text. Unfortunately, Netscape does not support this tag, so using the <!-- and --> characters is recommended.*

? What is the HTML <META> tag, and how do I use it?

The <META> tag sits at the top of the HTML document between the <HEAD> and <TITLE> tags and provides information that is invisible to the user. The <META> tag is usually used to define page topics for search-engine robots, set cookies on a user's browser, and set the page to refresh itself in the number of seconds that you specify. Newer browsers interpret <META> contents as if they were HTTP response headers. More recent uses of the <META> tag include setting the RSAC content rating, specifying who created the page, and defining the document's content type.

To correctly use <META> tags on a site, you can either learn the various attributes and formats pertaining to each type of <META> tag you want to implement, or you can copy and adapt a tag that has already been formatted. Because <META> tags use many formats, especially within the CONTENT attribute, simply copying pre-existing tags is quite a bit simpler.

Following are many of the uses for <META> tags, along with examples and explanations.

Defining Content

<META> tags allow you to define the content of your pages with both key words and a description.

```
<META NAME="Keywords" CONTENT="Computers, Sales, Intel, Compaq,
Discount">
META NAME="Description" CONTENT="We sell discount computers on
the Web!">
```

These lines of HTML summarize the page for a search engine by listing key words. The key words help place the page properly and competitively in site listings such as Excite, Alta Vista, Lycos, and InfoSeek.

Recreational Software Advisory Council Rating System

You can set an RSAC rating for your page by using a <META> tag such as the following example:

```
<META http-equiv="PICS-Label" content='(PICS-1.1
"http://www.rsac.org/ratingsv01.html" l gen true comment "RSACi
North America Server" by "inet@microsoft.com" for
"http://www.microsoft.com" on "1997.06.30T14:21-0500" r (n 0 s 0
v 0 l 0))'>
```

The Recreational Software Advisory Council rating system provides a standard to rate the content of Web sites. Users can set Microsoft Internet Explorer 3.0+ to exclude sites that contain such topics as nudity and violence. This example HTML is from Microsoft's home page. In the code, the r (n 0 s 0 v 0 l 0) indicates, appropriately, that the page contains zero nudity (n), sex (s), violence (v), and obscene language (l). For more information on RSAC ratings, visit http://www.w3.org/pub/WWW/PICS.

Controlling the Caching of Pages

Microsoft Internet Explorer supports a <META> tag that defines the date on which the content expires:

```
<META HTTP-EQUIV="expires" CONTENT="Mon, 12 May 1998 00:36:05 GMT">
```

Microsoft Internet Explorer, if set to first look to the browser's cache, uses a cached version each time a visitor revisits a page until the expiration date set by the <META> tag is reached. For pages that you don't want cached, set the expiration date to a date that has already passed.

Setting a Page to Change or Refresh the URL

You can use the <META> tag to change URLs in a specified number of seconds:

```
<META HTTP-EQUIV="refresh" CONTENT="5; URL=http://host.domain.com/
index.html">
```

This example calls a new page five seconds after the current page has loaded. This can be set to the same page that the <META> tag is on to allow the page to refresh itself.

Language

The <META> tag allows you to set the language:

```
<META HTTP-EQUIV="content-language" CONTENT="en">
```

English is en, French is fr, and esperanto is eo. For a complete listing, visit http://vancouver-webpages.com/multilingual/iso639a.txt.

Robot Information

It is possible to tell friendly robots to index a page but not follow the links:

```
<META NAME="ROBOTS" CONTENT="INDEX, NOFOLLOW">
```

Other options for the CONTENT attribute include NOINDEX and FOLLOW.

? Cheating on <META> Tags

To avoid the trouble of constructing your own <META> tags from scratch, visit http://www.apple.com and http://www.aol.com and view the HTML source for some great examples.

Another option is to visit the META Builder page shown in Figure 10-2. On that page, you can construct <META> tags by simply filling out forms. The META builder page can be found at http://vancouver-webpages.com/VWbot/mk-metas.html.

? Is it possible to prevent my page's background from scrolling with the HTML in my page?

Internet Explorer 2.0 introduced a BGPROPERTIES attribute for the <BODY> tag. This attribute prevents a tiled page background from scrolling when it is set to fixed. Preventing the background from scrolling in Netscape is not possible. Following is a sample HTML <BODY> tag which

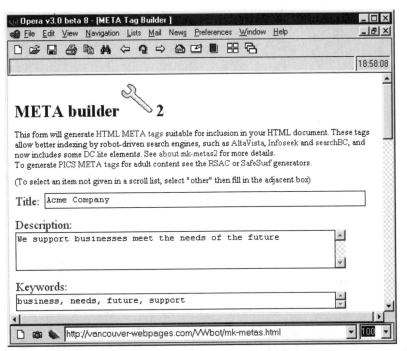

Figure 10-2 On the Meta builder page, you can build your own <META> tags online by using simple form input fields.

defines a background that does not scroll in Microsoft Internet Explorer:

```
<BODY BACKGROUND="tile.gif" BGPROPERTIES="fixed">
```

? When I put line breaks at the end of my table cell, Microsoft Internet Explorer 3.0 ignores them. How can I fix this?

Microsoft Internet Explorer 3.0's ignoring of line breaks at the end of table cells is a common problem. For example, this code renders the table cells shown in Figure 10-3:

```
<TABLE BORDER=1>
<TR><TD WIDTH=100>I would like three line breaks<BR><BR><BR></TD>
<TD WIDTH=100></TD></TR>
</TABLE>
```

To force Internet Explorer to read the line breaks, simply place any character or an invisible nonbreaking space ( ) after the <BR> tags.

Empty cells that are completely solid in tables with cell borders is another common problem. To force a table cell to appear empty, insert a single character or a nonbreaking space ( )

? What is the <LAYER> tag, and what browsers support it?

The layer tag is a new Netscape-specific tag that was introduced with Netscape Navigator 4.0. The tag allows you to group sections of HTML, and, using the NAME attribute, define a name for the group. With the WIDTH and HEIGHT attributes, you can confine content to a certain area and

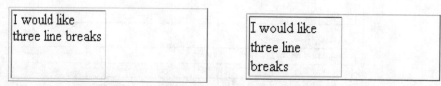

Figure 10-3   The same table displayed in Microsoft Internet Explorer (left) and in Netscape Navigator (right). Notice how the lines break differently.

thereby create a sort of floating table. The CLIP attribute enables content to be cropped to a certain size. The TOP and LEFT attributes enable you to specify screen coordinates for display positioning. For example, you could make graphics and text overlap. The ABOVE, BELOW, and Z-INDEX attributes allow relative Z depth to be specified so that graphics overlap in the right order. The VISIBILITY attribute can be set to SHOW, HIDE, or INHERIT to effectively turn on or off a block of HTML through JavaScript. Combining multiple <LAYER> tags can result in graphic effects without the need for images, such as the Web page shown in Figure 10-4.

Perhaps the most exciting aspect of the <LAYER> tag is being able to combine it with features introduced with dynamic HTML. Using JavaScript with the <LAYER> tag, a <LAYER> attribute can be changed by JavaScript, even after the page has loaded. Graphics, HTML, Java applets, and so on can all be animated over and under each other to a position anywhere on the screen.

Figure 10-4 The <LAYER> tag allows absolute positioning and layering as a few of its many features. This screen was created using a number of <LAYER> tags without the use of images.

A few tools on the market allow dynamic HTML scripting with the Netscape <LAYER> tag without the user having to

How Well Do You Know HTML Text Tags?

You may think you know all the HTML tags, but some of the more obscure tags may surprise you.

The following tags have been around for quite a while but are rarely used on the Web. With these tags, you can spice up your pages and still keep them compatible with Microsoft Internet Explorer and Netscape Navigator. Many of these tags, however, are rarely used for good reason. Frequently, the exact same effect can be achieved with common tags such as italics <I>, bold <B>, and variations of the <FONT> tag. Since many of the least-used tags are, for all practical purposes, redundant, a well-supported effort is under way to remove many of them from future HTML specifications. Follow is a list of some lesser-used tags for formatting text:

Tag	Intent of Tag	How It Is Implemented
<EM>	Emphasize text	Italics
<CITE>	For citations	Italics
<STRONG>	Make text stand out	Bold
<BIG>	Increase text size	Increase font size
<SMALL>	Decrease text size	Decrease font size
<S>	Strikeout text	Line through middle of text
<STRIKE>	Strikeout text	Line through middle of text
<SUB>	Subscript text	Small text set lower than surrounding text
<SUP>	Superscript text	Small text set higher than surrounding text
<BLINK>	Blink text	Text rotates between displayed and hidden
<TT>	Teletype	Fixed-width font; usually Courier
<ADDRESS>	Address	Italics
<CAPTION>	Table captions	Places standard text above or below tables
<KBD>	Keyboard	Fixed-width font; usually Courier

Tag	Intent of Tag	How It Is Implemented
<XMP>	Example	Fixed-width font, usually Courier, with space above and below the text
<SAMP>	Samples	Fixed-width font; usually Courier
<VAR>	Variables	Italics
<WBR>	Word break	Words that span line returns will break at the tag
<PLAINTEXT>	Plain text	Fixed-width font, usually Courier, with space above and below the text
<LISTING>	Lists	Fixed-width font, usually Courier, with space above and below the text
<U>	Underline	Underline
<BLOCKQUOTE>	Quotes	Line break above and below with added margin space

know JavaScript or HTML. Macromedia's Dreamweaver is currently the market leader for this functionality.

❓ How can I add a link that brings up a site visitor's e-mail application with the To: line filled in with a specific e-mail address?

Adding client-side e-mail functionality to a Web page is essentially the same as adding a hyperlink to a mail application. The syntax is as follows:

```
<A HREF="mailto:user@domain.com">Click here to
e-mail user@domain.com</A>
```

An e-mail client will open on the user's computer. On the client is a blank line for writing an e-mail message and, on the To: line, an already-filled-in e-mail address. Probably the browser brings up the system's default e-mail client. There is no way to specify which e-mail application to open. It is important to note that, to send e-mail, visitors to your site must have an e-mail account or at least an e-mail application that is set up to send messages.

Both Microsoft Internet Explorer and Netscape Navigator hyperlink to their own built-in e-mail packages by default. In order to link e-mail links to a different e-mail package, a user must edit the browser's preferences. To support users who have not associated their external e-mail application with their browser, it helps to include the actual e-mail address along with the text that is clicked. This way, users can manually copy the address to their e-mail client if they wish.

Netscape and Mosaic browsers also allow you to enter the contents of the subject line of the e-mail that is started with the Mailto: line. This feature results in invalid e-mail addresses in e-mail messages launched from Microsoft Internet Explorer. The syntax of a client-side e-mail that specifies a subject is as follows:

```
<A HREF="mailto:user@domain.com?subject=This is the subject">
```

 Note: *A Web site visitor can send e-mail even if he or she does not have an e-mail application or an e-mail account. By combining CGI scripting and HTML forms, it is possible to construct a page that uses server-side e-mail. With server-side e-mail, far more possibilities are open for e-mail formatting and addressing. To read more about server-side e-mail, see Chapter 11.*

If I use the <EMBED> tag for a plug-in element, how can I display an alternative for browsers that do not have the plug-in installed?

Without using JavaScript, you cannot display alternative HTML for browsers that both support the <EMBED> tag and do not have the necessary plug-in installed. For browsers that do not support the <EMBED> tag, you may use the <NOEMBED> and </NOEMBED> tag to display alternative HTML.

For Netscape 3.0 and later browsers, you can detect whether specific plug-ins are installed with JavaScript and write out the appropriate HTML by using JavaScript. Unfortunately, this method does not work with Netscape 2.0 or Internet Explorer browsers.

A little known attribute for the <EMBED> tag, PLUGINSPAGE, allows you to specify a hyperlink to an alternative page for those who do not have the needed plug-in.

How can I include externally stored HTML in my Web page using HTML?

Unfortunately, externally stored text cannot be included on Web pages the same way that graphics and other screen elements can. To include this functionality on a page, you need to use a server executable of some sort. A number of publicly available CGIs include this functionality. The easiest way to include a script of this sort on a page is to use server-side includes. For more information on server-side includes and custom server applications, see Chapter 11.

Is it possible to create a text hyperlink that is not underlined?

A simple method of hyperlinking text without underlining it is available with Netscape Navigator 4.0 and Microsoft Internet Explorer 3.0+. Unfortunately, because style sheets are necessary, other browsers simply ignore the STYLE attribute. The following HTML defines hyperlinked text that is not underlined:

```
<A HREF="newpage.htm" STYLE="TEXT-DECORATION: NONE">Click Here</A>
```

How can I link to sections of a page that would normally require scrolling?

To link to a section of a page that isn't at the very top, you first need to give it a name. In the HTML, find the area on the page to which you want to link and add the following code:

```
<A NAME="recipes"></A>
```

If you want to link to this section from a different section on the page, use the following code:

```
<A HREF="#recipes">Click here for recipes</A>
```

To link from other pages, use standard hyperlink syntax with a # sign and the section name at the end of the link, like so:

```
<A HREF="mypage.html#recipes">Click here for recipes</A>
```

Keep in mind that section names are case-sensitive in many browser versions. It is always a good idea to stick to lower case with regards to section titles.

FRAMES

What is the syntax for creating a basic frames-based page?

Two types of tags are used for creating frames-based pages: <FRAMESET> and </FRAMESET> tags and the <FRAME> tag. The <FRAMESET> tag defines a set of rows or columns and their individual widths or heights. The asterisk character (*) specifies that the remaining space in the browser window be used by each column or row. Following is a sample <FRAMESET> tag that defines three columns, the first 50 pixels wide, the second 100 pixels wide, and the third the remainder of the browser width:

```
<FRAMESET COLS="50,100,*"></FRAMESET>
```

Other options for the <FRAMESET> tag include the ROWS attribute, which divides the window vertically and is a replacement for the COLS attribute. Using a percentage figure instead of number of pixels is also acceptable. A <FRAMESET> tag that divides the window vertically and specifies the percent for row height is shown here:

```
<FRAMESET ROWS="*,80%"></FRAMESET>
```

Next, individual URLs need to be specified and a name needs to be given to each frame. Each frame defined by the <FRAMESET> tag needs its own <FRAME> tag. A <FRAME> tag at its simplest defines just a URL and a name, like so:

```
<FRAME SRC="http://www.yahoo.com" NAME="search">
```

A hyperlink from any frame or browser window that specifies TARGET="search" will now update the search frame.

All frame tags should be placed directly following the </HEAD> tag in an HTML page. The full HTML for a simple frames page is shown here:

```
<HTML>
<HEAD><TITLE>Page Title Here</TITLE></HEAD>
<FRAMESET ROWS="*,80%">
    <FRAME SRC="http://www.yahoo.com" NAME="search">
    <FRAME SRC="home.html" NAME="bottom">
</FRAMESET>
</HTML>
```

❓ How do I create an alternative page for browsers that do not support frames?

To create a page for browsers that do not support frames, include <BODY> and </BODY> tags after the last </FRAMESET> tag. Next, add <NOFRAMES> and </NOFRAMES> tags between the two <BODY> tags. Content that you insert between the <NOFRAMES> and </NOFRAMES> tags appear in older browsers as an alternative to frames.

A sample frames-based page with alternative text is shown here:

```
<HTML>
<HEAD><TITLE>Page Title Here</TITLE></HEAD>

<FRAMESET ROWS="*,80%">
    <FRAME SRC="http://www.yahoo.com" NAME="search">
    <FRAME SRC="home.html" NAME="bottom">
</FRAMESET>

<BODY BGCOLOR="#FFFFFF">
<NOFRAMES>
You need to download a frames-based browser to view this page.<BR>
We recommend <A HREF="http://www.microsoft.com">Internet Explorer</A>
and <A HREF="http://www.netscape.com">Netscape</A>
</NOFRAMES>
</BODY>
</HTML>
```

? How do I create a more complex frames-based page with multiple rows and columns?

To build a frames-based page that is anything other than simple vertical columns or simple horizontal rows, you need to nest frames. Frames can be nested in two ways. Either fill a single row or column with a Web page that is itself frames-based, or use more <FRAMESET> and </FRAMESET> tags in place of <FRAME> tags. To divide a page into two horizontal columns with the right column divided into two rows, use the following code:

```
<FRAMESET COLS="100,*">
    <FRAME SRC="menu.html" NAME="menu">
    <FRAMESET ROWS="*,100">
        <FRAME SRC="main.html" NAME="main">
        <FRAME SRC="bottom.html" NAME="bottom">
    </FRAMESET>
</FRAMESET>
```

? How can I remove the frame borders for Netscape Navigator 3.0 and Microsoft Internet Explorer 3.0 and later browsers?

A number of <FRAME> and <FRAMESET> attributes are treated differently in Microsoft Internet Explorer and Netscape Navigator. Fortunately, however, there is a trick for getting borderless frames in each browser. To create borderless frames for Netscape Navigator 3.0 and Microsoft Internet Explorer 3.0 and later, add FRAMEBORDER, FRAMESPACING, and BORDER attributes to all <FRAMESET> and <FRAME> tags. Make sure to add <FRAMEBORDER="no"> and <FRAMEBORDER="0">. A borderless set of tags for a frame-based page looks something like this:

```
<FRAMESET COLS="100%" ROWS="40,*" FRAMEBORDER="0"
FRAMEBORDER="no" BORDER="0" FRAMESPACING="0">
    <FRAME NAME="topmenu" SRC="topmenu.html" FRAMEBORDER="no"
FRAMEBORDER="0" FRAMESPACING="0">
    <FRAME NAME="main" SRC="main.html" FRAMEBORDER="no"
FRAMEBORDER="0" FRAMESPACING="0">
</FRAMESET>
<NOFRAMES>
```

How can I open up a new browser window from a hyperlink?

To open up a new browser window from a hyperlink, use the following syntax:

```
<A HREF="mypage.html" TARGET="_new">
```

This example opens a new browser window each time it is clicked. If a name other than "_new" were used—say, "mypage"—the new window would be assigned the name "mypage". Each time a hyperlink is clicked in a currently open browser window that uses TARGET="mypage", the mypage window is updated.

If you want a hyperlink to change the page of the browser window that opened the current window, use the syntax TARGET="_parent".

Both the Microsoft and Netscape browsers allow new windows to be opened with a specified width and height and without the usual browser attributes such as navigation buttons, URL line, menus scroll bars, and so on. To add this functionality, JavaScript is necessary. For more information about opening new windows with JavaScript, read Chapter 13.

How can I clear all of the frames that are dividing my Web page?

To clear all of the frames that are contained in the browser window, use TARGET="_top" in an <A HREF> tag, as in the following example code. This clears even the nested frames on a page.

```
<A HREF="page2.html" TARGET="_top">
```

How do I allow content to be downloaded through my Web pages to a user's hard drive?

Web content that is mapped to MIME types that a Web browser is equipped to display or play will display or play. If a MIME type is not playable through your Web browser, you are given the option of saving the file. To allow a file to be downloaded, simply put it on the Web server in a Web-accessible directory that is not an executable or a CGI directory and provide a hyperlink to the document in your HTML. A Microsoft Word document that sits in the same directory as the HTML document to which it links may be downloaded by clicking on the following HTML:

```
<A HREF="MyDocument.doc">Click to Download</A>
```

+ ***Tip:*** *When providing downloadable documents on a Web site, listing their file size is a good idea. A site visitor may not realize that a file is impractical to download until the download is well underway. If your site is visited by Web novices, explaining how long a file may take to download at different connection speeds is also a good idea.*

? How can I include a hyperlink on my page that works like the Previous button on my Web browser?

HTML does not offer any tags that link visitors automatically to the previous page. However, two methods can be used to offer "previous button" functionality: JavaScript's document.history.back(), and the environment variable HTTP_REFERER that is available to server scripts and executables.

For more about these two methods, read Chapter 13 about JavaScript and Chapter 11 about server scripting.

FORMS

? What are the different form elements and their attributes?

The HTML language includes tags for creating check boxes, passwords, radio buttons, text-entry fields, multiple select boxes, drop-down menus, and text areas. Each form element has a slightly different syntax in HTML. For the form elements to be functional, all form elements must sit within <FORM> and </FORM> tags. Netscape Navigator browsers do not display form elements without a <FORM> tag and an ACTION attribute.

Radio Buttons

The radio button tag is defined with the TYPE="RADIO" attribute. The NAME attribute defines the name of the variable that is being set. If the CHECKED word is present in the tag, the radio button is pre-selected. Two radio buttons with the same NAME attribute toggle when selected. When one is clicked, the other is deselected automatically. Following is a sample <INPUT> tag that defines a pre-selected radio button such as the one shown in the margin.

```
<INPUT TYPE="RADIO" NAME="myradio" CHECKED>
```

Check Boxes

The check box is similar to the radio button but does not offer the toggle functionality. Check boxes should each have unique NAME parameters. Like the radio button, the text CHECKED prechecks a check box. Following is a sample <INPUT> tag that defines a pre-selected check box form element such as the one shown in the margin.

```
<INPUT TYPE="CHECKBOX" NAME="checkvariable" CHECKED>
```

Drop-Down Menus and Multiple Select Lists

Drop-down menus allow one option to be selected from many. Any number of drop-down options may be set by adding more <OPTION> tags. VALUE is an optional parameter. To turn a drop-down menu into a multiple select list, you need to add a SIZE attribute to the <SELECT> tag. SIZE specifies the number of visible rows in the list. If SELECTED is placed in one of the drop-down menu options, the browser preselects that element. The sample code listed below defines a drop-down menu and multiple select list such as the two shown in Figure 10-5:

```
<SELECT NAME="gender">
    <OPTION SELECTED--Unknown--
    <OPTION>Male
    <OPTION>Female
</SELECT><BR><BR><BR>
<SELECT NAME="country" SIZE=3>
    <OPTION>USA
```

```
            <OPTION>Canada
            <OPTION>Mexico
            <OPTION>Belize
            <OPTION>Costa Rica
            <OPTION>Nicaragua
      </SELECT>
```

Text-Entry Fields and Password Fields

Text-entry fields and password fields differ in HTML definitions only with the TYPE parameter. Plain text fields are defined with TYPE="TEXT", and password fields are defined with TYPE="PASSWORD". In terms of functionality, the only difference is the use of asterisks in place of visible characters as words are typed. The MAXLENGTH field indicates the maximum number of characters that can be entered in the field. SIZE indicates the visible size of the form element on the screen. The VALUE element is optional and allows text to be pre-entered in the fields. Listed below is HTML defining both a text entry field and a password field both containing pre-filled-in text as defined in the value parameters. The HTML results in visible screen elements such as those shown in Figure 10-6.

```
<INPUT TYPE="TEXT" NAME="address" VALUE="Enter
address here" SIZE=20 MAXLENGTH=20><BR>
<INPUT TYPE="PASSWORD" NAME="password" VALUE="Enter
address here" SIZE=20 MAXLENGTH=20>
```

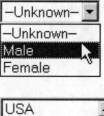

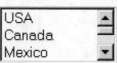

Figure 10-5   Drop-down lists

Figure 10-6   Text-entry field and a password field

Text Area Elements

A text area element allows large text entries to be made. The NAME attribute sets the variable name, while ROWS specifies the number of visible rows of text that appears on-screen. Likewise, COLS specifies the number of visible rows of text. To enter default text in the text area element, simply place the text between the <TEXTAREA> and </TEXTAREA> tags. Following is HTML that defines a text area form element such as the form element shown in Figure 10-7:

```
<TEXTAREA NAME="email" ROWS=4 COLS=50>
Message here
</TEXTAREA>
```

? What is the difference between the GET and POST methods in a form?

When you create a form in HTML you are faced with a decision to use GET or POST as part of the METHOD attribute of the <FORM> tag:

```
<FORM ACTION="FormParse.cgi" METHOD="POST">
```

The difference between POST and GET has to do with the way that data is actually sent to the Web server. GET sends all of the form's variable names and associated data along the URL line, whereas POST sends the data separately.

Figure 10-7   A text area for entering large amounts of text

The key limitation to using the GET method is its length restriction. The URL lines of many browsers restrict the number of characters that can be sent. If you are using the GET method, restricting the amount of characters to no more than 128 minus the length of the URL path to the destination CGI is a good idea. The URL line also needs to hold the HTTP path to the server script that will process the data. Therefore, only the remaining character space is available to the form data. Form content is also URL-encoded, which converts illegal URL line characters to legal codes that can be converted back. A typical form that uses GET submission with one TEXT input field with the NAME attribute set to "search" may resemble the following when the words *mom's cooking* have been submitted:

```
http://www.domain.com/cgi-bin/site_search.cgi?search=mom%27s+cooking
```

POST submissions are not restricted by the URL line and do not share the limitations of GET data.

For more about form processing, read Chapter 11 on server scripting.

? How can I prevent my <TEXTAREA> input field from scrolling endlessly to the right when users enter data?

Microsoft Internet Explorer 3.0 and later automatically wrap text that is entered into a <TEXTAREA> field. Unfortunately, Netscape Navigator does not wrap text this way. However, a WRAP attribute to the <TEXTAREA> tag was introduced with Netscape 2.0 that allows several different wrapping options:

WRAP Attribute	What It Does
WRAP="Off"	The text entered into the text area scrolls to the right until the RETURN or ENTER key is pressed.
WRAP="Virtual"	Text entered in a text area wraps when it reaches the end of the text area input box. When the data is submitted to the server, it is received as if the text didn't wrap at all. The only line breaks received by the server are those made by pressing ENTER or RETURN.

WRAP Attribute	What It Does
WRAP="Physical"	Text wraps, just as it does with WRAP="Virtual", only when the text is actually submitted line breaks are inserted at every point where the text wrapped.

? How do I submit invisible information via a form?

A certain form type allows data to be hard-coded into a page and submitted with other, visible form elements. Like other forms, hidden forms must reside between <FORM> and </FORM> tags in a Web page. It is important to realize that even though information is hidden in the browser window, the data can still be seen by viewing the HTML that makes up the page. Following is an example of a hidden form input field:

```
<INPUT TYPE="HIDDEN" NAME="MyVariable" VALUE="The user cannot
see me">
```

? If I use a drop-down menu, how can I submit text that is not part of the visible drop-down list?

There are two ways to specify what information is sent to the Web server from a drop-down list. The first method is to simply use a number of <OPTION> tags without setting any additional attributes. In this case, the text sent to the server is the same as that which is seen in the drop-down list. If a user selects the "I am male" option from the drop-down list, for example, the variable set in the <SELECT> tag is sent to the server with the value "I am male," as this code demonstrates:

```
<SELECT NAME="MyList">
    <OPTION>---Select one of the following---
    <OPTION>I am male
    <OPTION>I am female
    <OPTION>I would rather not say
</SELECT>
```

Often, specifying a variable for each drop-down list item makes parsing easier for the script that receives the data. To specify a value for each drop-down option, you need to add a VALUE attribute to each <OPTION> tag, like so:

```
<SELECT NAME="MyList">
    <OPTION VALUE="">---Select one of the following---
    <OPTION VALUE="male">I am male
    <OPTION VALUE="female">I am female
    <OPTION VALUE="unknown">I would rather not say
</SELECT>
```

? My drop-down lists are not wide enough to display all of the text that they contain. How can this be fixed?

Anyone who creates a number of forms has probably come across a drop-down list that is too narrow. From time to time, Microsoft Internet Explorer and Netscape Navigator fail to provide lists with enough width. This problem occurs most frequently with Internet Explorer 3.0. With Navigator, the problem sometimes occurs after the page is loaded when you dynamically change the contents of a drop-down list with wider content.

To force a drop-down list to be wider, simply add a string of nonbreaking spaces after the longest drop-down option, as in this example:

```
<SELECT NAME="ProductUses">
<OPTION VALUE="B">Business Use       
<OPTION VALUE="H">Home Use
</SELECT>
```

The series of   elements forces the drop-down list to display with an increased width.

? My site visitors complain about radio buttons being invisible. What is happening?

Netscape Navigator browsers have had problems with radio buttons disappearing. Users can fix this problem by minimizing and then opening the browser window again. The redrawing of the window should make the radio buttons reappear. No authoring solution can be found for the disappearing radio button problem.

TECHNIQUES

? **How can I simulate what other Web surfers see without installing a dozen different browsers on my machine?**

Most Web developers are cursed with having to install every browser version under the sun to ensure that visitors see their sites correctly. Nothing beats installing all the different browsers, but you can take several steps to simulate other browser environments. Turning off Java, JavaScript, cookies, and graphics is possible in Netscape Navigator browsers. In Microsoft Internet Explorer, you can turn off sound, ActiveX controls, and VBScript as well as images, JavaScript, and plug-ins.

For even more options, it is possible by means of a publicly available Perl script to keep a browser from seeing certain tags and families of tags . The Backwards Compatibility Viewer allows developers to view pages without tables, frames, <FONT> tags, <CENTER> tags, and other elements.

To use or download the Backwards Compatibility Viewer, visit http://www.delorie.com/web/wpbcv.html.

? **Is it possible to convert other file types to HTML easily?**

A number of file converters have been written for converting data to HTML. Certain file types may be opened and converted using Microsoft Word. In Word 97, you can save data with the Save as HTML command on the File menu. You can do the same with an add-on for Word 95.

For a comprehensive list of conversion tools, visit http://www.w3.org/hypertext/WWW/Tools/Filters.html.

? **How can I design a Web page that prints well from a printer?**

When you print a page from a Web browser, the page is converted from HTML (the language was never intended to be a publishing or printing language) to PostScript or your printer's proprietary language. HTML is intended to be window size-independent, whereas the language that a printer uses must provide exact sizes for printing.

Browsers assume that Web pages are printed on paper that is 8.5 inches, or about 600 pixels, wide. Converting the data from HTML to PostScript or your printer's proprietary language doesn't always go smoothly. Designing a page that prints well from different browsers and on different printers requires a little trial-and-error experimentation. Netscape Navigator 3.0 and 4.0 both include a print preview feature for viewing a page before actually printing it.

Graphics from a Web page always print poorly because they are optimized for file size and a 72 dpi monitor. Most printers support much higher resolutions (300 to 600 dpi), so printed Web graphics often look blocky.

Printing from frames also causes a few more headaches than one might expect. Printing more than one frame at a time, from either Microsoft Internet Explorer or Netscape Navigator, is simply not possible. For a specific frame within a page to be printed, the frame must be the last one clicked. You make a frame active simply by clicking the background of that page.

? How can I pre-load images so my larger pages don't take so long to download?

To effectively pre-load images, you need a page that is pretty "light" in terms of total kilobytes (the sum of the HTML, graphics, and any other screen elements). The page must be light in order to show up before the other pages appear. If you have a light page, add the graphics that you want to pre-load at the bottom of the page. Set both the WIDTH and HEIGHT parameters of the image tag to one pixel. The following HTML pre-loads and caches a graphic that may be significantly larger than one by one pixel:

```
<IMG SRC="MyBig.gif" WIDTH="1" HEIGHT="1">
```

? How can I tell if my HTML is correctly constructed?

Checking HTML for errors, also known as *validation*, is a great idea. Netscape Navigator 2.0+ and Microsoft Internet Explorer versions 3.0+ offer a great deal of built-in error-correction mechanisms for finding incorrectly formatted HTML.

Correcting errors makes life easier for the Web site visitor, but tougher for developers. Developers can no longer merely check the code in their favorite browser and be sure that the HTML is correct. A number of large Web sites, including http://www.microsoft.com, have realized how important correcting errors is, and they have introduced policies that require HTML to be validated before it can be posted on their Web sites.

Some of the more common errors that validation tools find are

- Incorrectly formatted tables, such as tables that lack </TD> tags

- Tags that have been left unclosed, such as a single <B> tag

- Characters that should be defined with HTML ISO representations, such as the trademark character (™), which should be represented in HTML as ™

A number of HTML validation tools are available both online as well as for downloading. HTML Validator is a stand-alone PC tool available for downloading at http://www.htmlvalidator.com/. For a list of validation tools, visit http://www.cre.canon.co.uk/~neilb/weblint/validation.html.

Chapter 11

Server Scripting

Answer Topics!

Server Scripting @ a Glance

If you have seen a page counter or bulletin board, or submitted a form from an HTML page, you have used a *server script*.

In order to process forms, generate dynamic pages, connect with databases, and otherwise enhance the functionality of a site, adding software to the server is necessary. Enhancing server-side functionality to a site may be as simple as adding a string of characters to your page that tells your Web server to embed the date within the page, or as complex as writing custom-compiled software that takes advantage of the Web server's API. Extending a site's functionality with server software is often called *CGI programming* or *server scripting*, but both names are often misnomers. Frequently, server scripts do not use the Common Gateway Interface. In fact, server scripts may not be scripts at all. Compiled applications are technically not scripts, but the name has stuck due to the proliferation of server scripts.

Implementing custom server functionality can be done using a variety of methods and languages. Fortunately, the basic framework behind methods of server scripting is the same. Essentially, scripts are called with or without additional information being passed along (form submissions or commented out information in the URL line) and the scripts, in turn, return HTTP-compliant syntax to the Web browser. The server script may be essential in that the data that it sends the browser can only be provided through a dynamic executable on the server (e.g., a search engine or browser detection), or the server script may provide invisible functionality to the user (updating a database, updating a text file, incrementing a counter). In any case, server applications are a necessary part of all kinds of site functionality.

This chapter covers these important topics:

Server Scripting Basics explains the different types of server scripting and the advantages and disadvantages of each. It explains environmental variables as well as providing tips about how to find out which language a site uses for its dynamically generated pages.

- **Server-Side Includes (SSIs)** covers the ins and outs of SSI and provides examples of the most common SSI tags.
- **Common Gateway Interface (CGI)** offers an overview of CGI and explains what it takes to add a CGI program to your server. Standard HTTP headers and source code for a bare-bones CGI are included in both C and Perl.
- **HTML Embedded Scripting** explains what HTML embedded scripting is and what products support it.
- **Web Server API Applications** points out the advantages and disadvantages of programming with a Web server's native application programming interface (API).

SERVER SCRIPTING BASICS

❓ What is server scripting generally used for?

Whenever a server responds to a request for anything besides an already existing HTML page, a server application of some type beyond your basic Web server is required. Server scripts can also perform a variety of tasks that are transparent to the user. For example, server scripts can send e-mail, save data from forms to a text file, and redirect the user to a different location on the Web.

Server scripting is most commonly used for the following types of Web site features:

- Form handling (saving data on the server)
- Counters
- Searches
- Bulletin Board Service (BBS)
- Browser detection
- Server redirects to new pages
- Database connectivity
- Time-stamps

? What is the difference between server-side and client-side scripting?

Both server-side and client-side scripting can provide some degree of decision branching to determine what appears on a Web page. For example, a server- or client-side script can display a picture of a home after 6 p.m. or a picture of an office building before 6 p.m. On many occasions, however, server- and client-side scripts do not overlap in terms of what they are capable of doing. Client-side scripts, for example, cannot by themselves update text files or databases. Server-side scripts are finished with a page after the content on the page has been generated. No interaction occurs with a server-side script until a hyperlink is clicked or a form is submitted and a request is made to the server.

In general, client scripting such as client-side JavaScript requires less server processing time, but it requires a browser that is compatible with the language being used. Client-side scripting is not Web server-dependent, so pages may be moved between Web servers without making any changes. Server-side scripting is more processor-intensive on the server end, but is capable of generating HTML that is compatible with all Web browsers. Server scripts are often Web server-dependent. They need to be customized or recompiled when moved to a new Web server.

Client-side scripting has been available to Web developers since the introduction of Netscape 2.0. Client-side scripting involves embedding script, usually JavaScript or VBScript, within the HTML of a document. Client-side scripts allow the user and the page to interact, the page and the URL line to interact, or the page and time to interact. Client-side interactivity is limited in what it can do and frequently cannot perform the functionality that is desired.

Following is a list of client-side functions that are available through all JavaScript-compliant browsers:

- Form validation
- Time-stamps
- Frame interactivity
- Creating floating windows
- Reading and writing cookies

● Generating custom HTML as a page is loaded

For more information about JavaScript, read Chapter 13.

? What types of server programming are available to developers?

Generally speaking, four general types of server programming are available to Web developers:

● Server-side includes (SSIs)
● Stand-alone Common Gateway Interface (CGI) executable scripts or compiled applications
● HTML embedded scripts
● Web server API applications

Each type of programming is discussed in detail in this chapter. In short, here is a description of each type of programming:

● SSI code snippets are the fastest to execute and the easiest to write.
● Stand-alone CGI executables are usually the most flexible, but often suffer from speed problems under high loads.
● HTML embedded scripts are usually parsed by another application that has been written using the Web server's API.
● Web server API applications are typically compiled applications that interact very efficiently with the Web server by using the server's application programming interface.

? How can I tell if a Web page is generated from a server-side script and, if so, how can I tell which language was used?

It is impossible to tell conclusively whether a Web page is generated from a script or from static HTML sitting on a server. Most Web servers allow any file extension, including .html, to be mapped to the server-side scripting method of your choice. If you install a Perl run-time engine on a Web

Server Applications and ISPs

Unfortunately, many Internet service providers and Webmasters don't allow custom server scripts on their Web servers. Why? For security reasons. Simply put, being able to execute an application on a server is a potential security problem. If a hacker or rogue Web author obtains write permissions to a Web server directory and those permissions allow files to be executed, the hacker has a clean point of entry and can wreak havoc on the server. At an ISP it is likely that a number of sites will be hosted on the same Web server. Bugs in server scripts have the potential to bring down the entire Web server, affecting sites other than your own.

Some scripting languages, such as server-side VBScript and JavaScript (implemented with Microsoft Active Server and Netscape's LiveWire), try to address this issue through a server scripting environment very similar to the sandbox in which Java operates on the Web client. A recent survey estimated that as many as 66 percent of all Web sites do not use server-side scripting. Unfortunately, Webmasters all too often use this as justification for restricting custom server programs on their servers.

server, you can most likely call Perl scripts with the standard .pl, .plx, and .cgi extension, as well as any other file suffix you want to use. Keep in mind, however, that when you map a scripting engine to a file suffix and the file suffix is also being used for files that are being served from read-only directories, you get an "insufficient permissions" error when you try to request the read-only files.

Table 11-1 lists common file extensions and their associated languages.

? What are environment variables?

Environment variables are variables that store request information for a particular HTTP request as well as server information such as the port being used, the server's name, and what software the server is running. Environment variables may be referenced from server scripts and can be extremely useful.

Extension	Language
.asp	Active Server Pages (Microsoft); probably HTML embedded VBScript or JavaScript
.cfm	Cold Fusion Markup Language
.cgi	Any common gateway interface language
.class	Java
.dll	Dynamic Link Library; probably Internet Server API application
.exe	Any binary compiled language or Microsoft Visual Basic
.htx	Server macro language (Internet Factory); also may be a template used with .idc files
.idc	Internet database connector (Internet Information Server file type)
.js	Server-side JavaScript (Netscape LiveWire); probably HTML embedded
.lp, .ls, .lsp	Lisp
.pl, .plx	Perl
.py, .pyc	Python and compiled Python, respectively
.qry	Tango (EveryWare Development)
.shtm, .shtml	Server-side include (SSI) HTML embedded tags
.wo, .woa, .wos	Web objects

Table 11-1 Common Files Extensions and Their Associated Languages

In general, there are two types of environment variables: variables provided by the browser and passed along by the server and variables provided by the server. Environment variables are essential for Web site features such as server-side browser detection and form processing. It is important to note that not all browsers send the same environment variables. Table 11-2 explains the common environment variables.

Environment Variable	Sample Value	Description
HTTP_ACCEPT	image/gif, image/x-xbitmap, image/jpeg, image/pjpeg, */*	Accepted MIME types for the browser making the request

Table 11-2 Common Environment Variables

Environment Variable	Sample Value	Description
HTTP_ACCEPT_CHARSET	iso-8859-1,*,utf-8	The character set that the browser supports
HTTP_ACCEPT_ENCODING	gzip, deflate	Types of encoded files the browser supports
HTTP_ACCEPT_LANGUAGE	en-us,en-ca	Language accepted by the browser (U.S. English in the example)
HTTP_CONNECTION	Keep-Alive	HTTP connection type supported by the browser
HTTP_COOKIE	EGSOFT_ID=205. 139.115.177-20596 17088.29150672	Report of cookies assigned to current URL
HTTP_HOST	www3	Host name of Web server
HTTP_REFERER	http://www.yahoo.com/ Computers/Software/	Referring URL, if one exists
HTTP_USER_AGENT	Mozilla/4.0 (compatible; MSIE 4.0; Windows NT)	The reported name of the browser
QUERY_STRING	name=Franklin& lastname=Roosevelt	URL-encoded information passed along the URL line following the *?* character; empty if no question mark is present
SERVER_PORT	80	Port number of the Web server
SERVER_SOFTWARE	Microsoft-IIS/3.0	Web server software

Table 11-2 Common Environment Variables (*continued*)

Following are examples of environment variables sent from Web browsers along with requests. This list of environment variables was provided by Microsoft Internet Explorer 4.0:

HTTP_ACCEPT:application/vnd.ms-excel, application/ msword, image/gif, image/x-xbitmap, image/jpeg, image/pjpeg, */*

HTTP_ACCEPT_LANGUAGE:en-us,en-ca

HTTP_CONNECTION:Keep-Alive

HTTP_HOST:ikonia

HTTP_REFERER:
http://www.yahoo.com/Computers/Software/

HTTP_ACCEPT_ENCODING:gzip, deflate

HTTP_USER_AGENT:Mozilla/4.0 (compatible; MSIE 4.0; Windows NT)

HTTP_COOKIE:EGSOFT_ID=205.139.115.177-205961708 8.29150672

This sample list of environment variables was provided by Netscape Navigator 4.0:

HTTP_ACCEPT:image/gif, image/x-xbitmap, image/jpeg, image/pjpeg, */*

HTTP_ACCEPT_LANGUAGE:en

HTTP_CONNECTION:Keep-Alive

HTTP_HOST:ikonia

HTTP_USER_AGENT:Mozilla/4.01 [en] (WinNT; I)

HTTP_ACCEPT_CHARSET:iso-8859-1,*,utf-8

HTTP_COOKIE:EGSOFT_ID=205.139.115.177-162917910 4.29137851

SERVER-SIDE INCLUDES (SSIs)

? What are server-side includes?

Server-side includes (SSIs) are a semi-standard set of HTML-like tags that are parsed out of a Web document on the Web server and are replaced with the appropriate text whenever a page is requested by a browser. SSIs only work on pages that are requested from a Web server. For SSI tags to be correctly parsed, the Web server must support the specific server-side includes that you use. What's more, the Web server may also have to be configured to parse all the documents that sit in a particular directory or all the documents with a particular file extension. The file extension .shtml is often used to indicate which documents should be parsed by the Web server.

SSIs are great alternatives to what would normally be short CGI scripts. Date- and time-stamping, sharing HTML between pages on a server, and including the date that a file was last modified on a Web page are all examples of tasks that are easy to accomplish with SSIs. Because the format is within <!-- and --> characters, SSI tags that fail to parse out on the server are commented out on the Web page.

? How do I use server-side includes on files that have been set up to be parsed by the server?

Because SSI tags are very similar to HTML codes, you can use server-side includes by placing tags that provide the functionality you desire (make sure the tags are compatible with your Web server) in your HTML document where you wish the output to appear. If the SSI is a date-stamp, for example, place the tag where you would like the date to show up. Following are explanations of the most commonly supported SSI functions and their associated tags.

Adding the File Size of a Document or Downloadable File to a Page

```
<!--#fsize file="/DownloadFile.zip"-->
```

Adding the file size of a downloadable file is considered good netiquette. Using the <#fsize> tag as it is used in the following example is one of the easiest ways to add file size automatically:

```
<A HREF="/DownloadFile.zip">Latest file
<!--#fsize file="/DownloadFile.zip"--> bytes</A>
```

These lines of HTML and SSI result in HTML that allows a user to see a document's file size and download the file. If the downloadable file is replaced with a larger file with the same name, the HTML does need to be changed to account for the new size. Because SSI is parsed out server-side, viewing source from a browser would only reveal numbers where the <#fsize> tag once was.

Inserting Environment Variables

```
<!--#echo var="HTTP_USER_AGENT"-->
```

This tag will be replaced by the user's browser name and version number. HTTP_REFERER returns the URL of the document from which the user linked, if the user linked from another URL and if the browser used reports the HTTP_REFERER variable.

Inserting HTML from Another Document

```
<!--#include virtual="/template/MenuBar.html"-->
```

This example will be replaced by the contents of MenuBar.html. Obviously, if this SSI tag is within the <BODY> tags of an HTML page, MenuBar.html should not contain the <HTML>, <BODY>, <HEAD>, or <TITLE> tag. This tag is known as a <#include> (pronounced "pound include") and is particularly useful when data that may change is included in multiple HTML documents. For example, using the <#include> tag allows you to add a menu item to a universal menu that is part of a number of pages simply by changing the HTML of one file.

For further consideration, the following line indicates a relative path to the included file:

```
<!--#include file="..../MenuBar.html"-->
```

Adding the Last File Modification Date to a Page

```
<!--#flastmod file="/DownloadFile.zip"-->
```

This example demonstrates a handy way to keep lists of downloadable files up-to-date with regard to the date on which they were last modified. To include the file-modification date of the page being requested, it may be easier to use

```
<!--#echo var="LAST_MODIFIED"-->
```

✱ ***Note:*** *A good tutorial on SSI can be found at http://
www.carleton.ca/~dmcfet/html/ssi.html. NCSA Web server
SSI information can be found at http://hoohoo.ncsa.uiuc.edu/
docs/tutorials/includes.html. Microsoft SSI information
can be found at http://www.microsoft.com/salesinfo/qa/
iis018.htm. Apache 1.2 information is available from
http://www.apache.org/docs/mod/mod_include.html.
CERN Web servers do not support SSI, but a Perl script that
adds SSI functionality is available at http://sw.cse.bris.ac.uk/
WebTools/fakessi.html.*

COMMON GATEWAY INTERFACE (CGI)

❓ What is a CGI application, and how does it work?

CGI, which stands for Common Gateway Interface, is a
simple protocol that allows a Web server and a stand-alone,
compiled application or script to communicate. When a
browser requests a page from an executable directory, the
Web server launches the script or compiled application that
is referenced in the URL line. The server makes a number
of variables associated with the request available to the
executable as environment variables. As the program executes,
information specific to the request, such as the URL line, the
browser type, and form submission information, are all
easily accessible to the program, if necessary.

For example, the CGI application may connect to a
database or send information via e-mail, but ultimately all
CGI applications need to print, and to do this they need to
use their language's standard output method. At least one
line of text is necessary for the request to be complete. When
the request is complete, the text is routed through the Web
server back to the Web browser that made the request. If the
CGI application's output was HTML, the HTML that the
browser receives looks as though it came from a static
HTML file.

Although the Common Gateway Interface (CGI) protocol
is easy to use, it is slow and performs poorly when a large
number of people use an application at the same time. The
Web server is forced to spawn a new process to execute the
CGI each time a user requests the CGI. The speed hit

involved in spawning a new process is minor, but the speed of the Web server is affected when numerous hits arrive each second. The advantage of CGI applications is that they run independently of the Web server. If a CGI application crashes, the Web server does not crash with it.

CGI applications may be written in any language. Typically, CGIs are written in Perl, C, Java, AppleScript, and Visual Basic. For more information on the CGI interface, visit the NCSA Web site at http://hoohoo.ncsa.uiuc.edu/cgi/.

? What does a CGI need to write as standard output for a minimal HTML page to be generated?

In order to generate a minimal HTML page that contains one line of visible text, the standard output of a CGI needs to print the following lines of text:

```
Content-type: text/html

<HTML>
<HEAD><TITLE></TITLE></HEAD>
<BODY>
Hello, World!
</BODY>
</HTML>
```

On the following pages is source code in both C and Perl to generate this output. Note that two line-returns appear after the content-type MIME definition. Both line-returns are necessary (they are part of the HTTP protocol) for the output to return correctly to the browser that requested it.

Soure Code in C

Following is the source code in C:

```
#include<stdio.h>
main(){
printf("Content-type: text/html\n\n");
printf("<HTML>");
printf("<HEAD><TITLE></TITLE></HEAD>");
printf("<BODY>");
printf("Hello, World!");
printf("</BODY>");
printf("</HTML>");
}
```

Source Code in Perl

Following is the source code in Perl:

```
#!/usr/bin/perl
print "Content-type: text/html\n\n";
print "<HTML>";
print "<HEAD><TITLE></TITLE></HEAD>";
print "<BODY>";
print "Hello, World!";
print "</BODY>";
print "</HTML>";
```

? What does Content-type do in the HTTP header line?

Content-type sets the MIME type of the document. If you were dynamically generating a Microsoft Word document, for example, you would begin the data stream with the following:

Content-type: application/msword

? Do I need to include any other HTTP header information?

Most CGIs only define the Content-type header or, in the case of redirections to a new URL, only define the Location header. Other headers, such as Date, the HTTP status code, and the server software are added by the Web server automatically. The Content-type header is the only critical header for a CGI that is sending actual content.

You may wish to add two types of optional headers to the Content-type header: standard and user-configurable HTTP headers. HTTP headers are a standard set of headers that define a detailed list of properties in a document. User-configurable headers are open to discretion but should precede standard HTTP headers. A number of non-standard headers such as "set-cookie" have worked their way in as de facto standards for the Web. Table 11-3 explains the most common HTTP headers.

Often, adding header information via CGI is not necessary. The functionality available through <META> tags on many of the newer browsers makes defining variables from a CGI unnecessary.

For more information on HTTP headers, visit http://www. w3.org/Protocols/HTTP/Object_Headers.html.

HTTP Header	Example	Description
Last Modified	last-modified: Tues, 12 Aug 1997 21:12:20 GMT	Lists the date and time that the file was last modified.
Content Language	content-language: en	Specifies the language of a Web page. Especially necessary for languages that use different alphabets. The language is specified with an ISO code.
Location	location: http://www.ikonic.com	Presents another method of redirection. When this is used, Content-type should not be specified.
URI	URI: http://www.gmcanada.com	Presents one method of server redirection. Best to use Location: as well. When this is used, Content-type should not be specified.
Date	date: Tues, 12 Aug 1997 23:30:20 GMT	Lists the current date and time.
Expires	expires: Wed, 13 Aug 1997 00:20:54 GMT	Specifies that the document is still sent, but many browsers do not look to their cache for a document that has expired. This is one method for persuading browsers to refresh versions of documents that are used frequently.
Server	Server: Microsoft-IIS/3.0	Lists the server software that is being used.
Set Cookie	set-cookie: MC1=GUID=e0cf8812135a22d1 bb080000f84; expires=Wed, 15-Sep-1999 19:00:00 GMT; domain=.microsoft.com; path=/	This is the accepted standard for setting client-side persistent cookies from the server.
Content-Length	content-length: 8110	Lists the content length in bytes. Especially important for binary files.

Table 11-3 Common HTTP Headers

➕ *Tip:* *Following any HTTP headers to a CGI's output, make sure that a double line-return appears after the last header only. The double line-return is absolutely necessary for any CGI and marks the end of the HTTP headers and the beginning of the HTML document.*

❓ How do I redirect a Web request to a different URL using a CGI?

To redirect a user to a new location from your CGI, simply output the following line followed by two line-returns:

Location: http://www.domain.com/

A few older browsers, rarely used now, also require a URI line for redirection. Although most CGIs don't bother with the URI line, adding it to your CGI's output doesn't hurt. To add a URI line, use the following syntax (notice the single line-return after Location and the double line-return after the line beginning with URI):

Location: http://www.domain.com/

URI: http://www.domain.com/

❓ I want to launch a CGI, but I don't want it to update or change the browser window. How can I do this without getting an error?

If you want to launch a CGI from a Web browser but you do not want the page to reload or redirect to a new page, try returning a no content header to the browser. The no content header will not produce an error in your browser. To generate a no content header, your CGI should return this text followed by two line-returns:

Status: 204 No Content

❓ How can I configure my Web server to support CGIs?

Three things are necessary on a UNIX or Microsoft Windows NT machine for a CGI to execute from a Web server:

● A correctly installed and compatible runtime engine or virtual machine must be on the server; or, if the application is compiled, it must be compiled for the machine on which it is running.

● The directory in which the CGI resides must be recognized by the Web server as a CGI directory.

● The CGI itself must be given executable file permissions as part of the operating system's security permissions settings.

CGIs in UNIX

To set executable permissions on a CGI file in UNIX, use the following syntax:

```
chmod 755 CgiFileName
```

CGIs in Windows NT

To set security on a Windows NT file, right-click the file and select Properties, then select the Security tab, and then press the button labeled Permissions. By selecting special status, you ensure that executable permissions are set for the correct users.

❓ My Perl script runs locally on my PC just fine, but when I upload it to my Web server it doesn't return anything. What is going on?

One of the most common mistakes people make when uploading scripts to a UNIX server is choosing to upload in binary instead of ASCII format. The ASCII characters used as line-returns in UNIX are different than the characters used in most PC text editors. All FTP applications allow you to choose whether to transfer files as ASCII or binary. A file that has been edited and saved on a PC does not have correct line-returns when it is FTPed bit for bit as binary. As part of an ASCII transfer, however, the line-returns are modified and converted to a UNIX-compatible format.

Many script editors, such as Bare Bones's BBEdit for the Macintosh and Allaire's Homesite for the PC, include a setting on the Preferences menu by which UNIX file returns can be included in text documents when they are saved. By saving a document in the correct setting, you can upload files as binary in your FTP client.

Another distinct possibility is that your CGI is not set to be executable. To make your CGI executable, follow the instructions in "How can I configure my Web server to support CGIs?" earlier in this chapter.

Will converting my CGI to FastCGI speed up its performance?

A number of options are available to Web developers for significantly speeding up the performance of server-side, Web-based programs. Two protocols associated with specific servers are Internet Server API (ISAPI) for Microsoft Internet Server and Netscape's Netscape API (NSAPI) for Netscape servers. Unfortunately, very few servers other than these support ISAPI or NSAPI, and, as a result, many have turned to a more open standard. Additionally, server APIs are usually tied to one or a few programming languages and don't lend themselves to simply converting existing CGIs. FastCGI, on the other hand, is currently the most popular open solution to the problem of multiple process spawning.

FastCGI is currently supported on NCSA httpd 1.5.2, Apache 1.1.1 and later (with a patch), Stronghold Secure Webserver 2.01, and Open Market Secure WebServer 2.0. To convert and run an existing CGI, two things are necessary:

- You must have a Web server that is compatible with FastCGI.
- A FastCGI application library must be written for the language in which your CGI was written. Currently, the only languages supported with FastCGI application libraries are Java, C, C++, Perl, and TCL.

FastCGI has the additional benefit of living separately from the Web server. When a FastCGI application crashes, it is unlikely to bring down the whole server. This benefit alone has won the favor of ISPs. Many ISPs would like to offer a faster solution than CGI to the sites they host, but they can't afford to support every developer's attempts to write an ISAPI or NSAPI at the risk of bringing down a Web server.

For more information on FastCGI, download the FastCGI developer's kit from http://www.fastcgi.com/applibs/.

CGIs for Nonprogrammers

That you have to be an experienced programmer to write a CGI application is a common misconception. CGIs are simple and are, in fact, a good way of learning basic programming skills. Scripts that address the most common CGI-based Web site features are freely downloadable from a number of sites on the Web. Using well-tested, public domain scripts is often safer than writing your own. As far as security goes, popular CGIs are usually safe if they have been around for more than a few months.

Before you upload CGIs to your Web server, make sure to read any applicable readme files. You may have to configure the server for the application to run. Also, if the CGI is a script, such as Perl or Python, and the server is running UNIX, you may need to change the path to the scripting language's run-time engine listed at the top of the script. The standard directory path to the Perl run-time engine is

```
#!/usr/bin/perl
```

To locate your scripting language's run-time engine on a UNIX machine, use the following syntax from the command prompt:

```
where perl
```

Popular download sites for scripts include

- Matt's Script Archive: http://www.worldwidemart.com/scripts/
- Kira's Web Toolbox: http://lightsphere.com/cgi/
- NCSA's Script FTP site:
  ftp://ftp.ncsa.uiuc.edu/Web/httpd/Unix/ncsa_httpd/cgi/
- Selena Sol's Public Domain CGI Script Archive:
  http://www.extropia.com/Scripts/

HTML EMBEDDED SCRIPTING

? What is HTML embedded scripting?

HTML embedded scripting is one of the easier methods of adding server-side functionality to a Web site. Unlike CGIs, which are stand-alone files that print out HTTP headers and HTML, HTML embedded scripts sit in the HTML document itself. Like SSIs, embedded scripts are parsed out of the HTML document and executed, and the results are returned before the document leaves the Web server. The tools that allow embedded HTML scripting let authors include and use environmental and server system variables along with a full suite of useful functions and macros.

Because the software that controls the parsing and execution of HTML embedded scripts is usually written in a Web server's native API, HTML embedded scripting is often done in a multi-threaded, server-optimized environment. Similar to daemons in UNIX, these run-time environments allow scripts to run without having to spawn a new process with each request.

? What HTML embedded scripting environments are available?

A number of Web servers include built-in scripting support. What's more, you can add a few solutions to existing server environments and thereby extend their functionality to include HTML embedded scripting. Following is a short list of environments:

- Microsoft Active Server is an extension for the Microsoft Internet Information Server environment. It includes built-in support for HTML embedded VBScript and JavaScript. Active Server has been ported to Netscape Server as an NSAPI called Chili!Asp by ChiliSoft. For information about Microsoft IIS and ChiliSoft, respectively, visit these sites:
  - http://www.microsoft.com/iis/
  - http://www.chilisoft.net/

- Netscape LiveWire, an extension for Netscape's Server, allows JavaScript to be included in HTML and executed on the Web server instead of the Web browser. For more information about Netscape LiveWire, visit http://merchant.netscape.com/netstore/servers/livewire.html.

- Cold Fusion is designed as a Web server API. It includes built-in support for database connectivity and dynamic page creation with HTML embedded Cold Fusion Markup Language. For more information, visit http://www.allaire.com.

- HTMLEx is an ISAPI (Internet Server Application Programming Interface) that works only on Microsoft Windows NT Web servers that run Internet Information Server. HTMLEx is a well-implemented, easy-to-use, and free scripting environment. For more information, visit http://erc.riteh.hr/HTMLEx/.

WEB SERVER API APPLICATIONS

? **What are the advantages and disadvantages of writing an application using a Web server's API?**

Applications written to take advantage of a Web server's API are almost always faster than other custom server applications. Your application essentially becomes part of the Web server itself. As part of the Web server, multi-threaded applications can run in an optimized environment without having to spawn new processes each time the application is called or needed. Applications written to take advantage of a Web server's API are usually written in C or C++. Other languages for writing server API applications include Borland's Delphi for the PC.

The major disadvantage of writing an application using a Web server's API is that the application is tied specifically to the Web server whose API you want to use. Rewriting an application that was written for one API so that it can be used by another Web server's API can be quite difficult. Even if the Web server is cross-platform, your Web server API application at the very least needs to be recompiled. More likely, your Web server API application needs to be extensively modified to work on a different platform.

Another disadvantage of writing an application that uses a Web server's API is the fact that its fate is tied to the fate of the Web server. If your application crashes, the server most likely will crash as well. When a CGI crashes, the process that is dedicated to the CGI is terminated. A program that modifies the Web server's API is essentially modifying the server.

Chapter 12

Client-Side Persistent Cookies

Answer Topics!

Client-Side Persistent Cookies @ a Glance

Cookies, or *client-side persistent cookies* as they are officially known, have gathered a large amount of press and attention since Netscape introduced them with Netscape Navigator 2.0. Cookies were introduced to help solve a basic deficiency in the hypertext transfer protocol. HTTP is stateless, which means that every time a request is made to a Web server, the server behaves as though the request were being made for the first time. In order to tell for certain that a request was made by the same browser that requested a page five minutes ago, setting state is necessary.

Essentially, *setting state* means to set a variable that is available to both the Web pages and the Web site itself. The variable is available even after the site has been visited many times and the computer restarted. Since the IP address is the only identifying variable available to the Web server, and the IP address may be shared by any number of machines over time, it was determined that a client-side solution is a better idea. Client-side persistent cookies have become the client-side solution to storing state. Compared to complex server-side applications that assign session IDs and often utilize databases for tracking, persistent cookies are a cheap and simple solution.

If you want to find out how many times a user has visited your site, assign a unique user ID that is remembered from week to week, or simply save form information to make filling out forms easier next time, cookies are probably your best bet.

This chapter covers these important topics:

Cookie Basics explains what cookies are, what is needed to write them, and the different methods you can use to create them.

Browsers and Cookies covers the limitations of cookies and how to determine what browsers support cookies.

Writing Cookies with JavaScript shows how to read, write, and delete cookies. Also included are pointers to JavaScript source code repositories where you can find more examples of using JavaScript with cookies.

Writing Cookies with Web Server Scripts and Applications includes an example and an explanation of the HTTP set-cookie header as well as Perl and Java source code for writing cookies from a CGI script. A VBScript example for writing cookies from Active Server pages is also included.

COOKIE BASICS

? What are cookies? Should I allow them, or are they a threat?

Client-side persistent cookies are simply a method of storing snippets of information on a site visitor's hard drive. This data is stored in a text file, or, in the case of Internet Explorer, in numerous text files locally in an area that is readable and writeable by a Web browser. Information that is stored in your cookie file or files can only be accessed by pages from a specific Web site or a section of a specific site. In most cases, the site that has access to the cookie information is the same site that stored the information there in the first place.

? What information is needed to write a cookie?

To write a cookie, the following information is needed:

- The date when the cookie should expire
- A URL that includes, at minimum, the domain for which the cookie information is accessible
- The name of the cookie variable
- The data itself that is associated with the cookie variable

Once the cookie information is collected, it needs to be sent to the browser in a format that allows the browser to actually write it to the appropriate cookie file. The three ways to create a cookie in a browser are with a server-side script or application, with <META> tags, and with JavaScript.

Server-Side Script or Application

In response to a page request, a server-side script or application can generate an HTTP header that passes information to the browser. Cookie-capable browsers read the header and store the information on the computer's hard drive, while other browsers simply ignore the header. Writing cookies from a server-side application or script is supported by a slightly higher percentage of Web browsers than the <META> tag or JavaScript methods. With server-side cookie generation, cookies may only be written at the time a page is actually requested. Server-side applications may also be used to read any cookies currently assigned for a particular site.

<META> Tags

The easiest way to generate a cookie is through the use of the <META> tag. By simply placing a correctly formatted <META> tag at the beginning of an HTML document, the Web browser saves the information. Unfortunately, <META> tags can only save information that is hard-coded within the HTML document. It is impossible, for example, to increment the number of times a site has been visited by a particular user because there is no way to see the existing number and add one. Likewise, it is impossible to add the date, a user's name, or form information without JavaScript or some form of server-side executable. However, <META> tags are a useful way of writing cookies if you simply want to know whether a user has been to a site before.

JavaScript

JavaScript allows cookies to be both read and written when a page loads or when triggered by a user event. The syntax of JavaScript is not as simple as it could be, but numerous publicly available examples can be found on the Web.

Strictly speaking, both JavaScript and VBScript can be used to generate cookies and can do so with surprisingly similar syntax. JavaScript, however, is the overwhelming client-side language of choice for cookies because both Netscape Navigator and Microsoft Internet Explorer support it. VBScript is only supported by Microsoft Internet Explorer.

? How do I delete a cookie?

There is no built-in command to delete cookies. Instead, you may delete a cookie by choosing one of the methods used for creating the cookie in the first place. Simply overwrite an existing cookie by specifying the same variable name and domain name as the cookie you want to erase, but specify an expiration date that has already passed. Browsers delete cookies whose expiration dates have passed.

If you are writing a cookie that you want to remain on the client for a while, choose a date that is no more than a couple of years in the future. Because browsers can only handle a finite number of cookies, setting an expiration date for cookies when you wish to stop using them or no more than a few years in the future is a common courtesy.

*   ***Note:*** *To delete cookies, make sure that the expiration date is at least as recent as 1970. Dates before 1970 are assumed to be after the year 2000 and will, therefore, keep your cookie around for a good while to come.*

❓ What are cookies actually used for on the Web sites that are using them?

There are a number of practical uses for storing data on a person's hard drive so that the data can be retrieved later. Some of the more practical uses are as follows:

● A Web site wants to track how many times a particular visitor has been there, when the visitor was there last, and what the visitor's path through the site was.

● An ad delivery service wants to know how many times a particular advertisement has been seen by a user.

● A Web site contains a number of forms and wants to help its visitors by filling in the data on forms that has already been collected.

● A Web site wants to let visitors personalize a link on its home page.

● A site wants to assign a unique ID to a particular site visitor for better site personalization.

● A site wants to collect and track demographic data over multiple site visits.

● A secure site wants to let a user enter without having to re-enter his or her user name and password.

● Storing information for dynamically generated content on a site.

? Are cookies a threat to my site visitor's security?

Cookies are not a threat to a user's security. Many have argued that cookies are a threat to Web surfers' privacy and anonymity, and although this is true, it is important to note that cookies don't do anything that can't be done by more difficult means on the Web server. In fact, the only really useful information that a cookie file can store is information that the Web server gets already when visitors fill out a form or merely visit a site in the first place.

Frequently, information associated with cookie files is already stored in a Web server's log files, a Web server's database tables, or a Web server text file that stores information submitted on forms. Cookies can only store text information. As a result, cookies cannot be executed on a computer like a virus or a trusted ActiveX control.

Keep the reading and writing of cookies down to a reasonable level as a courtesy to site visitors. Don't write more than a few cookies to a browser unless it is absolutely necessary. Try sharing the same cookie variable for storing multiple pieces of information.

? How does a Web server receive cookie information?

A Web server receives all cookies associated with its domain from browsers as part of the HTTP GET request for graphics and pages. If a browser has a variable set through cookies for a given site and it has not yet expired, the variable is sent automatically to the server with every request. Most Web servers make any cookie variable available to CGI applications as environment variables.

BROWSERS AND COOKIES

? Where are my browser's cookies stored?

Cookies are stored in a text file that is located in the area on the hard drive where your browser has permission to both read and write text files. By opening your cookie file, you can debug your cookie programming better and understand the process as well. Note that some browsers do not update their associated cookie files until the browser has been closed.

PC

Netscape Navigator 2.0 and 3.0 store cookies in a file called cookies.txt that is located in the Netscape folder on the hard drive. Netscape Navigator 4.0 also places cookie information in a file called cookies.txt. The file is located in a directory called Profiles in a directory named after your user name. The easiest way to find a Netscape browser cookie file is to simply do a search on cookies.txt.

Microsoft Internet Explorer for Windows 95 and Windows NT store cookie files in slightly different directory paths. Windows NT uses Winnt\profiles\log-in name\cookies, whereas Windows 95 uses the path Windows\Cookies. You will notice a large number of files in the cookie directory on both operating systems. Microsoft Internet Explorer creates a different cookie file for each domain that sets a cookie.

Macintosh

Netscape Navigator for the Macintosh stores cookies in a file called MagicCookie that is stored in a folder called Netscape under Preferences in the System Folder.

Microsoft Internet Explorer for the Macintosh stores cookies in a text file called Cookies that is located in a directory called MS Preference Panel under Extensions in the System Folder.

? What are the physical limitations of cookies?

According to Netscape, its browsers can store a total of 300 cookies. Each cookie can be no longer than 4KB, as defined by the size of the name combined with the OPAQUE_STRING. Only 20 cookies are allowed per server or domain. So what happens if you write too many cookies or write one that is too long? If the 20 cookies per site or the 300 maximum limit is exceeded, Netscape Navigator deletes the least recently used cookie to make room for the others. Cookies that are too long are still written, but they are cut off when the 4KB limit has been reached.

For more on Netscape cookies, visit Netscape's Persistent Client State HTTP Cookies page at http://www.netscape.com/newsref/std/cookie_spec.html.

Microsoft Internet Explorer 3.0 and 4.0 create a new cookie file for each site. Rumor has it that each cookie file has a maximum size of 4KB, but the size limit is poorly documented. Unlike Netscape Navigator, Internet Explorer allows more than 20 cookies to be set per page.

Which browsers support cookies?

An extremely comprehensive list of all browsers, their various versions, and whether or not they support cookies is available at http://www.research.digital.com/nsl/formtest/stats-by-test/NetscapeCookie.html.

To summarize the list, Netscape Navigator 2.0 and later supports cookies, as does Microsoft Internet Explorer 2.0 and later. Problems have been reported with beta versions of these browsers, but the problems were corrected at the time of the final release. Keep in mind, however, that Web site visitors can turn off cookie acceptance by means of the browser preference settings in most cookie-enabled browsers.

How can I tell whether a browser supports cookies?

There are two ways to tell whether a browser supports cookies: by using the HTTP_USER_AGENT variable or a JavaScript property, and by writing a test cookie.

You can simply use the HTTP_USER_AGENT environment variable on the server or the navigator.appVersion JavaScript property on the browser to detect which browser is being used. If the browser is supposed to support cookies, then, *voilà*, you can assume that cookies are supported. Unfortunately, this method doesn't detect whether cookies have been turned off by the user. Netscape 3.0 introduced the option of manually denying cookies with a dialog box such as the one shown in Figure 12-1. Microsoft Internet Explorer 3.0 introduced the option of disabling cookies altogether based on a browser preference. Therefore, assuming that certain browsers always support cookies is not always a safe bet.

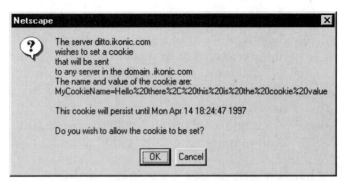

Figure 12-1 Netscape 3.0 introduced the option of rejecting cookies.

The second method of determining whether a browser supports cookies is to write a test cookie and then try to read it. If you can't read the cookie, either the browser doesn't support cookies or the Web surfer isn't accepting them.

WRITING COOKIES WITH JAVASCRIPT

? How can I use JavaScript to write or delete a cookie?

A number of publicly available JavaScript source code repositories can be found on the Web. On these sites you can find code for reading and writing cookies. The following code writes a cookie to the Web browser. Make sure that the first four variables are set to the variables that you wish to use for your cookie. To delete a cookie, match its name and domain using the following code, but make sure to specify a negative number for the monthsuntilexpiration variable.

```
<SCRIPT LANGUAGE="JavaScript">
<!--
function writecookie ()
{
/**Change the next line to your domain name**/
var domain = ".domain.com";
/**Change the next variable to the number of**/
/**months that the cookie will last**/
/**a value of -1 will delete the cookie**/
```

```
var monthsuntilexpiration = 6;
/**Next line is the name of the cookie with no spaces**/
var variablename = "CookieName";
/*Following is the value that you wish **/
/**to store in the cookie*/
var cookievalue = "Hello, world";
var expirecookie = new Date ();
var month = 2635200000; /*milliseconds in a month*/
cookieexpiredate =
expirecookie.setTime((expirecookie.getTime() +
(monthsuntilexpiration * month)));
document.cookie = variablename + "=" + escape (cookievalue) +
"; expires=" + expirecookie.toGMTString() +  "; path=/; " +
"domain=" + domain + ";";
}
writecookie ();
//-->
</SCRIPT>
```

For more information about setting cookies with JavaScript, visit the following section of the JavaScript Tip of the Week site: http://webreference.com/javascript/961125/.

Creating Cookies with the <META> Tag

Creating cookies with the <META> tag is the easiest way to write a cookie. To create a cookie with the <META> tag, you can either create one from scratch or follow the syntax listed below. Place the <META> tag at the very top of your HTML document, and change MyVar to the name of the variable you wish to set. Change Hello to the text that you wish associated with your variable.

```
<META HTTP-EQUIV="Set-Cookie"
CONTENT="MyVar=Hello;expires=Thursday, 30-Dec-99 04:31:12
GMT; path=/">
```

For more on <META> tags visit http://vancouver-webpages.com/META/metatags.detail.html.

? How can I use JavaScript to read a cookie?

Getting cookies that have been set for your site to all of the users is simply a matter of using document.cookie in JavaScript. Unfortunately, the information returned is a string of all the variables and their settings in a URL-encoded format. The string isn't easy to read, so it needs to be parsed. The following code takes the name of the variable that you wish to retrieve and parses out its value. To use it, simply set the name *variable* to the name of the variable that you want to retrieve.

```
<SCRIPT LANGUAGE="JavaScript">
function viewcookie() {
/*Following is the name of the variable you wish to retrieve*/
var name = "CookieName";
var fullcookie = document.cookie;
if (fullcookie.indexOf(name + "=")!=-1){
var partialcookie =
fullcookie.substring(fullcookie.indexOf(name + "="),
fullcookie.length);
if (partialcookie.indexOf(";")==-1) partialcookie =
partialcookie.substring(name.length + 1,partialcookie.length);
else partialcookie = partialcookie.substring(name.length +
1,partialcookie.indexOf(";"));
document.write(unescape(partialcookie));
}
else document.write("Cookie does not exist");
}
viewcookie();
//-->
</SCRIPT>
```

More examples of JavaScript code for reading cookies is available from these two sites:

- http://www.cookiecentral.com/demomain.htm
- http://www.ozemail.com.au/~dcrombie/cookie4.html

WRITING COOKIES WITH WEB SERVER SCRIPTS AND APPLICATIONS

? What are the HTTP headers and formats necessary for creating cookies from a Web server?

Only one HTTP header is needed to generate a cookie on a site visitor's computer. The set-cookie header needs to be added to the other Web server response headers when HTML is being sent back to a Web browser after a page has been requested. The format for the HTTP header is as follows:

```
Set-Cookie: NAME=VALUE; expires=DATE;path=PATH; domain=DOMAIN; secure
```

Following is an explanation of the different parts of this format:

- **NAME:** The Name variable is simply the name that is used to reference the cookie data that is set. "Phone," for example, may be used for a cookie that stores a user's phone number from information submitted on a form.

- **VALUE:** The value that you wish to store as a cookie. Phone=415-555-8000, for example, is a valid combination of NAME and VALUE.

- **DATE:** Unfortunately, the expiration date for cookies must be set in the following format: Day, DATE(two numbers)-MONTH(three letters)-Year(four numbers) Hours:Minutes:Seconds GMT. It is significantly easier to simply edit an existing example of a date, as in this example:

  Tuesday, 08-Nov-1999 21:11:22 GMT.

- **PATH:** Path is used to restrict a URL to a subset of a domain. If a cookie is only intended to be used within www.mycompany.com/employee/, for example, /employee would be in the PATH variable.

- **DOMAIN:** Domain is simply the domain in which the cookie can be read. A sample DOMAIN setting is www.domain.com. A domain must include at least two periods for it to be valid.

- **SECURE:** If the word *secure* is at the end of the cookie line, the cookie will only be sent along secure connections such as SSL.

Following is an actual set of HTTP headers that includes a set-cookie header (this example is from www.amazon.com):

```
HTTP/1.0 405 Because I felt like it.
allow: GET, POST
content-type: text/html
set-cookie: group_discount_cookie=F; path=/;
domain=.amazon.com; expires=Monday, 20-Oct-97 08:00:00 GMT
server: Netscape-Commerce/1.12
date: Monday, 13-Oct-97 05:52:29 GMT
```

For more on the cookie specification, visit Netscape's cookie page at http://home.netscape.com/newsref/std/cookie_spec.html.

❓ How can I write a cookie from a CGI written in Perl or Java?

The following two source code listings are for CGI applications that, when called, will write a cookie to the Web browser and redirect the browser to a different page. Both code listings print out HTTP headers that include the set-cookie header followed by a location header for redirection to a new URL. Both also include a double-line return to signify the end of the HTTP headers.

Perl

First, the Perl code:

```
#!/usr/local/bin/perl
print "HTTP/1.0 200 OK\n\r";
print "Content-type: text/html\n\r";
print "Set-Cookie: MyVariable=Hello_There; path=/; domain=.domain.com;
expires=Tuesday, 08-Nov-1999 21:11:22 GMT\n\r ";
print "Location: http:www.domain.com\n\r\n\r"
```

Java

Cookies can be written with both client-side and server-side Java. For more on client-side Java, visit http://www.cookiecentral.com/javacook2.htm.

Following is a simple server CGI written in Java. It writes a cookie and redirects to a different URL:

```
Public class WriteCookie
{ Public Static Void Main(String[] args)
   {
   System.out.println("HTTP/1.0 200 OK");
   System.out.println("Content-type: text/html");
   System.out.println("Set-Cookie: MyVariable=Hello_There; path=/;
domain=.domain.com; expires=Tuesday, 08-Nov-1999 21:11:22 GMT");
   System.out.println("Location: http:www.domain.com\n\r");
   }
}
```

? How can I read and write cookies, server-side, from a Microsoft Active Server page?

Microsoft has not provided full documentation for writing cookies from Active Server pages. To write a cookie with Active server, embed the following lines of code at the top of your HTML document:

```
<%
Response.Cookies("MyVar")="dinner"
Response.Cookies("MyVar").Expires = Date + 365
Response.Cookies("MyVar").Path    = "/"
%>
```

To read cookie files, simply reference the cookie by name with Request.Cookies(). The following code, placed between <BODY> and </BODY> tags on your Active Server page, prints the contents of the cookie variable:

```
<%
MyVar = Request.Cookies("MyVar")
response.write(MyVar)
%>
```

Chapter 13

JavaScript

Answer Topics!

JavaScript @ a Glance

Over the past few years, JavaScript has become one of the most popular scripting languages on the Web. The language's simple, Java-like syntax makes it one of the easiest ways to add interactivity to a site. JavaScript started out as a client-side scripting language for adding simple interactivity to Web pages. With Netscape Navigator 4.0 and Microsoft Internet Explorer 4.0, however, JavaScript blossomed into a full multimedia scripting language that allows everything from animation to database connectivity.

But JavaScript's value is not limited to client-side functionality. Both Microsoft's Internet Information Server and Netscape's Enterprise Server allow server-side JavaScript programming. Now a single language can be used for a variety of programming solutions for both client- and server-side Web site features.

This chapter is not intended to teach the syntax of the language itself. This chapter helps those who are new to the language understand what it is and help those who are familiar with JavaScript solve common problems and learn a few tips and tricks in the process.

This chapter covers these important topics:

JavaScript Basics explains what the language is and the difference between the various implementations of the JavaScript language. Also discussed is the new ECMAScript standard and its implications for JavaScript.

JavaScript Programming Methods covers techniques you can use to solve a number of JavaScript problems. Explained are some of JavaScript's limitations. You'll also find a comprehensive list of JavaScript events and HTML tags that support them.

JavaScript Programming Examples includes source code and explanations for different features that may be added to a site with JavaScript. JavaScript for non-JavaScript browsers, drag-down page navigation, and custom status messages are just a few of the Web site features that are covered.

Debugging JavaScript addresses some of the most common stumbling blocks in the JavaScript language and the various JavaScript-compliant Web browsers.

JAVASCRIPT BASICS

? What is the difference between JavaScript, LiveScript, LiveWire, JScript, and JScript for Active Server pages?

JavaScript and LiveScript are both Netscape implementations of what is most commonly called the JavaScript language. LiveScript was the original name, but for a number of reasons, including marketing reasons, Netscape chose to go with JavaScript. You can use either <SCRIPT LANGUAGE="LiveScript"> or <SCRIPT LANGUAGE="JavaScript"> in your Web pages, but using LANGUAGE="JavaScript" is recommended.

JScript is Microsoft's version of Netscape's JavaScript. JScript is extremely similar to JavaScript, but is not always 100-percent compatible. JScript's object model differs slightly, as does some of its native functionality. Microsoft

Internet Explorer also supports the <SCRIPT LANGUAGE="JScript"> tag, but be sure to note that Netscape does not. Again, using LANGUAGE="JavaScript" is recommended.

LiveWire is Netscape's implementation of server-side JavaScript, and ActiveServer is Microsoft's implementation. Both development environments are similar in that both allow developers to include HTML-embedded JavaScript that is executed on the Web server. LiveWire and Active Server offer CGI-like functionality in an integrated multi-threaded server environment. LiveWire is designed to work with Netscape Web servers, and Active Server is designed to work with Internet Information Server and other ISAPI-compliant servers. Active Server pages can also be run on Netscape servers with ChiliSoft's Chili!Asp NSAPI filter.

The following sites offer more information about the JavaScript language:

- **Microsoft's JScript language reference:** http://www.microsoft.com/jscript/
- **Netscape's JavaScript 3.0 language reference:** http://home.netscape.com/eng/mozilla/3.0/ handbook/javascript/
- **ChiliSoft:** http://www.chilisoft.net/

What is ECMAScript?

ECMAScript is an attempt to define "a general-purpose, cross-platform programming language." The language is based heavily on JavaScript and has been embraced by both Netscape and Microsoft. Officially known as ECMA-262, ECMAScript is largely implemented in both Netscape and Internet Explorer 4.0. The ECMA group, an international group for standardizing information and communication systems, is a major participant in the International Organization for Standardization (ISO). ECMAScript is eventually expected to become an ISO standard.

For more on the ECMAScript standard, visit http://www.ecma.org.

? **Will ECMAScript-compliant browsers still possess scripting incompatibilities in the future?**

Because the ECMAScript specification does not currently include an object model specification, Microsoft and Netscape use slightly different object models. An effort is underway to come up with an agreed upon object model specification, but until Microsoft and Netscape agree on a model, we will likely see a high number of incompatibility issues with the latest JavaScript features.

? **What are the limitations of client-side JavaScript?**

JavaScript has firm boundaries in the access it has to client-side information and functionality. Netscape 4.0 has introduced signed JavaScript in order to overcome these restrictions. Following is a list of basic things that are not possible with client-side JavaScript:

- E-mail
- Printing
- Reading, creating, and updating files on the server or browser
- Securely applying security to a page
- Executing applications anywhere other than through a Web server

Moreover, Microsoft Internet Explorer 3.0 and Netscape Navigator 3.0 and earlier cannot do the following:

- Affect the HTML layout once the page has loaded
- Capture keystrokes
- Change on-screen text that is not part of a form element
- Animate and change the visibility of any on-screen HTML elements, including graphics and text

Although JavaScript, especially JavaScript 1.0, has a very limited feature set, some surprising things have been done with it. Two of the more impressive examples are

- The JavaScript Lisp Interpreter, which interprets and runs the Lisp programming language, by Joe Ganley, available at http://www.cs.virginia.edu/~jlg8k/applets/jslisp.html.

- ASCII Space Invaders, which is compatible with JavaScript 1.0, by K.Moriyama, available at http://www1.nisiq.net/~jimmeans/game03w.htm.

? What JavaScript features work with which browsers?

Any JavaScript programmer will agree that the most difficult part of programming in JavaScript is not, as you might think, getting the script to work. The biggest challenge with JavaScript is getting the script to run on all browsers without an error. Remembering which features work with which browser and which browser version (and in the case of Internet Explorer, which JScript interpreter) can be very difficult.

Netscape's most notable JavaScript language changes have occurred between the 2.0X, 3.0X, and 4.0X browsers. However, Microsoft's changes are a little trickier to understand. Internet Explorer 2.0 does not support JScript. Internet Explorer 3.0, 3.01, and 3.02 all originally shipped with Microsoft's JScript.dll version 1.0. Microsoft released JScript.dll version 2.0 in early 1997, but, because it can be installed separately, two browsers whose versions are the same on the same OS may not support the same JavaScript functions. To make things more complicated, Microsoft uses a different dll for the object model. This object model dll changed between version 3.0 and version 3.01 of Internet Explorer. As a result, the syntax for calling a number of different methods changed or broke completely.

Table 13-1 lists basic JavaScript features that are compatible with at least one of the version 3.0 browsers. Table 13-2 lists the browsers' associated compatibilities.

? How can I tell which version of JScript my version of Microsoft Internet Explorer for Windows is running?

To determine which version of JScript your Windows Internet Explorer browser is using, you need to view the

Feature	IE3	IE3J2	IE4	NS2	NS3	NS4
Reading and writing cookies	✓	✓	✓	✓	✓	✓
Dynamic images (mouse-over images)*			✓		✓	✓
<NOSCRIPT> tag support	✓	✓	✓		✓	✓
Accessing Java properties**	✓	✓	✓		✓	✓
Open floating window	✓	✓	✓	✓	✓	✓
File upload			✓		✓	✓
Dynamic drag-down menus			✓		✓	✓
Externally stored scripts***			✓		✓	✓
Plug-in/MIME-type detection					✓	✓
Adding text to the browser status bar	✓	✓	✓	✓	✓	✓
Change layering of windows (on Focus)			✓		✓	✓

* The Macintosh release of Internet Explorer 3.0 does support this feature.

** There is little or no documentation for JavaScript to Java communication with Internet Explorer 3.0.

*** The Microsoft Internet Explorer 4.0 browser uses a different method (Scriptlets) than the Netscape 3.0+ browser.

Table 13-1 JavaScript Functionality Reference for Different JavaScript-enabled Web Browsers

version property of JScript.dll. To find JScript.dll on a Windows 95 or Windows NT computer, follow these steps:

1. Press the Start button on the Taskbar.

2. Select Find, and then Files or Folders.

3. Enter **jscript.dll** in the Named field on the Name & Location tab.

4. Click the Find Now button.

5. Right-click jscript.dll and select Properties.

6. Click the Version tab, shown in Figure 13-1.

Code	Browser Name and Version
IE3	Microsoft Internet Explorer 3.0X with JScript.dll version 1.0
IE3J2	Microsoft Internet Explorer 3.0X with JScript.dll version 2.0
IE4	Microsoft Internet Explorer 4.0X
NS2	Netscape 2.0X
NS3	Netscape 3.0X
NS4	Netscape 4.0X

Table 13-2   Codes Used for the Different Browsers Used in Table 13-1

? What is the relationship between browsers and JavaScript versions?

Each implementation of JavaScript has a corresponding JavaScript version. By the way, the JavaScript version shouldn't be confused with Microsoft's jscript.dll version number. Currently, all JavaScript-enabled browsers associate themselves with JavaScript 1.0, 1.1, or 1.2. Unfortunately, just because two browsers both associate themselves with

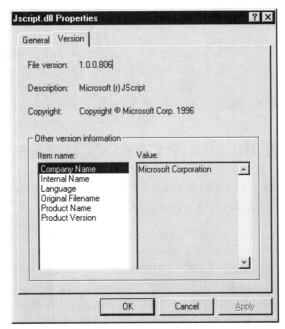

Figure 13-1   Viewing the properties of a PC's jscript.dll reveals which version of Microsoft's JScript is installed on your computer.

the same JavaScript version does not mean that they are compatible as regards a particular feature. In fact, knowing the JavaScript version number for your browser is only useful if you are using the version number as a method of browser detection as part of a script.

The JavaScript version number and Web browser associations are as follows:

Browser Version	JavaScript Version
Internet Explorer 3.0X (jscript.dll versions 1.0 and 2.0)	1.0
Internet Explorer 4.0X	1.1
Netscape Navigator 2.0X	1.0
Netscape Navigator 3.0X	1.1
Netscape Navigator 4.0X	1.2

What is signed JavaScript?

Netscape 4.0 introduced the ability to digitally sign your JavaScript code. Much like ActiveX controls, digitally signed JavaScript has access to many more operating system-level features than unsigned JavaScript. Signed files must be re-signed each time they are changed to ensure that scripts are not changed and reposted by those who did not create them. Signed JavaScript adds to the JavaScript feature set the ability to access files locally on a user's machine, read all browser preferences, send documents to the printer, and send e-mail.

JAVASCRIPT PROGRAMMING METHODS

What methods can I use to trigger JavaScript events?

JavaScript uses event handlers to trigger scripts being run. Whether it is clicking on an object or changing the order of the browser windows, JavaScript events are very important to any Web page on which the language is used. Any JavaScript code that is not within a function is treated as if it was called by the onLoad event handler. Table 13-3 describes JavaScript event handlers.

Event	Tags That Event Works with on Most JavaSccript Browsers	Called When
OnLoad	<BODY>, <IMG>, <APPLET>, <EMBED>	Document loads
OnUnload	<BODY>	A user exits a Web page
OnClick	<A>, FORMS	A user clicks an object, form element, or text
OnBlur	WINDOW, FORMS, <BODY>	A browser window is no longer the front-most browser window, or when a cursor moves out of a form element
OnChange	FORMS	A value has changed in a form element (for example, a drop-down list has the capability of triggering onChange when selected)
OnFocus	WINDOW, FORMS, <BODY>	A browser window changes position to become the front-most browser window, or when a cursor is inserted into a form element
OnSelect	FORMS	Text is selected in a form
OnSubmit	FORMS	A form SUBMIT button or graphic is pressed
OnError	<IMG>, <APPLET>, <EMBED>	An error occurs loading a plug-in, applet, image, etc.
OnAbort	<IMG>, <APPLET>, <EMBED>	A user stops an element from completely loading
OnMouseOver	<A>	A mouse moves over an object
OnMouseOut	<A>	A mouse moves off an object

Table 13-3   JavaScript Event Handlers and Their Associated Tags

FORM refers to one or more form element tags, including <INPUT>, <SELECT>, and <TEXTAREA>. WINDOW refers to changing the order of browser windows.

 Note: *Both Netscape 4.0 and Internet Explorer 4.0 have increased the number of events and the number of tags that can use the events. New events include ondblclick, onkeyup, onkeydown, and onmousemove.*

? Is it possible to use JavaScript to secure a section of my site?

JavaScript source code is always viewable through the Web browser, so securing pages through JavaScript is not a very effective solution. With enough time, any reasonable programmer can sort through your code and figure out how to bypass your security. For truly effective security, you need to secure your documents on the server. However, a few solutions have made great strides toward effectively hiding JavaScript from the end user. Jmyth, JAMMER, JavaScript Scrambler V1.0, and PageParser all attempt to hide JavaScript from the user. You can find the software a these addresses:

- **Jmyth:** http://www.geocities.com/SiliconValley/Vista/5233/jmyth.htm
- **Jammer:** http://www.geocities.com/SiliconValley/4274/jammer.htm
- **JavaScript Scrambler:** http://members.tripod.com/~tier/
- **Page Parser:** http://www.ozemail.com.au/~jbp/impressions/pageparser.html

? Can I use my browser URL line as a JavaScript debugger?

Any line of JavaScript can be run by itself in the URL line of a window with Netscape Navigator 2.0 or later or Internet Explorer 4.0 or later. To do this, simply type **javascript:** followed by your line of JavaScript code, as in this example:

```
Javascript:alert('Happy holidays!')
```

? Is it possible to share JavaScript between completely separate pages in a site without using frames?

Netscape allows JavaScript to be stored in an external text file with the extension .js. This method allows different pages to share the same JavaScript without frames being necessary. Unfortunately, Microsoft Internet Explorer does not support this method, so only Netscape can make use of shared JavaScript .js files. To use a shared JavaScript file in Netscape, use the following syntax on your Web page:

```
<SCRIPT SRC="MyJavaScript.JS">
This text is alternative text for non-supporting browsers
</SCRIPT>
```

For Netscape to properly include externally stored JavaScript, the .js file extension should be mapped to the MIME-type application/x-javascript on the Web server.

If you want to include this functionality with Microsoft Internet Explorer as well, try using server-side includes. You can achieve similar functionality by placing the JavaScript listed above into a MyJavaScript.txt file and placing the SSI tag, like so:

```
<!--#include virtual="/template/MenuBar.html"-->
```

Make sure that the Web server supports SSI tags and that the directory that the HTML is sitting in is set correctly for SSI.

Microsoft Internet Explorer 4.0 has introduced Scriptlets that offer similar functionality to externally stored JavaScript files. Scriptlets are imported through the <OBJECT> tag. Scriptlets expose not only their internal scripts, but may also take over a piece of on-screen real estate much like Java applets do. Following is a sample <OBJECT> tag for an Internet Explorer 4.0 Scriptlet:

```
<OBJECT WIDTH="100" HEIGHT="50" TYPE="text/x-scriptlet
"DATA="myscriptlet.htm">
</OBJECT>
```

For more on Scriptlets, visit http://www.microsoft.com/scripting/docs/scriptlets/scriptlets.htm.

JAVASCRIPT PROGRAMMING EXAMPLES

? **How can I create a JavaScript for one particular version of JavaScript or one particular browser?**

There are a number of different ways to tailor a segment of JavaScript code or an entire script specifically for one version of the language or one particular browser. Client-side, the two most common methods of doing this are to use variations of the <SCRIPT> tag or to use browser detection within your script with the navigator.appName or navigator.userAgent properties.

Using the <SCRIPT> Tag for Browser/Version Detection

To differentiate between JavaScript versions (Netscape Navigator 2.0 and Microsoft Internet Explorer 3.0, which use JavaScript 1.0; Navigator 3.0 and Internet Explorer 4.0, which use version 1.1; and Navigator 4.0, which uses version 1.2), you can specify the version number in the <SCRIPT> tag. JavaScript-enabled browsers recognize their own version of JavaScript and previous versions as specified in the <SCRIPT> tag. The following script will only be recognized by Netscape Navigator 3.0 and later and Internet Explorer 4.0 and later:

```
<SCRIPT LANGUAGE="JavaScript1.1">
document.write("Hello, world")
</SCRIPT>
```

Another method of browser detection in the <SCRIPT> tag is to use VBScript. Because Netscape Navigator does not interpret VBScript, the <SCRIPT LANGUAGE="VBScript"> tag is an easy way to create content only for Internet Explorer 3.0 and later. To create one client-side script for Navigator 2.0 and later browsers and one for Internet Explorer 3.0 and later browsers, use the following syntax:

```
<SCRIPT LANGUAGE="JavaScript">
<!--
if (navigator.appName == "Netscape")
{
document.write("Hello, Netscape");
}
//-->
</SCRIPT>
<SCRIPT LANGUAGE="VBScript">
<!--
document.write("Hello, Microsoft")
rem -->
</SCRIPT>
```

Note: *Remember that you need to script in VBScript within the <SCRIPT LANGUAGE="VBScript"> and </SCRIPT> tags.*

Browser Detection Within the Script Itself

To use different JavaScript for specific browsers and browser versions, you may use a combination of navigator.appName to distinguish between Microsoft Internet Explorer and Netscape Navigator, and the first character parsed from navigator.appVersion for a specific browser version number. The following script distinguishes between Internet Explorer 4.0 and Netscape 3.0 and other earlier JavaScript-compatible versions of the same browsers:

```
<SCRIPT LANGUAGE="JavaScript">
<!--
browserName = navigator.appName;
browserVer = navigator.appVersion;
/*Following grabs the first number to get the browser version*/
browserVer = browserVer.substring(0,1);
/*Following fixes an occasional bug in Netscape 2.0 for OS2*/
if (browserVer == '.') browserVer = 2;

if (browserName == "Netscape" && browserVer >= 3 || browserVer > 3)
{
/*insert JavaScript here for Netscape 3.0 and higher and Internet
Explorer 4.0 and higher here*/
}
else
{
/*insert JavaScript for other JavaScript-capable browser versions
here*/
}
//-->
</SCRIPT
```

? I am trying to write a few lines of HTML to the screen with JavaScript. For browsers without JavaScript, I would like an alternative to show up. How can I do this so it will work with all browsers?

One would think that adding alternative text for non-JavaScript browsers would be a relatively simple problem to solve. Unfortunately, Netscape 2.0 doesn't support the <NOSCRIPT> tag, so solving the problem is trickier than one might think. There are three ways of solving the problem. Each solution has it drawbacks, but tricking the browser with LANGUAGE="NotALanguage" has the most widespread browser support.

Using the <NOSCRIPT> Tag by Itself

The code below writes the current date to the screen using JavaScript. The code uses the <NOSCRIPT> tag to offer an alternative message for those without JavaScript or with JavaScript turned off. Netscape 2.0 users will see both the date and the alternative message. Netscape 3.0 and Communicator users as well as Microsoft Internet Explorer 3.0 and later users with default preference settings see only the JavaScript text. If these users have turned JavaScript off in their browsers, they see the alternative message.

```
<SCRIPT LANGUAGE="JavaScript">
<!--
var today = new Date();
mymonth = today.getMonth() + 1; mydate = today.getDate();
document.writeln('Today is: ' + mydate + ' / ' + mymonth)
//-->
</SCRIPT>
<NOSCRIPT>
You have Netscape 2.0 or a browser that does not support JavaScript.
</NOSCRIPT>
```

Using the <NOSCRIPT> Tag with Browser Detection

By using browser detection along with the <NOSCRIPT> tag, Netscape Navigator 2.0 users can be spared from having to see two sets of text. The example below writes the date on a Web page using JavaScript for all browsers except Netscape Navigator 2.0. Navigator 2.0, all non-JavaScript-enabled browsers, and those with JavaScript turned off will only see the alternative text that sits between the <NOSCRIPT> and </NOSCRIPT> tags.

```
<SCRIPT LANGUAGE="JavaScript">
<!--
browserVer = navigator.appVersion;
/*Following grabs the first number to get the browser version*/
```

```
browserVer   =   browserVer.substring(0,1);
/*Following  fixes  an  occasional  bug  in  Netscape  2.0  for  OS2*/
if  (browserVer  ==  '.')  browserVer  =  2;

if  (browserVer  >=  3)
{
var  today  =  new  Date();
mymonth  =  today.getMonth()  +  1;  mydate  =  today.getDate();
document.writeln('Today  is:  '  +  mydate  +  '  /  '  +  mymonth)
}
//-->
</SCRIPT>
<NOSCRIPT>
You  have  Netscape  2.0  or  a  browser  that  does  not  support
JavaScript.
</NOSCRIPT>
```

Tricking the Browser with <SCRIPT LANGUAGE="NotALanguage">

A third method of adding alternative text for non-JavaScript browsers is to not use browser detection at all but rather use <SCRIPT LANGUAGE="NotALanguage"><NOSCRIPT> at the beginning of your non-JavaScript alternative and </SCRIPT></NOSCRIPT> at the end. Netscape Navigator 2.0 ignores the <NOSCRIPT> tags but recognizes <SCRIPTLANGUAGE="NotALanguage"> as a scripting language that it doesn't know, and it ignores all content until the tag is closed with </SCRIPT>. Other JavaScript-enabled browsers recognize the <NOSCRIPT> tags and ignore everything between them. Microsoft Internet Explorer gives errors if the <NOSCRIPT> tags are not present, because it doesn't like the <SCRIPT LANGUAGE="NotALanguage"> tag. Following is code that uses this method to print the date for JavaScript-enabled browsers, and an alternative for all others. This solution will print the date to the screen for all JavaScript-enabled browsers and will not print two messages for Netscape Navigator 2.0 users. The only drawback of this method is that those who have manually disabled JavaScript will see neither the date nor the alternative text.

```
<SCRIPT LANGUAGE="JavaScript">
<!--
var today = new Date();
```

```
mymonth = today.getMonth() + 1; mydate = today.getDate();
document.writeln('Today is: ' + mydate + ' / ' + mymonth)
//-->
</SCRIPT>
<NOSCRIPT>
<SCRIPT    LANGUAGE="NotALanguage">
If I could tell you the date I would
</SCRIPT>
</NOSCRIPT>
```

? I would like to include a drop-down menu that allows page navigation. How can I do this?

The following code allows users to navigate immediately to a page by means of a drop-down menu. Netscape 2.0 has some problems with the onChangeevent being triggered, so a button is included as well. If you find that the button is not needed for any of your target platforms, simply delete the line beginning <INPUT TYPE="button".

```
<SCRIPT LANGUAGE="JavaScript">
<!--
function navto(){
var navselectitem = document.navselect.navlist.selectedIndex;
if (document.navselect.navlist.options[navselectitem].value != "stay")
location =document.navselect.navlist.options[document.
          navselect.navlist.
selectedIndex].value;

}
//-->
</SCRIPT>
<BR>
<FORM NAME="navselect">
<SELECT NAME="navlist" onChange="navto()">
<OPTION VALUE="stay">Choose a destination to link to...
<OPTION VALUE="http://www.americanexpress.com/travel/
">American ExpressTravel
<OPTION VALUE="http://www.wave.ca">Roger&#39;s Wave
<OPTION VALUE="http://www.cmpnet.com">CMP Net
<OPTION VALUE="http://www.planetdirect.com">Planet Direct
</SELECT>
<INPUT TYPE="button" VALUE="Go" onclick="navto()">
</FORM>
```

If you want the drop-down menu to be invisible to non-JavaScript-compliant browsers, use JavaScript to write the HTML. To do this, insert the usual<SCRIPT> tags around the HTML that makes up the drop-down form element. Next, place document.writeln(' at the beginning of all of the HTML lines beginning with <FORM> line and ') at the end of each line. Do this for every line until </FORM>, as in this example:

```
<SCRIPT LANGUAGE="JavaScript">
<!--
document.writeln('<FORM NAME="navselect">')
document.writeln('<SELECT NAME="navlist" onChange="navto()">')
document.writeln('<OPTION VALUE="stay">Choose a destination
to linkto...')
/*Add the rest of your form options here*/
//-->
</SCRIPT>
```

? I have seen gray JavaScript pop-up windows that allow the user to enter text. How is this done?

The alert method of popping up windows is the most popular way of bringing up quick messages and warnings without linking to a new HTML page. However, this method does not allow text-entry fields to be placed in the pop-up window. The prompt method, however, provides text-entry fields quite easily. The following code sets the variable password to the user input in the gray pop-up window shown in Figure 13-2:

```
<SCRIPT LANGUAGE="JavaScript">
<!--
var password = prompt("Enter your password","");
//-->
</SCRIPT>
```

Although it doesn't allow for a text entry field, another little-used alternative to the prompt method is the confirm method. With confirm, JavaScript supports another pop-up window method besides alert and prompt. The confirm method displays a gray box just like alert, only a question mark appears instead of an explanation point, such as the pop-up

Explorer User Prompt

JavaScript Prompt:

Enter your password

OK

Cancel

Figure 13-2 An example of the prompt method.

window shown in Figure 13-3. Also, the confirm method allows users to select either OK or Cancel. Following is JavaScript code that will result in a confirm pop-up window.

```
<SCRIPT LANGUAGE="JavaScript">
<!--
var learnmore = confirm("Would you like to learn more?");
//-->
</SCRIPT>
```

? Is there an easy way to add text to the status bar at the bottom of the screen when a mouse-pointer travels over a link on a page?

Customizing text in the status bar is an example of JavaScript functionality that works in all JavaScript-compatible browsers. To add text to the status bar, simply add an onMouseOver attribute to your <A> hyperlink tag and set the window.status property with it. If you want the message to disappear when the mouse leaves the area, you need to add an onMouseOut attribute to the <A> tag and reset window.status to blank. Following is code that displays the text "Look down at the status bar" when the mouse

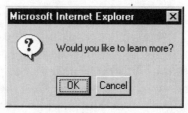

Figure 13-3 An example of a confirm pop-up window.

passes over the graphic. The message disappears when the mouse is no longer over the graphic.

```
<A HREF="home.html"
   onMouseOver="window.status='Look down in the status bar';return
   true"
   onMouseOut="window.status='';return true">
<IMG SRC="banner.gif" BORDER="0" WIDTH="100" HEIGHT="100">
</A>
```

? How do I add a last modified date to my pages with JavaScript?

To add a last modified date to a document, insert the following script between the <BODY> and </BODY> section of your HTML document:

```
<SCRIPT LANGUAGE="JavaScript">
<!--
   document.write("This document was last modified "
+document.lastModified);
// -->
</SCRIPT>
```

? How do I update two frames with one mouse-click?

To update more than one frame with one mouse-click, using something beyond just straight HTML is necessary. Using plug-ins, Java, and ActiveX controls is possible, but by far the easiest way to fully control frames is to use JavaScript.

To reference frames in JavaScript, you can reference the frame's array number:

```
parent.frames[0].location='http://www.excite.com';
```

or you can reference the frame's name:

```
parent.FirstFrame.location='http://www.excite.com';
```

When updating two frames from one click event in JavaScript, you may choose either of these methods:

● Update both frames from the same frame by using two JavaScript location lines.

● Simply use a traditional hyperlink that targets a new frame and place a JavaScript script in the new frame that updates a third frame.

Following is an example of the former solution that defines two HTML pages. Open the first HTML page in your browser to check it:

```
<HTML>
<HEAD><TITLE>Master Frameset</TITLE></HEAD>

<FRAMESET ROWS="100%" COLS="33%,33%,*">
    <FRAME NAME="FirstFrame" SRC="http://www.yahoo.com"
SCROLLING="AUTO"MARGINHEIGHT=1 MARGINWIDTH=1>
    <FRAME NAME="SecondFrame"
SRC="http://www.infoseek.com"SCROLLING="AUTO">
    <FRAME NAME="ThirdFrame" SRC="update.htm" SCROLLING="AUTO">
</FRAMESET>

<BODY>Your browser does not support frames</BODY>
</HTML>

<HTML>
<HEAD><TITLE>update.htm</TITLE></HEAD>

<SCRIPT LANGUAGE="JavaScript">
<!--
function update()
{
parent.FirstFrame.location='http://www.excite.com';
parent.SecondFrame.location='http://www.lycos.com';
}
//-->
</SCRIPT>

<BODY>
<A HREF="javascript:update();">Change Search Engines</A>
</BODY></HTML>
```

The previous update.htm uses a hyperlink to trigger one JavaScript script, which then updates two frames, shown in Figure 13-4.

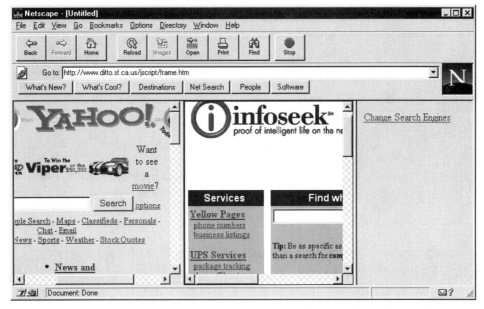

Figure 13-4   HTML to set up a three–column, frames-based page that contains two search engines and update.htm.

✱   ***Note:***   *In case you are wondering whether you can target another window with the <META http-equiv="Refresh"> tag, wonder no more. The <META> tag does not support this functionality.*

❓ How can I change the size or attributes of the current browser window?

You cannot change the size or attributes—for example, you can't remove the buttons or URL line—of the current window by using standard, unsigned JavaScript. You can influence window artifacts, scrollbars, buttons, and so on when opening a new window. The elements that can be influenced in opening a new browser window include

● Directories (whether the directory bar is visible)

● Height (the height of the window)

● Location (whether the URL line is visible or not)

- Resizability (whether the window can be resized or is of fixed dimensions)
- Scrollbars (whether scroll bars are present, not present, or automatic if they are needed)
- Status (whether the status bar is visible)
- Toolbar (whether the toolbar is visible)
- Width (the width of the window)

The following code opens a new window 100×100 pixels in size with no scrollbars, browser buttons, or menus:

```
<SCRIPT LANGUAGE="JavaScript">
<!--
floatingwindow = window.open("menu.html","floater",
"toolbar=no,location=no,directories=no,status=no,menubar=no,
scrollbars=no,resizable=no,width=100,height=100");
// -->
</SCRIPT>
```

? Is it possible to preload pages and images using JavaScript?

It is possible to preload images using JavaScript. The HTML of Web pages can also be preloaded, but less elegantly, using JavaScript or standard HTML. JavaScript techniques for preloading images are particularly useful for menu graphics and title graphics.

A graphic file named GraphicFile.gif can be preloaded with the following JavaScript:

```
<SCRIPT LANGUAGE="JavaScript">
<!--
MyImage = new Image;
MyImage.src="GraphicFile.gif";
//-->
</SCRIPT>
```

Another method of preloading graphics involves simply including a 1×1 pixel version of the image in an unobtrusive area of the page. This method is explained in Chapter 10.

Preloading Web pages in a way that is compatible with all JavaScript-capable browsers requires a trick. The trick that most programmers use involves opening a 1×1 pixel floating window that contains the HTML file and returns the focus back to the main browser window. An easier method for caching pages is to add a 1-pixel-high frame to your page and fill it with the HTML that you want to preload. If the background color matches and you use borderless frames, users will probably not notice the preloaded frame.

? How do I include double quotation marks in JavaScript when the script is defined within an <A> tag?

When JavaScript sits within an <A> tag , enclosing it with double quotes is often necessary and always a good style:

```
<A HREF="JavaScript:alert()"> Click Here</A>
```

Unfortunately, if you change the alert to alert("Hello"), the first set of double quotes will signify the end of the HREF attribute and close it. An error will result when the text is clicked. To add quotes within the alert, JavaScript allows single quotes to function the same as double quotes when they are enclosed within double quotes. For example, the following syntax will work:

```
<A HREF="JavaScript:alert('Hello')"> Click Here</A>
```

For JavaScript that is not within <A> tags, you may choose double quotes or single quotes to enclose text. If your text includes a few double quotes, then you should enclose the text in single quotes. If your text includes apostrophes, enclose the text within double quotes. If your text includes both single and double quotes, you may escape the punctuation that matches the punctuation in which it is wrapped with a backslash character (/). For example, to print

Don't say anything!
Do not say, "anything."
Don't say, "anything"

use the following JavaScript:

```
<PRE>
<SCRIPT LANGUAGE="JavaScript1.1">
<!--
document.writeln("Don't say anything!")
document.writeln('Do not say, "anything."')
document.writeln("Don't say, \"anything.\"")
    //-->
</SCRIPT>
</PRE>
```

? I am trying to get each site visitor's monitor height, width, color depth, and IP address without using a CGI. Is it possible to do this by calling Java methods from JavaScript?

Accessing Java methods through Live Connect in Netscape Navigator 3.0 and later is possible. Accessing monitor height, width, and resolution is not easy with JavaScript, but it can be done. Live Connect requires both Java and JavaScript to be active in the browser. As for detecting a user's IP address, I have found no way of reliably gathering it without a server-side script being involved in the process or a custom Java applet passing the variable to JavaScript.

Microsoft Internet Explorer, however, is a different story. There is no simple way to gain access to Java methods from JScript. Internet Explorer 3.0 has an undocumented explorer object that allows access to the width and height of the Internet Explorer window through explorer.height and explorer.width, but these objects were removed with the Internet Explorer 3.02 upgrade and give an error message (see:http://www.microsoft.com/kb/articles/q166/3/67.htm). Internet Explorer 4.0 has more properties and includes a window.visual property. Screen height, width, and color depth can be accessed with window.visual.hres, window.visual.vres, and window.visual.colorDepth respectively, but the visitor's IP address is still unavailable through JScript or VBScript.

The following code prints out screen width, height, and monitor resolution if they are available on a Netscape

Navigator browser (this code does not work on Internet Explorer):

```
<HTML>
<HEAD><TITLE>Using Netscape Live Connect</TITLE></HEAD>
<BODY>
<SCRIPT LANGUAGE="JavaScript">
<!--
BrowserVersion = parseInt(navigator.appVersion);
if (navigator.appName == "Netscape" && BrowserVersion >=3)
{
if (navigator.javaEnabled())
{
var toolkit = java.awt.Toolkit.getDefaultToolkit();
var MonitorSize = toolkit.getScreenSize();
var MonitorDPI = toolkit.getScreenResolution();
var PixelDepth = toolkit.getColorModel();
var MonitorColors = PixelDepth.getPixelSize();
document.writeln('Monitor Width: ' + MonitorSize.width + '<BR>');
document.writeln('Monitor Height: ' + MonitorSize.height + '<BR>');
document.writeln('Monitor Resolution: ' + MonitorDPI + 'dpi<BR>');
document.writeln('Color Depth: ' + MonitorColors + '<BR>');
}
}
if (navigator.appName == "Netscape" && BrowserVersion < 3)
{document.writeln('Netscape Navigator 2.0 and earlier does
not support thisfunctionality');}
// -->
</SCRIPT>
</BODY>
</HTML>
```

DEBUGGING JAVASCRIPT

? **How can I narrow down where my JavaScript errors are in my script?**

Different browsers give different error messages, and the messages are not always helpful in narrowing down a problem. It helps to understand the different categories of errors that result from bugs in code or weaknesses in the run-time engine itself:

- **Load-time errors** occur as a page is loading. Your browser's JavaScript interpreter scans the code for language syntax problems and immediately reports the errors it finds.

- **File transfer errors** are usually announced as load-time errors and occur when HTML files are transferred as binary to a different operating system. Different operating systems use different characters or sets of invisible characters for line returns. If the server does not recognize the line returns that are being used, it may send the document without any line returns at all. If a JavaScript script works locally but not from the server, then it is probably a file-transfer error. To detect this problem, view the source of the current document from your browser and check to see if the script contains line returns in the correct places. To fix the problem, transfer your text files to the server as ASCII files (an option found in almost all FTP applications). You may also have the option of changing the way your script editor stores line returns. Both BBEdit for the Macintosh and HomeSite for the PC include this feature.

- **Run-time errors** are caught while a script is actually running. Just because a script has the correct syntax doesn't mean the interpreter can handle the situations that the script creates for it.

- **Logic errors** are not caught by the JavaScript interpreter but result in incorrect output. A common mistake is converting numbers with decimal places to integers, a format that does not store decimal places.

? If browsers scan scripts for errors or incompatibilities at load time, how can you avoid errors with incompatible JavaScript that have been hidden with browser-detection "if" statements?

Load-time checking does not result in errors as long as scripts use proper syntax. If incompatible functions are correctly stored in browser-detection "if" statements, then the functions are safe from incompatibility errors. If the browser detection fails, however, the result is a run-time error. The following code contains Netscape 4.0-specific code, but because it is within browser detection, the code does not cause errors on other browsers:

```
<LAYER NAME="tart" LEFT="50" TOP="50">
This text will be positioned by Netscape 4.0 only through JavaScript
</LAYER>
<SCRIPT LANGUAGE="JavaScript">
<!--
browserName = navigator.appName;
browserVer = navigator.appVersion;
/*Following grabs the first number to get the browser version*/
browserVer = browserVer.substring(0,1);
/*Following fixes an occasional bug in Netscape 2.0 for OS2*/
if (browserVer == '.') browserVer = 2;

if (browserName == "Netscape" && browserVer >= 4)
{
document.tart.left = 200;
document.tart.top = 200;
}
//-->
</SCRIPT>
```

❓ I am having trouble getting cookies to work using JavaScript with Microsoft Internet Explorer 3.0. Are there any incompatibilities?

Unfortunately, cookies do not work with JavaScript on Microsoft Internet Explorer 3.0 when files are being viewed locally. Because cookies associate themselves with a domain, and because you are not using a domain when you view files locally, cookies will not work. If you upload your pages to a Web server and access them through HTTP, you shouldn't have any problems with Internet Explorer and cookies.

❓ Why won't my floating menu window and ad banners stay on top of the other windows in Internet Explorer the way they do in Netscape?

The Window.focus() method is necessary to keep one window on top of others. Because window.focus does not work with Microsoft Internet Explorer 3.0, floating windows move to the back when other browser windows are clicked and will stay there until they are reselected.

? I am using a JavaScript mouse-over on my site and it works fine under Microsoft Internet Explorer 4.0 and Netscape Navigator 4.0, but Navigator 3.0 is not making the mouse-overstate disappear. How can I fix this?

Netscape Navigator 3.0 uses a different technique for dynamically changing images. After both mouse-over and mouse-out versions are cached, the browser treats them like flash cards, with one in the front and one behind. If the graphic in the front has transparency, the graphic behind is visible.

The work-around for this problem is to simply make your graphics opaque in order for them to work with Netscape Navigator 3.0.

? My browser is printing text from my JavaScript script to the screen even though the JavaScript is correctly formatted. What is happening?

Netscape has a problem writing HTML with JavaScript that sits within an HTML table. The symptom is almost always strange characters appearing on the screen in the middle of the HTML document. For example, the following JavaScript will frequently fail:

```
<TABLE><TR><TD>
<SCRIPT LANGUAGE="JavaScript">
<!--
document.write("This is a test");
//-->
</SCRIPT>
</TD></TR></TABLE>
```

The work-around for this problem is to write all of the HTML table tags from JavaScript. Keep in mind that you need to print the HTML for all tables that surround the HTML that is generated from JavaScript with document.write tags. The following HTML works in Netscape browsers:

```
<SCRIPT LANGUAGE="JavaScript">
<!--
document.write("<TABLE><TR><TD>");
document.write("This is a test");
document.write("</TD></TR></TABLE>");
//-->
</SCRIPT>
```

Chapter 14

Java and Shockwave

Answer Topics!

Java and Shockwave @ a Glance

You can use Java and Macromedia's Director to add significant client-side functionality to Web sites. The technologies are implemented differently, but the functionality that they make available through the Web browser is very similar. Java uses applets to embed content in Web pages; Director uses the Shockwave file format and, with Director 6.0, also exports Java byte-code.

Both technologies support the ability to add low bandwidth and client-side functionality to a Web page, both of which normally are available only through standalone executables. Functionality that requires a connection to the server, the inclusion of externally stored content, and high levels of interactivity are all available, without any server programming, with a visual element that sits directly within the Web browser window.

The purpose of this chapter is not just to compare the two technologies, but to explain their possibilities and limitations. Shockwave Flash, Authorware Shockwave, Director Shockwave and Java are all covered in this chapter:

Java Basics introduces Java language terminology and the different Java implementations. This section also covers the browsers that support Java.

Shockwave discusses Macromedia's Shockwave format, how to implement and troubleshoot Shockwave on your site, and how to weigh the pros and cons of using Shockwave and Java.

Developing with Java and Using Java discusses issues such as speeding up applet downloads, protecting your code, and maximizing your use of the <APPLET> tag parameters.

Troubleshooting Java covers the most common questions and problems that surround building and including Java applets on a Web site.

JAVA BASICS

? **Is Java a language or a type of object that can be placed on a Web page?**

The terms that apply to Java can be confusing and are frequently used incorrectly. Java, which was invented by Sun Microsystems, is an object-oriented programming language. Java is largely based on C++ and is intended to be a simple yet powerful language for creating cross-platform applications.

The Java language can be used to program a wide variety of application types, including Web servers, CGIs, servlets (persistent server-side applications similar to Fast-CGI), and Web page applets. Someone who claims to have Java on his or her Web page more likely has an applet, written in Java, that is embedded within the Web page. Applets are just one of the many types of Java implementations. However, because Java applets are the most visible, they are frequently referred to as simply "Java."

? **Do I have to pay royalties when I create Java applets or include them in my Web pages?**

Java is an open specification and is freely available from Sun Microsystems. Using the language costs nothing and Sun has published a royalty-free license for developers. In fact, the Java Developers Kit is freely available from http://www.sun.com/java/.

? **What is the difference between Java and Java byte-code?**

When the Java language is used to write an application or applet, the source code is generally stored as a text file with the file extension .java. In order to run Java, the code must be byte-compiled. Byte-compiled Java always has the .class extension. Because compiled Java is cross–platform, it is compiled into byte-code instead of lower-level machine code. This byte-code is not readable to a person, but is much easier for a computer to read than Java source code. For a Java application to run, the source code is not needed. As a result, we only see byte-compiled applets on the Web.

For Java applications to run, a Java virtual machine must be installed. The virtual machine is similar to the projector that is used to run Macromedia Director applications. It installs with the latest Netscape and Microsoft Web browsers as well as with the majority of Java development environments. Some operating systems, such as IBM's OS2 Warp, have begun shipping with a built-in Java virtual machine.

When Java applications run, the Java byte-code is interpreted by the Java virtual machine and executed. Since Java virtual machines only need Java byte-code to run an application, many programming languages can be translated to Java byte-code and executed with the virtual machine. The virtual machine only reads Java byte-code and cannot distinguish between Java byte-code compiled from different languages. Since Java byte-code compilers have been written for a number of different languages, a Java application could conceivably be written in the programming language TCL/TK, Python, or even Scheme and be executed as if it were written in Java.

? What are the functionality limitations of using Java within a browser window?

For security reasons, Java applets operate in Web browsers in what is known as a *sandbox*. The sandbox prevents malicious applets from propagating viruses, deleting hard drives, and so on. The main limitations of the Java sandbox are as follows:

- Read privileges are not allowed for any files on the browser's computer.
- Creating or modifying files on the browser's computer in any way is not allowed.
- Reading directories is not allowed on the browser's computer.
- Network connections to any computer other than the original host are not allowed.
- Applications on the browser's computer cannot be launched.

> ✱ *Note:* *In Netscape, there are some differences in terms of sandbox permissions between Java applets run locally and Java applets run from a Web server. Java applets run locally have a few more permissions in order to make development easier.*

❓ What browsers and platforms support Java applets?

Netscape Navigator 2.0 was the first popular browser to offer built-in Java support. Unfortunately, the original release of Navigator 2.0 for the Macintosh did not support Java. Microsoft Internet Explorer 2.5 for the Macintosh and Internet Explorer 3.0 for the PC were the first Microsoft browsers to support Java natively.

A strong degree of Java 1.1 support is claimed by Microsoft for Internet Explorer 4.0, but a few 1.1 features are notably missing from the browser. Netscape 4.0 supports many Java 1.1 features, but lacks a good number of the new functions. Netscape has announced full support for Java 1.1 in future browser releases.

SHOCKWAVE

❓ Should I use Java or Shockwave on my site?

The battle between Shockwave and Java for client-side interactivity is a big one and has been raging for several years. The battle may resolve itself with the Director 6 Java Export Xtra that adds Save-As Java functionality to Director. But the dispute runs deeper than merely what run-time engine and byte-code format is used.

Essentially, the differences between Java and Shockwave are rooted in the battle between designers and programmers. Designers prefer Shockwave for its easy development environment, strong built-in color palette, audio support, and the fact that turning it into a stand-alone application is easy. Programmers lean toward Java's flexible class libraries, object-oriented programming paradigm, and the fact that they do not have to install any plug-ins to make it run on the latest browsers.

Before you select a technology, ask the following questions:

- **Do your site visitors have the Shockwave plug-in or mind downloading it?** Shockwave requires a plug-in or ActiveX control for each of the different Shockwave technologies (Director, Flash, and FreeHand). Each Shockwave player may be installed separately or be installed at once in an installation that requires several megabytes. Java is built into most major browsers and requires no special installations.

- **Do your graphics and sounds need to be reproduced accurately or streamed from a server?** Director, Authorware, and Flash Shockwave all support built-in streaming. Director's streaming of Shockwave Audio offers high-quality sound and requires no special configuration. Java only supports one, poorly compressed audio file format.

- **Are you or your developers strong programmers?** Programming in Director, Flash, and Authorware is significantly easier than programming with nonvisual Java code editors.

- **Can you afford development software?** Many Java compilers and editors are freely available on the Web. Macromedia's products must be purchased to create Shockwave applications.

- **Do you need to support Netscape Navigator 2.0?** On Netscape Navigator 2.0 browsers that support Java, Java runs slowly and is often less reliable than Shockwave.

- **Is your desired functionality already available as shareware?** Pre-built applets and Shockwave movies are available from a number of different repositories and may already be available to offer the functionality that you desire. Java shareware is more common and more configurable because it predominantly uses externally defined parameters. Two popular Java shareware repositories are Gamelan at http://www.gamelan.com and the Java Boutique at http://javaboutique.internet.com.

? How do I make a Shockwave movie and put it on my site?

Shockwave comes in many types. First, you need to have the Macromedia application associated with the Shockwave movie that you want to create. For Director Shockwave, you need a copy of Macromedia Director 4.0 or later. For Shockwave Flash, you need Macromedia Flash. For Shockwave FreeHand, Xres, and Authorware, you similarly need a version of FreeHand, Xres, or Authorware that supports Shockwave. So long as the application is not more than a year or two old, odds are it supports Shockwave.

Following are steps that explain how to create a Shockwave movie and put it on your site:

1. Create a movie or file with a page or stage size that matches the dimensions of the Shockwave movie you want to make. If you are using Director or Authorware, make sure that your movie does not contain any features that are not supported in the browser environment, such as file input and output to the local hard drive.

2. When your file is complete, select Export As from the File menu of your Macromedia application and select Shockwave as the export type. If you are embedding any external content, such as QuickTime movies, make sure that they are in a cross-platform format. (QuickTime movies made on a Macintosh should be flattened. See Chapter 9.)

3. Place your newly generated Shockwave files in a directory on your Web server that is accessible remotely through a Web browser. Make sure that the directory that the Shockwave files are sitting in is set to be a read-only directory in your Web server software.

4. Add MIME types to the Web server for all of Shockwave content that you want to use. Table 14-1 lists Shockwave MIME types.

5. Add an <EMBED> tag to the HTML that you want the Shockwave movie to run in. Specify WIDTH, HEIGHT, and BGCOLOR attributes (BGCOLOR specifies the background color of the movie while it is loading). Following is an example of an <EMBED> tag:

```
<EMBED SRC="MyMovie.swf" HEIGHT=290 WIDTH=510 SCALE="showall"
QUALITY="high" PLAY="true" LOOP="false">
```

 Tip: *If you want to test your movie from a Web server that does not have MIME types set, consider the fact that Netscape 3.x browsers allow MIME type to be specified within the <EMBED> tag. Because other browsers do not support the specifying of URLs within the <EMBED> tag, the practice is only recommended for temporary testing. Following is an example of an <EMBED> tag with a TYPE attribute set to specify the files MIME type for Netscape browsers:*

```
<EMBED SRC="MyMovie.spl" type="application/futuresplash"
WIDTH="100%" HEIGHT="100%">
```

Director Shockwave	File Extension
application/x-director	dir
application/x-director	dcr
application/x-director	dxr
Authorware	**File Extension**
application/x-authorware-map	aam
application/x-authorware-seg	aas
application/x-authorware-bin	aab
FreeHand MIME Type Mappings	**File Extension**
image/x-freehand	fh4
image/x-freehand	fh7
image/x-freehand	fh5
image/x-freehand	fhc
image/x-freehand	fh
Flash MIME Type Mappings	**File Extension**
application/futuresplash	spl
application/x-shockwave-flash	swf

Table 14-1   Shockwave MIME types

? **I would like to add a Get Shockwave button to my page and link it to an official download area. Where do I find out where and how to link?**

To include the Made with Macromedia logo on your Web site or the Get Shockwave button that links to a download area, you should first follow the Shockwave button and usage guidelines. Macromedia would like you to use a specific URL for each type of Shockwave download button. Also available for downloading are Web-ready versions of all the Macromedia graphics that are available for Web sites, such as those displayed on the Web site shown in Figure 14-1.

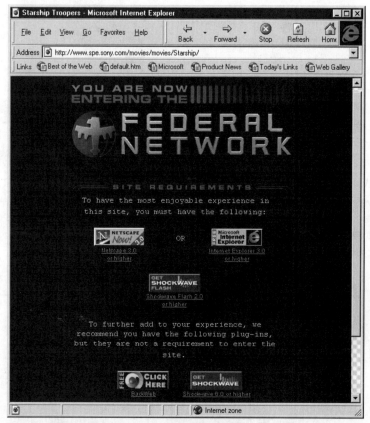

Figure 14-1 This page on the Sony Web site links to Macromedia's Web site, where users can download the latest Web browser plug-ins.

Macromedia's graphics, guidelines, and URLs are available from http://www.macromedia.com/support/programs/mwm/.

? Why is Shockwave still not working on my browser even though I downloaded the latest plug-in?

A common mistake people make with Shockwave is installing the wrong plug-in. Make sure that the Shockwave plug-in that you installed matches the Shockwave content type that you are viewing. If you try to view an Authorware Shockwave file with a Director Shockwave plug-in, for example, you cannot do it. An installation option is available from Macromedia's Web site that installs plug-ins for all of the Shockwave file types.

If you can view a matching Shockwave file type locally or from Macromedia's Web site, your plug-in probably isn't the problem. If MIME types are set incorrectly on the Web server, your browser may not know what to use to run the file.

DEVELOPING WITH AND USING JAVA

? What are Java servlets?

A common misunderstanding is that servlets are just CGI applications written in Java. This is not the case. Actually, *servlets* run—like FastCGI applications—persistently and are capable of handling any number of requests without quitting and having to restart a new process. For this reason, servlets are significantly faster than standard CGI applications.

That does not mean, however, that servlets are the answer for every server-side feature. Because servlets are a relatively new feature, the vast majority of Web servers do not support servlets without additional software. Fortunately, interest in servlets has been strong enough that extensions for making Java applications using the servlet API run are now available for most of the major Web servers. After your server is configured correctly, you shouldn't have any problems using servlets instead of CGI for your site's server programming.

For more information about Java servlets and software for running servlets on your Web server, visit these sites:

- http://www.livesoftware.com/
- http://jserv.javasoft.com/products/ java-server/servlets/index.html
- http://webreview.com/97/10/10/feature/index.html

Does Java support the display of animated and transparent GIFs?

Java 1.1 supports the display of animated GIFs. Earlier releases of Java support static GIFs and JPEGs only. By using animated GIFs instead of coding animations yourself, you can save significant development time.

Java does support the display of transparency in GIFs. Moreover, Java allows the background color that shows through the transparency to be specified.

I suspect that there is a bug in Java 1.1. Is this likely and where can I go to find out if there is a bug?

Java is still a relatively young language. As a result, bugs have yet to be fixed in the implementations of the language. Compilers, virtual machines, and in some cases even class libraries may be the source of your program's bugs. An official bug list is available at http://java.sun.com/products/ jdk/1.1/knownbugs/index.html.

How can I speed up my applet downloads?

Since many applets require numerous additional files such as graphics, sounds, and additional class files in order to run, you can package the files that your applet needs into one file. JAR, ZIP, and CAB formats all allow the multiple files that an applet needs to be wrapped together in a single compressed file. Using one of these three formats speeds up the delivery of applets because fewer requests are made to the server and the files are compressed.

The reason for three file formats has to do with differences between Microsoft Internet Explorer, Netscape Navigator browsers, and JDK 1.1. Unfortunately, the fact that there are three formats can make things a little confusing. Your best bet is to spend a few extra minutes and use all three formats for your applet.

The CAB Format

CAB, which is short for "cabinet," is only supported by Microsoft. Internet Explorer 3.0 and 4.0 both support the format. To use the CAB format, add a CABBASE parameter to your applet that points to the CAB file that you have created with the Microsoft Cabinet Software Developer's Kit. For more on cabinets, visit http://www.microsoft.com/workshop/prog/cab/.

The following <APPLET> tag and <PARAM> tag allow you to specify a cabinet file for browsers that support the cabinet format:

```
<APPLET NAME="BannerAd" CODE="Banner" WIDTH=200 HEIGHT=200>
<PARAM NAME="cabbase" VALUE="BannerAd.cab">
</APPLET>
```

The JAR Format

Java 1.1 introduced the JAR format (it stands for Java Archive). Internally, the JAR format is based on the ZIP format and is the only cross-platform format for bundling Java files. Netscape Navigator 4.0 and Microsoft Internet Explorer 4.0 both support the JAR format. Internet Explorer does not, however, support JAR files that have been digitally signed.

The following HTML example results in two JAR files being downloaded by browsers that support the JAR format. Other browsers will simply download the non-JAR file specified in the <APPLET> tag.

```
<APPLET NAME="BannerAd" CODE="Banner" WIDTH=200 HEIGHT=200>
<PARAM NAME="archives" VALUE="BannerAd.jar + SoundFiles.jar>
</APPLET>
```

The ZIP Format

The ZIP format is the same as the standard PC ZIP compression format that has been around for years. ZIP is the only file format supported by Netscape 3.0 for bundling Java files. To ZIP files, use a ZIP utility such as PKZip or

WinZip for the PC, or Stuff-It for the Macintosh. ZIP has been replaced by JAR in Netscape 4.0.

Adding the ARCHIVE parameter to the <APPLET> tag allows ZIP formatted files to be downloaded if the format is supported by the browser. Other browsers simply download the code specified with the NAME attribute. Following is a code sample that specifies a ZIP file for Netscape Navigator 3.0 browsers:

```
<APPLET NAME="BannerAd" CODE="Banner" WIDTH=200 HEIGHT=200
ARCHIVE="BannerAd.zip">
</APPLET>
```

All three formats can be supported using the ARCHIVE attribute and the ARCHIVES, and CABBASE parameters with the same applet. Following is code that includes all three formats:

```
<APPLET NAME="BannerAd" CODE="Banner" WIDTH=200 HEIGHT=200
ARCHIVE="BannerAd.zip">
<PARAM NAME="archives" VALUE="BannerAd.jar + SoundFiles.jar">
<PARAM NAME="cabbase" VALUE="BannerAd.cab">
</APPLET>
```

❓ What attributes are allowed in the <APPLET> tag?

The <APPLET> tag allows a number of useful attributes, many of which are rarely used. The following attributes may be used in the <APPLET> tag:

Attribute	Description
ALIGN	Similar to the ALIGN element for the <IMG> element. Allowed variables for this attribute include left, right, top, bottom, middle, absmiddle, absbottom, baseline, and texttop.
ALT	Allows alternative text for browsers that support the <APPLET> tag but do not display applets. This tag is rarely used because a scenario in which the ALT tag would be seen is so rare.
ARCHIVE	A Netscape-specific tag for compressed applets.
CODE	The applet name.
CODEBASE	The path to the location on the server of the Java applet. The applet that is referenced must be byte-compiled and therefore a .class file.

Attribute	Description
DOWNLOAD	Specifies the download order of any externally stored images in the applet.
HEIGHT	Number of pixels high that will be given to the applet for display.
HSPACE	Specifies the number of pixels that should cushion the applet to its left and right.
MAYSCRIPT	When included in the <APPLET> tag, the word MAYSCRIPT by itself indicates that the applet is accessible to JavaScript functions.
VSPACE	Specifies the number of pixels that should cushion the applet to its top and bottom.
WIDTH	Number of pixels wide that will be given to the applet for display.

I am using an applet that allows users to navigate to a different URL that I specify within a <PARAM> tag of an applet. Why doesn't my applet work when I specify a local path for navigation to another page?

A common misconception about Java applets is that they handle URLs specified in their external <PARAM> tags the same way Web browsers handle the variety of URLs that can be specified in the <A HREF> tag. Unfortunately, Java page navigation in its simplest form does not allow local page navigation. Most applets require a full path beginning with http://. Converting an applet so that it allows local navigation if the source is available is not difficult, but this is not always the case.

If source code is not available and local navigation is essential, use JavaScript to write the applet tag. Leverage JavaScript's ability to figure out the current URL or local file path and then write all the necessary <APPLET> and <PARAM> tags, adding in the current URL. Following is an example of JavaScript code with this functionality. The applet being defined is a drop-down menu applet that navigates the user to a different page when the mouse is released. The applet was written by Darryl Stoflet and is available from http://www.calweb.com/~dstoflet/.

```
<SCRIPT LANGUAGE="JavaScript">
<!--
/*the following clips the URL or file path to the current page*/
```

```
var ThisLocation = location.href.substring(0,
(location.href.lastIndexOf('/') + 1));
/*the following writes the <APPLET> and <PARAM> tags with the
correct domain path information.*/
document.writeln('<APPLET  CODE="link.class"  WIDTH=150
HEIGHT=33>');
document.writeln('<PARAM  NAME="target"  VALUE="mainframe">');
document.writeln('<PARAM  NAME="bgColor"  VALUE="#666666">');
document.writeln('<PARAM  NAME="number"  VALUE="3">');
document.writeln('<PARAM  NAME="link0"
VALUE="-------------------------------\\not  a  link">');
document.writeln('<PARAM  NAME="link1"  VALUE="Page1\\' +
ThisLocation + 'page1.htm">');
document.writeln('<PARAM  NAME="link2"  VALUE="Page2\\' +
ThisLocation + 'page2.htm">');
document.writeln('<PARAM  NAME="link3"  VALUE="Page3\\' +
ThisLocation + 'page3.htm">');
document.writeln('</APPLET>');
//-->
</SCRIPT>
```

TROUBLESHOOTING JAVA

? **I have been trying to use one particular GIF as my Web page's background and as part of a Java applet. Even though the colors are the same, I can't seem to make them match. What is going on?**

Different browsers use different Java virtual machines to render applets to the screen. Depending on which platform, browser, and version you are using and how color depth is set in your monitor, you may get varying results. The problem occurs with older browsers that use older Java virtual machines. For example, if you create a single-color GIF that uses the valid Netscape color cube RGB color 0,0,153 (00,00,99 for hexadecimal fans) and display the GIF in a Java applet running in a browser window, your results may be interesting. On a PC with the colors set to 8-bit (256 colors), my test results showed the wrong color in Netscape

Navigator 3.0 and dithering in Microsoft Internet Explorer. With the monitor's color depth set to 16-bit, both Netscape 2.0 and 3.0 dithered the graphic quite noticeably.

I have read that Java running in Navigator 3.0 actually uses a 125-color palette when displaying graphics. According to what I read, only the colors 0, 64, 128, 192, and 255 are valid for red, green, and blue. From personal experience I have found that Java applets in Netscape 3.0 dither these colors even worse than valid color cube colors (colors that only use 00, 51, 102, 153, 204, or 255 for RGB values).

So what can be done about graphics that display poorly through Java? Very little. Netscape Navigator 4.0 and Microsoft Internet Explorer 4.0 offer improved JIT (just-in-time) compilers that replace the older virtual machines and do a much better job of rendering graphics. One option for extremely simple pictures or basic blocks of solid color is to specify the RGB values within Java and draw the image manually. This technique does not help in most cases, but the older Java virtual machines are much more accurate when they display colors that have been specified within an applet. As a last resort, you can always just use simple colors that only involve combinations of 0 and 255 for RGB values.

? I have an applet that plays an audio file. Why do some audio files play while others do not?

Unfortunately, all versions of Java through version 1.1 use one very specific audio file format. For an audio file to play in Java, it must be in au format, be 8kHz mono, and use mu-law encoding. Unless all three sound requirements are met, the sound will not play in Java. A few programmers have claimed success with 16kHz mono au files, but sticking to the 8kHz specification is a safer bet.

A number of popular sound-editing utilities do not save with mu-law encoding. As a result, a correctly formatted au file that plays within Java may not play after it has been opened and saved in many sound-editing applications.

To find an application that saves correctly formatted sounds for Java, many developers have turned to older sound-editing utilities. For sound-editing utilities that work with the Java sound format specifications, try the following:

● Goldwave for Widows 95 (available from: http://www.shareware.com)

● SndConverter Pro for Macintosh (available from: http://www.shareware.com)

? Every platform uses different fonts. How can I be sure that the browsers my visitors use will display fonts as I want them to be displayed in Java?

Fonts can differ from platform to platform quite significantly. Even fonts with the same name display differently in different operating systems. Word spacing, letter spacing, letter height, and even letter shape can vary in appearance. You can't get exact font matches in a Java applet that is running on different operating systems without using graphics that already contain text instead of text from within Java.

However, Java 1.1 and Java 1.0 do offer a limited number of fonts that are certified to be either available or represented by a reasonable facsimile when they are displayed on the user's machine. Unfortunately, Java 1.1 actually reduced the list of certified fonts to Serif, Sans Serif, and Mono. Serif usually displays as some form of the Times family; Sans Serif as Helvetica, Arial, or a similar font; and Mono as a monospaced font such as Courier.

If you want to select a specific font for a particular system, a full list of fonts is available with the getFontList() function.

? I am trying to make the move from Perl to Java for server-side programming, but I have been surprised and frustrated by the fact that the Java language has no equivalent to regular expressions. How do I work around this problem?

No one defends regular expressions more rabidly than Perl and Unix veterans. Fortunately, Java programmers who want to use regular expressions can make use of two regular expression class libraries that are available for fast and efficient text parsing:

- http://www.pic-internet.or.jp/user/kojin/ender/java/packages_e.html#REGEXP
- http://www.win.net/~stevesoft/pat/

As to what a *regular expression* is, to give the short answer it is a language syntax for text pattern matching. For example, if you knew three letters of a word but not the correct order of the letters and you remembered seeing the word at the end of a line, one regular expression would most likely find it for you quickly. Regular expression support is built into languages such as Awk, Perl, Python, and Tcl. A large number of search engines, text editors, and even Unix implementations (through GREP) include regular expression support for those who know how to use it.

Following are two lines of Perl that use regular expressions to parse a variable TextString for <font> tags that are not closed with </font>. These lines add the </font> tag to those that are not already closed.

```
if (($TextString =~/\<font.*\>/)&&(!($TextString =~
/\<\/font\>/))){$TextString =~ s/(.*)\]/\1<\/font\>\]/;}
```

The cryptic syntax of regular expressions may offer power to the programmer, but it costs dearly in terms of simplicity and elegance. Decrypting a complicated and uncommented set of regular expressions can be extremely difficult. On the positive side, I have never heard anyone complain that regular expressions are not powerful enough and, speaking from experience, once a programmer knows the syntax he or she is hooked.

For more on regular expressions, visit the page maintained by Jeffrey Friedl, author of *Mastering Regular Expressions* (O'Reilly & Associates), at http://enterprise.ic.gc.ca/~jfriedl/regex/. You can also visit an MIT reference at http://wonder.mit.edu/misc/regex.html. For more useful Java Class libraries, visit http://java.developer.com/pages/Gamelan.programming.libraries.html.

✳ ***Note:*** *Netscape Navigator 4.0 supports a wide range of regular expression syntax with JavaScript within the String object. However, Microsoft Internet Explorer does not support this regular expression syntax.*

Why won't Netscape run the updated version of my applet, even after I have cleared the browser's cache?

Many Netscape browsers continue to run older versions of applets even after the browser cache has been cleared. This is caused by a bug in the browser and can often, but not always, be fixed by holding down the SHIFT key while pressing the Reload button. If Navigator still doesn't run the updated version of the applet, go to a page that does not contain the applet, clear your cache again, quit all versions of Navigator that are currently running, and restart the browser.

How do I reference a Java applet that is in a different directory than my HTML document?

Java applets must reside in a nonexecutable (read-only) directory on most Web servers. The CODE attribute of the <APPLET> tag, when used by itself, only allows Java applets to be placed in the same directory as the HTML page or CGI output that is calling them. Since CGIs are usually run from an executable directory, referencing an applet from a CGI with only the CODE attribute is impossible.

By adding a CODEBASE attribute to the <APPLET> tag, a base directory can be specified from your applet. For example, the following line references a Java applet that resides in the virtual root /media in a directory called JavaApplets:

```
<APPLET CODE="MyJavaApplet.class"
CODEBASE="/media/JavaApplets" Width="83" HEIGHT="33">
```

How can I prevent my applets from being used elsewhere, and how can I tell if anyone else has used my applets on the Internet?

Unfortunately, stealing and reusing most applets is not a particularly difficult task for the devious minded. However, reusing an applet without permission is against the law and is similar to publishing a book without the permission of the author or publisher.

Applet theft is a growing problem on the Web. Many people believe that simply changing an applet's parameters makes the applet different and distinct from the original. Not only is this practice illegal, but in many situations it is impossible to tell if an applet has been changed. Fortunately, applet owners can take certain steps to protect themselves against the unsolicited use of their code.

As long as an applet has a unique or at least a rare name, it is possible to conduct a search of all pages where it is being used. A few search engines, including Digital Equipment Corp's Alta Vista search engine, offer special features for searching for implementations of Java applets by applet name. However, for the search to be accurate, having an applet with a name that is not being used elsewhere on the Web helps a lot. Also, if the search engine allows it, be sure to screen out pages from your own site in the search.

From http://altavista.digital.com/, try using the following syntax to search for Web pages that are not on your site and contain applets with the same name as the applet that you specify:

```
+applet:MyApplet -host:MyDomain.com
```

To design an applet that is not reusable on other sites, try adding a function that checks the URL from which it is being served. Use getDocumentBase().getHost() to get the URL of the document that called the applet. If the host name that is returned doesn't meet the host name you specify within the applet, then kill the applet with System.exit(0).

It is important to keep .java source files out of Web-accessible directories if you want to protect your source code. Many authors place their .java source files in the same directory on the Web server as their .class files, making their applet's source code easy to download and therefore editable. A Java applet that has been stolen and heavily edited is often impossible to distinguish from the original. After functions have been renamed, the applet itself renamed and a little bit of code added, the applet has a different byte size and a different name.

But even without Java source code on your Web server, there remains the threat of your byte-compiled applet being decompiled, recoded, and then recompiled under a different name. Even checking the host name within the applet doesn't protect against this. Fortunately, a very small percentage of the Web-browsing community is savvy enough to decompile, recode, and recompile an applet. If you are still worried about the threat, a number of utilities are available for changing Java code in ways that make decompiled applets extremely difficult to reverse-engineer.

The following utilities can obfuscate Java byte-code:

- Hashjava: http://www.blackdown.org/~kbs/hashjava.html
- Mangler: http://www.schlund.net/axyz/projekts/ mangler/mangler.html
- Jobe: http://www.primenet.com/~ej/

A good article with a code example is available from http://www.webdeveloper.com/categories/java/java_jj_ applet_theft.html.

Chapter 15

Dynamic HTML

Answer Topics!

Dynamic HTML @ a Glance

Dynamic HTML, also known as DHTML, has given Web documents new life. For years, all Web documents were static with perhaps a few small areas of interactivity created by means of Java, Shockwave, or ActiveX. With Microsoft Internet Explorer 4.0 and Netscape Navigator 4.0, a full suite of multimedia features have been made available to Web developers. No longer do developers need costly programming environments, hefty run-time engines, complex programming techniques, or large file sizes to create interactive pages.

With the extended programming tools that are built into the DHTML browsers, developers can add a tremendous degree of interactivity to Web pages without ever leaving the HTML and JavaScript authoring environment. Fully interactive content is possible without the need for server-scripts, plug-in content, or Java applets. Whether it is functionality as simple as animating blocks of HTML on a page or as complex as opening direct links to databases with client-side content sorting, dynamic HTML is probably your answer.

The easiest way to imagine what can be done with dynamic HTML is to consider the interactivity that is available through a multimedia authoring environment such as Macromedia's Director or presentation tools such as Microsoft's PowerPoint. Fade ins and fade outs, animation, fancy buttons, audio synchronized with motion, overlapping graphics and text, and exact positioning are all possible without using any programming resources outside the HTML of the Web page.

As part of their dynamic HTML enhancements, Microsoft and Netscape have both added a great deal of internal enhancements. For example, you can subscribe to Web content, thereby allowing the browser to automatically download content for later browsing. And you can convert your browser window to a maximized, kiosk mode that does not contain the usual window artifacts.

This chapter answers questions that concern the major features of dynamic HTML and common problems that developers face. The best way to learn dynamic HTML is to read a book dedicated to DHTML such as Michele Petrovsky's *Dynamic HTML in Action* (Osborne/McGraw-Hill, 1998), but this chapter lays the groundwork for a thorough understanding of the subject.

Following are the important topics covered in this chapter:

New DHTML Features explains what dynamic HTML is and the methods you can use to implement its features in Microsoft Internet Explorer 4.0 and Netscape Navigator 4.0.

Dynamic HTML in Netscape Navigator 4.0 covers topics specific to developing with dynamic HTML for Netscape Navigator 4.0. The section takes a close look at the <LAYER> tag and how its attributes can be changed even after a page has loaded.

Dynamic HTML in Microsoft Internet Explorer 4.0 answers questions specific to Microsoft Internet Explorer 4.0 and dynamic HTML. Scriptlets, animation with DHTML, and the Microsoft Agent control are all covered in this section.

Channels is devoted entirely to Netscape's Netcaster and Microsoft's Active Channels. This section covers the new functionality and features that have been added with the two 4.0 browsers.

NEW DHTML FEATURES

? What programming language enhancements and new HTML tags should I use when creating dynamic HTML?

A number of different methods can be used to implement similar features of dynamic HTML. Some methods are compatible with both Netscape Navigator 4.0 and Microsoft's Internet Explorer 4.0, but others are not. Following are different methods that may be used for adding DHTML content and functionality to Web pages.

Cascading Style Sheets (CSS)

Cascading style sheets can be used for absolute positioning of graphics and the application of styles, such as font size or color, in one place. All of the new features in the 4.0 browsers are usually placed under the dynamic HTML category even if, like style sheets, they are not by themselves dynamic. Cascading style sheets are defined within the <STYLE> and

</STYLE> tags and use a format that can be a little cryptic to those who are used to standard HTML.

The style information presented here defines a font class named myFont and a positioning class named myGraphicClass. Once this style information is placed above the <BODY> tag on an HTML page, using <FONT CLASS="myFont"> anywhere inside the <BODY> and </BODY> tags results in display text that is green and 32 points in size.

Wrapping a block of HTML in <DIV CLASS="myGraphic-Class"> and </DIV> results in a block of HTML that is visible, positioned 150 pixels down the page, and positioned 50 pixels in from the left side of the screen.

```
<STYLE>
.myGraphicClass{
position:  absolute;
top: 150px;
left: 50px;
visibility: visible;
}
.myFont{
color: green;
font-size: 32pt;
}
</STYLE>
```

The W3C Web site is a good place to learn the syntax of CSS and the differences in implementation between browsers. The W3C site can be found at http://www.w3.org/Style/.

A cascading style sheet syntax wizard for generating correctly formatted cascading style sheet information is available on Netscape's site at http://developer.netscape.com/library/technote/index.html?content=dhtml/css/css.htm.

<LAYER> Tag

The layer tag, a Netscape-specific tag, allows positioning to be set for a block of HTML without the use of CSS. The HTML elements contained within a layer tag can be repositioned, rendered invisible, cropped, or otherwise tweaked by using the new document.layers object in JavaScript.

The following <LAYER> tag places HTML text 150 pixels down and 150 pixels to the right of the upper-left corner of the Netscape Navigator 4.0 browser window. Z-INDEX specifies a layer's depth in order to determine whether it is above or below another layer.

```
<LAYER NAME="HelloText" TOP=150 LEFT=150 Z-INDEX=10>
Hello, world.
</LAYER>
```

For more information on the <LAYER> tag, read "What is the <LAYER> tag and what browsers support it?" in Chapter 10.

<DIV> Tag

Strictly speaking, the <DIV> and </DIV> tags aren't new to HTML but, when coupled with new CSS settings, they can be used similarly to the <LAYER> tag. The <DIV> tag is supported by both Netscape Navigator 4.0 and Microsoft Internet Explorer 4.0. It is used to group blocks of HTML content together. A <DIV> tag coupled with style sheet settings allows for absolute content positioning, layering, visibility, sizing, and so on.

JavaScript

Both Netscape Navigator 4.0 and Microsoft Internet Explorer 4.0 offer JavaScript enhancements that allow Web page content to move, play media, and interact based on events such as user clicks, key strokes, and the passage of time. The object model of both browsers has expanded to allow for increased interactivity with blocks of HTML on the page and their attributes such as shape, color, positioning, and layer ordering. Other important JavaScript enhancements include the ability to detect screen resolution and color depth. With these enhancements, a site can tailor its content specifically to each client's display settings.

Although the object models for both browsers allow for similar functionality, the newest features are quite different and incompatible. For example, if you want to change the style setting of a section of HTML—you want to change a green font to purple, say—the syntax for completing this task in the two browsers is different.

For more on Microsoft Internet Explorer 4.0 JavaScript enhancements, visit http://www.microsoft.com/sitebuilder/ workshop/prog/ie4/jscript3-f.htm.

For more on Netscape Navigator 4.0 JavaScript enhancements, visit http://developer.netscape.com/ library/documentation/communicator/codestock.html

VBScript

Like JavaScript, VBScript offers new language features by which to control the same screen elements as JavaScript in Microsoft Internet Explorer 4.0. Netscape Navigator does not internally support the VBScript language.

Built-in Multimedia Controls

A number of multimedia effects have been blended into Internet Explorer 4.0 as style sheet filters and as ActiveX controls. The ability to include animated 3D objects, vector graphics, and filters such as blurs, drop shadows, and transition effects is controllable with client-side scripting and/or style sheets.

For more on Microsoft's Internet Explorer multimedia controls like the ones shown in Figure 15-1, select multimedia controls from the menu at http://www.microsoft. com/ie/authors/.

? Are the Netscape Navigator 4.0 version and Microsoft Internet Explorer 4.0 version of dynamic HTML compatible?

Netscape and Microsoft took different approaches to implementing dynamic HTML. As a result, the two browsers are largely incompatible. For very simple features such as positioning a graphic or block of HTML at exact coordinates on the page, it is possible to use compatible code. For more complex features such as animation coupled with interactivity, writing code that works in both browsers with the same code is virtually impossible.

Figure 15-1 Multimedia controls in Microsoft Internet Explorer 4.0 allow users to create and manipulate vector-based content within an HTML page.

To be specific, Netscape Navigator and Microsoft Internet Explorer both use the same syntax for cascading style sheets (CSS) but use a different object model for manipulating screen elements. You can place items on the page at exact locations using CSS, but if you want to move the items, you are stuck with the differences between the two versions of JavaScript.

The following example code displays the content of a <DIV> tag at a location specified in the page's style sheet. The code works in both Netscape Navigator 4.0 and Microsoft Internet Explorer 4.0.

```
<HTML>
<HEAD><TITLE>Absolute Positioning</TITLE></HEAD>
<STYLE>
.myPositioningClass{
position:  absolute;
```

```
top: 150px;
left: 150px;
visibility: visible;
color: #FF6600
}
</STYLE>
<BODY>
<DIV CLASS="myPositioningClass">
<H1>Hello, world.</H1>
</DIV>
</BODY>
</HTML>
```

If the 4.0 browsers use incompatible methods of creating dynamic HTML, how can I create a page that supports both?

If the functionality that you desire for your page is not supported through a common means on Microsoft Internet Explorer 4.0 and Netscape Navigator 4.0, you have three options:

- Create separate pages for each browser.
- Use browser detection within your script to separate the incompatible code elements.
- Use scriptlets and externally referenced layers to store incompatible content and scripts externally.

Create Separate Pages

If your content is spread across different pages, you can either redirect the user with a server-side redirection script that uses browser detection (a subject discussed in Chapter 11) or you can use client-side browser detection and redirect the user based on his or her browser type with JavaScript.

Use Browser Detection Within Your Script

To support incompatible dynamic HTML on the same page, you need to use client-side browser detection with JavaScript. For an explanation of how to add JavaScript browser detection to your pages, read Chapter 13 on JavaScript.

Use Scriptlets and External Content

Externally stored content is one of the easier ways to separate dynamic content from incompatible browsers. Microsoft Internet Explorer 4.0 supports the inclusion of externally stored HTML with the <OBJECT> tag. These tags point to content called scriptlets that are described in more detail later in this chapter. Navigator allows externally stored scripts and content through the SRC attribute of the <LAYER> tag. Because Internet Explorer ignores the <LAYER> tag and Navigator ignores the <OBJECT> tag, both sets of content are safely protected in incompatible browsers. The following is an example of a layer tag that references externally stored content:

```
<LAYER NAME="menu" SRC="menu.html" HEIGHT=300
WIDTH=100 LEFT=20 TOP=20 Z-INDEX=100
VISIBILITY="show"></LAYER>
```

Netscape has introduced a trick with the <LAYER> tag that allows you to comment out content within the <LAYER> and </LAYER> tags to browsers that do not recognize the tags. To comment out a <LAYER> tag, use the following syntax:

```
<!--&{typeof document.layers == "object"};
<LAYER TOP=100 LEFT=100>
Hello,world.
</LAYER>
-->
```

Also allowed by Netscape Navigator 4.0 are the <NOLAYER> and </NOLAYER> tags. These two tags hide content that sits between them from browsers that support the <LAYER> tag. Currently, Netscape Navigator 4.0 is the only browser that supports the <LAYER> tag.

Microsoft Internet Explorer 4.0 similarly allows externally stored scriptlets for content. Unfortunately, there is no equivalent to the <NOLAYER> tag in Microsoft Internet Explorer.

? Is it possible to define CSS information in one place and share it between Web pages?

The easiest way to include externally stored style sheet information is to use the <LINK> tag in place of <STYLE> and </STYLE> tags. Place the <LINK> tag above the </HEAD> tag in your HTML document. Following is a tag for an externally referenced style sheet that works with both Navigator and Internet Explorer:

```
<LINK REL="stylesheet" TYPE="text/css"
HREF="MyStyle.css"
TITLE="MyStyleSheet">
```

The MyStyle.css file referenced above should be a standard text document that contains content such as the following:

```
<STYLE>
.MyRedClass{color:#FF0000;}
.MyGreenClass{color:#00FF00;}
</STYLE>
```

? If I am using CSS positioning on my Web page, how can I make it backward-compatible for older browsers?

Creating a site that looks great in older browsers if you are also using CSS to position content is very difficult. The challenge is to make the site look great both with and without the <DIV> or <LAYER> tag being understood by all browsers. If you are going to use <DIV> or <LAYER> tags, follow the three useful rules of thumb that help make content more browser-friendly:

● Place everything in the page in the order in which you would like it to appear on the screen from left to right and top to bottom, even if you are using CSS positioning

● Use relative rather than absolute positioning

● Test frequently with browsers that you wish to support

DYNAMIC HTML IN NETSCAPE NAVIGATOR 4.0

? **How do I change attributes in the <LAYER> tag with JavaScript?**

Any attribute in the <LAYER> tag can be changed with JavaScript in Netscape Navigator 4.0. To change an attribute in a <LAYER> tag, set a variable to equal document.layers["YourLayerName"]. This variable can then be used to change any attribute with the syntax variable.attribute. The following example code changes the screen position, background color, and layering position of the layer BigText at the time the page loads. If you receive errors with this example, try moving the script to a position in your HTML below the <LAYER> and </LAYER> tags.

```
<LAYER NAME="BigText" TOP=150 LEFT=150 Z-INDEX=10>
<B>Hello, world.<B>
</LAYER>
<SCRIPT LANGUAGE="JavaScript">
var BigTextPosition = document.layers["BigText"];
BigTextPosition.top = 20;
BigTextPosition.zIndex = 4;
BigTextPosition.bgColor = "blue";
</SCRIPT>
```

? **How can I make a section of HTML be invisible with a mouse-click in Netscape Navigator 4.0?**

The easiest way to make a section of HTML disappear is to first wrap the HTML between <LAYER> and </LAYER> tags. If you do not specifically include a VISIBILITY attribute, the VISIBILITY attribute is automatically set to *inherit*, which means that the setting is literally inherited.

In the screen shown in Figure 15-2, clicking the Change Visibility hyperlink within the HTML page triggers the JavaScript function ChangeVisibility shown in the sample

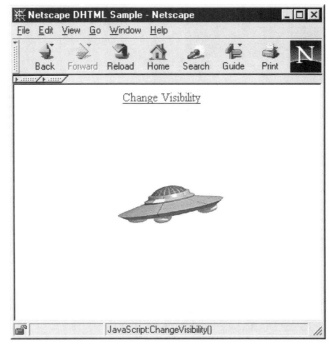

Figure 15-2   This object—a UFO—is rendered visible or invisible based on a mouse-click in Netscape Navigator 4.0.

code. This function determines if the UFO is currently visible or invisible and switches the UFO's visibility state.

```
<HTML><HEAD>
<TITLE>Netscape DHTML Sample</TITLE>
</HEAD>
<BODY>
<SCRIPT LANGUAGE="JavaScript">
<!--
function ChangeVisibility()
{
    var UfoState = document.layers["UFO"]
    if (UfoState.visibility == "show"){
        UfoState.visibility = "hide";
    }
    else{
        UfoState.visibility = "show";
    }
}
```

```
//-->
</SCRIPT>
<CENTER>
<A HREF="JavaScript:ChangeVisibility()">Change Visibility</A>
</CENTER>
<LAYER NAME="UFO" LEFT="125" TOP="125" Z-INDEX=10 VISIBILITY="show">
<IMG SRC="UFO.GIF" WIDTH="144" HEIGHT="52">
</LAYER>
</BODY>
</HTML>
```

? How do I create a simple animation with Netscape Navigator 4.0?

The ability to animate content around a Web page is perhaps the most exciting new feature introduced with DHTML. To animate content with Netscape Navigator, it is necessary to use JavaScript.

First, group the content that you want to animate with a layer tag and give it a name, like so:

```
<LAYER NAME="moon" LEFT="0" TOP="100" Z-INDEX=15>
<IMG SRC="moon.gif" WIDTH=189 HEIGHT=186 BORDER=0>
</LAYER>
```

Next, add a JavaScript function that moves the <LAYER> that you have defined:

```
<SCRIPT LANGUAGE="JavaScript">
<!--
var moonobject = document.layers["moon"];
moonobject.moveBy(5,0);
//-->
</SCRIPT>
```

This code moves the HTML within the <LAYER NAME="moon"> and </LAYER> tags 5 pixels to the right and 0 pixels down. The numbers set here define the number of pixels that the HTML moves each time it is redisplayed on-screen. If the code gives an error, try placing it beneath the HTML tags that define the layer.

To animate this HTML, it is necessary to place the JavaScript code into a function and include a setTimeout that allows the function to call itself after a set amount of time. This way, the time interval between each movement on the screen is specified to the millisecond.

Essentially, the function that moves the HTML is called once to initialize the animation. The function starts a counter that increments up each time the HTML is moved. The idea is for the animation to be stopped after a certain number of iterations. The function moves the HTML with the moveBy method and then calls itself with the setTimeout method.

The following code listing moves the layer named "moon" 5 pixels to the right every 30 milliseconds until the moon shown in Figure 15-3 has been moved 100 times:

```
<HTML>
<HEAD><TITLE>Moving Moon</TITLE></HEAD>
<BODY BGCOLOR=#000000 TEXT="#FFFFFF">
<LAYER NAME="moon" LEFT="0" TOP="100" Z-INDEX=15>
<IMG SRC="moon.gif" WIDTH=189 HEIGHT=186 BORDER=0>
</LAYER>
<LAYER NAME="Earth" LEFT="100" TOP="40" Z-INDEX=1>
<IMG SRC="earth.gif" WIDTH=437 HEIGHT=433 BORDER=0>
</LAYER>
<SCRIPT LANGUAGE="JavaScript">
<!--
var moonobject = document.layers["moon"];
var i = 0;
function MoveMoon(){
  /*Move the moon 5 pixels right and 0 down*/
  moonobject.moveBy(5,0);
  i = i+1;
  /*Only move the moon the first 100 times this function is called*/
  if (i < 100)
  /*Call this function again in 30 milliseconds*/
  setTimeout("MoveMoon()", 30);
else
  return;
}
/*Start the animation*/
MoveMoon()
//-->
</SCRIPT>
</BODY>
</HTML>
```

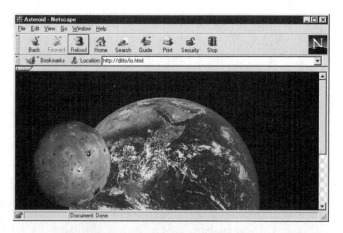

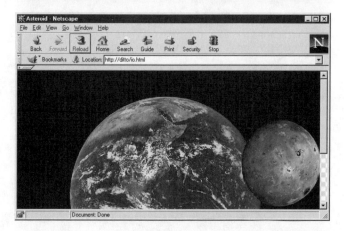

Figure 15-3 You can use JavaScript and Netscape Navigator 4.0 to animate a graphic across the screen, as in the example shown above.

DYNAMIC HTML IN MICROSOFT INTERNET EXPLORER 4.0

? **Microsoft Internet Explorer displays the ALT attribute as a pop-up tool-tip. Can I specify a tool-tip other than the ALT text in Internet Explorer 4.0?**

Microsoft Internet Explorer adds the TITLE attribute to just about any tag you wish. The TITLE attribute pops up as a tool-tip when the mouse pauses over it. Try adding the following code to your Web page and take a look at what pops up in Internet Explorer:

```
<B TITLE="This is a hot season in the Northern hemisphere">Summer</B>
```

? **I would like to center an object vertically on the screen in Microsoft Internet Explorer when the page loads. How do I do this?**

The Microsoft Internet Explorer object model has added clientHeight and clientWidth to its object model. Now JavaScript and VBScript can access the browser's window dimensions. The following sample code segment centers the image ufo.gif vertically within the visible area of the users Microsoft Internet Explorer browser window:

```
<IMG ID="ufo" SRC="ufo.gif" WIDTH=144 HEIGHT=52 BORDER=0
STYLE="VISIBILITY:hidden;POSITION:absolute;">
<SCRIPT LANGUAGE="JavaScript">
<!--
ImageHeight = 52;
ufo.style.top = ((document.body.clientHeight/2) - (ImageHeight/2));
ufo.style.visibility = "";
//-->
</SCRIPT>
```

By the way, this example code defines the graphic as being hidden with the STYLE attribute of the <IMG> tag. The graphic is then set back to being visible with JavaScript. It seems a little unusual, but if the graphic is defined as being visible all along, the graphic draws to the screen before the JavaScript is interpreted and, therefore, before the image is moved. The result is a visible jump effect. By keeping the graphic invisible until after the JavaScript executes, the image is drawn in the correct place the first time.

? How can I make a section of HTML be invisible with a mouse-click in Microsoft Internet Explorer 4.0?

To make a section of code invisible with a mouse-click, wrap your code between <DIV> and </DIV> tags. Use the STYLE parameter to set positioning and visibility for any HTML that you wish to make invisible. The figure shown here, like the Netscape Navigator figure that appeared earlier in this chapter, results in a page with a UFO graphic and the words "Change Visibility" in a hyperlink. Clicking "Change Visibility" changes the visibility of the object and renders it either visible or invisible. The following code was used to create Figure 15-4:

```
<HTML><HEAD>
<TITLE> DHTML Sample</TITLE>
</HEAD>
<SCRIPT LANGUAGE="JavaScript">
<!--
function ChangeVisibility()
{
    if (UFO.style.visibility == "hidden"){
        UFO.style.visibility = "";
    }
    else{
        UFO.style.visibility = "hidden";
    }
}
//-->
</SCRIPT>
<BODY>
<CENTER><A HREF="JavaScript:ChangeVisibility()">Change Visibility</A></CENTER>
<DIV ID="UFO" STYLE="POSITION:absolute;LEFT:125;TOP:125;Z-
INDEX:10; VISIBILITY:;">
<IMG SRC="UFO.GIF" WIDTH="144" HEIGHT="52">
</DIV>
</BODY></HTML>
```

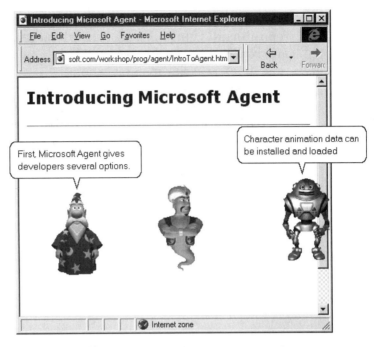

Figure 15-4   Microsoft Agent allows characters to be controlled via Web page scripts as they talk and move around the screen.

What are scriptlets?

Microsoft Internet Explorer 4.0 has introduced scriptlets to contain and display externally stored DHTML content. *Scriptlets* are simply external HTML files that may also contain DHTML features. This content can be included on a page through the use of the <OBJECT> tag. The WIDTH and HEIGHT attributes of the <OBJECT> tag specify the area of the page in which the scriptlet displays. Because scriptlets can be stored externally, they can be shared between several pages on the same site. Scriptlets are also self–contained, so they can be run without conflicts between similarly named variables or functions in your page and in your scriptlet.

The idea behind scriptlets is two-fold. First, scriptlets function like Java applets and can be used for Java-like functionality on a page without the hassle of having to write an applet or ActiveX control. Second, the fact that scriptlets are self-contained and don't conflict with script content on the page means that they lend themselves to scriptlet repositories. Unlike JavaScript, which can be difficult to copy and reuse within pages, scriptlets can be used without touching the script inside of them.

To create a scriptlet, create an HTML page with the functionality that you desire and then save it. Next, include an <OBJECT> tag with a DATA attribute that points to the source and TYPE="text/x-scriptlet" to help your browser determine its MIME type. Following is a set of <OBJECT> tags that reference a scriptlet:

```
<OBJECT STYLE="position:absolute;
        width:100%;
        height:100;
        top:50;
        left:50;"
        TYPE="text/x-scriptlet"
        DATA="BannerAd.htm">
</OBJECT>
```

? What is the Microsoft Agent?

Microsoft has developed a client-side software agent that can speak and move around the screen independently of the browser window. Agents can be controlled through a number of different languages, including Web page scripts, and can interact with the user. Microsoft Agent has three characters (shown in Figure 15-4) from which to select and new characters can be created manually.

Microsoft Agent does not install as part of the Web browser but is available without cost from the Microsoft Web site. For more information about Microsoft Agent ActiveX controls, visit http://www.microsoft.com/msdn/sdk/inetsdk/help/msagent/agent.htm.

CHANNELS

? What are channels?

Both Netscape and Microsoft have introduced functionality with their 4.0 browsers that both companies are calling *channels*. The functionality is surprisingly similar, yet incompatible. Both browsers now offer off-line browsing and a global, graphical set of links.

Microsoft's channel feature is an integral part of the Internet Explorer browser and may be activated by pressing the channel button on the toolbar or, with integrated desktop mode, by pressing the channels icon on the Taskbar. Netscape's channels are delivered through Netcaster and have a different look and feel than Microsoft's. To launch Netcaster from Netscape Navigator 4.0, select Netcaster from the Window menu.

When you subscribe to a channel in both browsers, a new button is added to your list of subscriptions. The button is essentially just a hyperlink that takes you to the page that is represented by the button. The buttons may also have submenus with other links that are similar to the bookmarked links that are found in folders in the bookmark feature of many browsers.

Unlike bookmarks, channels are predefined. Channels can also be added at the click of a button, while adding a bookmark involves using the browser's built-in menus. A site that offers a channel feature is essentially offering a set of links to different sections at a click of a button. As part of the subscription process, channel subscribers are able to specify whether Web site content should be downloaded in the background and cached to the hard-drive. This process eliminates both the need to wait for content and the need to be connected to the Internet to view a site.

By some estimates, as few as 30 to 40 percent of all installed browsers actually contain bookmarks that have been set by their users. Channels have been introduced to help newcomers to the Web find and navigate to new sites. The name "channels" represents a desire to create a more television-like interface for the Web. You subscribe to channels that interest you just as you select cable channels from the local cable company.

What do I need to do to my server to configure it for channels?

Channels require no special server configuration. A channel is essentially just a text file that points to existing page content that could sit on any Web server. To place a channel definition document on a server, you need to either place it in a nonexecutable directory (i.e. the same directory as your HTML content) or you need to generate the document from an executable such as a server script.

? Are channels really push content or are they client pull?

Contrary to much of the rhetoric, Netscape's channels and Microsoft's channels are client pull. When you subscribe to a channel, you set your channel to automatically update when new content becomes available. What you are actually doing is telling your browser how often to check for content that has been modified since it was last cached. If content has a newer file modification date than the locally cached version, the browser downloads the content to update its cached version.

? How do I create a channel for my site?

Fortunately, both Netscape Navigator 4.0 and Microsoft Internet Explorer 4.0 have introduced surprisingly simple formats for creating channels. To create a channel for your site, simply create a text file that is named appropriately, either .cdf for Microsoft Internet Explorer or .js for Netscape Navigator, add the text (correctly formatted), and place a hyperlink to the new page on your site.

Microsoft Internet Explorer

Microsoft Internet Explorer uses the channel definition format CDF to store channel information. CDF files contain information in XML format that describes the graphics used to represent the channel as well as any submenu links and the destination of those links. CDF files are also capable of scheduling updated downloads of site content for those who have chosen to schedule automatic downloading and caching of channel-linked pages.

To create an Internet Explorer channel, three graphics—194 x 32, 80 x 32, and 16x16 pixels in size—are needed to create the channel bar and menus. A simple channel file that defines one large channel button with two submenu links is shown in the figure. Once channel code such as that shown in the figure has been created, save it as an ASCII file with a .cdf file suffix and place it on your site. Adding a simple hyperlink to the file brings up subscription options that are built into Internet Explorer. Following is the source code for a simple CDF file that contains two sub-menus. This code, when saved in a .CDF file and hyperlinked from a Web page, allows users to subscribe to the Kung Fu Apocalypse Web site shown in Figure 15-5.

```
<?XML version="1.0"?>
<CHANNEL HREF="http://www.jps.net/kungfu">
<TITLE>Kung Fu Apocalypse - Channel</TITLE>
<LOGO HREF="http://www.jps.net/kungfu/img/channel
/smalllogo.gif" STYLE="ICON"/>
<LOGO HREF="http://www.jps.net/kungfu/img/channel/medlogo.gif"
STYLE="IMAGE" />
<LOGO HREF="http://www.jps.net/kungfu/img/channel
/largelogo.gif" STYLE="IMAGE-WIDE" />
<ITEM HREF="http://www.jps.net/kungfu/html/movie_set.html">
<LOGO HREF="http://www.jps.net/kungfu/img/channel/
movielogo.gif" STYLE="ICON" />
<LOG VALUE="document:view" />
<TITLE>Movie Reviews</TITLE>
<ABSTRACT>Great movie reviews of 70's kung Fu movies</ABSTRACT>
</ITEM>
<ITEM HREF="http://www.jps.net/kungfu/html/game_set.html">
<LOGO HREF="http://www.jps.net/kungfu/img/channel
/gamelogo.gif" STYLE="ICON" />
< LOG VALUE="document:view" />
<TITLE>Interactive Game</TITLE>
<ABSTRACT>Interactive Kung Fu game</ABSTRACT>
</ITEM>
</CHANNEL>
```

Another option for generating Microsoft Channels is to use the Microsoft CDF Generator, which is available through Microsoft's Internet Client Software Developers Kit. The Microsoft Internet Client SDK is available from http://www.microsoft.com/msdn/sdk/inetsdk/help/default.htm.

Figure 15-5 The Kung Fu Apocalypse site has been added as a channel in Microsoft Internet Explorer 4.0.

Netscape Netcaster Channel

To create a Netscape Netcaster channel, you need to either code a little JavaScript or use the "Add Channel Button" wizard on Netscape's site, shown in Figure 15-6. Since you may need upwards of ninety lines of code for your channel and Netscape's wizard is extremely easy to use, using the wizard is probably a good idea. To use the wizard, visit Netcaster Developer Central at http://developer.netscape.com/one/netcaster/index.html.

For more on Netcaster, visit the Netcaster FAQ at http://home.netscape.com/comprod/products/communicator/netcaster_faq.html.

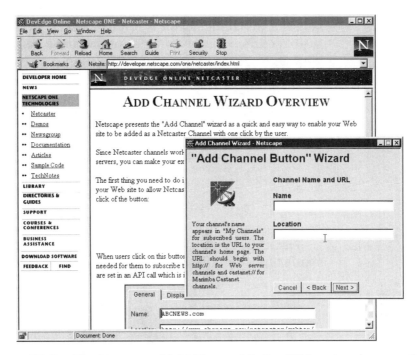

Figure 15-6   The Netscape "Add Channel Button" Wizard makes creating
a Netscape channel easy.

? **Many of my site's advertisers are concerned because, with channels and automatic downloading of content, many ad impressions are not being seen. How can I determine if the content is being downloaded automatically or manually?**

Microsoft Internet Explorer 4.0 actually uses a different browser identifier when it requests pages automatically. If your Web server logs HTTP_USER_AGENT HTTP headers, counting the number of times a specific ad graphic was requested by an Internet Explorer automatic download should be a simple task. Keep in mind that automatically downloaded content is not necessarily seen by the user. If site content changes and is re-downloaded by the browser, the old cached content may be overwritten before it is ever viewed. Not knowing if content is being seen complicates billing practices for advertisers.

When downloading content automatically, the Microsoft Internet Explorer 4.0 HTTP header for Windows 95 changes from

```
Mozilla/4.0 (Compatible; MSIE 4.0; Windows 95)
```

to

```
Mozilla/4.0 (Compatible; MSIE 4.0; MSIECrawler; Windows 95)
```

Netscape's Netcaster channel feature does not offer similar functionality.

Chapter 16

Server-Side Features

Answer Topics!

Server-Side Features @ a Glance

A Web server that only serves prewritten content is often not enough for a site. Whether on a bulletin board, chat area, or live images on the Web, server-side features are a great way to jazz up visitors' online experiences. And preparing and developing server-side features are easier than you might expect.

Developers are free to choose between a number of different methods when it comes to server functionality. Everything from custom programming to shrink-wrapped, off-the-shelf products can be used to add search services, bulletin board services, and other capabilities. Knowing the limitations of your server environment, what your budget is, and which skills your site's developers possess helps you determine what approach to take to enhance your site with server-side functionality.

In fact, your Web server may already have the necessary components for the features you want. Knowing what features are already built in to your software and what tasks are necessary to implement additional features is an important part of building a feature-rich site.

This chapter covers these important topics:

Basics of Server-Side Functionality lists the common types of server functionality and explains the factors that determine how difficult or easy integrating them in a site is.

Automated Up-to-Date Information covers developing features for updating content automatically. Live Web cameras, "What's New" pages, time/date stamps, and real-time stock quotes are discussed.

People-to-People Features explains how to add features that allow individuals to communicate with your organization or with each other via the Web. People-to-people features include chat areas, guest book registration, server-side e-mail, and bulletin boards.

Web Site Functionality Enhancements discusses the issues and the benefits of adding search, recommendation engine, and electronic commerce functionality to a site.

BASICS OF SERVER-SIDE FUNCTIONALITY

? **What common server-side features can I add to my site?**

The following server-side features can be added to most Web server environments. None of the features listed here are experimental and all can be found on a number of sites currently on the Web.

- Live chat areas
- Bulletin board services (BBSs)
- Live Web cameras
- Real-time stock quotes
- Recommendation engines
- Search engines
- Web commerce
- Last-modified dates on pages

- Current time/date stamps
- True push content
- Automatically generated "What's New" pages
- Personalized content
- Ad servers
- Web based e-mail
- Virtual whiteboards
- Page counters
- Guest books

? **What factors make server-side features more or less difficult?**

Before you decide which server-side features to add to your site, consider your Web server environment. The difference between a site hosted on a shared server at an Internet service provider and a feature-rich Web server environment that you have direct access to is great indeed.

Internet service providers usually offer very few, if any, server-side features because only a certain number of sites may be hosted on the same machine. If they are offered at all, common features such as search and "What's New" pages must be shared by all of the sites that are hosted on the server. ISPs usually allow sites to use server-side includes and CGI applications. CGIs and server-side includes should be enough to provide features such as BBSes and guest book registration, but CGIs and server-side includes are usually inadequate for full-featured e-commerce and chat functionality.

People who host their own sites have a great deal more control over server customization. Before you start building or downloading and reusing custom feature solutions, take a look at the features that are included with your Web server. More and more Web servers ship with built-in or easily integrated software that provides many of the server features described in this chapter.

If you want to add a number of features to your server that aren't there already, look for a flexible language engine or software solution that can meet your challenges. Using both Perl for a page counter and Java servlets for serving personalized content, for example, may require two different run-time engines and negatively affect your server's performance. Using a number of different technologies also makes a site more difficult to maintain.

AUTOMATED UP-TO-DATE INFORMATION

 How can I add an automatically generated "What's New" page for new and recently changed content?

Looking for new or recently updated content on a site you visit frequently can be frustrating. As a developer, you have the option of adding a static "What's New" page that is updated manually each time you update your site. However, maintaining a "What's New" page can be a repetitive and slow process, especially if the site's content changes often. The solution is to use a server application to generate a "What's New" page automatically based on the file modification dates of Web pages on the site. Any server programming environment can handle this functionality as long as it is able to access a list of files in a directory and view the associated file modification dates.

In general, there are two methods for creating "What's New" pages. One method is to write or use an already existing server application—one written in Perl, Java, or Visual Basic—that is scheduled to run automatically on the server to generate a Web page in a Web-accessible directory at intervals. For example, the application could run every day or every week. The second, slower method is to write the application as a CGI or similar application that generates the "What's New" listing each time the request is made to the Web server. Instead of being cached, the listing is sent directly to the browser that requested it.

You can probably find a customizable script on the Web that fits your needs, but understanding the basic steps that server applications use to generate a page is helpful. For scheduled pages, a server scheduling system of some sort (scheduling systems are included in most operating systems) is configured to run the application as frequently as is desired. Most likely, the script runs every day or every week, depending on how up-to-date you want the page to be.

The application looks in Web-accessible directories for content ending in .html or .htm for files that have been modified within a certain period of time, such as the past week. For new pages, the application needs to create an external text file that contains a catalogue of the site's pages. By creating the catalogue, the application can compare current files with files that existed last time the application was run and in so doing identify new pages that were added to the site. The application then generates an HTML file with hyperlinks to new and recently modified pages, updates the look-up file, and quits.

"What's New" pages that are generated on the fly when the user requests them go through essentially the same steps as scheduled server applications. However, the output is sent directly to the user's browser instead of being saved as an HTML file on the server.

A C++ CGI with "What's New" functionality can be downloaded from http://hjs.geol.uib.no/Software/WhatsNew/CplusWhatsNew.html-ssi.

? How do I add a page counter to my site?

Page counters have become a common feature across the Internet. Counters simply count the number of requests that have been made for a page since a specific date and list the number of requests. Page counters are either numeric text that is included on the page or they are text strings in the form of image tags that reference a different graphic for each digit (e.g., 12 is represented as <IMG SCR="1.gif"> <IMG SCR="2.gif">). Regardless of which style is used, the basic process behind both page counter display types is very similar.

To include a counter on your page, you can use either a counter service or your own script to track the number of visits to your site and publish the results. A counter service takes care of the work for you for free or at a small cost. If your site is hosted by an ISP, you may have a counter service already available to you at no cost and with minimal effort from the ISP.

If you want to use your own script, it is simply a matter of executing a script, which is easily done through a server-side include tag such as <!--#include virtual="/cgi-bin/counter.cgi"-->. Keep in mind that not all servers provide built-in server-side include support. For more information on server-side includes, read the server-side include section in Chapter 11.

Most counter CGI scripts simply open a text file, read the number that it currently stores, increment the number by one, update the text file with the new number, and output the number through standard output for inclusion on the page. If you want to use graphical numbers, output each number individually with <IMG SRC= preceding the digit and .gif BORDER=0> following it. A comprehensive collection of graphical digits, such as those shown below, is available from http://www.counterart.com/.

`0 2 1 8 4 9`

Commercial services are available from the following sites:

- http://www.digits.com/
- http://www.asoftware.com/

Web counter scripts are available at these sites:

- Kira's Web Toolbox (http://lightsphere.com/cgi/#lk3)
- Matt's Script Archive (http://www.worldwidemart.com/scripts/counter.shtml)

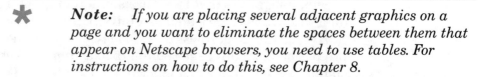

Note: *If you are placing several adjacent graphics on a page and you want to eliminate the spaces between them that appear on Netscape browsers, you need to use tables. For instructions on how to do this, see Chapter 8.*

What is involved in adding a last-modified date or current time/date stamp to my pages?

Last-modified dates and time/date stamps are added to pages by means of server scripting, SSI by itself without any referenced scripts, or client-side JavaScript. Virtually every server-scripting environment offers the necessary functions to add time/date stamps and last-modified dates. Keep in mind, however, that if you are calling a script such as a Perl script from a server-side include, the last modification that is given may be the date for the script itself and not the file that called it. You can avoid this problem by using the last-modified date feature that is available within SSI. The following code outputs the date and last file modification date.

For a server-side include:

```
<!--#echo var="LAST_MODIFIED"--><BR>
<!--#echo var="DATE_GMT"--><BR>
```

For JavaScript (client-side):

```
<SCRIPT LANGUAGE="JavaScript">
<!--
var today = new Date();
document.writeln('Today is: ' + today + '<BR>');
document.writeln('Last modified date:' +
document.lastModified);
//-->
</SCRIPT>
```

What is involved in adding a live Web camera to my site?

Live Web cameras offer up-to-the-minute glimpses of real places. Web cameras have been used to spy on traffic, enjoy amazing views, and peek into college dorm rooms. A live camera that points at something interesting that changes from moment to moment, such as the live image of the San Francisco Bay Bridge shown in Figure 16-1, is a sure way to attract visitors. A number of different configurations are possible for Web cameras, but the most common configuration requires the following:

- A video or digital camera
- A computer within a reasonable distance of the camera
- A video capture card or device
- Software to grab a still video image and send it to the Web server

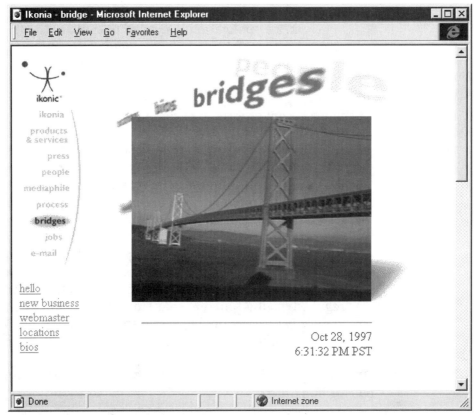

Figure 16-1   The www.ikonic.com Web site features an up-to-the-minute view of San Francisco's Golden Gate Bridge. The image is captured from a video camera and processed using Snappy! Hardware and software.

● A constant connection either to the Internet or directly to a Web server

● Script to push or update the captured image to the Web server

The process of capturing images starts with the camera. If you are using a video camera, video is constantly fed to the computer via a video capture card or a device such as Play's Snappy. Keep in mind that many video cameras can only send video short distances, often as little as 15 feet, over conventional cables. Another option is to use a digital camera and plug it directly into the computer. Digital cameras do not usually need special computer hardware in order to upload images.

Next, an application is needed to capture the frame and convert it to a Web-ready format such as GIF or JPEG. Using the GIF format may mean paying licensing fees, so JPEG is usually the format of choice. Most digital cameras and many video capture cards are now sold with software that grabs images, converts them automatically to a Web-ready format, and saves them. If your Web server is on the same machine or on a local network, set your application to save your images to a Web-accessible directory. If your Web server is only available through the Internet, you need to transfer the files via FTP. Some image-capture software transfers images for you, but if yours doesn't, you need to write a script that creates a connection to your Web server through FTP, enters the necessary user name and password, transfers the image, and overwrites the old image. Either schedule the script to run regularly (say, every 30 seconds) or have the script regularly call a function that transfers the file. Scripts are generally written in UNIX as a shell language, on Windows as a batch file (.bat), or on the Macintosh in Applescript.

? How can I add real-time stock quotes or news feeds to my Web site?

For publicly traded companies and financial sites, such as the Pacific Stock Exchange site shown in Figure 16-2, real-time stock information can be a great asset. Pages that otherwise change once every quarter can attract repeat visitors with their dynamic, up-to-date stock information. News feeds can be a great way to automatically offer up-to-date information on a site. News feeds and stock quotes are an incentive for visitors to bookmark a site or make it a channel.

Real-time stock feeds are available for a fee from a number of different vendors. A few vendors, such as PC Quote, offer interfaces that were specifically designed to interface with Web server applications. To include a real-time stock feed on your Web pages, you need a server-side application that is capable of requesting and receiving HTTP data from other Web sites. Your application can request information from the stock feed each time the page is requested, or an application can request the stock feed every thirty seconds or every minute and store the data as a Web-accessible HTML file. With either solution, the server application must

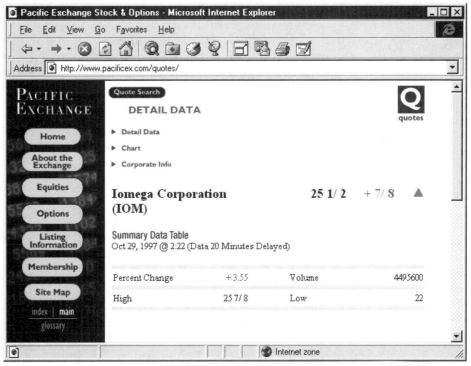

Figure 16-2   The Pacific Stock Exchange provides free 20-minute-delayed stock information to site visitors from PC Quote.

be able to parse the data that is received from the feed and insert HTML tags for formatting.

Adding a news feed to a site is very similar to adding a stock feed. Articles are usually made available through usenet but sometimes through FTP or the Web. The text files can be requested by an application on your server and cached or immediately incorporated into Web pages. For a fee, services such as ClariNet and UPI provide news feed services that can be incorporated into pages on Web sites.

On a heavily trafficked site, the server application should request stock quotes or news feeds from the server no more than once every thirty seconds. The best way to cut down the number of requests to the service is to schedule or loop an application. The application grabs the information from its source and caches it as a text file or incorporates it into static HTML files. This method significantly reduces the processing time on your server and the information feed server during peak hours.

If real-time stock quotes are too expensive for your budget, consider 15-minute-delayed stock quotes. Stock quotes that are more than 15 minutes old are significantly cheaper and can even be acquired in exchange for posting advertisements. Time-delayed news stories are also less expensive than stories that compete with those on the large news sites.

PEOPLE-TO-PEOPLE FEATURES

? How do I add a guest book to my site?

There are two types of guest books on the Web: guest books that simply record information and those that also publish the information on a Web page. A guest book that visitors can sign and browse can be a nice feature on a site that receives a limited number of visitors, such as the Dancing Donkey site shown in Figure 16-3. Visitors can e-mail each other if e-mail addresses are included and the result could be an online community. On a popular site, however, a guest book that can be updated and browsed quickly grows to be unmanageable in size.

Figure 16-3 At the Donkey Dancing site, visitors can post messages in the guest book for other dancing donkey fans to read.

A typical guest book starts with a Web-based form that asks users for information such as their names and comments about the site. The form information is then submitted to a server application such as a Perl script or Active Server page, where the information is screened for illegal characters and field lengths and recorded in a database or appended to a plain text or HTML file. When visitors view a guest book, they see the content from the database or a text file on a Web page. In the case of an HTML file that has been appended, the HTML file is sent to visitors.

Guest books that share their contents over the Web were a popular feature in the early days of the Web but are less common today. Today's guest books come in the form of site registration features that simply record data for the owners of the Web site. If the right questions are asked, site registration can be a powerful tool for learning who your audience is. A good place to start designing a guest book is at one of the many script repositories on the Web.

Guest book scripts are available from these sites:

- Matt's Script Archive (http://www.worldwidemart.com/scripts/guestbook.shtml)
- Magna Software's Write Wall (http://chat.magmacom.com/software/WriteWall/)

? How do I add a bulletin board feature to my site that allows visitors to post information and respond to postings?

Bulletin boards are frequently used to exchange information on the Internet. News servers allow the creation of newsgroups that offer BBS functionality (such as those available through Usenet), but many people prefer a Web front end for posted information. A bulletin board system works much like a guest book that publishes user-entered information on a Web site. However, bulletin board systems can be much more complicated than guest books if users can create new topic areas or link responses directly to an original posting.

Building a bulletin board system from scratch is entirely possible but usually takes more time and causes more problems than using a preexisting system. Publicly available bulletin boards have been written in almost every popular server-side language. Most bulletin boards store data in text files, but a number of solutions use a database instead.

For more information about bulletin board systems and bulletin board software that works with Web servers, visit the Bulletin Board FAQ at http://www.sysopworld.com/bbsfaq/text/faqmain.htm.

! ***Warning:*** *On a Web site where visitors can add their own comments to a live Web page, you always run the risk of someone posting profanity, racial or sexual epithets, and even subtle innuendoes that negatively impact a site. Any system that involves automatic Web publishing, no matter how strong the filtering, is open to abuse. To fully protect your site, you have to review the content yourself.*

? What is necessary to implement a live chat area on my Web site?

Anyone who has participated for more than a few minutes in a live chat recognizes the value, or at least the attraction, of real-time chat on the Web. Because the Web uses a request method rather than a push method for transferring content, chat does not lend itself well to a regular, HTML-based, interface. As a result, most major chat applications require either a Java-based client, an ActiveX client, or a browser plug-in for participants. Web-based chat areas that do use HTML-based clients require a <META> refresh tag to pull down the latest text every five or ten seconds.

For large-scale chat solutions that can handle large numbers of concurrent visitors, a commercial chat server is usually necessary. Commercial systems offer a number of features, including

- Automatic opening of new virtual chat areas when others fill up
- The ability to moderate chat areas
- The ability to send private messages to others who are online
- The ability to safely embed HTML, such as links or font color, into messages
- The ability to create temporary or permanent password-protected areas
- The ability for users to create private chat areas
- Profanity filters
- *Avatars* (graphical representations of participants)
- The ability to bring people on guided tours of Web content from chat rooms

In general, the more features and the fancier the chat client, the more expensive the software is. Effective, free chat software does exist, but in terms of scalability and features it rarely competes with large-scale commercial chat systems, such as ichat, shown in Figure 16-4 in use on Sony's popular "The Station" Web site.

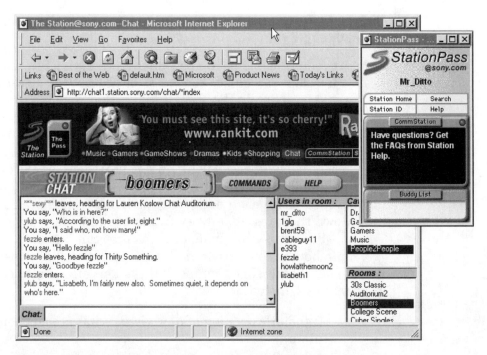

Figure 16-4 Sony's "The Station" Web site offers a full–featured, Java-based chat area that uses ichat software.

Chat areas can be an effective means of building a community on a Web site. Chat areas are not meant for every site, however. People cannot chat in an area by themselves, so unless your site attracts enough visitors to keep a chat area stocked with at least two people, the chat area won't be used.

A list of different chat software is available from http://www.yahoo.com/Computers_and_Internet/Internet/ World_Wide_Web/Chat/Software/.

How can I add the ability for site visitors to send e-mail even if they don't have an e-mail account?

Using <A HREF="mailto:user@domain.com"> may be an easy way to add e-mail to your site, but the method only works for people who have a preconfigured e-mail application.

By adding form-based e-mail to your site, on the other hand, users can send e-mail without an e-mail application, mail server, and so on. To add e-mail to your site, you need a Web server application that takes form-submitted data and sends it, correctly formatted, to a mail server. With a server application, you can customize the formatting of the subject and the body of the e-mail that is sent.

Form-based e-mail is often used to request more information, to e-mail comments to the Webmaster of a site, and to order products. The easiest way to add e-mail to your site is to write your own or customize an existing server-side mail script. Different server platforms use different methods of connecting to mail servers, so mail scripts written in scripting languages that run on your server may not interface correctly with your mail server. Most UNIX systems, for example, are already configured with sendmail, an application that allows scripts to easily send e-mail.

For more on sendmail, visit the sendmail FAQ at http://www.landfield.com/faqs/mail/sendmail-faq/. For a number of different CGI form mail applications, visit http://www.cgi-resources.com/. For a COM object that allows form-based e-mail through Active Server pages, visit http://www.serverobjects.com/products.htm#Aspmail.

+

Tip: *When processing Web-based e-mail messages on the server, appending an easily identifiable string of text to the beginning of the subject line of the e-mail message is a good idea. For example, if the user enters "You have a great Web site" as the subject line, change the subject to:*

[Website Mail] You have a great Web site

If the e-mail is sent to someone who also receives personal e-mail, changing the subject line makes e-mail from the Web site easy to distinguish from personal e-mail. A common string in the subject line of Web-based e-mail also makes e-mail filtering and sorting significantly easier. There is always the danger that someone will send 500 e-mails from the Web site and bury someone's personal mail on the receiving end.

WEB SITE FUNCTIONALITY ENHANCEMENTS

? ## What does it take to add a search feature to my site?

Adding an effective search engine to a site can be one of the easiest or hardest tasks in Web development. What makes search engines difficult is the fact that they must perform a number of different functions. Good search engines do the following:

- Allow users to search with a variety of search parameters
- Run constantly as daemons or services on the Web server
- Continuously index Web site content
- Break up search results into pages that contain a limited number of hits
- Prioritize, or rank, pages that have been found
- Allow a high degree of customization in the search results pages
- Index <META> tags for prioritized page listings

An effective search engine must do so many tasks that installing, debugging, and customizing the output is often a challenge. If you already have a Web server installed, there is a chance that a search engine is also installed. Netscape Enterprise server, for example, ships with Verity Search Engine, shown in use in Figure 16-5, and Microsoft's Site Server package includes Microsoft Index Server. Using search engines that are bundled with your server is usually a good idea. A bundled search engine will have been tested for compatibility and speed. Besides, you already purchased it, so the software is available without additional cost.

After search engine software has been installed, it needs to be configured. Your search engine needs to know which documents to index. You may be able to specify virtual roots that have been set by the Web server or you may need to specify file paths to Web directories. You may also need to filter certain types of content, such as scripts, based on file suffix or directory. You need to configure your HTML form to

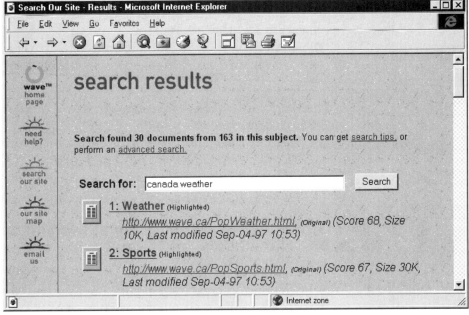

Figure 16-5 Roger's Wave Cable allows site visitors to search their site using the Verity search engine that installs with Netscape Enterprise Server.

send the correct parameters to the search engine application. Parameters may be included as form elements hidden within the page or hard-coded into a text file, such as an .ini file. Parameters that need to be specified for site searches often include

- Directory restrictions on which content to include in the search
- Maximum number of total hits to return
- Maximum number of hits to display per page
- Types of documents to include in the search (e.g. HTML, Microsoft Word, Adobe PDF)

Once the data has been submitted, search engines display the search results in a template page, usually a CGI or a static HTML page with special tags that are interpreted by the search engine when the results are listed. This page or script needs to be edited to give the search results page the look and feel that you desire.

A comprehensive list of site indexing software is available at http://serverwatch.internet.com/tools/search.html.

!

> ***Warning:***   *Installing persistent server applications on a Web server decreases the amount of CPU processing available for Web page delivery. Depending on the size of your site, the frequency with which the content changes, and the software you use, a search engine may require significant amounts of RAM and CPU time.*

?

What is required to add a recommendation engine to my site and what benefits can it offer site visitors?

Recommendation engines are a relatively new feature on the Web. With a recommendation engine, the user enters personal profile data by filling out a form or answering questions. Moviefinder, for example, asks users to rate movies. As the user rates movies, the engine builds a personal profile. After all the data has been collected, the user's profile is compared with that of others whose preferences are similar and a recommendation is made. A recommendation engine may review a user's profile information and notice, for example, a fondness for science fiction books by Neil Stephenson and William Gibson. The recommendation engine examines the user profiles of others who like the same books. The engine then recommends books that have been rated highly by others whose profiles are similar. Barnes and Noble offers a similar automated collaborative filtering system on their Web site shown in Figure 16-6.

The process of comparing user preferences is known as *automated collaborative filtering.* Commercial recommendation engines can make recommendations based on as many as tens of thousands of other user profiles. The service offers a great deal to site visitors, but putting a recommendation engine on a site requires a great deal of thought and configuration. Before you decide that a recommendation engine is right for your site, ask the following questions:

- Does my site offer products or services that would benefit from a recommendation engine?
- Do I have the infrastructure to support the database and software requirements?
- Does my site attract enough visitors to make automated collaborative filtering worthwhile?

These popular software packages offer automated collaborative filtering:

- Firefly, at http://www.firefly.com
- Affinicast, at http://www.affinicast.com

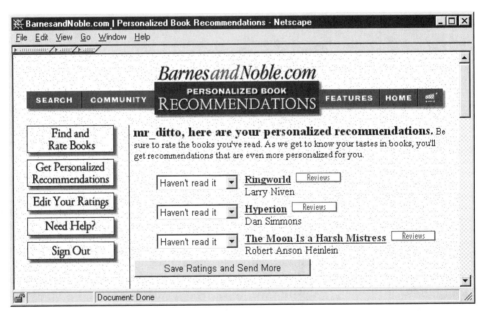

Figure 16-6 Barnes and Noble uses automated collaborative filtering to recommend books to its customers.

? What does my site need in order to add electronic commerce functionality?

Online commerce has proven an effective means of handling automatic transactions. Goods and services can be sold in a number of different ways over the Internet. Unfortunately, the simplest methods are the least secure. The following methods are frequently used for selling products online:

- E-mail
- 800 numbers
- Order forms that can be printed and faxed
- Insecure HTML forms for sending credit card data
- Secure HTML forms for sending credit card data
- Secure transaction using First Virtual
- Secure transaction using DigiCash, CyberCash, and SmartCards

Allowing visitors to purchase products by sending e-mail messages, sending fax transmissions, or dialing an 800 number may seem an inexpensive addition to a site or business. However, these sales methods all require someone on the other end to manually verify whether a credit card number is valid. These methods also have the potential for security holes. Sending standard HTML forms through an insecure connection isn't much safer than e-mailing credit card information over the Web.

A good e-commerce solution requires a secure connection such as a secure sockets layer between the Web browser and the Web server. Commerce servers offer a number of security features and can process transactions automatically without human involvement. Developing an e-commerce site can be challenging and potentially quite expensive, depending on which software and methods are used.

If your company offers a small number of products, experiences a low sales volume, or simply doesn't have the development resources to build a secure online commerce solution, try using a third-party e-commerce server that is already set up and maintained. Only payment information has to be secure, so the majority of pages on your site can probably remain. For a third-party solution, place your order form on the secure commerce server and make sure that any sensitive data that is returned is also sent through a secure connection. Be aware that sites that offer e-commerce services often take a percentage of sales revenue as well as a hosting fee.

Whether you intend to build an e-commerce solution yourself or you need a third-party to handle sales transactions, look for the following popular e-commerce features:

- Transaction verification
- Secure connections
- Database connectivity
- Fault tolerance
- Flexible payment methods (i.e. First Virtual or Cybercash)

For more information about electronic commerce, visit Internet.com's Electronic Commerce Guide at http://e-comm.internet.com/. For a listing of Commerce servers, visit http://serverwatch.internet.com/tools/secure.html.

Chapter 17

Online Advertising

Answer Topics!

Online Advertising @ a Glance

Online advertising is becoming more popular across the Internet. It is almost impossible to spend any time online without running into the familiar rectangular banners that define an online advertisement. Advertisements can be a strong source of online revenues. Now more than ever before, sites are considering using advertisements or are looking to revamp their current advertising methods.

Advertising means more than simply adding a graphic to your site and charging for it. To make the most out of hosting advertisements, you must take every step—from signing contracts to analyzing the data—very carefully. Done properly, advertising has the potential to be your site's greatest source of revenue.

This chapter covers the following topics:

Why Advertise? gives an overview of why companies advertise on the Web and what factors you should consider before puttings ads on your site.

Advertising Deals discusses the details that go into contracts as well as the factors that effect the price of advertisements on the Web.

Advertising Standards covers the current file size restrictions and popular pixel dimensions of online advertisements. Also covered are the two new types of online advertisements: interstitial ads and floating ads.

Managing Ads offers different methods of handling ads along with a little advice on what technique is best for your site.

Driving Up the Price of Ads explains how to get more money for the ads on your site.

WHY ADVERTISE?

? Why do companies advertise on the Web?

Today, the majority of Web site revenues come from advertising. Revenues from subscriptions and commerce have not lived up to expectations. As a result, many sites sustain themselves by advertising alone.

The Web advertising industry took off in the last few years largely as a result of one thing, demographics. The 40 million or so people worldwide who surf the Web are mostly college graduates. Half are either working professionals or managers. The average Web surfer is in his or her early thirties and earns an annual income well above the national average. Over half of all Web users have a Web connection at work and, not coincidentally, the peak Internet traffic time in most areas is around lunch time.

Advertising on the Web is one of the easiest ways to target people with money to spend and a desire to spend it. Every company has its own reason for advertising, but most advertise for one of two reasons:

- To increase brand recognition
- To drive people to purchase

How popular does my site need to be before I can consider adding advertising banners?

Advertising on the Web is different from advertising in traditional media such as print, radio, and television. And although the front page of a Web site is often referred to as a *home page,* placing an ad on your site is quite different from placing an ad in front of a house. No one would pay to put a billboard on a front lawn because so few people would see it—not so on a Web page. Because most Web advertising models are based on the number of times an ad is seen by site visitors (the number of *impressions*), advertisement space on a page that does not attract a lot of traffic may still make money. Advertisers are especially interested in sites that attract visitors with highly focused or specialized interests, because advertisers can target the specific types of people who visit those sites.

Are there special factors that I should take into consideration before I add advertising banners to my site?

A number of factors play important roles in the success of online advertising. Before you place advertisements on a site, consider the following questions:

- Is setting up software on my site to schedule and track ads realistic?

- Will advertisements distract from the content on my site?

- Does my site attract the type of demographics that an advertiser would want?

- Will the return on investment be higher than the cost involved in adding advertisements to my site?

- Does my Internet service provider's "terms of use" or my company's policies allow advertisements to appear on my site?

These questions may raise even more questions, but carefully finding the answers should make it clear whether advertising is a legitimate option for your site.

Banners on Smaller Sites

Advertisers who pay on a per-impression basis often prefer to place ads on low-volume sites that specialize in one topic because the visitors to those sites usually spend more time looking at each page. The typical visitor to a large site, such as a search engine, usually browses through pages very quickly in search of one piece of information. On pages in which visitors stop and take the time to view the content, the exposure time for each advertisement is greater. Longer exposure times mean a better effect from exposure to a company's logo or message. This increase in exposure also increases the chances that a site visitor will both remember and click an advertisement.

Low-volume sites that offer specialized content give advertisers the opportunity to target people with specific interests, and advertisers can do that without paying a premium for sites that use sophisticated targeting software. For example, take a quick visit to www.motorcycle.com and you will find advertisements for motorcycles and parts that you probably can't find elsewhere on the Web. Paying for an advertisement that pops up when someone searches with a search engine for a keyword like "motorcycle" is usually more expensive than advertising on a site that already specializes in motorcycles.

ADVERTISING DEALS

? What is in a typical advertising contract?

Price is not the only factor in most advertising deals—far from it. Many advertisers are interested in other factors, such as guaranteed click-throughs, and write them into contracts. Making sure that all of the conditions of a contract can be met is important. As you negotiate a contract, make sure that the amount charged for advertisements and the promise of visitors who see the advertisements makes the deal lucrative for both parties.

Ad spots are almost always bought on the basis of cost-per-thousand banner impressions (CPMs), the number of click-throughs, or a hybrid of the two pricing models. Therefore, using ad management software that can measure the number of impressions served and click-throughs is critical. Large contracts, especially contracts that involve time-critical advertisements, usually state that the conditions of the contract must be met within a certain time period. Agreeing on an advertising contract that is both lucrative and contains specific terms that can easily be met may be quite difficult.

A typical advertising contract, for example, may include the following conditions:

● Eight different ad banners, with all banners placed in a central location across the top of a page

● 350,000 total impressions

● All banners served over one calendar month

● Limit of two exposures per banner per user (based on IP address), unless all banners have been shown twice

● Guaranteed 500 click-throughs (1 percent for all impressions), or ads will continue to be served until that number is reached

● Thorough reporting of click-throughs and impressions served

On a busy site, contracts with several different advertisers may require ads to be placed in the space on the same set of pages at the same time. In cases like those, the site has to balance the requirements of several different contracts. A flexible ad server can understand, for example, that one banner is doing better at 3 o'clock in the morning in one area of the site than another banner. The flexible ad server can increase a banner's display percentage in one area and move another banner aside to make room.

How much do most sites usually charge for advertisements?

The method of pricing advertisements on the Web is still being settled. At the moment, the majority of sites use the CPM model, by which the advertiser is charged based on the number of impressions (ad banners) served. Not everyone is satisfied with this pricing model. Compared to advertising in

The Click-Through Model

Rather than pay for advertisements based on the CPM model, the majority of companies that place ads would rather pay based on the number of click-throughs. A *click-through* is when a Web surfer clicks on an ad banner and hyperlinks to the advertiser's site. Counting the number of click-throughs and comparing the number to the cost of placing the ad is often the easiest way for an advertiser to measure the success and effectiveness of an ad.

A typical quote range for an untargeted, full-sized banner ad at 468×60 pixels is $20 to $50 per one thousand impressions. A site that serves 40,000 pages a month with one ad on every page can expect somewhere between $800 and $2,000 in monthly ad revenues in a fully sold month. Keep in mind that a fully sold month with advertisements for every page in a site is not common. A site that has sold half to three-quarters of its ad spots is thought to have done well.

traditional print and broadcast media, Web advertising tends to be more expensive on a cost-per-exposure basis.

? What factors are advertising prices based on?

The price that a site charges for advertising is typically based on four variables:

- **Size:** A strong correlation has been drawn between the size of an ad in total number of pixels (height × width) and the likelihood that it will be both noticed and clicked. Large ads that take up a higher percentage of the Web page tend to do better, but they are more expensive than small ads.

- **Position on the page:** The closer an ad is to the top of the page, the more likely it will be seen. Ads in the lower part of the page are less likely to be seen because users have to scroll down the page to see them. Ads at the bottom of the page, curiously, are usually more successful than ads in the middle of the page, because visitors who have scrolled down the page are often more tempted to click on a banner there than they are to scroll up the page again.

- **Targeting:** User targeting is a factor that drives advertisement prices up. Sites that offer keyword searches, such as search engines, and sites with areas that attract visitors with specific interests, often attempt to serve ads that match these interests. Targeted ads are much more likely to hit users who are interested in what they have to offer. A travel ad that is displayed when the name of a foreign city is typed as the search criteria on a search engine site is a good example of an ad targeted to specific user interests. The higher prices that are usually quoted for targeted ads are often necessary to cover the expensive software that makes the targeting functionality possible. Being able to demonstrate the effectiveness of targeting on a site is important. Promising a client that you will only serve their ad to residents of New York, for example, is not realistic.

● **Reporting:** Being able to provide data on who saw an advertisement, as well as who clicked on it, is a strong selling point for advertisers. In addition, live reporting on ad delivery and well-presented, timely reports increase the value of advertising on a site.

Optimal Ad Placement

A recent study by students at the University of Michigan compared the click-through rates of advertisements placed in different positions on pages at a site called www.webreference.com. The results: The highest click-through rates were recorded in banners placed in the lower-right corner of the browser window next to the scroll bar. In general, high click-through rates were recorded in ads placed next to the scroll bar.

ADVERTISING STANDARDS

? What are the usual dimensions of ad banners?

The Internet Advertising Bureau has proposed a voluntary standard for the size of online advertisement banners. Most ads are designed to be one of the eight sizes in Table 17-1.

Three of the most popular sizes of ad banners include: a) square buttons, b) micro buttons, which often link to software that can be downloaded, and c) the ubiquitous full banners that grace the tops and bottoms of many Web pages.

b) A micro button at 88 × 31 pixels

a) A square button at 125 × 125 pixels

c) A full banner at 468 × 60 pixels

Width*	Height*	Size Name
468	60	Full banner
392	72	Full banner with vertical navigation bar
120	240	Vertical banner
234	60	Half banner
125	125	Square button
120	90	Button #1
120	60	Button #2
88	31	Micro button

* Sizes are in pixels.

Table 17-1 Internet Advertising Bureau Voluntary Standards for Online Advertisement Banner Sizes

How the Standards Originated

The size of magazine and newspaper advertisements are based on predetermined factors such as page size and column width. No such predetermined factors exist for the Web, but the need for advertisement standards in the online world is as important as it is in other media. Advertisers that place ads on a number of different sites prefer banner sizes to be consistent across sites. Consistency of size makes it easier to compare a banner's effectiveness in different sites. Consistency also means that fewer banners need to be constructed.

? What are the standard file-size restrictions or standards for online advertising?

There isn't much in the way of standards when it comes to how big or small the file size of an ad can be. A good estimate is 8 to 15KB. Sites that cater to visitors who access the Web via a T1 line, for example, allow file sizes to be larger because visitors can take advantage of the higher bandwidth. Taking into consideration the bandwidth of visitors to your site is extremely important.

DoubleClick currently puts the cap on file sizes at 8KB for full banner ads. The limit at Infoseek ranges from 10KB for a static GIF to 12KB for a GIF animation. If a large percentage of visitors are using a modem, keep in mind the number of seconds that having a large banner adds to a page's download time.

You can expect the standards for file sizes and file formats to change in the future as high-resolution computer screens become more common, new browsers are introduced, and bandwidth increases.

? What are the standards for floating ads and ads that show up between pages?

Ads that float in their own windows and ads that show up between pages, called interstitial ads, are a recent development. Both types of advertisements are different from traditional banner ads and have attracted a bit of attention. In terms of ad size, no standards like the de facto standards for banner ads have been declared for these types of ads.

Interstitial Ads

After the hyperlink has been clicked, an interstitial ad takes up the whole screen. A typical ad appears from five to ten seconds before it is replaced by the user's intended destination. Interstitial ads are usually designed for a screen area no larger than 485 by 320 pixels, the default window area when Netscape Navigator 2.0 is opened on a Macintosh. The ads are designed to load quickly and use minimal text. With only five to ten seconds of opportunity, site visitors rarely click on interstitial ads and often can't read more than a few words. Interstitial ads, however, do get noticed. For this reason, they are often considered prime opportunities to increase consumer exposure to corporate brands and messages. The success of an interstitial ad is less likely to be measured in click-throughs.

As you create an interstitial ad, keep in mind that optimal connection speed is important. A home user connected with a 14.4 baud modem may require ten seconds to display a 10KB interstitial ad and another five seconds to read it, whereas a visitor connected through a T1 line may grow frustrated at having to wait longer than eight seconds before being redirected to the next page.

Creating an Interstitial Ad

To create an interstitial ad, simply create a simple HTML advertisement page and add the following line of code to the very top of the HTML document:

```
<META HTTP-EQUIV="Refresh" CONTENT="5; URL=NewPage.html">
```

After the page is displayed for five seconds, the browser requests NewPage.html. Rename NewPage.html with the page to which you wish to redirect the user. Change the number 5 to the length, in seconds, you want the interstitial ad to be displayed.

Rarely used browsers do not support the META refresh tag listed here. If users of these browsers are important to your site, make sure to ad a hyperlink to the destination page, or the user will not be able to navigate to the intended page. Also, if you place your hyperlink for browsers that do not support the refresh META tag within <NOSCRIPT></NOSCRIPT> tags, it will be hidden from many of the browsers that do support the refresh tags.

Floating Ads

Floating ads use JavaScript to create a floating window that is the same size as the ad banner containing no drop-down menus, URL line, navigation bar, or scroll bars, such as the window shown in Figure 17-1. The floating window contains an ad banner. When the banner is clicked, the main browser window content is updated with the URL specified by the ad and the floating window disappears. Browsers that support floating ad banners include Netscape Navigator 2.0 and later and Microsoft Internet Explorer 3.0 and later.

Note: *Chapter 13, which covers JavaScript in detail, offers source code for creating a floating advertisement with JavaScript.*

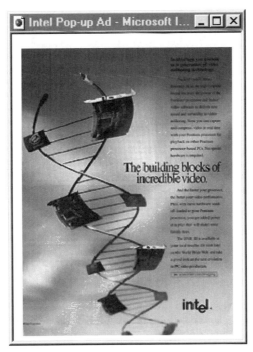

Figure 17-1 A floating advertisement

MANAGING ADS

What are the main methods of managing the serving of advertisements?

At first glance, managing ads doesn't seem to be very difficult, but it can consume a great deal of time and effort. Except for sites that have only one sponsor that buys all the ad space for a given amount of time, managing ads can be difficult. In fact, you probably need special software or an outside agency to help manage and possibly serve the advertisements.

You can deal with the complexities of hosting ads in one of four ways:

● Brute-force human labor, possibly coupled with a few server scripts, JavaScript, and Java applets

● Contract out to an agency that schedules and serves ads

● Build your own ad server software
● Purchase ad server software

✱ ***Note:***   *Many ISPs prohibit the use of certain types or even all types of custom server software. If you use an ISP, check the "terms of use" conditions that you agreed upon when you signed up.*

What is involved in managing ads by hand?

For small sites with few advertisers, managing advertisements by hand isn't unrealistic. Anyone who tracks and reports by hand, however, should pay very close attention to the contract requirements. If an advertiser finds that its click-through statistics don't match yours, you may be in for a rough conflict resolution.

What are ad brokering services, and how do they make money?

Contracting out to a service that sells and manages ads for your site is the simplest and often the most economically feasible method of hosting advertisements. Companies that offer this service are known as advertising representatives, or brokers. Serving ads on the Web is a new industry, so a number of disreputable companies either underpay or pay late. The stable and reliable services require a minimum number of page impressions per month, ranging from 100,000 to 1 million, depending on the broker.

Sites are usually paid a percentage of the revenue made from selling ads on a site. Depending on the volume of ads sold, the percentage ranges from as low as 25 percent to as high as 80 percent. The more pages that a site serves, the better deal you get. Companies that offer brokering services include DoubleClick, AdSmart, ClickThrough, FlyCast, and Banner Media.

Most brokering agencies are proud to tell you who their most prominent clients are. However, checking to see if the clients are still using the agency and whether ad space on their sites is actually being sold is always a good idea. The percentage of revenue to which a site is entitled is often higher for long-term contracts. For example, if you sign a three-year contract with an ad broker, a higher percentage is usually paid to you.

Another thing to consider when choosing an ad broker is speed. Many agencies still use the slower CGI-based applications or scripts to tabulate statistics, tabulate demographics, and place ads. The processing time of CGI-based ad delivery may cause ad graphics to appear slowly on a site.

What are the risks involved in building ad software?

Building their own software is the first thought that enters most programmers' minds when they hear the prices that are quoted by commercial ad servers for handling ads. Prices range from $6,000 to $60,000 for a good ad server, so it is easy to get cold feet at the thought of hosting your own ads. Unless a programmer has successfully written ad server software before, however, building a server is probably a bad idea. Maintaining the server, not to mention corporate liability for software errors, makes building your own server risky.

Small sites that deal with only one or two advertisers and a small number of impressions and ads can consider a number of easily implemented, client-side solutions. Freely available JavaScript code and Java applets can be used to monitor, rotate, and track ads. To find client-side solutions such as these, visit www.gamelan.com, www.webreference.com/javascript/, and the Java Boutique at www.j-g.com.

You can also manage ads with Web database applications. However, make sure that you understand database applications and their development environments very well before you attempt a database-driven ad management solution. Constructing a Web-based ad server from a Web-connected database application is often possible, with a small amount of programming, for under $1000.

What should I look for when shopping for a commercial ad server?

The first thing most people notice when shopping for commercial ad server software is the price. Today's ad server solutions are as expensive as e-commerce servers were a few years ago. Until an industry leader like Netscape or Microsoft steps in, ad management software will most likely remain expensive.

A half-dozen software companies offer high-end solutions, and another half-dozen offer mid-range solutions for ad management and serving software. As you compare ad server software, look for a solution that includes the following:

- ease of use
- targeting capabilities
- allows remote administration
- allows you to choose from a number of databases for tracking and targeting functionality
- offers reliable customer service hours in your time zone
- offers live statistics on the number of ads being served

Beware of companies that make most of their income from consulting on their own software product. Companies that offer ad servers include NetGravity, DoubleClick, ClickOver, Accipiter, and Homegrown.

Building vs. Buying and Outsourcing Ad Management Resources

A very thorough cost study of outsourcing, buying, and building ad-hosting solutions was conducted by Forrester Research, Inc., at the beginning of 1997. The study compared the costs of hardware, software, outside fees, and human resources at small, medium, and large sites. The conclusion: Small sites should go with an outside agency. For medium sites, choosing an outside agency or buying software is a toss-up. Large sites, meanwhile, should buy the software and manage the ads themselves. The study serves to confirm what many large sites have found out after dedicating countless hours on ad serving solutions before stepping outside the company for a pre-built or even a third-party, off-site solution.

DRIVING UP THE PRICE OF ADS

? **What are the main ways to drive up the prices of ads on my site?**

You can take advantage of a number of methods to increase the amount that you can charge for ads. If you are serving your own ads, the following techniques help:

- Create a media kit for advertisers
- Offer to create the actual ad banners
- Target ads
- Have a third party audit statistics
- Offer thorough, well-explained ad statistics to advertisers
- Avoid "fire sales" by which you sell unsold space at the last minute
- Offer live reporting

? **What are media kits, and what is involved in creating one?**

Media kits are a great way to sell a site to advertisers. Include advertising rates, site statistics, and any demographic information you can get your hands on in a media kit. Use a media kit to brag about click-through rates and your targeting capabilities. Include success stories in the media kit. Make sure to include ad banner sizes, deadlines, file types, maximum file sizes, and prices. If you have collected data about your site through online registrations, contests, and so on, include that data in the media kit. Printed, hard-copy media kits are useful, but online versions are more convenient in most cases.

? **How does creating ads for a client drive up the price of advertising?**

Making the services of a graphic artist part of a package is especially useful for targeting first-time advertisers and smaller, less-technical advertisers. Offer in-house expertise to demonstrate what works in a banner and what doesn't work. Not all companies have their own advertising agency or their own graphic artists to create the graphics they need for a successful campaign.

Even if a company has its own advertising agency, the agency may lack experience with the Web. Use your online advertising experience as a selling point. Companies, of course, like to hear success stories about the ads you created in the past. Know what works and what doesn't, and sell this knowledge as an advantage to advertising on your site.

? What is targeting, and how does it increase the amount that I can charge for advertising?

Targeting, which is new to the Web, means to match a user's interests with a specific advertisement. Someone who uses a search engine to search on automobiles, for example, sees an advertisement from a car company, such as the ad shown in the search results page in Figure 17-2. Most high-end ad servers include the targeting capability as part of their software. However, adding the ability to target to a site can be extremely difficult.

Targeting software may not be necessary for sites that already attract visitors with specific interests. Visitors to a site that rates movies, for example, obviously watch movies. Movie advertisers may pay more per impression for an add on a move site because the ad automatically targets movie fans.

To make targeting a part of their site, sites that generate content from relational databases can add advertising categories into the database and match the categories with content served or with topics that have been requested in a search. Search engines can do the same thing. Companies that offer advertising server software with targeting capabilities include NetGravity, DoubleClick, Bellcore, and Accipiter.

Companies that include software and/or services that help to customize content, including ads, to specific types of users include FireFly, Engage, BroadVision, and NetPerceptions.

? Is third-party auditing of statistics necessary?

Many major advertisers on the Web require site statistics to be audited by a third party. Whether ads are priced based on

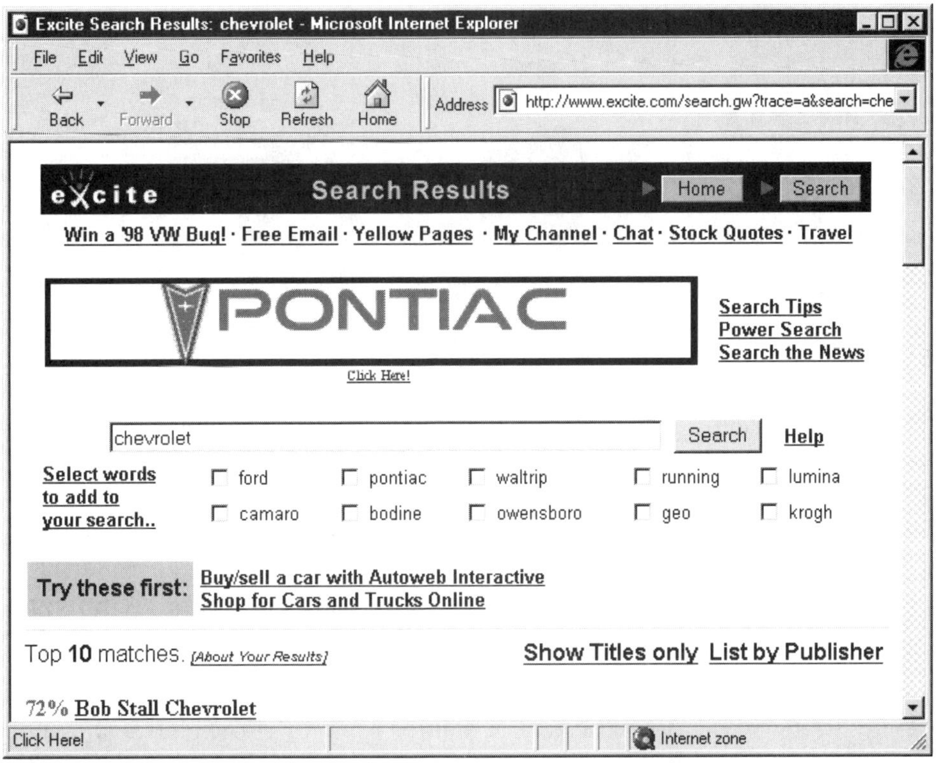

Figure 17-2 Search engines like this one use targeting to match search criteria with the appropriate advertisement. Here, the results of a search on *Chevrolet* trigger an ad for Pontiac.

the number of click-throughs or CPM, advertisers are wary of sites that artificially increase their site statistics in order to increase revenue. Advertisers don't want to be charged when the same ad is served to the same person five times or when most of the people who view the ad work for the company that runs the site on which it appears. A third-party audit simply makes sure that advertisers are not cheated.

Web-based statistical packages that keep track of user sessions and IP addresses are available. The packages can estimate how often a particular visitor retrieved an ad, image, or content from a cached file or from the server. Tell your advertisers which ad-tracking methods you use before you place ads to avoid conflicts in the future. Companies that offer auditing services include I/PRO, BPA International, and NetCount.

Consistent Tracking Is Difficult

Counting how many times an ad is seen is not as simple as it sounds. With the caching of ads on proxy servers and local hard drives, some ads are seen but never logged on the server and therefore cannot be counted. And when a Web surfer uses an off-line browser that automatically hits and caches every page in a site for viewing later, there is no way to know if anyone ever viewed those specific pages and ads.

? Are "fire sales" a good way to clear out unsold advertising space at the end of a sales cycle?

Some Web sites sell unsold advertising space at a discount near the end of a sales cycle or right before the space becomes available on their site. "Fire sales" like these are bound to cause at least a few advertisers to hold out each month for cheaper CPM rates. Keep in mind that fire sales can devalue your ad space and anger advertisers who paid the full price.

One way to handle unsold space is to exchange it with a site that doesn't compete with your site and create a cross-promotional opportunity. Place a banner on another site in exchange for hosting a banner on yours. In the long run, swapping ad space may drive up the number of site visitors and thereby increase the number of ads that can be sold next time.

? Do advertisers see any value in live reporting on site and advertisement statistics?

Creating a page on your site that offers live, or at least daily, statistics is a great selling point for most advertisers. Tracking click-through rates on specific banners as well as the total number of each banner served helps advertisers manage their advertising campaigns. Banners with low click-through rates can be replaced quickly with more effective banners. Recognizing an extremely effective campaign, an advertiser may decide to buy more impressions.

Increasing Click-Throughs

One way to increase a site's value to advertisers is to offer suggestions for increasing the click-through rates of ad banners. Following is a list of common techniques that help increase click-through rates:

- **Clear text:** Strange messages may increase click-throughs, but if the wrong visitors are attracted they may feel deceived and never return again.

- **Branding:** Displaying the company logo brings legitimacy to an ad.

- **Click me messages:** Simple, action-toned messages such as "Click here" and "Don't press" can increase click-throughs by 40 percent or more.

- **Interactivity:** Find out guidelines for ad banners on sites that you have selected for a placement. Many sites allow Shockwave, Flash, Java, and HTML. These banners always attract more attention. Met life, for example, has created a popular interactive advertisement using HTML with tables and a form element that allows navigation to a number of different pages from one banner, as shown here.

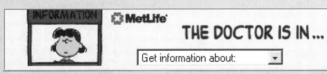

- **Color:** Bright but simple blocks of color attract attention. Use background colors that do not match page backgrounds. Subtlety is the enemy.

- **Animation:** Simply animating a banner often increases click-through rates by 25 percent.

- **Test banners:** Test a number of ad banners on a small scale and weed out banners that do not produce results. Live reporting often helps to do this quickly.

- **Choosing locations wisely:** Try to target your best possible demographic by choosing sites, sections of sites, and keywords wisely. Try to find a location where people are looking for what you have to offer.

- **Size and Placement:** Choose different sizes and placement areas on a page to distinguish your ads from standard banner ads at the top of the page.

- **Rotate frequently:** Click-through rates decrease significantly after a user has seen an ad banner for the second time. An ad that is being displayed on different sites by different Web servers is almost certain to be seen by the same person more than once. With lots of banners, the chance of repeat exposures is decreased.

- **Keep contests, sweepstakes, and limited-time offers to a minimum:** Contests, sweepstakes, and limited-time offers frequently reduce click-through rates because entering sweepstakes and contents requires the user to enter personal data, a practice that many Web surfers abhor. However, gathering demographic information from contests and sweepstakes may be more valuable to a company than doubling click-through rates. Collecting information this way helps to generate specific demographics that can be used to evaluate the success of an ad or suggest other marketing opportunities.

Chapter 18

3D on the Web

Answer Topics!

3D on the Web @ a Glance

In order to overcome the size and functionality limitations of flat Web pages, a handful of technologies have been developed to bring 3D interactivity to the Web browser. 3D Web sites may not be commonplace on the Web today, but few doubt that someday in our future the Web will be an interactive 3D experience.

Before we see widespread adoption of 3D on the Web, a number of changes need to take place: Hardware and software advancements, 3D definition language specifications, and public acceptance of 3D space. Some of these concerns are being addressed today with technologies such as Intel's MMX hardware and ISDN Internet connectivity to the home. At present, a number of true 3D and pseudo 3D technologies are available that can make any Web site more intriguing. VRML, Superscape's SVR, Apple's QuickTime VR, Microsoft's Direct Animation, and Sun's Java 3D API all offer methods of adding an element of virtual reality to a Web site.

Whether you add a completely separate 3D space to your site or you embed a 3D technology directly into an existing Web page, 3D is available and in use today.

This chapter covers these important topics:

VRML introduces Virtual Reality Markup Language and explains the basics of viewing VRML worlds and adding them to your site.

Developing with VRML offers tips for creating VRML worlds for your site. 3D file format conversion tools, multiuser VRML servers, and the enhancements made with the VRML 2.0 specification are all covered in this section.

Alternatives to VRML introduces Superscape's SVR and Apple's QuickTime VR, as well as Microsoft's Direct Animation and Sun's Java 3D APIs.

VRML

? What is VRML?

VRML (Virtual Reality Modeling Language) was accepted as a standard in 1995. VRML has blossomed into VRML 2.0, which offers greatly enhanced functionality. With only a few years behind it, VRML is still in its infancy and only a small percentage of the Web has adopted VRML.

What VRML offers the Web is interactive three-dimensional space. Objects are described with X, Y, and Z coordinates; lighting; atmosphere; textures; motion; and much more. But hardware limitations, lack of software, and lack of public awareness and acceptance are all hurdles that VRML faces today.

Even though VRML has not been adopted by the mainstream, adding a VRML section to a Web site, such as Mediadome's 3D Dilbert shown in Figure 18-1, can give the site the extra attention it needs. Creating a VRML world is not as difficult as it may sound. New tools offer VRML export functionality and the quality of the tools keeps getting better. VRML browsers are also improving. With VRML functionality being introduced in the newest releases of Microsoft and Netscape Web browsers, we are likely to see sites jumping head-first into VRML in the next few years.

? What do I need in order to view a VRML world?

To view a VRML world, you need a stand-alone VRML viewer, a Netscape VRML viewer plug-in, or a VRML ActiveX control from one of the companies that offer viewers. Because VRML is designed to be platform-independent, you may view VRML worlds on any platform as long as you have a viewer.

Netscape Communicator 4.0 was released with Silicon Graphics Cosmo Player 1.0. Microsoft Internet Explorer 4.0 includes VRML 2.0 Viewer version 1.0, which is based on Intervista Software's WorldView 2.0. Netscape Navigator 3.0 was released with Netscape's Live3D plug-in, which supports VRML 1.0.

The VRML viewers that have been released recently usually display scenes at higher quality than older viewers.

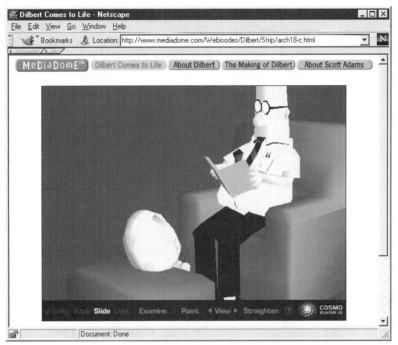

Figure 18-1   Mediadome has created a number of 3D Dilbert comic
strips, complete with moving camera angles and speech.
Because the cartoon is written in VRML, users can select
from a number of different viewers on different platforms
and change viewing positions while the cartoon plays.

This is especially true with VRML viewers that support the
VRML 2.0 standard defined in 1996. In addition, VRML
viewers that take advantage of native APIs on your
computer for rendering (Microsoft's Direct X and Silicon
Graphics Open GL, for example) perform better than those
that do not. Don't be afraid to try several viewers before
choosing one you like.

A number of significant features are still not part of the
VRML specification. Many of these features have to do with
streaming content, binary encoding, and the multiuser
worlds in which visitors interact. A few different companies
are pushing for their own standards to become part of the
VRML specification. As a result, some worlds contain
viewer-specific code and may only work with viewers made
by one company.

Companies that offer VRML viewers include

Company	Viewer Name	URL
Holger Grahn	GLView 3.1	http://www.snafu.de/~hg/
Intervista	WorldView 2.0	http://www.intervista.com/
Live Picture	RealSpace Viewer	http://www.livepicture.com/products/index.html
Microsoft	VRML2.0 Viewer	http://www.microsoft.com/vrml/
Newfire	Torch	http://www.newfire.com/pinfo/index_frames.html
Platinum Technology	WIRL	http://www.platinum.com/products/appdev/vream/wirl_ps.htm
Silicon Graphics	Cosmo Player	http://cosmo.sgi.com/
Sony	Community Place	http://www.sonypic.com/vs/
Superscape	Viscape	http://www.superscape.com

? What is the advantage of adding VRML to my site now?

With the release of Netscape Navigator 4.0 and Microsoft Internet Explorer 4.0, a large percentage of Web browsers now contain built-in VRML 2.0 support. The fact that very few sites have taken advantage of VRML doesn't mean that you should avoid VRML. In fact, now is probably the best time to surprise visitors with a 3D interactive experience. Following is a list of benefits that VRML can bring to a site:

● **Attracting media attention:** Pepsi used VRML to create a lightweight 3D animated advertising banner, shown in the following illustration. The number of people who actually saw the ad is smaller than those who read about it, but press coverage made the ad a great success. Pepsi was seen as breaking new ground by using cutting edge technology on the Web.

- **Increased time spent on your site:** Whether yours is an immersive 3D world or a simple, 20-second VRML animation, the site visitor is likely to spend more time on your 3D site. Animated GIFs, Java, and background sound do not have the same staying power as a rich and interactive VRML world.

- **Increased brand or message retention:** Visitors remember a site with a rotating ad banner in a 3D environment that they can walk around. Visitors also remember a 3D Web page better than they do a passive Web page.

- **Potentially smaller file sizes than animated GIFs:** Using VRML in place of animated GIFs for Web animations could lead to 30-second banner commercials that still fit within the tight file size restrictions for ad banners imposed by many sites.

What file format is used with VRML files?

VRML files are currently saved as text files much the same way that HTML files are. A binary file standard is now being investigated, but for now VRML are text files with a .wrl file extension. VRML files may also be stored in a gzip compression format, usually defined with the extension .wrl, .gz, or .wrz. Texture maps are usually saved in JPEG format and, with compressed files, the graphics are included in the single compressed package.

Is a special server configuration necessary for VRML?

For standard VRML 2.0 files, no server configuration is necessary other than the setting of MIME types. The .wrl file extension should be mapped to the MIME type, like so:

    model/vrml

? **What challenges must VRML technology overcome before it is embraced by the Web development community?**

Before VRML or another true 3D technology is embraced by Web developers, a number of difficult challenges must be overcome. Following is a list of the hurdles that VRML technology currently faces:

● **Computer hardware limitations:** 3D rendering involves very large computations. High-end computers are required for smooth renderings and high frame rates with seamless animation. This is especially true of highly detailed 3D scenes.

● **Lack of well-established, time-tested VRML viewers:** All of the VRML viewers currently on the market are relatively new. As a result, many are slow and suffer from display and compatibility problems. Many viewers have included proprietary enhancements to the VRML language, which improves functionality at the cost of compatibility.

● **Lack of development tools for creating interactive 3D environments:** A number of development tools are available, but many are expensive, difficult to use, and limited in terms of functionality.

● **Limitations of the current VRML 2.0 specification:** 3D space shared by multiple users and binary encoding are just two of the numerous features developers are expecting in future VRML specifications.

● **Lack of a good navigational metaphor for moving around in a VRML world:** Most users have difficulty using the navigation systems built into current VRML browsers. To overcome this problem, different input and display devices for personal computers may be used eventually.

● **Dependence on equipment designed for two-dimensional navigation:** The computer industry's dependence on the mouse, the keyboard, and the two-dimensional display screen make it difficult to develop intuitive, immersive methods of navigation in three-dimensional space. Shutter glasses, 3D mice, data gloves, head-mounted displays, force feedback devices, and 3D audio equipment have yet to be accepted in the personal computer marketplace.

? Is it possible to embed a VRML world into a Web page?

Embedding a VRML world into a Web page is actually quite a simple task. Just use the <EMBED> tag and specify WIDTH and HEIGHT attributes. For example, a VRML ad banner may use the following tag:

```
<EMBED SRC="AdBanner.wrl" HEIGHT="60" WIDTH="468">
```

To remove navigation bars, specify image quality, and so on, you need to look at the specifications of your particular browser. Cosmo Player and VRML 2.0 Viewer each support the following parameters:

```
VRML_DASHBOARD = FALSE
SGI_DASHBOARD = FALSE
VRML_IMAGEQUALITY = BEST, SMOOTH, SMOOTHEST
SGI_IMAGEQUALITY = BEST, SMOOTH, SMOOTHEST
```

Each DASHBOARD and IMAGEQUALITY attribute provides the same functionality, but using both is best to comply with a wider variety of browsers. A browser that doesn't understand one or more parameters simply ignores them. The following tag embeds a VRML world into a 468 by 60 pixel rectangle with no visible navigation controls and "best" image quality:

```
    <EMBED      SRC="AdBanner.wrl" HEIGHT="60" WIDTH="468"
                VRML_DASHBOARD = "FALSE"
SGI_DASHBOARD = "FALSE"
VRML_IMAGEQUALITY = "BEST"
SGI_IMAGEQUALITY = "BEST"
>
```

DEVELOPING WITH VRML

? Is it possible to convert existing 3D models to VRML format?

Most major 3D graphics applications now support the VRML format and export data to that format. Be sure to note the VRML version that your 3D application supports. 3D models look worse in VRML 1.0 than they do in VRML 2.0. If you don't achieve the effect that you are looking for with your 3D application's export function, try importing it into another 3D application and using its VRML export feature.

Tools are available to convert VRML 1.0 files to VRML 2.0, as well as import models that import the DXF format. This conversion will most likely increase compatibility with the VRML 2.0 browsers (some of which do not fully support VRML 1.0). Keep in mind that many of the best feature enhancements of VRML 2.0 are not included in your converted file because your conversion tool is not likely to add additional detail to your world.

The following software packages offer "save as VRML" functionality or VRML 1.0 to 2.0 file conversion:

Application	VRML Conversion Functionality	URL
3D Webmaster	Imports VRML 1.0, 2.0, and SVR and supports save as VRML 2.0 and SVR	http://www.3dwebmaster.com/
Crossroads	Imports many formats and supports save as VRML 1.0 and 2.0	http://www.europa.com/~keithr/
doomToVrml2	Converts Doom WAD files to VRML	http://vrml.sgi.com/tools/ doomtovrml2/
Extreme 3D to VRML Converter	Converts Macromedia Extreme 3D files to VRML	http://www.intervista.com
MAX VRML Exporter	3D Studio MAX plug-in that supports VRML file export	http://www.ktx.com

Application	VRML Conversion Functionality	URL
PolyTrans v2	Imports many formats and supports save as VRML 1.0 and 2.0	http://www.okino.com/
Ray Dream Studio	3D modeling tool	http://www.raydream.com/
Various SGI Utilities	A number of utilities are available for converting 3D files to VRML on the Silicon Graphics platform	http://webspace.sgi.com/Tools/index.html

? Is it feasible to build a VRML world with a text editor or should I use a tool that exports VRML code?

A number of books and online tutorials demonstrate how to write a VRML world from scratch. However, to create more than a handful of primitive shapes, you will have a significantly easier time using either a 3D graphics application that exports VRML or a VRML world creation tool. Large VRML worlds usually exceed several megabytes in file size. Entering this much information by hand can be extremely difficult and is likely to produce many errors.

It is always possible to open up a VRML world that has been created by VRML tools and edit the code by hand. As VRML world creation tools improve and become more accessible to the average developer, editing VRML worlds by hand will become less necessary. If you jump from HTML to VRML, you will probably be frustrated by VRML's programming language structure. VRML doesn't use tags the same way that HTML does, which takes a little bit of getting used to.

3D Technical Terms

Following are definitions of common 3D technical terms:

ambient light: Light that doesn't have a specific source. Increasing the ambient light increases the lighting on all objects evenly.

camera: The position that defines where the viewer "stands" in a 3D world. Moving around a 3D world primarily involves moving the camera that acts as the viewer's eyes.

directional light: A light source in a 3D world with a specific angle and brightness that results in a "cone" of light. Moving or changing the brightness of a directional light changes the brightness of objects that fall inside the cone.

FPS (frames per second): For animation and movement through a 3D world, the number of renderings per second is important. Viewers with high FPS counts animate smoothly; viewers with low counts see choppy landscapes.

gouraud shading: A method of rendering 3D data to the screen. Gouraud shading is a standard 3D graphics display option in 3D tools and viewers. It produces lower quality images than Phong, but renders faster to the screen and, as a result, allows more frames per second.

phong shading: A standard 3D graphics display option that renders images to the screen. Phong shading produces higher quality renderings than Gouraud shading, but renders more slowly.

polygon count: Every 3D model is made up of polygons. Detailed models have more polygons and, hence, a higher polygon count. Worlds with high polygon counts take longer to render but provide more detail.

rendering: The computer process of converting 3D model data, viewpoints, lighting, and so on to a flat image for onscreen display or printing. Rendering can vary from high to low quality. Different methods can be used, such as Phong and Gouraud shading, to produce a variety of results.

texture map: A 2D image that is wrapped around a 3D image to give it color and the appearance of texture. A brick texture map, for example, may be applied to a 3D rectangle to give it the appearance of a brick wall.

yaw, pitch, and roll: Different methods of rotation in 3D space. For example, if you imagine your head as a 3D object, yaw is the motion of looking from left to right, pitch is the motion of looking up and down or nodding, and roll is the motion of leaning your head from one shoulder to the other. Using 3D navigation controls, users can adjust their yaw, pitch, and roll, as well as move forward and backward for 3D navigation.

Z-buffer: An algorithm that removes hidden sides of 3D objects and remembers the layering order of pixels that are rendered. Z-buffering is important for optimal rendering performance.

? Do I need to create an entire "world" or can I create a single object in VRML?

The term *world* is used loosely when describing VRML content. A VRML world can be a single object or a complex set of objects. Likewise, a VRML world can employ lighting atmospheric effects and behaviors, or it can simply not define these effects and use the defaults instead.

For example, the following is VRML code for a red sphere with no defined light source:

```
#VRML V2.0 utf8
Shape{
appearance Appearance{
    material Material{
        diffuseColor 1 0 0
        }
    }
geometry Sphere{
    radius 10
    }
}
```

? What primitive shapes are available in VRML?

Primitives are basic 3D shapes that can be used as building blocks. Spheres, cubes, cones, and cylinders can all be created in VRML without specifying individual vertices. You can also create primitives by specifying vertices, but highly detailed spheres and cones increase the file size of a VRML file significantly.

Text may also be placed within a VRML world without defining individual vertices for characters. Font faces can be defined with the FontStyle setting. Three typefaces, serif, sans serif, and typewriter, are available along with these font styles: bold, italic, and none.

? Are prebuilt 3D objects available online?

There are a number of VRML object libraries. You can even find a large number of 3D object libraries that offer objects that can be converted to VRML. Most of the objects in the libraries are free. Many are available at different resolutions, so you can choose the ones that suit the needs of your world. Large, highly detailed models slow down the rendering speed of a virtual world. 3D world authoring tools include 3D clip art and often come bundled with comprehensive object libraries.

A good listing of VRML object libraries is available from the VRML repository at http://www.sdsc.edu/vrml/.

? What are the differences between VRML 1.0 and 2.0 and what features can we expect in the future?

VRML 1.0 was the first pass at developing an open 3D standard for the Web. VRML 2.0 has made great strides in improving the VRML standard by adding a number of new features and functionality. The following features have been added to VRML in the 2.0 specification:

● The ability to create irregular terrain for ground surfaces. Previously, only a flat plain could be used for the base of a VRML world.

- The introduction of animation allows motion in what were previously static worlds. Characters and objects are capable of containing their own set of movements.

- Interaction with the 3D environment, including collision detection and triggered events that occur based on actions that take place in a VRML world.

- Scripts may be used to add behaviors and responses to triggered events.

- Syntactical language changes have improved the structure and flexibility of the VRML language.

? What are the limitations of the VRML 2.0 standard?

Alhough VRML 2.0 has brought a number of significant advances to the VRML standard, there are drawbacks to using it for interactive 3D on the Web. Many drawbacks are not necessarily caused by the specification. Issues such as speed and rendering quality are implementation problems, but they stem from VRML's ASCII file format and the need for cross-platform support. The VRML 2.0 standard is by no means the final VRML standard. Many of VRML's current difficulties are being addressed by members of the VRML Consortium.

Following are some of VRML 2.0's drawbacks:

- **Slow rendering speeds on all VRML viewers:** Compared to 3D games such as ID Software's Doom and Quake, VRML often displays with a low frame rate and poor image quality. Some argue that insufficient detail in the file format is partially responsible for rendering performance.

- **Object behaviors difficult and often inefficient to add:** Scripting is allowed but not strictly defined or integrated into the VRML specification. The EAI (External Authoring Interface) is less than ideal and has trouble coping with dynamic worlds. However, some blame only the hardware.

- **Lack of direct support for VR input, feedback, and display devices:** VRML viewers rely on traditional monitors, mice, and standard keyboards. Head-mounted displays and 3D input devices such as data gloves and 3D mice should be included in the specification.

- **No built-in multiuser support:** Companies such as Blaxxun are developing multiuser APIs, but they are not strictly part of the VRML specification.

- **No byte compilation standard supported:** The current plain text file format allows source code to be viewed and places a greater computing burden on the viewer at the time of rendering.

? What is necessary to add a multiuser interactive 3D world to my site?

Multiuser 3D worlds are the newest 3D attraction to hit the Web. Visitors can interact with others in a virtual 3D environment. Many multiuser VRML sites offer text chat capabilities as well as visual interaction.

Keeping track of the spatial position of each site visitor and updating every browser with every other visitor's location requires special server software. At the moment, only these companies offer multiuser VRML servers:

Product	Company	URL
Community Server	Blaxxun	http://www.blaxxun.com
OZ Virtual	OZ	http://www.oz.com
World's Chat Gold	World's Inc.	http://www.worlds.net

Avatars

An *avatar* is a virtual representation of an individual in cyberspace. To see other people in a multiuser space, they must be represented by a form of some kind. Most multiuser spaces let you select or create your own avatar when you enter the 3D space. In the Blaxxun Community Server, shown here, custom-built avatars interact in a 3D environment.

Avatars can be quite complex. Some can walk, talk, and make facial expressions. Prefabricated avatars are available for downloading at avatar repositories on the Web.

The word *avatar* is a spiritual term that refers to the embodiment of a belief or philosophy. Neal Stephenson first applied the word to virtual reality in his book *Snowcrash*.

ALTERNATIVES TO VRML

What is SVR and how does it differ from VRML?

VRML is not the only file format for creating 3D content on the Web. Superscape, Inc. has developed an alternative called

SVR. SVR is a proprietary file format for creating interactive 3D worlds for use with Superscape's Viscape viewer, shown in Figure 18-2. SVR was developed by Superscape outside the boundaries of the VRML Consortium. Although the Viscape browser also supports VRML, using the SVR file format with Viscape offers a number of advantages over VRML.

Following are some advantages and disadvantages of the SVR format.

Advantages of SVR

First, the advantages:

● **Faster rendering speed**: Unlike VRML, SVR is a binary file format. Unlike ASCII files, binary files are already optimized for display when received by the browser. SVR files frequently offer greater detail and faster frame rates than VRML files.

Figure 18-2 The Cy-Berlin site is an SVR virtual model of Berlin. As the picture shows, it includes the Brandenberg Gate. SVR is an alternative file format to VRML.

- **Complex object behaviors built in to the file format**: Movement, gravity, and friction can all be added by using Superscape's authoring tools. Visitors to SVR worlds can interact with and manipulate objects in 3D worlds.

- **Small file sizes**: SVR's binary file format results in worlds that are significantly smaller than VRML worlds. Additionally, the source code is not accessible to those who are running the files.

- **Stability**: One browser means fewer viewer compatibility issues. The Viscape browser is quite stable and SVR worlds function more consistently as a result. One of the biggest complaints about VRML is browser instability.

Disadvantages of SVR

And here are the disadvantages:

- **Limited browser support**: At the present time, the Viscape browser is the only browser that supports SVR. However, this can also be seen as an advantage because cross-browser compatibility creates more development difficulties.

- **Limited choices for development tools:** Superscape's development tools output both VRML and SVR files, but other tools do not currently support the SVR format.

To download the Viscape browser or visit 3D sites that present SVR worlds, visit the Virtual World Wide Web at http://vwww.com.

? What is Apple's QuickTime VR and is it really 3D?

QuickTime VR, a technology that was first released by Apple a number of years ago, is usually viewed over the Internet through a browser plug-in. Because you can rotate around a point or pivot on a point, QuickTime VR gives the viewer the perception that he or she is viewing three-dimensional space. QuickTime VR is not actually 3D in the sense that it makes use of a coordinate system. Objects in a scene do not rotate slower if they are closer to you, for example.

As you view a QTVR scene like the one shown in Figure 18-3, you can only rotate, zoom in and out, and scroll up and down. Zooming in on a scene creates an image with a lower resolution because the pixels are stretched on the screen. To navigate a QTVR scene, hold down the mouse button and move it in the direction that you want to scroll. By pressing the SHIFT key, you can zoom in; press the CTRL key to zoom out.

By using multiple QTVR movies and connecting them by means of what are essentially hyperlinks embedded in the movie, you can create a particularly compelling 3D effect.

For more information on QTVR authoring and plug-ins, and to obtain samples of QTVR, visit Apple's QTVR site at http://qtvr.quicktime.apple.com/.

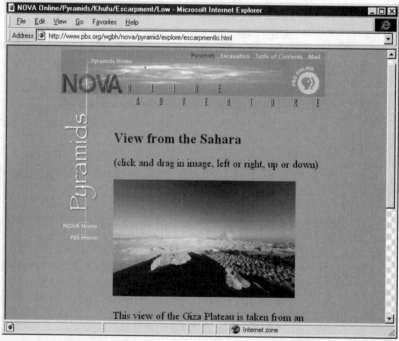

Figure 18-3 Nova uses Apple's QuickTime to illustrate what Egypt's Giza Plateau looks like from the Sahara desert. Visitors to the Nova site can rotate the view 360 degrees as well as zoom in and zoom out.

? What are the advantages of using QTVR?

QTVR offers a number of advantages over VRML and other coordinate-based 3D technologies. Following are some of the advantages:

- QTVR movies can be constructed completely from photographs. Stadium scenes, concert hall scenes, and outdoor scenes can all be created using a special 360-degree camera or by digitally "stitching" multiple images together.

- QTVR movies are often less than 200KB in size. Compared to VRML, the file size of a QTVR movie is often quite small. VRML worlds can get quite large when texture maps and complex 3D objects are added to a scene. QTVR scenes can be made from 3D-rendered scenes as well as from photographs. The complexity of a 3D model affects the file size of a QTVR movie in a small way.

- Many 3D modeling tools allow rendered scenes to be saved in a format that is easy to convert to QTVR panoramas.

- QTVR tools are inexpensive and viewers are freely available from Apple's Web site. QuickTime VR Authoring Studio is an Apple product with a wide variety of QTVR authoring tools.

- Newcomers to the Web have a much easier time using QTVR than they do navigating the 3D space of a VRML world.

? Are any types of QTVR movies available other than panorama?

Besides panoramas, QTVR movies can be made of objects. The movies themselves are often more difficult to create, but the effect can be quite compelling, particularly when displaying a single item against a solid color background. With object movies, the user grabs the object (clicks and drags) and spins it into a different position instead of scrolling left, right, up, and down, as shown in the Axisimages Web site seen in Figure 18-4.

Figure 18-4 Axis Images has created a QTVR movie of a Mercedes Benz that can be grabbed and rotated with the mouse.

Depending on how the movie was made, objects can be turned either on one or two axes. Most object movies allow an object to be spun 360 degrees on one axis, but creating an object that can be rotated along an X or Y plane is possible. To create either type of object movie, pictures need to be taken of the object at precise intervals around the object (e.g. every 15 degrees). It is also necessary to point the camera directly at the center point of the object with each photo for maximum effect. You can purchase or make hardware to make the process easier. Instructions for creating QTVR movies and a list of QTVR service companies are available from Apple's QuickTime VR Developer World at http://qtvr.quicktime.apple.com/dev/dev.html.

What is Direct Animation?

Direct Animation, a Microsoft API, allows you to build applications using features such as these: the ability to stream, 2D vector graphics, 3D geometry, and sound and video content. Direct Animation features can be accessed in Web pages through the use of ActiveX controls and client-side scripting or through Java applets. Microsoft provides a number of ActiveX multimedia controls that allow you to use many of the Direct Animation features with Internet Explorer 4.0.

For more information about using Direct Animation, visit the Direct Animation SDK site at http://www.microsoft.com/msdn/sdk/inetsdk/help/dxm/da/.

What is Java3D?

Java3D is an API and a subset of the Java Media and Communications APIs. With Java3D, entire scenes complete with atmosphere, lighting, 3D shapes, and so on can be generated.

Java3D uses specific APIs such as Microsoft's Direct3D, Silicon Graphics' Open GL, Sun's XGL, and Apple's QuickDraw3D as its underlying rendering engine. Although Java3D was never intended for high-frame-rate, interactive game play, it can be used to create compelling cross-platform scene renderings at run-time.

Java3D is a new API. As a result, it lacks the graphical development tools found with other 3D technologies such as VRML.

Chapter 19

Site Monitoring and Content Management

Answer Topics!

Site Monitoring and Content Management @ a Glance

- Running a Web site doesn't finish when the site goes live on the Internet. Whether it is maintenance, monitoring, or content updates, a Web site always needs some form of attention. By understanding the common problems associated with running a successful site, you can anticipate the site's needs.

- Site monitoring and management involve everything from keeping the site up and running to updating the content. Every good site needs a process. Your site's process may be as simple as assigning one person the job of taking care of the whole site, or as complex as keeping a whole team working with a fully featured automated publishing system.

- A well-thought-out process not only improves visitors' experience at the site, it also saves time and money. By streamlining publishing and maintenance procedures, you can spend more time attracting and keeping visitors.

- Much of this chapter is dedicated to pointing out the danger signs of a mismanaged site and recommending methods and processes for keeping ahead of problems. Much of the advice offered here applies only to large sites; much only applies to those who do their own hosting. Even if some of the advice doesn't apply to your site right now, it may in the future. Yahoo!, one of the most successful sites on the Internet, started as a handful of pages. Plant the seeds now to reduce growing pains in the future.

- This chapter explores these important topics:

- **Monitoring Web Server Software** explains the importance of monitoring a Web site, discusses what to look for in monitoring software, and describes what typically causes Web server problems.

- **Media Management** covers different methods of maintaining a site. You also learn techniques for ensuring that new content meets the necessary standards for online publication.

Dealing with Frequently Changing Content discusses the
difficult topic of managing a site that contains frequently changing
content. The different methods that are typically used and software
that can be used to implement each method are outlined.

MONITORING WEB SERVER SOFTWARE

What is site monitoring and how important is it for my site?

Anyone who has ever received the "connection to the server
could not be established" error after following a hyperlink
has probably seen the result of a Web site failure. When your
Web server crashes, anyone who requests a page from your
site receives an error. No Web server is perfect. If your site
remains up for any length of time or receives a reasonable
number of hits, your Web server probably suffers an
occasional hiccup.

The key to minimizing a Web server's downtime is to
respond to Web server problems as quickly as possible.
Unfortunately, knowing whether you have a problem is not
as easy as it sounds. The contact e-mail address and phone
number posted on your Web site are not accessible to visitors
after a server failure. Site monitoring is simply the mechanism
for determining whether a Web site is up and running.

A system that involves checking a site regularly is highly
recommended for every Web server. The solution may be as
simple as assigning an individual to actively check the home
page every few hours during the work day or as complex as
running automation tools to check the server constantly and
page you when a problems occurs. If you are wondering
whether a monitoring system is important for your site, ask
yourself how long it would take you to react and bring a site
back online if your site were to be suddenly turned off or
unplugged. Would getting the site back up take as long on the
weekend as at night? If you aren't satisfied with the time it
would take, you should consider a good site-monitoring plan.

? Does 24/7 site monitoring mean that someone needs to be near the Web server at all times?

Twenty four hour a day site monitoring does not mean that someone has to be around your site's Web server at all times. A number of applications are available that can check your Internet services and page or e-mail you or someone else if the site goes down. Most Web servers are capable of being administrated remotely, so restarting or reconfiguring a Web server or even an operating system from any computer with a telnet application and an Internet connection can be done.

To add automatic site monitoring capabilities to your server, you need to install site-monitoring software. For a comprehensive list of site-monitoring software and performance tools, visit http://serverwatch.internet.com/tools/monitor.html.

Tip: *A well-configured site will reboot itself and restart any Web services if the operating system crashes. Web servers can go back online after certain types of crashes without humans being involved. However, a server that is having problems and constantly restarts is hard to detect when everything is automated. If your server is set up to restart automatically, adding a startup script that e-mails or pages you with a quick note that tells you that the server restarted is worthwhile.*

Common Causes of Web Server Failure

The following problems may cause a Web server to stop responding or to stop altogether:

● **Full hard drive** is often a result of Web server log files that have not been removed from the server. Some operating systems have difficulty starting without enough hard drive space. Some Web servers also require hard drive space in order to operate.

- **Programming error** caused by a custom application such as a CGI. Even though a crashing CGI shouldn't directly affect the Web server, it may crash the operating system or overutilize the system resources.

- **Too many requests** cause many Web servers to crash. You can fix this problem by optimizing your site for performance. See Chapter 5 for details.

- **Memory leaks** can be caused by any server application including the operating system itself. Memory leaks can be cured temporarily by rebooting the server. To permanently cure memory leaks, eliminate or update the offending program.

- **Free server software expires** and so cannot be used. It may sound obvious, but it isn't uncommon for companies to rely on free, time-limited trial versions of software. Mark your calendar a week in advance of the date that free software expires and do what needs to be done to remove or properly register the software.

? What should I look for in an automated server-monitoring tool?

Server-monitoring tools offer a number of useful features. Knowing what is available will help you choose the tools that best meet your needs. Some of the features require software to be on the server itself, while others must be installed on other machines, so a number of tools may be necessary to implement the features that you desire. Following is a list of monitoring tool features to help both anticipate future problems and figure out problems that have already affected your Internet services:

- Performance monitoring checks for speed slowdowns.
- Hard drive space monitoring checks for waning disk drive space.
- Remote pinging checks the connection to the Web server.

- HTTP monitoring checks preset Web pages and scripts to ensure that they are returning data.

- Performance deviation monitoring determines whether a site is functioning correctly but also deviating from historically logged performance trends.

- CPU monitoring makes sure that the server's CPU utilization isn't overburdened.

- Site link analysis verifies Web site links.

- E-mail, pager, and PCS notification lets the right person know, day or night, when a problem has arisen (PCS is a telecommunications protocol by which alphanumeric messages are sent to electronic devices such as cellular phones).

MEDIA MANAGEMENT

? What is the best way to specify how content should be updated, added, and approved on my site?

The Web is not so different from other forms of media when it comes to process and publishing guidelines. Magazines, academic institutions, newspapers, and publishing houses all use style guides to make sure that the editorial tone of their publications, the look and feel of graphics, and branding and formatting are all consistent. On a Web site, a style guide is like an "owner's manual" for keeping content up to date, for organizing content, and for making sure that content remains up to the specifications that the site was originally designed for.

A style guide should include the following specifications concerning design, HTML, and testing and quality assurance.

Design

As far as design goes, the style guide should do the following:

- Cover font sizes, colors, and styles. Specifying exact <FONT> tags used for different styles is best.

- Include the HTML for any material that is included in multiple pages, such as menu bars and page footers.

- Present detailed instructions about how to adapt a new template page for a newly added section.

- List the locations of any master art such as high-resolution, layered Adobe Photoshop files.

- List all color palettes used for the site and list which sections use which super palette.

HTML

As to HTML, the style guide should do the following:

- List file naming conventions.

- State new folder creation guidelines to prevent deeply nested directory structures.

- Specify which WYSIWYG HTML generation tools, if any, are allowed for creating pages.

Testing and Quality Assurance

The style guide should also set these rules for testing and quality assurance:

- List the browser versions for which the site should be designed and tested.

- List the maximum allowable file size per page.

- List the language run-time versions for any site-scripting languages or byte-compiled applications such as Java. Listing the pages that are affected by each scripting language update is also useful so that testing can be done more thoroughly on pages that are affected.

- Explain the approval process for pages.

Everyone who is involved in updating online content should at the very least have a Web browser. Therefore, you should write or convert your site's style guide to HTML format so everyone can read it.

? What are the symptoms of a site whose content, design, or server configuration has been mismanaged?

You may not realize if your site has been mismanaged. Following are the symptoms of a disorganized internal structure, poor maintenance, and loose review and approval structures:

- Broken links to external Web sites
- Broken links to graphics and pages within a site
- Script errors
- Documents buried more than two directory levels deep in a site
- Frequent Web server crashes
- Visible Web site directory indexes
- Ninety percent of site traffic visits only a handful of pages
- Inconsistent graphic design
- Search engines that fail to find recent documents
- Outdated content

? How can I tell when a page was last modified?

If you are looking at a document from the Web server itself locally or through FTP, you can identify when it was last updated by examining the attribute that the operating system assigned to the file. From a Web browser, the task can be tricky and the results not always accurate. Server applications such as CGIs always generate content dynamically, with the result being a last file modification date that either is not specified by the file or is the same date that your request was made.

Here's a tip: use a Netscape Navigator browser and go to the page you want to check. Next, add about: before the http:// part of the URL line, as in the following example:

about:http://www.mcgraw-hill.com/

Netscape Navigator will list a number of attributes including the last modification date.

Here are some other tricks you can do with a Netscape browser:

about:cache	View the attributes of cached files.
about:global	See a history of where your browser has been.
about:image-cache	View images and information regarding images that have been cached on your browser's hard-drive.
Control-alt-f	Navigate to Netscape's Amazing Fish Cam page.
Control-alt-s	Cause the status bar to disappear or reappear.
ftp://username@ftp. domain.com	Log onto a secure FTP server (use this format when using your Netscape browser). Files may be uploaded by selecting Upload File from the File menu. Although it isn't documented, Microsoft Internet Explorer also allows access to secure FTP directories using the syntax ftp://*username*:*password*@*ftp.domain*.com in the URL line.

Avoiding Web Site Sprawl

A Web site that has been updated by a number of different developers and Webmasters can grow into a complicated site that is difficult to understand and manage. Not unlike urban sprawl caused by unregulated growth, Web sites that are not carefully managed can suffer from inconsistent naming conventions, complicated directory structures, and too many different scripting technologies and styles.

A small but growing specialty has arisen in the past few years around the gentrification of untamed and mismanaged Web sites. Cleaning up a site can be labor-intensive and difficult, but cleaning up large and popular sites that wish to either speed up or simplify updates is crucial. To keep your site from slipping into a state of Web site sprawl, consider the following recommendations:

Content

As regards content:

- Define a common superpalette for all GIFs on your site. Different palettes on the same page may cause color display problems on monitors set to a 256-color display.

- Define common font sizes and styles to be used in all headings and menu graphics.

- Define a common <BODY> tag or selection of <BODY> tags for every page on the site.

- Provide an HTML template or series of templates for all newly created pages.

- Validate all HTML before it is placed on your site.

- Provide instructions for adding new sections to your site.

- Enforce consistent capitalization and formatting of HTML documents.

- Define a naming convention for all graphics and HTML pages.

Server Configuration

As far as server configuration is concerned:

- Place all virtual roots side by side at the directory level on the Web server.

- Use different virtual roots for each section of the site.

- Create a standard for linking between pages (i.e., always specify links beginning with a virtual root such as /virtualroot/page.html instead of using relative linking such as .../page.html).

- Try to keep an actual server directory tree for files similar to the menu navigation tree on your site.

- Don't split a site over different servers unless all servers are using the same operating system and the same Web server software.

Programming

As regards programming:

- Use only one scripting language or environment for all server executables that are custom developed.

- Use common libraries for any scripts that use libraries.
- Enforce commented code.

Maintenance

When it comes to maintaining a site:

- Schedule link validation software reports regularly and correct any broken links that are found.
- Run software that finds and reports on unlinked content (orphans).
- Keep an up-to-date map of your site.
- Avoid, if possible, outsourcing to many different developers and designers.
- Write site development requirements into service contracts with all outside developers that work on your site.

? What is the best way to screen content on a site before it is posted?

All content that is posted to a publicly accessible Web site should be screened to ensure that it is

- Legal
- Relevant
- Accurate

Screening content is not a task that can be automated. Usually the task is handled by one individual or a select few who act as gatekeepers. The role of the gatekeeper is to screen all content before it is uploaded to a live, publicly accessible server. Gatekeepers may simply approve or reject content, or their powers may extend to managing the individuals who create the content. In any case, establishing a single point of review as the last stage before publicly posting content is always a good idea.

On a site where content is updated frequently, reviewing content can be a challenging task. To minimize the risk of inappropriate content being posted to the outside world, many Web sites assign the role of gatekeeper to the individual or individuals who actually upload the content to the Web server. This individual must be very familiar with the structure of the site as well as all publicly accessible content. On sites that are simply too large for one person to screen the content, the role of the gatekeeper should be distributed among several people, each of whom is assigned a specific section of the site.

Reviewing content is best done on a development or review Web server that closely resembles the configuration of the publicly accessible server. For most organizations, review and development servers are not an option. One way to review content on sites that don't have review servers is to post updated pages with slightly different names so the pages can be reviewed before they are renamed and then written over the old content. For new pages, post pages to be reviewed before you post or update the pages to which they will be linked. With this method, content can be reviewed in the "orphan stage" before it is linked from existing pages on the site. Keeping a copy of a site's contents locally can also be a useful way to develop and review content.

The Importance of Screening Personal Sites

Many corporate sites allow employees to create their own Web pages. What employees put on their pages needs to be checked for legality and accuracy. Comic strips, details regarding research and development, sales information, client names, and other content may be inappropriate for the Web server.

Strict content guidelines should be established for sites on which employees are allowed to post their own content.

DEALING WITH FREQUENTLY CHANGING CONTENT

? How do I manage a Web site with frequently changing content?

Managing and updating content on a Web site that changes frequently can be a very difficult challenge. Sites generally deal with the problem in one of four ways:

● **Manual labor:** Hands-on HTML work written and edited manually and posted to the site.

● **Database-driven:** Each page request instigates a call to a database where content is kept up to date.

● **Dynamic caching:** Although the term is an oxymoron, dynamic caching is generally the term used to refer to a database-driven site that automatically generates static pages each time content changes in the database.

● **HTML generating development tools:** Developers use prebuilt tools to insert changing content and to generate, or publish, a complete page that replaces an existing page on the Web server.

? What are the advantages to using manual labor for frequently changing pages?

In terms of startup costs, nothing beats manual labor when developing a system for frequent site updates. Anyone who knows HTML is able to update the site and no site-specific technology or methods are necessary. Changes are immediately reflected on the site and the only tools needed are a text editor and an FTP program.

In the long run, however, the manual labor approach causes pages to get sloppy. You end up with inconsistent HTML and a lot of extra files hanging around your hard drive, especially if a number of different people work on the same pages over time. If you are going to use human labor for sites, create a blank template and require laborers to use the template each time a page is created. Having a style guide also helps for consistency's sake. Besides, the person who creates content may not know HTML and an extra step may be required to update existing pages.

Designing a Site for Manual Content Changes

If individuals will edit the copy of Web pages by hand, formatting the HTML so that content can easily be identified and changed is a good idea. That way, anyone can make changes to the page without affecting the HTML layout. Separating content from formatting tags such as table cells and menus is easy to do with the use of hard returns and comments.

For example, instead of listing HTML for a title as:

```
<TABLE><TR><TD WIDTH=100><BR></TD>
<TD WIDTH=400><H2>Bob's Fishing Page</H2></TD></TR></TABLE>
```

separate out the text and comment it such as the following:

```
<TABLE><TR>
<TD WIDTH=100><BR></TD>
<TD WIDTH=400><H2>
<!--Below is the page heading-->
Bob's Fishing Page
</H2></TD></TR></TABLE>
```

 How does the Web page publishing process work on database-driven sites?

One method of presenting up-to-date information on a Web site is to use scripts that query a database each time a page is requested. By separating a site's frequently changing content from the HTML template that surrounds it, pages can be updated with a minimum of HTML.

By using client-server applications that provide a front end to the content database, it is possible to update or change content without having to create a new text file, open an HTML document, or even use an FTP application.

Changes to the database are reflected immediately in the site itself and, with a good design, content can be "rolled back" to previous versions. Client-server applications for updating databases can be built using a variety of tools, including Microsoft's Visual Basic and Powersoft's PowerBuilder products.

Web-browser-based tools for updating database content are also popular. As is the case with any tool that provides remote administration, security is critical.

Database-driven sites work with scripts or compiled server applications. Pages that contain database information are either script-embedded or are completely generated from scripts. Netscape's Livewire, Microsoft's Active Server Pages, and Allaire's Cold Fusion provide script-enabled pages. Java servlets, OraPerl, and Python generate pages from scripts.

Data is requested from the database by the scripts themselves. Embedded SQL queries, calls to stored procedures that are in the database itself, or proprietary database languages can be used to specify which information is wanted from the database. To actually link to databases, you can use a variety of methods. For Web servers that run Microsoft Windows, ODBC (Open Database Connectivity) may be used to link to most databases. For Java, JDBC (Java Database Connectivity) is the most common method for communicating with databases. Database servers provide an API and possibly even programming libraries that allow a server's applications to connect. Integrated database and scripting environments such as Allaire's Cold Fusion and simplified database connectivity tools such as Macromedia's Backstage provide database connectivity without the hassle of learning complex APIs or connection protocols.

However, database-driven sites do not come without a cost. Every page request made to database-driven pages requires running a server application such as a script, establishing a connection with a database, and processing and sending out the response from the database. Frequent connections to a database from a Web site can slow down the Web server and cause slower Web site responses.

? What is dynamic caching and how does it work?

Dynamic caching is most effective for pages with frequently changing content but no server-side personalization. For example, if everyone who visits your site at any given time receives the same page and the content on the page is frequently updated, the page is a prime candidate for dynamic caching.

One method of dynamic caching is to query a database when a page is requested for the first time and generate an HTML page after combining a page template with the content that is stored in a database. The user that made the request is served the newly created page. Each subsequent request for the page is directed to the cached static page. When the database fields that are used to create the page are updated, an event is triggered that deletes the cached page. The next request for the page generates a new, updated page, which again is created from a new database query.

The advantage of this system is that pages are served very quickly. Serving static HTML pages is not a difficult task for a Web server. A dynamic caching system offers many of the same advantages as database-driven pages because the pages reflect the latest content entered into the database.

Another similar method of delivering frequently changing content from a database—one without the speed disadvantage of having to query a database with every page request—is to constantly run server applications such as fast-CGI or Java servlets. From a constantly running server application, spawn a thread at load time that queries the database periodically and updates a global variable. For example, you could use a Java servlet init method to do this. The global variable is included in the output of the application with each page request.

Vignette's Story Server offers a dynamic caching solution for a number of major Web sites, including CNet. Other vendors are at work on similar solutions for high-traffic sites with frequently changing content.

? What methods are available that allow the creation of static pages without content creators accessing HTML page templates?

A site that is updated by inexperienced or careless authors runs the risk of broken JavaScripts and invalid or broken HTML. The risk of broken content is even greater in complicated templates that include tables, style sheets, and JavaScript features such as mouse-over states for graphics. With complex templates, deleting a single character can cause an entire page to fail to display. Hiding template information can also help in the creation of new pages. Instead of cutting and pasting what could potentially be hundreds of lines of HTML and JavaScript with each new Web page, new pages can be created with only a handful of lines.

Two methods can be used to keep page template information out of the way of Web site authors:

- Template information can be stored externally as text files and included in Web pages on the Web server by means of server-side include tags

- Content can be published with custom-built tools or off-the-shelf applications such as Microsoft's FrontPage or NetObject's Fusion

Storing template information away from the text that will be edited in Web documents reduces the risks associated with inexperienced or careless authoring. With the right tools, developers can develop content that is published to a local drive and transferred to the Web site or published directly to the Web site via FTP. Publishing has different meanings for different tools but, essentially, publishing involves combining page content with defined template information and then generating complete HTML files. Page content may be a graphical representation of page information, as is the case with NetObject's Fusion, or it may be textual with specially defined tags that represent large blocks of predefined HTML.

Another publishing solution is to create your own publishing system. By combining a database application such as Claris's FileMaker Pro with scripts, database fields can be combined with template scripts and published as HTML text files. Similar solutions are available with applications such as Microsoft Access and Microsoft FoxPro.

A Case Study: Standard & Poors' Web Site

The production team for Standard & Poors' Web site, faced with building a mega-site from the ground up in a limited time frame, needed a flexible tool for content management, so they developed a proprietary HTML generation tool based on a group of related Filemaker Pro databases. The team created records in the databases that represented pages and elements on the site. Content was then poured into the database and assigned to individual pages. Relationships were created between database records in order to position pages in the site hierarchy and to associate JavaScript code and images with pages.

Having filled the database with content, complete HTML code for the site's pages was created via scripts and calculated fields. The resulting code was then exported and processed with a Perl script to produce the site. Large-scale changes to the templates could be done in one place and applied universally. The site could be regenerated to reflect changes with the push of a button. The first screenshot below was used to assign a "location code" that established parent-child relationships in the site hierarchy. The HTML in the second screenshot shows the resulting generated HTML code before it is exported as individual HTML files.

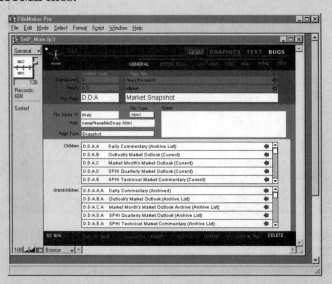

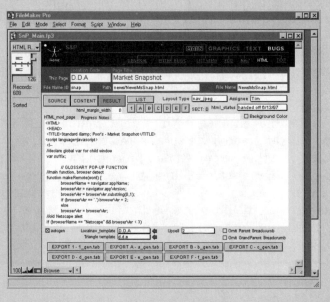

How can SSI help in the creation of page templates?

Most Web servers support server-side includes and provide the ability to combine externally stored HTML content with a Web page before the document leaves the server. Cutting out HTML elements that are complex or shared among several pages makes page editing easier. For content that is shared between pages, you get the added benefit of being able to edit template HTML that affects more than one page in one place. By using this method to edit content throughout a site, background colors, text styles, and menu graphics can all be updated merely by changing only one text file.

The HTML below defines a typical Web page with a menu of graphics on the left side and a title at the top of the page. This example isn't particularly complex, but the risk of an author inserting content in the wrong place or editing table tags that must be included remains present.

```
<HTML><HEAD>
<TITLE>Company Name</TITLE>
</HEAD>
<BODY BACKGROUND="/livent/images/background.jpg"
BGCOLOR="#000000"
TEXT="#FFFFFF" LINK="CC9900" ALINK="#990099" VLINK="#0033FF">
<TABLE CELLSPACING=0 CELLPADDING=0 BORDER=1 WIDTH=640>
<TR><TD WIDTH=140 VALIGN=TOP ROWSPAN=2>
<!--Menu Items are listed here-->
<A HREF="people.htm"><IMG SRC="MenuGraphic1.gif"
BORDER=0></A><BR>
<A HREF="places.htm"><IMG SRC="MenuGraphic2.gif"
BORDER=0></A><BR>
<A HREF="things.htm"><IMG SRC="MenuGraphic3.gif"
BORDER=0></A><BR>
</TD>
<TD VALIGN=TOP ALIGN=MIDDLE>
<!--Page title goes here-->
<IMG SRC="PageTitle.gif" WIDTH=300 HEIGHT=100>
</TD></TR>
<TR><TD>
<!--Frequently changing content goes here-->
Content should be inserted here
</TD></TR>
</TABLE>
```

```
</BODY>
</HTML>
```

With SSI, the frequently edited portion of this page can be reduced to a few lines of HTML with two SSI tags. The menu, title, and table information at the top of the page can be stored externally in one text file, while the closing table tags at the bottom can be stored in another text file. The code contained within the resulting three documents is listed below.

First, the actual HTML page that is called by the browser can be reduced to a few lines of HTML with the original HTML template information being replaced by SSI tags as follows:

```
<!--Do not delete or alter the following tag-->
<!--#include file="Protected_Dir/top.txt" -->
<!--Content goes here-->
```

Here is some sample content.

```
<!--Do not delete or alter the following tag-->
<!--#include file="Protected_Dir/bottom.txt" -->
```

Next, the top half of the original HTML template information, as shown below, can be placed in a text file by itself. For this example to work the HTML should be stored in a directory named Protected_Dir and the file should be named top.txt:

```
<HTML><HEAD>
<TITLE>Company Name</TITLE>
</HEAD>
<BODY BACKGROUND="/livent/images/background.jpg"
BGCOLOR="#000000"
TEXT="#FFFFFF" LINK="CC9900" ALINK="#990099" VLINK="#0033FF">
<TABLE CELLSPACING=0 CELLPADDING=0 BORDER=1 WIDTH=640>
<TR><TD WIDTH=140 VALIGN=TOP ROWSPAN=2>
<!--Menu Items are listed here-->
<A HREF="people.htm"><IMG SRC="MenuGraphic1.gif"
BORDER=0></A><BR>
<A HREF="places.htm"><IMG SRC="MenuGraphic2.gif"
BORDER=0></A><BR>
<A HREF="things.htm"><IMG SRC="MenuGraphic3.gif"
BORDER=0></A><BR>
```

```
</TD>
<TD VALIGN=TOP ALIGN=MIDDLE>
<!--Page title goes here-->
<IMG SRC="PageTitle.gif" WIDTH=300 HEIGHT=100>
</TD></TR>
<TR><TD>
```

The following code contains the template information for the bottom of the Web page. For this example to work it should be stored in a separate file, named bottom.txt and stored next to top.txt.

```
</TD></TR>
</TABLE>
</BODY>
</HTML>
```

? Why is my site experiencing broken links as a result of it being moved from a Windows NT Web server to an identically configured UNIX or Macintosh Web server?

File names on UNIX and Macintosh operating systems are case-sensitive, but the names of Windows NT files are not. Case-sensitivity carries over to hyperlinks and URLs. URLs on a Windows NT machine are case-insensitive, so links do not break as a result of incorrectly capitalized hyperlinks. Hyperlinks on UNIX and Macintosh Web servers that are incorrectly capitalized cause 404 (page not found) errors.

Authoring HTML pages with consistent file names and matching hyperlinks is a good way to make sure that the pages work after files are moved to other platforms. A few Web servers offer a "case-insensitive URLs" feature in their Web server administration interfaces. However, choosing this option slows down the performance of the server and is not recommended as a long-term solution.

Chapter 20

Legal Issues

Answer Topics!

Legal Issues @ a Glance

The laws and regulations that govern the Internet are anything but well defined. The Internet makes geographical boundaries irrelevant both technically and in terms of the user experience, but the laws and regulations that govern the Internet are deeply tied to place. U.S. laws that govern the transport of material over state lines as well as many countries' export and import laws have been used to prosecute Web sites that simply posted content that users requested. Due to the strong ties between law and place, people have been prosecuted by localities that they never visited under rules that don't apply in their own communities.

Courts have had a very difficult time deciding which medium most closely resembles the Internet and which medium therefore should be the model for writing Internet law. Most laws that are applied to the Internet were written before the Internet as we know it today existed. Rules originally intended to regulate television and radio broadcasting, mail services, print publications, and telephone communication have been used to try Internet cases in courts. This chapter focuses on U.S. law, but many of the measures discussed here to protect your site against unwarranted prosecution are applicable everywhere.

Efforts are being made worldwide to update laws and regulations to recognize the Internet and clarify its legal boundaries. In the meantime, Internet law is cloudy, but fortunately a few real-life cases have been decided, and we can use these cases as a starting point for determining how the law treats the Internet. This chapter focuses on the cases in which the court ruled on the Internet not to uncover a strict definition of the laws, but to find out in general how the law treats the Internet. Additionally, understanding the liability and copyright issues that pertain to Web sites, and making sure that your contracts and agreements cover issues such as ownership copyright and liability, is very important.

If you anticipate legal trouble, consult an attorney who is experienced in the field of online law. For an in-depth coverage of online legal issues, read *Netlaw* by Lance Rose (Osborne/McGraw-Hill, 1995). Meanwhile, this chapter covers these important topics:

Content Ownership and Copyright explains basic U.S. copyright law and Web content ownership issues. Issues regarding the public distribution of code and the GNU public license are also covered in this chapter.

Web Site Liability explains the basics of Web site liability and steps that you can take to reduce personal liability at your site. Included is a case study of the successful Heat.net site and the legal problems that SegaSoft, the builder of the site, was forced to overcome.

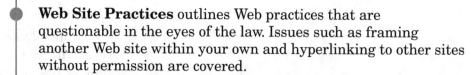

- **Web Site Practices** outlines Web practices that are questionable in the eyes of the law. Issues such as framing another Web site within your own and hyperlinking to other sites without permission are covered.

- **Contracts** covers both contracts with Web site developers and online contracts with Web site users.

CONTENT OWNERSHIP AND COPYRIGHT

? I would like to legally prevent my site's content from being used elsewhere. Do I need to register my copyright anywhere?

Registering a copyright with the Copyright Office may be of some benefit if a lawsuit ever arises, but legally you do not need to register a copyright to receive copyright protection for content. If you are faced with a lawsuit over your site's content, having registered a copyright helps establish the date when you created your content. Registering a copyright also greatly increases your chances of recovering legal costs and statutory damages if a legal action arises. Another way to establish a copyright date for important material is to print the media to paper and have it notarized with the date.

Using the copyright symbol (©) with a date indicates copyright. You do not have to register the material in order to use the copyright symbol. Using the symbol is an effective way to indicate to others that you are serious about protecting your copyright.

For information about copyrights and instructions for officially registering a copyright, visit the U.S. Copyright Office Web site at http://lcweb.loc.gov/copyright/.

? I recently paid someone to develop an applet for my Web site. Who now owns the code and who holds the copyright?

Whenever content is created, a number of different rights come into play, including publicity rights, copyrights, and trademark rights, to name a few. However, the right that is of most concern, especially where software development is concerned, is the copyright. Inside the United States, copyright laws fall under Title 17 of the United States Code. If your applet can be seen on the Internet, the question of who owns the copyright may also fall under the Berne Convention, which governs international copyrights.

Material that has been produced this decade in the U.S. is automatically protected by U.S. copyright laws, regardless of whether it contains the copyright symbol and date. The question of who actually owns a copyright is more difficult to answer. When work is produced for a company by one of its employees, the company has full copyright ownership. However, when the work is produced by another company or by someone who works independently, the contract determines who owns the copyright. If the contract says that the rights to the material are assigned to you or if the contract was a "work-for-hire" agreement, you can probably safely assume that you have full rights to the material. But if you don't have this kind of agreement and the material was outsourced, the copyright is likely owned by the individual or company that created the material.

Not owning the copyright to an applet places limitations on how it can be distributed and who profits by it. The individual or company that developed the applet may be the applet's co-owner and may therefore be entitled to a percentage of any profits. In addition, depending on the contract, you may not own the rights to the applet's source code.

If you want full control over an applet that was developed by someone else, it pays to write a clear contract from the beginning that specifies who owns the material that is produced. If you have difficulty establishing ownership, seek the counsel of an experienced attorney.

? How can I allow others to use my code and at the same time restrict their ability to profit from it without permission?

Sometimes people who create code with useful functionality or programming methods wish to distribute it for free. To keep others from legally profiting from the code without permission, attach a copyright notice that clearly explains the rights that you are giving up and just as clearly restricts types of usage that others can make of the code. Catching those who violate these rights, however, is a very difficult challenge.

Following is an example of a copyright notice that addresses these concerns:

```
1997 Ikonic. All rights reserved. Permission to use this code is
granted only if copyright notice remains intact. No rights to sell or
profit from this code is included in this license. For further information
contact Ikonic, 2 Harrison Top Floor, San Francisco, CA 94707. No warranty is
expressed or implied.
```

? To what extent can I use software protected by a GNU public license on my site?

The GNU public license is a popular method for protecting shareware. Programmers who want to keep their code in the public domain without the threat of others profiting from it may distribute it with the GNU license. Software distributed with the GNU license must be made available along with any source code.

A number of extremely useful pieces of software are distributed under the GNU licensing agreement and are available for free on the Web. Perl, GNU Emacs, gzip, and GCC are a few popular GNU programs. If you want to use software that is protected by GNU, you need do nothing special. Read the associated readme file for special instructions. If you want to sell software that is protected by GNU, you may. The GNU license allows you to charge as much as you want. You can also bundle the software with software support that you provide. Software that is developed using GNU-protected languages (Perl scripts, for example) or compiled with CNU compilers (applications compiled with the GNU C Compiler) can be copyrighted and sold without the restrictions of the GNU General Public License.

If you modify a piece of software that is distributed under GNU licensing and you want to release it to the public, you must distribute it with the GNU license. The GNU license requires you to make the source code and the licensing agreement available.

For the complete text of the GNU General Public License and more information about GNU, visit the Free Software Foundation Web site at http://www.fsf.org.

❓ What content can I legally use from other sites on the Web?

Putting together a large site with text, graphics, and music can be a challenging task given the ever-present fear of copyright infringement. A copyright is assigned to original works when they first appear in a reasonable setting. If you use content from another site, you need permission from the copyright owners.

Very few sites give away permissions to reuse the text and graphic content that they have created. Shareware sites for graphics do exist but the shareware is often of poor quality. For Java shareware, a number of sites offer applets that you can download and reuse. Permission to reuse these applets is often included in a commented out section at the top of the source code.

Keep in mind that creating content that is similar to the content found on other Web sites may also be a copyright infringment. For example, Delrina sold a screen-saver package that contained thirty different screen-savers, one which featured a cartoon character interacting with a flying toaster. Berkeley Systems, a software company that competes with Delrina in the screen-saver market and is well known for its flying toaster animations, accused Delrina of infringing its copyright to flying toasters. Even though Delrina didn't copy the toaster graphics directly from a Berkeley Systems product, the company was forced to stop selling its screen-saver package.

Similarly, the look and design of a Web site may be protected by the copyright laws. In a well-publicized case, an online magazine called The Fray accused another online magazine called Salon of stealing its HTML design. In fact, Salon included The Fray's design in an article and credited The Fray for inspiring the coding. The case has not yet been decided, but it brings up a number of issues regarding site design. It is difficult for a designer to avoid being inspired by the designs on different Web sites. If your site's design starts to resemble the design of another site, you may reconsider the design and try for another.

WEB SITE LIABILITY

? **What are the liability issues that pertain to my Web site?**

Legally speaking, Web sites have been judged under laws that were originally intended to regulate industries such as broadcasting, publishing, and telecommunications. But the Web is unique. The new medium has presented a number of difficult challenges with regard to free speech in the United States.

Certain types of speech and expression are not protected by the First Amendment, which protects the right to free speech. As far as online content goes, three types of expression are not protected: child pornography, obscenity, and defamatory language. How to define these forms of expression has been well argued in the courts. The courts have devised specific or implied tests for determining whether expression is protected under the law.

A more difficult task is the determination of liability. Who is liable for material on a Web site? If the owner of a Web site posts content on his or her own site, who is liable for the content is quite clear—the owner is liable. On the other hand, when content is posted to a Web site by a visitor, who is liable for that content is much less clear. The matter of who is liable for user-updated content in online chat areas, bulletin boards, and even employee Web pages on a company site is still relatively uncharted territory.

? **How can I protect myself from lawsuits that target a site that I personally own and operate?**

If you own and operate a Web Site under your own name and someone sues you, the legal cost of defending yourself against the lawsuit could negatively affect your personal finances. A drawn out lawsuit with high legal costs could leave you with no choice but to declare bankruptcy. One way to protect yourself financially from lawsuits is to run your site as an incorporated business. You may still be held liable for your personal role in an incident, but as to your personal liability for lawsuits against your site and for the actions of employees and contractors, you are on much safer ground legally.

The cost of incorporating a business in the United States ranges from a few hundred to over one thousand dollars, depending on the state in which you incorporate. Small companies frequently choose Delaware because it charges low fees and is friendly to businesses that want to incorporate from out of state.

Incorporated businesses must operate as businesses legally and financially. Taxes, bookkeeping, bank accounts, and so on all have different restrictions and guidelines. Before deciding to incorporate, consulting an attorney is worthwhile.

? **What can I do to avoid liability for content posted to my Web site's chat areas and bulletin boards?**

How to avoid liability for content posted by site visitors is a problem that online services have faced for years. Despite having a thorough understanding of the laws and precedent-setting cases, online services still end up in U.S. and overseas courts over issues of liability. How liable a Web site is for the content that visitors post still remains unclear.

In the following situations, a site's liability for content is considered high:

● You contributed toward the posting of the material either by directly posting part of it yourself or by encouraging others to post it.

● The posted material was of financial benefit to you. For example, you allowed material that infringed on another's copyright to be posted.

When it comes to supervising a site's public posting areas, Webmasters face a dilemma. If the postings are carefully screened and an illegal piece of content makes it through, you are more liable because you are considered negligent. On the other hand, if you do not screen material at all, the chances of troublesome content making it onto your site are significantly higher, but a personal negligence claim is more difficult to make in court. Large ISPs such as Compuserve, Netcom, and Prodigy have all taken a hands-off approach to restricting material because of the massive burden of screening material. Most ISPs also require users to sign a "Terms of Use" agreement that restricts the type of materials that can be posted.

Reducing the Risks from User-Updateable Content

Chat areas, discussions threads, and bulletin boards are all areas in which undesirable material may be posted. The following techniques can help reduce the risks of visitors posting undesirable content that is visible to others:

- Clearly define your Web site's policies regarding posted content and post them prominently on pages where visitors can post content. Justifying the removal of content that is clearly in violation of site policy is easier when policies are clearly defined.

- Post disclaimers where content posted by others can be read. Some people mistakenly believe that postings represent the opinions of the site on which they are posted. A disclaimer makes it clear that this is not so.

- Formulate a well-defined management policy for posted content and follow it carefully when screening content. If you remove some content but not other content, others can argue that you are giving approval to one piece of content over another. A firm policy gives you criteria for selecting which content to remove.

WEB SITE PRACTICES

? Is it OK to frame another site within my own?

Framing other sites is a practice that has been around since Netscape Navigator 2.0 introduced frames. When a Web site is broken up into frames, a number of different Web pages may be placed in each frame that the browser window is divided into. This practice may not be apparent to the site visitor. Often site visitors get the impression that the page is actually made up of only one HTML document. Filling one of the frames with a page from another site is a simple task.

Web sites that do not object to being linked to other sites by means of standard hyperlinks often prefer not to be included within another site by means of frames. Essentially, framing allows one site to wrap another site in different branding. Framing often gives the impression that the content in the site being framed is actually part of the framing site. A strong argument can be made for copyright infringement when one site frames another in such a way that the site being framed appears to be part of the first site.

The best way to avoid legal problems from framing is to avoid the practice altogether. If you are worried about losing visitors, open up a new instance of the browser window for the hyperlink by using the TARGET="_new" attribute in your <A HREF> tag. Opening up a new browser window isn't necessarily great net etiquette, but it can keep your site from disappearing altogether when a hyperlink to another site is clicked. Even if you receive permission to frame another site, subsequent hyperlinks from the site that you frame may cause other sites to be included in you site's frames.

? I would like to link to a number of other sites. Do I need to go through the hassle of obtaining permission for each link?

Hyperlinking between sites is the primary means of navigating the Web. If it weren't for hyperlinks, the Web

Preventing Someone from Framing Your Site

If you suspect or know that another site is including your site in one of its frames, you can take steps to end the practice once and for all. JavaScript makes it easy to detect whether a page is included inside another page. With the right code, a page can tell whether it is being framed and kill all the other frames, thereby leaving it maximized in the browser window.

To prevent your pages from being framed, include the following JavaScript between the </HEAD> tag and the <BODY> tag on your page:

```
<SCRIPT LANGUAGE="JavaScript">
<!--
if (self != top) {top.location = self.location}
//-->
</SCRIPT>
```

wouldn't be the as popular as it is today. The truth is that the vast majority of hyperlinks were included without first obtaining permission. Logic indicates that the more hyperlinks that lead to a site, the more visitors the site will get. But before you surreptitiously add hyperlinks to other sites without permission, consider a handful of lawsuits, and in particular a Georgia law, that have put this practice under question.

The state of Georgia passed a law that bans the practice of hyperlinking to Web sites in Georgia without obtaining the permission of site owners. How can you tell where a Web site server is located without contacting the owners or operators? You can make an educated guess by looking at the domain registration and trace route information, but it is impossible to tell conclusively where a Web server is. Whether the Georgia law will be enforced is unknown, but it does indicate that people believe strongly in obtaining permission before hyperlinking between sites.

A yet to be resolved case involving Microsoft and Ticketmaster has received a great deal of attention in the press. Microsoft's Sidewalk service contained a direct link to content that was deep within Ticketmaster's site. By linking directly to content deep in the Ticketmaster site, visitors from Microsoft bypassed advertisements in the Ticketmaster site that promoted a competitor to Microsoft's Sidewalk service. Visitors from the Microsoft site would have seen the advertisements if they had entered through Ticketmaster's home page.

A similar case involves an online newspaper called The Shetland News that provided news headlines with links to articles deep inside other news services' Web sites. As in the Ticketmaster case, the news sites that hosted the articles were troubled by the fact that links bypassed advertisements that visitors would have seen on the higher-level pages. The Shetland News dispute took place in Scotland. No decision has been made on the case and the issues at stake have not been resolved.

If you want to be protect yourself from the risk of hyperlinking to other sites without permission, get permission from other sites before you add the hyperlinks. And if you choose to hyperlink without permission, you are safer linking to other sites' home pages.

A Case Study of Heat.net

Before SegaSoft could launch a large online gaming community, a number of legal issues needed to be addressed. The following goals were part of SegaSoft's overall legal strategy:

- Educate members about the rules of participating in an online community.
- Prevent members from breaking the rules.
- Allow members to report harassment and offensive remarks or behavior made by others online.
- Protect members, especially minors, from exposure to content posted by users who break the site's rules and whose postings slip through the site's screening mechanisms.

- Discipline members in a fair and consistent manner.

- Protect SegaSoft from being liable for user-updated content that breaks the rules of the online community.

Heat.net's chat area, person-person messaging, and personal home page features offered the biggest legal challenges to SegaSoft. The Heat.net team approached the issues one at a time in a thoughtful fashion. Without having to sacrifice the technologies that enabled the online community to succeed, SegaSoft managed to create an environment that protected the interests of site members as well as the company.

The Heat.net team took the following steps to address legal issues and concerns:

- The entire site was restricted to adults 18 years old and over. This protected Heat.net from restrictive laws concerning minors. If anyone breaks the rules and manages to post or say something offensive, minors are not exposed.

- Screen names are run through a number of tests to check for potentially offensive words and phrases, including swear words and racial epithets.

- A set of rules and a disclaimer for content posted to personal pages and chat areas was prominently displayed. Users are restricted from posting content that is previously copyrighted or offensive to others.

- Files may not be uploaded to the Heat.net site. Heat.net wanted to give users the ability to upload graphics to their personal pages, but decided against it before the site was launched due to the high risk of copyrighted or offensive graphics being added to the site.

- The ability to turn off person-person messaging was added to the site. With the person-person messaging feature, users can send quick messages directly to other users who are online. When a member is harassed through a message, the member can disable person-person messaging.

- A clear reporting process was put in place. A prominent e-mail link to the Webmaster was added to make troublesome material and activity in the online community easy to report to those running the site. A process was devised for investigating and dealing with troublesome content and users.

- A clear and consistent mechanism for discipline was added to the community. Users who violate the rules are barred from using the service either temporarily or permanently, depending on the infraction.

CONTRACTS

? Do I have to sign a contract with a Web site developer or is a simple agreement sufficient?

Most medium-to-large Web site development projects that involve an outside party include a contract of some sort. Usually, contracts are extremely detailed and are filled with legal jargon that protects the developer and the client from confusion in the event of unforeseen circumstances.

Signing a contract with a Web developer offers one significant advantage and one significant disadvantage. First, the advantage: If the developer decides that they aren't making enough money or the job is tougher than anticipated, the developer is still bound by the terms of the contract and must finish the job. Usually, the developer can't drop you as a client without notice or leave you without the material you need to finish a project. Now the disadvantage: A contract can restrict you from firing the developer or dropping the project in a way that prevents the developer from fair compensation for work that was completed or anticipated.

A growing trend in the Web development industry is to begin developing Web sites with what is often known as an "authorization to proceed" letter. This short and to-the-point letter spells out the estimated costs or fixed costs of the initial stages of a project or its entire development. By signing the letter, development can begin before any legal contract issues have been ironed out. More and more often, the "authorization to proceed" letter carries through the entire project without the parties signing a detailed legal document.

? **Are online contracts with my site's users legally permissible even though I don't have a handwritten signature?**

Handwritten signatures are a convention of the business world but, strictly speaking, they are not necessary for a contract to be legally binding. In a contract between a Web site and its online users, making users read the contract and click an "I agree" button usually suffices. Allowing the user to disagree with the contract and exit the area that requires agreement is important. Giving users the chance to disagree is usually done by providing a "Disagree" or "Cancel" button at the end of the contract.

Contracts with users can be as simple as an agreement not to use offensive language in the chat areas or as complex as a several–page-long agreement regarding an online sweepstakes. A contract with users is also a good place to publish disclaimer information.

The more prominently displayed an agreement is, the better. Users can completely bypass a hyperlink to a stand-alone Web page disclaimer. Require users to agree to the contract before they enter areas of your site that require specific behavior or an understanding of some kind. To verify that users actually agreed to the contract, record the time, date, and information about users separately from your log files.

Appendix A

Glossary

active server: A server-side, HTML-embedded scripting environment that supports both VBScript and JScript scripting with Microsoft's Internet Information Server. (See Chapter 13.)

ad brokering services: Services that sell advertisements and place them on different sites, usually in exchange for a percentage of the advertising revenue. (See Chapter 17.)

ad server: A Web site feature for delivering ads to Web pages. Ad servers are usually controlled by an administrative interface that allows ad tracking, scheduling, and often targeting. (See Chapter 16.)

AIFF: A sound file format developed by Apple. AIFF is supported by many Web browsers. (See Chapter 9.)

alpha channel: The region of a graphic that contains transparency. Both PNG and GIF image file formats support transparency. (See Chapter 8.)

ambient light: Light that doesn't have a specific source in a 3D world. Increasing the ambient light increases the lighting on all objects evenly. (See Chapter 18.)

anti-aliasing: The blending of colors in a graphic, usually a result of resizing graphics or remapping a graphics palette. (See Chapter 8.)

applet: A Web-browser-based application composed of Java byte code. (See Chapter 14.)

AU: A sound file format natively supported by Java and a number of popular Web browsers. (See Chapter 9.)

authorization to proceed letter: A popular way for businesses and Web development companies to initiate a project without having to sign a contract.. (See Chapter 20.)

automated collaborative filtering: See *recommendation engine.*

AVI: A natively supported Windows movie format. (See Chapter 9.)

banner: An advertisement on a Web page. (See Chapter 17.)

banner exchange services: Service organizations that place ads for sites on Web sites. Usually, one site's ad banner is placed on other sites, and, in exchange, other sites can place their ad banners on the first site. (See Chapter 7.)

benchmark: A test that measures performance that is often applied to Web servers. Benchmarks for specific activities allow different software and hardware to be compared. (See Chapter 5.)

brittle software: Software that is easily broken by creating unexpected parameters. (See Chapter 6.)

browser detection: A technique for finding out which browser is currently requesting or displaying content. Browser detection is a common method of displaying content in different browser types. (See Chapter 13.)

bulletin board services (BBS): A Web site feature whereby users can post content to an area on the site that is accessible to others. (See Chapter 16.)

CAB (Cabinet): CAB files are a bundling mechanism for transporting Java or ActiveX applications over the Web along with any necessary libraries and media content. CAB files are supported by Microsoft Internet Explorer. (See Chapter 14.)

camera: The camera position defines the viewing position in a 3D world. Moving around a 3D world primarily involves moving the camera that acts as the viewer's eyes. (See Chapter 18.)

CERT (Computer Emergency Response Team): The CERT organization tracks security problems on the Web and posts warnings about security problems. (See Chapter 6.)

CGI (Common Gateway Interface): The most common programming interface for writing custom applications for the Web. (See Chapter 6.)

channels: A site navigation method offered by Microsoft Internet Explorer 4.0 and Netscape Navigator 4.0 with Netcaster. Channels offer off-line browsing and site navigation through a global set of graphical links. (See Chapter 15.)

chat: Web site feature whereby two or more visitors can exchange messages in real time. (See Chapter 16.)

CIAC (Computer Incident Advisory Capability of the Department of Energy): CIAC regularly posts updates about security problems on the Internet. (See Chapter 6.)

click-through: A link to a site from an advertisement. (See Chapter 17.)

client-side image maps: Information stored within the HTML of a document that allows Web site visitors to hyperlink to different destinations by clicking different parts of a graphic. (See Chapter 8.)

client-side persistent cookies: See *cookies*.

co-branding: When one site adds another site's branding to its site. Often done in exchange for links to a site or other online partnership deals. (See Chapters 7 and 17.)

content-type: An HTTP header that defines a document's MIME type when delivering it across the Internet. See also *MIME*. (See Chapter 4.)

cookie: A mechanism for storing on the browser rather than the Web server. Cookie variables may be stored on the browser and accessed later by the Web site that set them. Also known as *client-side persistent cookies*. (See Chapter 12.)

Cool Site awards: Web site awards that usually serve as recommended sites for Web surfers. (See Chapter 7.)

courtney: A set of scripts that analyze network traffic for suspicious behavior in order to detect malicious attacks. (See Chapter 6.)

CPM (cost per thousand impressions): A unit used when selling advertisements. (See Chapter 17.)

crack: A program that attempts to break a password by submitting an extremely large number of word combinations derived from a dictionary. (See Chapter 6.)

cross-promotion: When two or more Web sites mutually promote each other, usually by means of links or banners. (See Chapter 7.)

CSS (Cascading Style Sheets): A W3C-defined mechanism for applying styles such as color and typeface to text on a page. More recently used in Netscape Navigator 4.0 and Microsoft Internet Explorer 4.0 for defining absolute positioning, visibility, and more. (See Chapter 15.)

daemon: See *service.*

default document: The document that the Web server looks for if no page is specified on the URL line. If no page is found, an error page is served. (See Chapter 4.)

demographics: Statistics that define the habits, tastes, and composition of an audience. (See Chapter 17.)

DHTML (Dynamic HTML): A new suite of multimedia features that have been made available to Web developers in Netscape Navigator 4.0 and Microsoft Internet Explorer 4.0. DHTML content can be redrawn and redisplayed on a Web page without the need for reloading. (See Chapter 15.)

digital still cameras: Cameras that store images in an electronic format and are easily converted for use on the Web. (See Chapter 8.)

digital video cameras: Video cameras that record images digitally without using film. (See Chapter 8.)

directional light: A light source in a 3D world with a specific angle and brightness that results in a "cone" of light. Moving or changing the brightness of a directional light changes the brightness of objects that fall with in the cone. (See Chapter 18.)

directory indexing: An option on most Web servers that lists the files in a directory if no default document is provided. (See Chapter 4.)

directory listings: Web site listings that are organized into category trees for easy navigation. (See Chapter 7.)

DNS (domain name server): A database used to look up the IP addresses associated with a domain name. (See Chapter 3.)

document root: The home directory of a Web server. If a page is specified along the URL line and there is no associated directory, the page is probably being served from the document root. (See Chapter 4.)

domain name: A registered name that acts as a street address for a Web site. Domain names are a word followed by three-letter extensions: .com, .edu, .org, .mil, .net. Country codes such as .ca (Canada) can also follow the domain name. (See Chapters 2 and 4.)

dynamic caching. The term used to refer to a database-driven Web site that automatically generates static pages each time content changes in the database. (See Chapter 19.)

dynamically generated graphics: Graphics that are automatically manipulated, changed, or otherwise processed on a Web server. (See Chapter 8.)

ECMA Script: A standard language based heavily on JavaScript and designed as a cross-platform scripting language. (See Chapter 13.)

e-commerce: See *Web commerce.*

ego-surfing: Surfing the Web for references to yourself. (See Chapter 7.)

environment variables: Process variables available on the Web server that are commonly used in CGI applications. (See Chapter 11.)

executable directories: Directories on Web servers that execute any content that is requested from them. (See Chapter 5.)

FastCGI: A protocol that was developed to address many of the speed deficiencies of the CGI protocol. (See Chapter 11.)

fire sales: The practice of selling unsold advertising space on a site at discount prices at the last minute. (See Chapter 17.)

firewall: A system that protects a computer or network from receiving undesired data types from the network or the Internet and that also prevents a computer or network from sending out undesired data types. (See Chapter 6.)

Flash: A Macromedia Shockwave technology that allows vector animations to be run within Web browsers. (See Chapter 14.)

floating ad: An ad that is in its own floating window. (See Chapter 17.)

FPS (frames per second): The number of frames per second displayed in any 3D movement in a 3D world or a movie such as a QuickTime or AVI movie. The number of frames per second is important for smooth video, movement, and animations. (See Chapter 18.)

gamma settings: Monitor settings that affect the way colors look on computer monitors. (See Chapter 8.)

get: A method of sending data that is provided in HTML forms. Get data is URL-encoded and concatenated to the URL line during transfer across the Web. See also *post*. (See Chapter 10.)

GIF: A lossless file type for Web graphics that allows up to 256 colors to be used. (See Chapter 8.)

GNU General Public License: A popular method of protecting shareware. (See Chapter 20.)

gouraud shading: A standard 3D graphics display option in 3D tools and viewers. Gouraud shading is a method of rendering 3D data to the screen. Gouraud shading produces lower quality images than Phong but renders faster to the screen and will, as a result, allow more FPS. (See Chapter 18.)

guest book: A Web site feature whereby visitors fill out form data and either post it to a live Web page or allow it to be privately read by Web site operators. (See Chapter 16.)

hexadecimal: A number system based on sixteen instead the ten. Most often used for defining colors on Web pages. (See Chapter 8.)

HTML-embedded scripting: Scripting syntax that is embedded into a Web page, stripped out, and run on the Web server with the results being returned to the Web page before the page is sent to the Web browser. Examples of HTML-embedded scripting environments include Netscape's Live Wire, Microsoft's Active Server Pages, and Allaire's Cold Fusion. (See Chapter 11.)

HTTP headers: The initial lines of information sent between Web browsers and Web servers and vice versa. HTTP header information is sent at the beginning of an HTTP packet with both HTTP requests and responses. (See Chapters 5 and 11.)

HTTP status codes: Status codes that are given to every HTTP request by the Web server. For example, 200 is "OK" and 404 is "Page not found." (See Chapter 4.)

HTTP (hypertext transfer protocol): The transfer protocol used across the Internet for Web documents. (See Chapter 3.)

HTTP_REFERER: A variable tracked by the Web server indicating the Web page and/or site from which a user linked to a certain page. (See Chapters 7 and 17.)

hyperlink: A connection mechanism, usually text or a graphic, on a Web page that users can click and in doing so request another Web page. (See Chapter 10.)

image map: A graphic the different parts of which a Web visitor can click to link to different destinations. An image map is essentially a set of coordinates with associated URLs in a format that can be interpreted by a server or browser. (See Chapter 8.)

impressions: The number of advertising banners that were sent to Web browsers. (See Chapter 17.)

industry awards: Web site awards that seek to recognize the creators and maintainers of Web sites. (See Chapter 7.)

interlaced GIF: A GIF image whose rows of data are stored in such a way that a blocky-looking version of the graphic can be seen as the graphic is downloading. (See Chapter 8.)

interstitials: Advertisements that are shown for a few seconds between Web pages. (See Chapter 17.)

ISDN (Internet Services Digital Network): A type of telephone line that requires special modems but is extremely fast at transmitting data. Often the fastest available connection to the home. (See Chapter 3.)

JAR (Java Archive): A format designed to bundle and compress Java applets with associated libraries and media for transport across the Web. (See Chapter 14.)

Java: A byte-compiled programming language developed by Sun Microsystems and capable of creating a variety of applications, including applets and servlets. (See Chapter 14.)

Java 3D: An API and a subset of the Java Media and Communications APIs. (See Chapter 18.)

JPEG: A lossy file type for Web graphics that is very effective at compressing pictures with large numbers of colors. (See Chapter 8.)

JScript: Microsoft's implementation of the JavaScript language. (See Chapter 13.)

keyword directories: Search engine listings that are listed based on a keyword or keywords that were chosen as the search criteria. (See Chapter 7.)

kilohertz (kHz): A measurement of the number of samplings taken per second in a recorded sound. (See Chapter 9.)

live reporting: Site or advertisement statistics that are offered in real time. (See Chapter 17.)

live Web camera: A camera that offers an up-to-date image that is displayed on a Web page and updated automatically. (See Chapter 16.)

LiveScript: An earlier name for JavaScript. Rarely used today. (See Chapter 13.)

LiveWire: A server-side, HTML-embedded JavaScript scripting environment available for Netscape Web servers. (See Chapter 13.)

load balancing: Splitting data between servers to reduce demand on one server, or mirroring data on multiple servers and allocating users to one server either randomly or based on which server is deemed most available. (See Chapter 5.)

log file analysis tools: Tools that read server log files and produce documents that summarize the information. (See Chapter 4.)

log files: Text files that contain information regarding requests that were made to a Web site over a given period of time. (See Chapter 4.)

lossless compression: Compression of graphics wherein all the original information is retained. (See Chapter 8.)

lossy compression: Compression of graphics wherein some of the original data is lost or approximated in order to better compress an image. (See Chapter 8.)

low source (LOWSRC): A Netscape-supported attribute of the <IMG> tag that allows lower resolution images to be displayed while higher resolution images are being downloaded. (See Chapter 8.)

mailto: A format for writing hyperlinks. With a mailto hyperlink, the user's e-mail client is opened automatically with the e-mail address of the recipient already filled in. (See Chapter 8.)

Mbone (Multicast Backbone): A sub-network of servers across the Internet that support IP multicasting. Mbone can support the multicast media packets that are particularly useful for Web broadcasts. (See Chapter 9.)

media kits: Sales information regarding a Web site designed to attract advertisers for the site. (See Chapter 17.)

MIDI: An interface for storing musical sounds. MIDI is different from other formats in that it essentially stores notes rather than pre-recorded songs. MIDI files may be played in many Web browsers and tend to be quite small in size. (See Chapter 9.)

MIME (Multipurpose Internet Mail Extensions): Used for defining a file's content type so an end user's operating system knows which application to use to open it. (See Chapter 4.)

monitoring software: Software that monitors a servers performance and records or notifies an individual when certain criteria are met. (See Chapter 19.)

MPEG: A highly compressed, extremely high quality movie file format. (See Chapter 9.)

multi-homing: Hosting more than one domain name on one Web server. (See Chapter 4.)

NetShow: A highly compressed Microsoft interactive streaming movie format. (See Chapter 9.)

NSLookup (Name Server Lookup): A search that queries a DNS (domain name server) for the IP address of a domain's host or associated name server. (See Chapter 4.)

OnAbort: A JavaScript event triggered when a user stops an element from completely loading. (See Chapter 13.)

OnChange: A JavaScript event that is triggered when a value has changed in a form element. For example, a drop-down list option can trigger onChange when it is selected. (See Chapter 13.)

OnClick: A JavaScript event that is triggered when a user clicks a specific object, form element, or text string. (See Chapter 13.)

OnError: A JavaScript event that is triggered when a browser plug-in, applet, or image fails to load correctly. (See Chapter 13.)

OnFocus: A JavaScript event that is triggered when a browser window changes position to become the front-most browser window or when a cursor is inserted into a form element. (See Chapter 13.)

OnLoad: A JavaScript event that is triggered when a document loads. (See Chapter 13.)

OnMouseOut: A JavaScript event that is triggered when a mouse moves out of a specific area or away from an object. (See Chapter 13.)

OnMouseOver: A JavaScript event that is triggered when a mouse moves over an object on a Web page. (See Chapter 13.)

OnSelect: A JavaScript event that is triggered when text is selected in a form. (See Chapter 13.)

OnSubmit: A JavaScript event that is triggered when a submit button is pressed. (See Chapter 13.)

OnUnload: A JavaScript event that is triggered when a user exits a Web page. (See Chapter 13.)

page counter: A Web site feature that gives a graphical or numeric representation of the number of visitors to a site or Web page. (See Chapter 16.)

palette: A limited set of colors that are available for use in a graphic or graphics. (See Chapter 8.)

Perl: An uncompiled programming language that requires a run-time engine to execute. (See Chapter 11.)

personalized content: Content that is catered directly to an individual based on implicit or explicit profiling data. (See Chapter 16.)

phong shading: A standard 3D graphics display option in 3D tools and viewers. Phong shading renders slower to the screen than gouraud but provides a higher quality rendered image. (See Chapter 18.)

ping: A mechanism used for checking whether a server is still online. Ping is also a protocol and a service on the server. (See Chapter 3.)

platform detection: A technique for detecting which operating system is currently requesting or displaying content. Platform detection is a common method for displaying different content on different operating systems. (See Chapter 13.)

PNG (Portable Network Graphics): A lossless, highly compressed graphics format that supports a very large number of colors. (See Chapter 8.)

polygon count: Every 3D model is made up of polygons. Detailed models with more polygons have a higher polygon count. Worlds with high polygon counts take longer to render but provide more shape detail. (See Chapter 18.)

post: A method of sending data over the Web that has been provided by forms. Post allows more data to be sent over the Web than its alternative (See *get*), but the information is not directly accessible from the URL line. (See Chapter 10.)

PPP (Point to Point Protocol): A protocol that allows TCP/IP information packets to be sent over phone lines. (See Chapter 3.)

progressive JPEG: A way of saving a JPEG image wherein a low-quality preview of the image appears as the graphic is downloading. (See Chapter 8.)

protocol: A defined system for sending information over the Internet. The Web uses HTTP and FTP. (See Chapter 2.)

Python: A programming language that may either be byte-compiled or left uncompiled and executed with a run-time engine. (See Chapter 11.)

QuickTime: A highly compressed Apple movie format that is supported natively on the Macintosh and through a plug-in on the PC. (See Chapter 9.)

QuickTimeVR (QTVR): A file format that allows interactive panoramas and object views to be embedded in a Web page to create an effect that is similar to true 3D. (See Chapter 18.)

RAID: The fastest hard drive configuration available. RAID stands for *redundant array of independent disks*. (See Chapter 5.)

RAM (random access memory): Where the operating system, application data, and files sit after they have been requested from a permanent storage device such as a hard drive or floppy disk. More memory means less frequent disk access. (See Chapter 5.)

read-only directories: Web content directories that contain content that is not executed or altered on its way out of the Web server. Also known as *static content*. (See Chapter 5.)

Real Audio: A proprietary streaming audio format by Real Networks that supports real-time recording and broadcast over the Web. (See Chapter 9.)

real-time stock quotes: Stock quotes on a Web site that are up-to-date. Usually quotes are fed to the Web site through scripts and a live stock feed mechanism. (See Chapter 16.)

recommendation engine: A Web site feature whereby visitors enter information and receive recommendations based on the preferences of others who were determined to have similar tastes. Also known as *automated collaborative filtering.* (See Chapter 16.)

redirection application: A Web server executable that simply redirects users to URLs that are outside of a site. Redirection applications are used to track traffic on a site. (See Chapter 7.)

rendering: The computer process of converting 3D model data, viewpoints, lighting, and so on and converting it to a flat image for onscreen display or printing. (See Chapter 18.)

round-robin DNS: A method of balancing Web site requests among a number of different Web servers. Round-robin DNS sends requests one at a time to different servers. When it gets to the first server again, the process starts again. (See Chapter 5.)

RSAC (Recreational Software Advisory Council Rating): A rating system designed to allow Web content to be labeled by sites and blocked at the browser level. (See Chapter 10.)

sampling size: A measurement of the number of increments between the base and the peak of a recorded sound wave. Sampling size is to sound what the color depth measurement is to graphics. Also known as the *bit rate*. (See Chapter 9.)

SATAN (System Administrator Tool for Analyzing Networks): A tool used to test the security of a Web server. Can also be used maliciously to look for holes in other Web servers (See Chapter 6.)

scriptlets: Externally stored Dynamic HTML pages that can be included in Microsoft Internet Explorer 4.0 Web pages much like Java applets. (See Chapter 15.)

search engine: A site feature, enabled on the Web server, whereby users can search for Web site content based on keywords. (See Chapter 16.)

security hole: A weakness in a computer or network's security. A security hole is a potential access or disruption point for malicious users. (See Chapter 6.)

seek time: The average amount of time it takes for a storage device such as a hard drive to read the first bit of a file. (See Chapter 5.)

server-side image maps: Image maps that are stored on the server like CGIs. (See Chapter 8.)

service: An application that runs continuously on a computer. Also known as a *daemon*. (See Chapter 5.)

servlet: A Web-server-based Java application that is not burdened by the performance drawbacks of CGI. (See Chapter 14.)

Shockwave: A Macromedia technology that allows Director, Authorware, Flash, or Freehand multimedia content to be run in Web browsers. (See Chapter 14.)

SLIP (Serial Line Internet Protocol):   A protocol like PPP that allows TCP/IP information packets to be sent over phone lines. (See Chapter 3.)

sound card: A piece of computer hardware that allows computers to play sounds. The majority of PCs require sound cards in order to become audio-enabled. Macintoshes have the ability to play sounds already built into their motherboards. (See Chapter 9.)

SSI (server-side include):   A semi-standard set of tags that, if they are so configured, can be parsed out of a document by many Web browsers and replaced with appropriate data when a page is requested. (See Chapter 5.)

streaming: A technology or media type that allows playback before downloading has been fully completed. Apple QuickTime movies, for example, are a streaming technology because they have the ability to begin playing before they are downloaded completely. (See Chapter 9.)

SVR: An alternative file format to VRML developed by Superscape. (See Chapter 18.)

T1, T2, T3:   Bundles of twisted pair wires. Respectively, the equivalent of 24, 96, and 673 regular phone lines. (See Chapter 3.)

tag: A string of characters beginning with a left angle bracket (<) and ending with a right angle bracket (>) that is used in the HTML language to describe the layout of a Web page. (See Chapter 10.)

targeting: Narrowing down a potential audience based on interests, spending habits, and so on. Targeting can be done by monitoring a user's actions at a site or by analyzing the data collected on forms. (See Chapter 17.)

Telnet: A protocol for passing command line information back and forth between a user and a server. Often used as a control mechanism for administrating Web services and for changing file and directory permissions. (See Chapter 3.)

texture map: A 2D image that is wrapped around a rendered 3D model to give color and the appearance of texture. A brick texture map, for example, may be applied to a 3D rectangle to give it the appearance of a brick wall. (See Chapter 18.)

third-party auditing: An unbiased and independent group that analyzes site statistics to assure advertisers that they are not being cheated. (See Chapter 17.)

tool-tip: A small yellow rectangle with a brief description of content that pops up in many Microsoft applications, including Internet Explorer 3.0 and later. (See Chapter 15.)

twisted pair: A standard telephone line, often used in association with modems. (See Chapter 3.)

UDP (user datagram protocol): A method of sending packets over the Internet that is friendly to streaming media and leads to faster file downloads. (See Chapter 9.)

virtual memory: A method of using hard drive space as memory storage when no RAM is available on a computer. (See Chapter 5.)

virtual root: An aliased directory that does not need to sit within the document root. (See Chapter 4.)

watermarking: Electronically tagging an image, visibly or invisibly, in an attempt to prevent theft or other copyright infringements. (See Chapter 8.)

WAV: A predominately PC file format that many browsers have recently begun supporting. WAV offers similar file sizes to AIFF. (See Chapter 9.)

Web commerce: Refers to processing online transactions and filling orders made online. Also known as *e-commerce*. (See Chapter 16.)

Webmaster: The central coordinator and one who maintains a Web site, its content, and its servers. (See Chapter 2.)

WHOIS: A method for determining whether a domain name is taken and, if so, by whom. (See Chapter 2.)

world: Refers to a 3D scene. (See Chapter 18.)

WYSIWYG: "What you see is what you get," a term used to describe visual development tools that allow a user to edit a file and see as he or she does so what the file will look like in its final form. (See Chapter 10.)

XML: A language specification that is in the process of being developed for the Web. XML is a superset of HTML and is far more flexible and extensible than HTML. (See Chapter 10.)

Z-buffer: An algorithm that removes hidden sides of 3D objects and remembers the layering order of pixels that are rendered. Z-buffering is important for optimal rendering performance. (See Chapter 18.)

ZIP: A standard PC compression format. Also used as a standard file format for bundling and compressing Java applets with associated libraries and media for transport across the Web. Supported by Netscape Navigator 3.0 and replaced by JAR in Netscape Navigator 4.0. (See Chapter 14.)

Index

About Ikonic

Ikonic is a leading Web consulting and development company that builds businesses on the Web. Ikonic's strategy, architecture, and implementation services enable some of the world's largest companies to extend their brands onto the Internet.

Founded in 1985 as a developer of interactive applications, Ikonic quickly earned a reputation for easy-to-use, human-centered interface design that propelled the company from its origin in interactive travel videodisks into other new media technologies including CD-ROMs, interactive kiosks, and interactive television. Now, with offices in New York and San Francisco, Ikonic is building a reputation for creating world-class Web sites which deliver return on investment through revenue generation, cost reduction, and increased customer loyalty. With a staff of almost 100 professionals experienced in all aspects of the Web—from strategic and marketing planning to project management, branding, graphic design, information architecture, content development, database design, custom programming, systems integration, site maintenance, and promotion—Ikonic provides the expertise, creativity, and processes required to build global brands online.

Ikonic. We Build Businesses on the Web.[sm]